SAILOR'S TALES

Thanks mainly to the novels of C S Forester, Patrick O'Brian and Dudley Pope, there has been an upsurge of interest in the navy and sea life in the age of sail. This new series of contemporary memoirs and autobiographies fully supports the old notion that truth is stranger than fiction, since the best of the sailors' own tales are just as entertaining, informative and amusing, while they shed faithful light on the curious and outlandish world of the seaman. Avoiding the oft-reprinted or anthologised pieces, 'Sailors' Tales' offers only the rarest and most authentic accounts; but just as importantly they have been selected for their entertainment value, much enhanced in these newly designed editions.

REMINISCENCES OF A NAVAL OFFICER

A Quarter-Deck View of the War against Napoleon

Captain A Crawford RN

Introduction by Tom Pocock

CHATHAM PUBLISHING

LONDON

Publisher's Note

This edition was typeset from the original two-volume edition
of 1851, kindly supplied by Michael Tapper. Apart from some minor
stylistic changes, the addition of chapter titles and the removal of chapter
contents, the text is reproduced as originally published.

Published in 1999 by
Chatham Publishing
61 Frith Street, London W1V 5TA

Chatham Publishing is an imprint of Gerald Duckworth & Co Ltd

First published in two volumes in 1851 by Henry Colburn, London

British Library Cataloguing in Publication Data
A catalogue record for this book is available from the British Library

ISBN 1 86176 109 0

Introduction © Tom Pocock 1999

Type format of this edition © Chatham Publishing 1999

Printed and bound in Great Britain by
The Cromwell Press, Trowbridge, Wilts

CONTENTS

Introduction
by Tom Pocock

One Trafalgar Night, the late Lieutenant-Commander Peter Kemp – wartime keystone of Naval Intelligence, Admiralty Librarian and naval historian of infinite erudition – was proposing the traditional toast to 'The Immortal Memory of Lord Nelson'. But, instead of the customary words of praise for the admiral, he coupled him with innumerable other naval officers, although none was named. He asked the company to raise their glasses to the great hero *and* to his contemporaries, the young captains, commanders and lieutenants, who had commanded the smaller ships – the frigates, brigs, sloops and gunboats – and lived, fought and died in the same cause but without the fanfares.

On reading this rare book, Captain Abraham Crawford's *Reminiscences of a Naval Officer*, those men and that toast come to mind. Like other naval memoirs, these were written in retirement – Crawford was born in 1788 and his book was published in two volumes by Henry Colbourn in London in 1851 – and the opening pages are touched by the verbosity of the early Victorians. Indeed, the reader might fear that the dramatic memories of the young officer might be overlaid by the arch meanderings of a retired captain. Yet, read on. Quickly, the veneer is torn away by the vigour of his memories, springing from the past like boarders with cutlass, pistol and boarding-pike.

Thirty years on, the memory of the wait before a night action came into sharp focus: 'When the guns are all cleared and laid . . . when expectation and anxiety by the protracted chase are raised to a painful degree – and a silence, a stillness almost breathless, only broken at times by a whispered order from a Lieutenant . . . I own I have felt at such a time a thrilling solemnity, approaching to awe, which I never knew when the broad, clear day gave light to such scenes. Then the dusky sailors with arms bared and heads and loins girded for the strife . . . appear of larger proportions seen by the doubtful light and, with folded arms and bent, determined brows, they pass from time to time with silent step between you and the fighting lanterns...'

No wonder Crawford's memories lay fresh for so long but wonder is due at the quality of the writing he could bring to bear. Here are not only descriptions of the sea and action of high quality but accounts of people that give life to what could otherwise have been stiff little portraits like those sad, unidentified miniatures of naval officers that regularly appear in the salerooms. 'I think he is now before me,' writes Crawford of one lieutenant, describing 'his face, habitually rosy and, which after dinner assumed the hue of an unripe mulberry, rendered more so by contrast with a broad, white neck-cloth that displayed to great advantage the more than common length of his attenuated neck and from its tightness prevented his looking to the right hand, or left, without turning his whole body – his lower man encased in tight pantaloons, over which were drawn a pair of Hessian boots that idly flapped against his calfless legs at every step he took.'

This is – 'is' rather than 'was', so alive they are one of many. Some are rescued from anonymity, others seem to ring bells: the pen-portrait on page 24 might be a description of Patrick O'Brian's Captain Aubrey. Others are minor figures who now assume shape, like the future Sir Charles Parker – 'mirth and frolic laughed in his joyous, sunny eyes' – and the admiral's secretary, the brother of the publisher John Murray, who joined their ship with a library of four thousand books. More importantly, Crawford paints portraits of major historical characters – notably Lord Collingwood, when old and ill – so sharply-drawn that they they seem to look from the page like Nelson's friend Ben Hallowell, whose 'countenance was open, manly and benevolent, with bright, clear grey eyes, which, if turned upon you, seemed to read your most secret thoughts'.

Captain Crawford missed Trafalgar and the death of Nelson – 'Instead of shouts and songs of triumph and gratulation, the subject was mentioned in broken whispers . . . as if each individual had lost a friend' – but he was seldom far from action in the Channel, Atlantic and Mediterranean, where he took part in the blockade of Toulon, Duckworth's expedition to Constantinople and operations off the east coast of Spain. Happiest when about to put his ship's company's skill in seamanship and gunnery to active use, he found himself involved in the new technology of torpedoes, or 'carcasses'. 'This species of warfare, unmanly, and I may say assassin-like, I always abhored', he confesses but describes how it was done, as the captain of a Trident submarine might describe his own duties.

It is not only men of action and the action itself that Crawford describes so well but the background to it all: the sea. 'Just then,' he writes, 'an enormous sea, whose dark and ominous bulk was crowned with foam that shone and glistened' struck his ship, which 'yielding to the mighty pressure, lay almost broadside to the sea, stunned and writhing, as it were, beneath the blow.' The sea may be unchanged but there are constant reminders that ashore was the England of Jane Austen and Thackeray; and Ireland, too, for he was an Anglo-Irishman from Lismore. After a ball, there are the complaints from young ladies of Hastings that 'the lieutenants – alas! for poor human nature! – were both very tipsy; and so redolent of onions were your own messmates that they were quite unapproachable.' Or the magnificent dinner prepared at Minorca by the chef Pierre Brissat, who had been Admiral de Brueys' cook in *L' Orient* and had survived the Battle of the Nile: 'dressed in a linen jacket of spotless purity, from whose too strict embrace his portly person seemed struggling to be free – a cotton cap, varied at times for one of paper, on his head . . . Pierre presented the beau ideal of a *professeur*'.

Or, the transformation of the quarterdeck into a ballroom: 'The carronades are dismounted and, when the slides are slewed fore and aft, cushioned and covered with flags, you have as luxurious seats and sofas as were ever fashioned by the most expert upholsterers.'

Abraham Crawford soon becomes a friend, a guide to his lost world of the sailing Navy, which we know in imagination but he knew in reality, and he tells us exactly what it was like. Wondering what had happned to him, I turned to William O'Byrne's *Naval Biographical Dictionary* of 1849 and was delighted to find him there. His last appointment was to the *Magnificent* at Port Royal, Jamaica, in 1829 but was invalided home the same year. Two years later, he married a clergyman's daughter named Sophia Mockler in County Cork and settled down to write his memoirs, living to the age of eighty-one and dying in the year of the births of Neville Chamberlain, Mahatma Gandhi, Stephen Leacock and Henri Matisse. To turn O'Byrne's 1341 pages of biographical notes is to be reminded of all those unsung naval officers, who could have told stories such as Captain Crawford's. Very few of them did and their stories have been whirled away on the winds of time. But Abraham Crawford did tell his story – and what a story it is! We must give thanks for his immortal memories.

Tom Pocock
London 1999

ix

REMINISCENCES OF A NAVAL OFFICER

1: Joining the Navy

I have long been of opinion that if people, even in my humble walk in life, were to keep an abstract of the various scenes and occurrences through which they pass, with their observations on current events, it might prove salutary and useful. It would furnish the writer, as his narrative proceeded, with ample food for reflection, leading him to perceive how little real value is to be attached to those concerns which engaged his ardent pursuit, and to form a juster estimate of what his true happiness consists in; and to those who might read the transcript, it might serve as a beacon to guard against the dangers by which their course in this world is beset, and guide them into that haven where bliss and virtue only are to be found. This idea has pressed itself latterly with greater urgency upon my mind, inasmuch as I feel that my health is beginning to give way, and that there is no longer time for deliberation, if there be for the execution of my design. Besides, the occupation would amuse me, and render the confinement of a sick room less solitary and irksome. But to put this in execution demands energy of mind and purpose – greater, I fear, than I now possess – a resolution to shake off the torpor, which I feel too well has, for some time, been creeping upon me – a ransacking of memory and memoranda that I feel myself almost unequal to. Some time soon, but not to-day, I will make the effort.

Weeks, ay months, are dead and buried since the foregoing was written, and yet I have not summoned courage to begin. So perishes many a good resolution – many a well-concerted scheme! What our thoughts and meditations over night suggest to us, however wise, judicious, and necessary they be, are too often paralyzed and defeated by delay, – by that withering self-indulgence which whispers to us – 'to-day I am not in the mood – to-morrow will do as well.' Alas! for you tomorrow may never come! – the light of another morrow may never dawn for you! For the last time for you, perhaps, the sun's rays are now illuming that prospect, which your eyes so often and so fondly dwelt upon!

Feeling the truth of these sentiments, I *will* make the effort – I *will* arouse me to the task, and free myself, if I can, from the lethargy, which day by day is gathering around me, and numbing all my energies.

Then the question suggests itself, where ought I to begin? – from what period of my life? Ought it to be from the day that I first left my father's roof, and was launched into the world? the day that first saw me separated from home, from kindred, and from friends?

It was in May – the twelfth, if I remember – as bright and sunny a day as ever the pleasant month of May gave birth to: but before proceeding further, perhaps it may be as well to say, in few words, from whom I am, and to give a short account of the place of my nativity.

I was born in the south of Ireland, in the pleasant village, or rather town of Lismore, of which my father was one of the vicars. He had also a small living in another part of the diocese, which, with his vicarage, enabled him to bring up respectably a family of eleven children. Of these I was the youngest; and the same day that my eyes first opened upon this busy world saw my poor mother's closed for ever upon its many cares and sorrows.

The first thing I have any distinct recollection of, is being under the care of my eldest sister, who, at a very early age, was placed at the head of her father's house. Under her judicious management and affectionate guidance, I felt not the loss of a mother, but received from her all the watchful care and tender solicitude of the fondest parent. She taught me first to lisp my letters, to read and to write; and the same admirable instructress implanted in my youthful mind those seeds of religion which, dormant indeed and unproductive for many a year, though never wholly dead, are now germinating, I trust, and should life be spared a little longer, likely to produce good and wholesome fruit.

At the age of six I left my sister's gentle sway to mingle with ruder spirits, and undergo the drudgery of Latin. My father, who taught his own sons, was an excellent classical scholar, and under his tuition I soon made considerable progress in Latin, and some in Greek; though I must say that I acquired, with much greater facility, the gymnastic accomplishments of ball, running, leaping, and swimming, at all of which, even beyond my years, I was exceedingly expert.

A knowledge of Latin and Greek was alone considered a liberal education when I was a child; and the study of modern languages and sciences, which are far more useful, was too frequently neglected.

When I was between twelve and thirteen years old, my father, unwillingly, I believed, determined upon sending me to sea. Two of my brothers were already in the King's service; one in the army, and the other in the navy; and my eldest brother, from whose presumed abilities my father once augured much, was but recently dead. He had been idle in college, where he spent much more money than he ought, and after disappointing the sanguine expectations that were entertained of his academical success, was appointed to a regiment on the eve of sailing for the West Indies, where he contracted a disease, that in less than two years obliged him to return to Europe; and a few months after saw him consigned to a premature grave.

My father then, having two sons already in the King's service, and now no other at home but myself, felt unwilling to part with me. The great expense which my eldest brother had caused him, and his total failure in college, disheartened him from sending another son there. Moreover, he felt that he ought not to risk a similar waste of money; and I conclude I held forth no early promise of being more thrifty, either of my own time or of his pocket. As a friend had some time before made him the offer of receiving me into his ship, the sea was, therefore, fixed upon as my destination; and his resolution, however reluctantly made: short was the time and few were the preparations necessary for my equipment.

I cannot now call to mind that I had any preference for the life of a sailor, before I was asked if I should like to be one; but as soon as it was announced, and I was told that it depended on myself to make the choice, I most joyfully acceded. My young heart instantly began to swell with the recollection of all I had heard or read of the bold and daring adventures and successes of sailors – the histories of Sinbad, of Robinson Crusoe, but, above all, of Anson and his gallant crew. I remembered their privations, their enduring fortitude, their heroism, and final success. How noble to follow so bold an example, and after burning and plundering a city, fighting and taking a rich galleon, and sailing round the world, sit down a Peer and the first Lord of the Admiralty!

My mind filled with such thoughts, and the idea that I was about to follow the career of our great sea-captains, I went to bed; and no wonder if that night my childish slumbers were for the first time disturbed by dreams of battles, storms, conquests, shipwrecks, and I know not what besides.

A week sufficed for my moderate preparations, the intervening time being employed in visiting and bidding adieu to youthful friends and neighbours.

Though I felt proud and elated at soon becoming an officer, and not a little pleased at being released from books and school-boy tasks, still I can now remember, that, child as I was, it was not without a pang that I was about to part from dear, dear friends and playfellows – a home that I had never slept a night from, and which was endeared to me by so many ties and happy recollections.

Let it not be matter of surprise, then, that young as I was, I should visit in the last days of my sojourn at Lismore, most of my old familiar haunts. Once more, perhaps for the last time, I wandered through the desolate halls and chambers of its half-ruined castle, whose broken walls and nodding buttresses I had so often clambered to look for the nests of the owl, the hawk, and the daw, then its only inmates. Once more I explored its woods and groves – I penetrated its glens, and lay me down, a young and solitary enthusiast, by the banks of its bounding and beautiful river. And when the morning arrived that was to witness my final departure, I arose at an early hour, went again to the dear old garden, and spent most of the time until breakfast in wandering through its walks and fondly-remembered alleys, and in taking a last view of shrubs and flowers that were planted and reared by my own and my little sister's hands.

At length the moment of parting arrived, and with tears and sobs, which I had not then learned to restrain, I embraced and bid a long adieu to my sorrowing sisters.

How calm and peaceful appeared my native village the morning that, accompanied by my father, I took the road to Cove, whilst my childish heart was struggling with strange and unwonted emotions! Lismore! when I first left thee, thou wert a happy and a quiet spot! No angry feuds, no party nor religious contentions, disturbed and divided thine inmates! No insidious demagogue, with specious eloquence, had as yet learned to rouse thy latent passions into fury! – but all was peace, content, and friendship.

Something I would say of my birth-place, and though I feel it impossible to do justice to its site and scenery, I will attempt to sketch a faint outline of them.

Lismore, from Lis, a fort, or enclosure, and More, great, had also been named Dunsginne, and in remoter times Maghsgiath, or the Chosen Field. It is beautifully situated high over and somewhat retiring from the classic Avonmore of the Poet Spencer, now the Blackwater. It gives name to a Bishop's See, now united to those of Cashell and Waterford, and formerly, that is, in times long gone by, it was a place of note, but now is reduced to the condition of an Irish village, and in itself possesses nothing to attract, save its unequalled situation, its cathedral, bridge, and half-ruined castle. Tradition and the Irish annals inform us that it once contained twenty churches and other religious houses, with an university, whose reputation for learning was so great, that numbers flocked to it for instruction from foreign countries, as well as from all parts of Ireland. It also possessed numerous cells, and a hermitage; and so *holy* and *uncorrupt* were its 'Religious', that women were forbid to enter the quarter of the town where those devout men chiefly inhabited. In the year 1179, one of its bishops assisted at the Council of Lateran. It was burned to the ground, with all its churches, in 1207; and in that fire perished all its magnificence. No trace or memorial of its former extent and consequence at present exist, and I cannot find that it ever after attained to any note or eminence.

The church, or rather cathedral, which is in the form of a Greek cross, and was founded by St Carthagh in the seventh century, stands high over the river, surrounded by trees of venerable growth. The side windows are lancet, that in the eastern end, giving light to the altar, being of the pointed Gothic, light and elegant, whilst the one at the opposite extremity, evidently very ancient, is circular, or of Saxon form.

Originally built by King John, and crowning the opposite height to the westward, not many hundred yards from the cathedral, rises the now dilapidated castle. Its northern face is reared on a precipice more than sixty feet high over the river, and commands the approach to the village on that side, which, from the north, is by a handsome and very picturesque bridge of nine arches, that crosses two rivers at the same time, the Blackwater and the Oun-a-Shead. Over this bridge, and passing between the church and castle, is the road that leads from the northern side of the river to the village. For many years the castle had been the residence of the Bishops of Lismore; but after many vicissitudes, suffering much from fire and siege, it was partially burned by Lord Castlehaven, who, with great difficulty, took it from a handful of men, by whom it was defended in 1645. It was once in the possession of Sir Walter Raleigh, who, being in want of money to complete the equipment of an expedition to America, sold it, together with large estates, to the first Lord Cork, and from him it has descended, in the female line, to its present noble proprietor.

East, west, and north, the castle commands a delightful prospect. To the right may be seen the river, wooded on both sides in all its windings for an extent of three miles, when the eye rests upon the picturesque village of Capoquin, and the extensive ruin of Kilbree, once a Preceptory of Knights Templars. On the left are the charming and highly ornamental grounds of Ballyinne, with a noble reach of the river beyond; and nearer at hand the salmon fishery, where the waters, struggling and foaming through the weir, have all the appearance, and produce the lulling sound, of a distant waterfall. Immediately in front there opens a deep, romantic glen, giving passage to the Oun-a-Shead (Anglicè, waters of the sprite, or fairy), whose chafed and rushing current, vainly obstructed by the huge masses of rock that everywhere cross its course, appears more bright and sparkling when contrasted with the sombre gloom of the woods that clothe the steep acclivities on either side; whilst high over all towers the cone-shaped Knock-mel-Doun, the giant guardian of the pass, reflecting in hues, now gloomy and dark, now joyous and bright, the ever-varying shadows of the atmosphere – like man, when stirred to good or evil, whose face, the faithful index to his mind, betrays the secret workings of those thoughts he vainly struggles to conceal.

Two men, who have added lustre to science and literature, were born in the Castle of Lismore, Robert Boyle the philosopher, and Congreve the poet and dramatic writer. Boyle was indeed a Christian philosopher; but Lismore, in after days, could boast of one that laughed at creeds and gloried in infidelity. I have heard that he was not without admirers, but, on the contrary, even in Lismore contrived to enlist a few silly followers, who, like their leader, by an affected singularity and *independence* of thought, hoped to attract some notice. This poor mistaken man, eschewing consecrated ground, and carrying his eccentricities to the grave, left directions in his will that he should be interred on the summit of Knockmel-Doun, nearly two thousand feet above the ocean. Numbers flocked to his funeral, and attended him to his resting-place, where they left him, if not in glory, most assuredly *alone*.

When I was a child, Lismore though remote, and so sequestered as to be in a manner unknown, contained, within its limited circle, that which would have reflected credit and respectability on a town of far more importance. I speak of its society, which at that time was highly respectable: and amongst several of enlarged minds and cultivated tastes was the Rev Mr Jessop, who, though he never published, except a few pieces of detached poetry, that appeared at different times in the 'Gentleman's Magazine', had written many things of great interest and beauty; of which the 'Reign of Queen Elizabeth', that I have heard highly commended by competent judges, who had been favoured with a sight of it, must alone have stamped the writer as an author of great merit and research. Mr Jessop had been induced to undertake the history of that Queen's reign from having accidentally met with some volumes of manuscript papers, which lay for years unnoticed and neglected in the old Castle of Lismore. These volumes contained copies of Orders in Council issued at the time, with letters to Lord Cork from one of his sons, who filled some situation at Elizabeth's Court, which enabled Mr Jessop to furnish many anecdotes, and illustrate many points in her character and policy.

Old people, too, used to laud the cordiality and good fellowship that formerly existed in the village; they spoke with enthusiasm of their pleasant meetings and cold bones, a name which I presume was given to what is now known by the not more significant term pic-nic – of the private theatricals held at Dromana, where his late Majesty, when in command of a frigate on the Irish station, as Duke of Clarence, condescended to be present. But to return to my journey.

My father and I proceeded on horseback, stopping by the way to call on one or two friends – he proud, no doubt, of exhibiting his boy in his newly-acquired character of sailor, and I as much so of my blue jacket and trousers. A little beyond the town of Tallow, four miles from Lismore, we joined the servant, who had a portmanteau, containing my then worldly goods, strapped behind him, on a long-tailed black horse, which, though coeval with myself, still retained in the family the name of the black *colt.* Here my father and I were to part; and though I wept plentifully at bidding my sisters farewell, no tear dimmed my eye when I received his final embrace and blessing. This seeming want of tenderness and feeling on my part made him afterwards say that I evinced much philosophy on the occasion. Such, in truth, was not the case; but my new position occupied so much of my thoughts – my mind was so filled with visions of I knew not what, that no space was left, I suppose, for thoughts or feelings of another kind. We parted, however, and I was left in charge of Jack Callahan, the name of my attendant.

Jack, though a faithful servant, and true to his trust, was neither in appearance nor equipment, a very first-rate groom – neither was I very splendidly mounted I suspect, or my sailor's dress in that part of the world might have attracted notice, and excited ridicule. Be the cause what it might, just as we passed a troop of schoolboys, taking their afternoon's airing in the neighborhood of Middleton, such an universal shout of laughter was raised at our expense as never greeted the ears of the Knight of La Mancha and his Squire as they ambled forth in quest of adventure. I own I felt grievously mortified at being the object of so much merriment, and debated for a moment whether, with my squire, I should not charge the whole body; but Jack's cooler head, reflecting that 'discretion is the better part of valour,' recommended peace; and as we quickened our pace, and left our tormentors behind, the peals of laughter fell fainter on my ears, and my equanimity was soon restored.

At length, for the first time, my eyes looked upon the sea, and I beheld the numerous vessels that crowded the harbour of Cove. The noble view gave birth to a thousand vague emotions – my heart actually danced with anticipated happiness, and in imagination I was already captain of one of the ships I saw at anchor.

Before the sun went down we entered Cove, and I was delivered to the care of a friend of my father, who kindly undertook to see that I was provided with whatever was necessary for my embarkation, and then to take me to the *Révolutionnaire* frigate, for a passage to join my proper ship the *Diamond*, at that time supposed to be at Plymouth.

When I stood, for the first time, on a frigate's quarter-deck, I thought I never should be satisfied with gazing – my eyes viewed, with increasing admiration, the novel sight – all was new and strange – shrouds, cordage, guns, the whole furniture of the deck and masts – every object was matter of fresh wonder and astonishment, and completely baffled and set at naught all my preconceived notions of a ship. I was not suffered long, however, to continue my inspection. The First Lieutenant desired that Mr Beauman might be sent for; and upon that gentleman answering the summons, I was consigned to his care, and desired to be introduced to my future messmates and new abode. If I were pleased and indeed agreeably surprised with what I had hitherto seen – the 'outward and visible' appearance of the frigate – I confess that I was not only a good deal *désen-chanté*, but my consternation was great, when, after descending two ladders, I beheld the dungeon (for such it appeared to me), into which my conductor led me, and said that that – the larboard berth, was to be my quarter in the *Révolutionnaire*.

The frigate was low 'between decks', much lower than I remember to have seen any other, and, in the half-dozen paces, between the hatchway and the berth, though a very little fellow, I had knocked my head as many times against the beams. The crib into which I was introduced was small even for a frigate, notwithstanding which the chests, belonging to its inmates, were ranged around (none being allowed in the steerage), just leaving in the centre sufficient room to admit a small deal table, which was then covered with a not over-clean cloth preparatory to dinner. In one corner of the berth was lashed a 'harness' or pickle cask, containing beef that was meant to serve for half the approaching cruise, and which, either from the heat of the weather, or that the preserving process had been imperfectly performed, already began to emit certain unsavoury smells, a mournful indication that the work of decomposition was fast proceeding, without the aid of previous mastication.

The ship was weak, and open in her 'top sides', and at sea, her yawn-ing seams, at every roll, freely admitted the water, traces of which, in lines of rust, were rendered visible through the 'dim obscure' by means of one lean and meagre tallow candle. My messmates, assembled for dinner, con-sisted of the before-named Mr Beauman, who was the caterer, two other *elderly* mates or midshipmen, and a youngster, to all appearance not much my senior, but of considerable standing at sea. The three first-mentioned had flourished before the mast; but as, in those days, midshipmen were not as 'plenty as blackberries', and their conduct and qualifications as good and steady seamen recommending them I presume to notice, Captain Twisden elevated them to the respectable situation which they then filled.

Dinner was soon served by a dirty boy, black and reeking from the 'galley'. It consisted of a piece of beef, baked in a deep tin dish, with potatoes under it. I tried to eat; but whether it proceeded from the earliness of the hour (twelve o'clock), to which I was unaccustomed, or was caused by the disagreeable sights and smells by which I was assailed, and which generally act as a 'preventive check' upon all appetites fresh from the shore, or a combination of all, I know not, but my stomach rebelled against food, and it was with difficulty I forced myself to swallow a morsel. Grog for the 'oldsters' and 'black-strap' (a very detestable mixture, resembling in taste a combination of sloe juice and logwood) for the youngsters, followed. The bare application of this beverage to my lips was sufficient. I could drink none; but whilst the more practised hands were imbibing their potations, I had leisure to reflect upon my new situation and future companions, and I honestly confess that, despite all my enthusiasm, and recent heroic aspirations after fame and adventure, my young heart sank within me when I compared it all with what I had left behind.

When I contrasted my father's house – large, roomy, and though not splendidly furnished, neat, commodious, and comfortable – with the dark confined hole, which in future was to be my only dwelling-place – those rough, uneducated men, whose very language was then unintelligible to me, and even the youngster, whose age more nearly approached my own, speaking upon matters which to me were altogether new, and giving utterance to sentiments and feelings that met with no responsive chord in my breast – when I compared all this with the home I had just left, and my former companions and associates – I own I felt such a despondency, such complete forlornness, that it was with difficulty I restrained my tears.

Years have since passed, and I have long got rid of such childish sensations; yet what I then felt is fresh in my memory, nor has time, nor the variety of scenes or situations through which I have passed, served in the least to weaken my remembrance of it. I soon perceived, however, that a midshipman's berth was no place for indulging such feelings; so gulping, as well as I could, my griefs and regrets, I mounted the deck, where I soon got acquainted with others of my shipmates, and before long I found myself as a 'Paddy' and a 'Johnny-Raw', the butt whereat many jokes and much sea-wit were levelled. All these I bore, I believe, with tolerable good humour; and perhaps the efforts that I was compelled to make to parry the good things which were pointed at me, served to divert my thoughts from other and more painful matters.

Tea at four, and supper at eight o'clock, served by the dingy boy in the same slovenly and comfortless manner as dinner, closed the first day I passed on board a man-of-war; and soon after I descended to the cable tier, where I found a hammock slung and hung up for me, by the care of my friend, Mr Beauman. Should any sailor, whose entry into the service does not date more than twenty years back, ever happen to glance his eyes over these pages, be it known to such, that in the steerage of the *Révolutionnaire* no hammocks were allowed. It was as innocent of the lumber of midshipmen in the night season as in the day, the cable tier alone being allotted for the sleeping apartment of those worthies. As I was a 'supernumerary', and moreover the last comer, my hammock was hung 'athwart ships', the fore and aft 'long-hers' being all occupied. In harbour and smooth water this was of no consequence, but it proved of grievous inconvenience and annoyance when rolling at sea.

When I joined the *Révolutionnaire*, it was expected that she would be ordered to Plymouth for repairs, of which she stood much in need; instead of which she was directed, in company with the *Ambuscade*, to see a West India convoy past Madeira; after which she was to cruise for six weeks; and then to return to Cork for further orders. Meanwhile, I began to be somewhat more reconciled to my companions and my new mode of life. I busied myself in learning the names and uses of the ropes, and in going aloft, whither I was permitted to soar unmolested, having first 'paid my footing' to the Captains of the tops.

At length the *Ambuscade*, the Commodore, arrived; the convoy was all assembled, and at four o'clock in the morning, in the early part of June, 1801, the boatswain's call, followed by the words 'all hands unmoor ship', and echoed by his mates, was heard through the frigate, and long before I could huddle on my clothes, the 'tierers' were already clearing away for their work. The *Révolutionnaire* was soon at single anchor, and 'hove short'; and at noon, having seen the last of the lingering convoy under-weigh, we made sail out of the harbour.

For the first time I found myself moving on the waters, and as the ship passed Spike Island, and shot by each point between it and the harbour's mouth, my mind was again the scene of varied emotions. Visions of successful adventure and unknown pleasures, which hope always presents to youth, on first entering into the world, in her brightest and gayest colours, contended with the sorrow and regret I felt for all I was leaving behind, and some doubts and misgivings as to the mode of life upon which I had embarked.

All thoughts, past and future, were, however, soon to vanish. We were now on the broad bosom of the ocean, and the frigate began to feel the influence of its heaving pulsations. Soon my head reeled – my eyes grew dim and dizzy – a faintness almost to death seized all my limbs, and before long I lay stretched on one of the chests in the berth in all the misery and helplessness of sea-sickness. Three mortal days did I continue in this wretched state, without the power to assist myself, and I verily felt as if fate had done its worst, and the bitterness of death was past. This agony, however, could not last for ever. Once more I was able to crawl, and contrived to get on deck, without the aid of that quickening remedy which was applied to 'Peter Simple' upon a similar occasion. There the fresh, invigorating air soon revived me. A few days more sufficed to restore my strength and appetite, and I felt no more sea-sickness.

The occurrences of this my first trip to sea were not numerous or varied – at least, they have left few traces on my memory. I recollect, however, that the night-watch was at first a very painful and trying occupation; and those who have never left their snug, warm beds at night, can hardly form a notion of the sufferings of a little fellow of twelve or thirteen, who, after being roused out at twelve o'clock at night, and shivering on deck, perhaps in wet and cold, is permitted, at the end of four hours, to return to his hammock, hung 'athwart ships' in the tier, where, at every roll of the ship, his head or his heels strike with an awakening force against the cables. Such was my initiation into his Majesty's service.

The young as well as the old kept watch in those days, and I do not hesitate to say that a service of three years gave greater experience, and, consequently, more practical knowledge, than double that number of years at the present time. In most ships, since the peace, considerably more than half their time is passed by the young officers of the rising generation in harbour.

Captain Twisden was, in figure, rather tall and slight, with a complexion unusually dark and saturnine, which, like a thunder-cloud before it explodes, became awfully black whenever things went wrong, and his ire was more than usually excited. He seemed a reserved and austere, but I believe a perfectly just man, and had the reputation of being a first-rate officer. His ship was a pattern of order and discipline, and splendidly manned; and of both ship and crew he was justly proud. She was pre-eminently the fastest sailer on the station, which procured for her the well-known sobriquet of the 'Irish Race-horse'.

Captain Twisden did not punish as often, nor as severely, as I have known some far less efficient officers to do; but his discipline was regular and systematic, never acted upon by whim or caprice. Slight offences were not visited with much severity, but he never overlooked a glaring fault; and if a man had the pledge of his 'sacred honour' (his usual emphatic asseveration, whenever he deemed the man's crime unpardonable), for a flogging, he was never disappointed.

Captain Twisden was not long permitted to command his fine ship's company. Upon his arrival at Plymouth to refit, a few days after I left the ship, an order was received to draft the 'Racehorse's' men, and no representation, however urgent and respectful, could induce Lord St Vincent, the First Lord of the Admiralty, to change his *dictum*, which, once promulgated, was as immutable as the laws of the Medes and Persians. The system of drafting ships' companies was much practised when Lord St Vincent presided at the Admiralty, and was intended, I conclude, to answer two purposes: first, to prevent men remaining idle in port, whilst their ships were undergoing any lengthened repairs, and, secondly, to obviate the necessity of raising more men to furnish those ships which only wanted a crew to take them at once to sea; thereby economising the public money – a great and ruling object with that highly respectable officer, though questionable statesman.

These objects, when viewed by themselves, without reference to other matters, seem sufficiently important; and if they were to be procured by the discomfort alone to officers and men, which the perpetual change of ships is sure to produce, the purchase, even at such a sacrifice, would be cheap. But discomfort to the crews is not the only evil which it causes; it is most injurious to good discipline, which, though pretty uniform throughout the navy in *generalities*, differs in many minute, though essential points, in different ships, according to the various methods adopted and put in force by their captains; so that what men learn in one ship they have to unlearn in the next, and new ships and new officers necessarily bring with them to the seamen, fresh lessons to be acquired. This would appear sufficiently harassing and disgusting, but the mischief it causes is not all told. The men lose that strong attachment to, and pride in their ship, which I have ever found to be a principal spur to activity and exertion on the part of a ship's company: besides, it seems hard and unjust, that men are not to have a little relaxation on shore after a cruise of six or eight months, but are for ever to be denied that indulgence which is granted to people of every other service or pursuit.

The system of drafting ships' companies, though not so general and frequent as during the sway of the noble lord in question, was much too prevalent up to the close of the late war; and I am confident that, combined with the too rigid and unnecessary confinement to their ships, it was the chief cause of that disgust and estrangement from the service, so general among seamen during that period. Since that time much has been done to ameliorate their condition, and make them better satisfied with the service. Amongst others, a great change for the better has been adopted with regard to rations; and the long leave from their ships, which enables the men to go home and see their friends after an absence of three years on foreign service, with the monthly payments of a portion of their wages that are now made to them, are decided improvements.

The loss of his ship's company was a heavy blow to Captain Twisden; he was greatly attached to his men, who had been long under his command, and on their parts were perfectly accustomed and reconciled to his peculiarities and mode of discipline. He thought himself unjustly treated, which preyed upon an irritable temper; and though he soon got a new ship's company, and retained the command of his favourite ship, the morning he sailed from Plymouth Sound something went wrong, that excited his anger to a more than ordinary degree, and after foaming with passion for some time, he left the deck and retired to his cabin. In half an hour after the First Lieutenant, who had gone to make some report, found him stretched speechless on a sofa, unable to move even to ring the bell for assistance, and in less than an hour more he was a corpse. It would appear, that unrestrained excitability of temper, working upon a predisposed constitution, produced apoplexy, which speedily terminated in death.

But to return to my narrative: I do not remember that anything remarkable occurred during our continuance with the convoy. After seeing them pass Madeira, and escorting them as far as the 'Trades', we parted company, and cruised as we were ordered. When Madeira was in sight my heart yearned, as it often did, to be once more on shore. I recollected that a military force had been recently sent there to assist in repelling some meditated attack of Bonaparte. My brain, which was always given to castle-building, was instantly at work. From a little middy in a blue jacket, without notice or consideration, I was transformed at once into a gay ensign, and with my regiment stationed in the island. I pictured to myself marchings and countermarchings, and then fancied the enemy at hand; and I thought storming a fortress or some rocky height might prove pleasanter work than a fight at sea, or cutting out vessels from an enemy's harbour. With the declining sun, and as the island was lost to our view, my castles fell into the ocean, and I found myself again pacing the frigate's quarter-deck.

We made no captures during our cruise – a piece of ill-luck that did not usually befall the *Révolutionnaire*, of whose performances, as a fast sailer, most marvellous stories were rehearsed. Everybody, even to the least boy in the ship, felt an interest in her fame; and the histories of the chase and capture of the *Bordelais* and *Déterminée*, two large French privateers, were so familiar to me, that I almost fancied I had been a sharer in the frigate's wonderful exploits upon those memorable occasions.

We chased and boarded several neutrals, one of which, I remember, gave us a run of a dozen hours and more. She was seen from the masthead, and sail made after her, early in the morning. The wind was light and variable most part of the day, and though we neared her considerably, she was six or seven miles from us at sunset, at which time the breeze freshened, and became steady; and we seemed to be coming up with the chase fast. As it darkened, however, we were still at a considerable distance, and it was with difficulty we kept her in sight. Suddenly a bright light appeared in the direction of the object of our pursuit, which, increasing in magnitude and vividness every moment, attracted all eyes, and the general supposition was that the chase was on fire. Captain Twisden, who was an old and wary cruiser, was not so to be taken in; his eyes did not long rest upon the fiery beacon; but after viewing it steadily for a few seconds, he swept the horizon with his nightglass, and soon discerned our friend broad on the larboard bow, with larboard studding-sails set, having altered her course several points to port. To alter our course, likewise, trim sails, and shift the studding-sails, occupied but a few minutes; and again we were ploughing through it with the chase on our starboard bow. The Captain of the stranger, finding himself foiled in his first attempt, tried no more 'ruses', and in another hour we were alongside of him. He proved to be an American, with papers quite correct and regular, and having nothing on board that could warrant detention.

Like most of his countrymen, who were greatly annoyed, and bitterly exasperated, against all 'Britishers', for exercising the right of search after British seamen, or for goods belonging to an enemy, or contraband of war, with an exactness, and in a manner which they considered offensive, the master of the American, the moment he observed the frigate in chase, was resolved to use every effort to baffle and escape us; or, at all events, to lead us such a dance as should cost both time and trouble. He was much mistaken, however, in thinking that any stratagem could deceive the caution and watchfulness of our practised commander, or that he could escape the legs of the flying *Révolutionnaire*.

Although I look upon the right of search as one of England's most valuable privileges and acquirements, and one that should never be relinquished (for, without it, the stability and integrity of her empire would not be secure), yet it should always be exercised with the utmost delicacy and caution. Every officer, however strictly and exactly he is required by duty to enforce it, should be gravely warned to avoid all harshness of manner, and every appearance of injustice, and to give no offence or unnecessary trouble; and should he ever remove a man from a neutral, under the plea of his being a British subject, he should always be sure, or, at all events, have the strongest reasons for supposing him to be one.

About the end of July (the period of our cruise being expired), we returned to Cove, where we found a few transports, with the Dutch troops, then in the pay of England, embarked, ready to be escorted to Portsmouth. With these under our charge, we sailed in a few days, and, after a very tedious passage, left them at the Isle of Wight. We then made the best of our way to Plymouth, at which place I left the *Révolutionnaire*, and, I confess, without regret. My treatment in her, though not rougher than that which all the other youngsters experienced, was not calculated to conciliate my affections for either the ship or the service; and I may say now, without being liable to the charge of a grumbler, that my perfect ignorance of a sea-life, and extreme youth, might have justified the exercise of some indulgence and consideration in my favour. Possibly, however, the two months I passed in her steerage may not have been without advantage. They may have taught me to view, by comparison, many things as light and trivial, which otherwise I might magnify into serious evils, and to endure those real ills and hardships with patience and good humour, to which sailors are at all times exposed, even in ships that are considered the most *comfortable* and indulgent.

The *Diamond*, the ship I was about to join, was at sea when I arrived at Plymouth, and until she came into port, I was to stay with Mrs Griffith, the Captain's wife, who received and treated me with the greatest kindness, seeing herself to the completion of my wardrobe and nautical appointments.

At length the *Diamond* arrived, and I joined my proper ship, and great reason I had to rejoice in the exchange I made from the *Révolutionnaire*. I found the berths larger, better ordered, and, consequently, far more comfortable; and instead of the midshipmen's chests being stowed in them, and their hammocks hung in the tier, they were allowed to have both in the steerage. I felt this order of things the more agreeable, when I compared it with the state of discomfort in which the first two months of my probation had been passed.

The ship, which wanted repair, was stripped and taken into dock; and the First Lieutenant, a rigid officer, saw that the Midshipmen, young and old, attended in their stations to what was going forward. But besides what must be learned by a punctual attendance on the various duties of the ship, and the different operations going on in harbour, an experienced seaman was employed a couple of hours each day in teaching the youngsters every practical part of a seaman's duty. We learned each knot and splice that was known to Matthew Walker himself; and when we were sufficiently instructed in them, we were put to rig a small ship, that stood in the Captain's cabin for the purpose. We were shown how to raise sheers, and get in the lower masts and bowsprit; then to cut out, mark and serve the lower rigging, reeve the girt-lines, and get it over the mast-heads, prepared also by us for that purpose; and, in fact, without entering more into particulars, we rigged and unrigged the ship, until we were pronounced perfect by our teacher.

As there was no schoolmaster in the ship, one of the elder Midshipmen, a *protégé* of the Captain, kindly undertook to give me lessons in mathematics and navigation, but I fear I did not profit much by his instruction; nor, indeed, did I ever after show any predilection or much aptitude for figures or abstruse calculations.

About this time the preliminaries of peace were signed; and I remember Captain Griffith asked me whether, from what I had seen of the service, I really felt no distaste to a sea life. 'It is now peace,' added he, 'and there is no foreseeing how long it may last. Should it be of long continuance, promotion will become every year more difficult to obtain. You have only been a few months from home, and much time has not yet been lost. Now is the moment to decide, either to persevere and never after waver, or at once to give up all thoughts of the profession, and return to your friends.'

This was wholesome and judicious advice at such a period, and most kindly and encouragingly put; yet notwithstanding this friendly address, and, indeed, almost advice to relinquish the service, on the part of my Captain – strange as it may seem, although I sighed for home – though my dreams of early distinction and advancement, dissipating, one by one, before my better acquaintance with the service and the realities of a Midshipman's situation, were completely dissolved by the announcement of peace – though I began to entertain a very sincere and cordial dislike to the sea, yet, from false shame, an unwillingness to turn my back upon a profession that I had once adopted, and to confess all I felt and thought about it, I told the Captain that it was the one of all others that I preferred, and I was allowed to persevere.

These feelings and opinions, with the youngsters of the service, I believe are not singular; at least, the majority of officers that I have conversed with on the subject, very heartily detesting the early years of a middy's life, and all the discomforts that attend it, known only to the initiated, would most willingly fly back to their quiet homes and fond mammas before a year of their apprenticeship was served – their visions of renown and bold adventure that first dazzled their young imaginations being quite blotted out by a short acquaintance with that curious world which is only to be found upon the waters – were they not restrained by some such morbid feeling of *mauvaise honte* as I experienced myself.

As it was now peace, there seemed to be no great hurry to get the *Diamond* ready for sea; and so the people of the dockyard also thought, and therefore they took matters perfectly easy. Captain Griffith, who always was in the habit of giving his young gentlemen the opportunity of acquiring as much useful knowledge and accomplishments as the brief time allowed for refitting ships in time of war permitted, gladly availed himself of our present lengthened stay in harbour to have such as desired it instructed in drawing, French, and dancing; and, with the view of not permitting us to forget all early habits, and, from change of element, become 'rude and boisterous children of the sea', he invited us frequently to his house, and introduced us to several of his friends.

These particulars of our early sea-education in the *Diamond*, and the manner in which our conduct as young officers and gentlemen was looked after and attended to by our excellent Captain, have been brought to my recollection by having lately heard more than one absurd and very sweeping condemnation of a system which has been denominated that of the 'old school'. I freely confess that there were many things, as practised in a number of ships, in that system, which were susceptible of amendment. As yet, I have not seen a great deal of the 'new'; but truth compels me to declare, that in very few things in what I have seen can I discover a marked improvement.

Navigation and marine gunnery, two most important branches of naval science, have undoubtedly been much more attended to since the peace, and creditable progress has been made in spreading a more general knowledge of them through the service. Beyond these, I am not aware that much has been added; but in practical seamanship, and the ready manœuvring and handling of a fleet or squadron, I am convinced there is a decided falling off: in proof of which, one has only to refer to the enormous disproportion of casualties, in wreck and loss of masts and spars, that has taken place since the peace, and which can be accounted for in no other way than by supposing the race of officers now serving to be less efficient than the one employed during the war.

2: Under Captain Owen

For several months the *Diamond* was suffered to remain quietly in Plymouth harbour; but in February, 1802, she was sent to cruise off the coast of Cornwall for the prevention of smuggling. Whilst on this service no *contrabandistas* fell into our hands, which, nevertheless, were not suffered to be idle or unemployed. They were fully occupied in guarding against the dangers of a winter's cruise upon that coast, and in providing for the safety of the ship, which, during the whole of the short time we remained on the station, was exposed to a continuance of as rough weather as I ever remember to have felt. She was frequently driven from her anchors, and blown out of Mount's Bay, into which we used to run for shelter during the prevalence of violent westerly gales.

One of these gales, and its not unusual result, that of snapping our cable, is now present to my memory, where it has been fixed by the following circumstance. Once, during an appearance of moderate weather that in the end proved deceitful, the Captain ventured to go to a ball and concert at Penzance, taking some of the youngsters with him, myself among the rest. Soon after midnight, when the dancing and singing were at an end, we returned with the Captain to the ship, where we soon danced another measure, and had our senses enlivened and our ears tingled with a far different melody from that to which they had just been listening in the concert-room.

At the time we got on board there was not much wind; but it was 'breezing up' – the sky was lowering, and threatening to the north-west, with every appearance of a fast-approaching gale. The wind continued momentarily to increase, and every preparation was made, and precaution taken to withstand its force and pressure. All, however, proved vain; for, at six o'clock in the morning, it blew such a hurricane as swept the *Diamond* and *Hunter* brig resistlessly before its breath out of the bay.

When the first hurry and agitation consequent upon a ship's being driven from her anchors were over, and things were put to rights, no further damage or inconvenience was felt by the *Diamond*, for the wind was off the land, and the sea, though lashed into foam by the fury of the blast, was comparatively smooth. Such was not the case, however, with the little *Hunter*. Her berth was considerably further in, and nearer the southern side of the bay, than ours. There, after veering and parting the first cable, a second anchor was let go; but that scarcely held for a moment, the cable seemingly offering no greater resistance to the blast than so much packthread.

By this time she had drifted far, and neared the shore considerably, and, before her head could be got round, the brig was driven by the force of the wind between a small island, which lies off the village of Mousehole, and the Main, when, after striking three or four times with great violence in much less water than she drew, the lifting of the surge and the strength of the gale carried her through the passage. So imminent was her danger, however, and so close was she to the shore, that a Lieutenant and several men jumped on the mainland to escape what they conceived inevitable destruction. The brig proceeded to Plymouth to have her damages examined and repaired; but, although obliged to keep the pumps going all the way, she did not require our escort.

Soon after this occurrence, the *Diamond* was also obliged to return to Plymouth, this tempestuous winter having so shaken her about the bows, and damaged the 'hawse pieces', that she again required assistance from the dockyard. In order to get conveniently at that part of the ship which needed repairs, perfectly smooth water was necessary, and we went into Barn Pool. Whilst there, one of those accidents, which seem alone to paralyse the energies of a sailor, and deprive him of his self-possession, befel the ship.

It was noon, and the ship's company were all below at dinner. Suddenly the fearful and appalling cry of 'the ship's on fire!' resounded through the ship, followed by a simultaneous rush to all the hatchways, and that confused murmuring noise which always proceeds from a multitude in a state of doubt and alarm. Men, women, and children, thronged every approach to the ladders, and it was with the utmost difficulty that I squeezed myself through the press, and made my way upon deck. When there, I observed that the fire proceeded from the fore part of the ship. Already it had caught the booms, and the flames, every instant advancing more and more, were menacing the foremast.

For an instant irresolution and dismay seemed to possess the crew. Several exclaimed, as they observed the ascending flames, and the danger was magnified to their eyes by their own fears, that it was impossible to save the ship, and that the only way now left to preserve their lives, was to slip the bridles and let her drift on shore. Others, again, had the yard and stay-tackles in their hands, and were already in the act of preparing to hoist out the two remaining boats, the rest being absent on duty at the dockyard.

At this moment, the First Lieutenant reached the deck, and his voice, heard high above the din, in an instant commanded silence, and put a stop to the confusion. A few threatening gestures and expressions sufficed to shame and awe the timid, whilst his perfect self-possession, and clear and encouraging orders and directions, inspired confidence in all. The roll of the drum beating to quarters was now heard, and at its sound every one flew to his proper station. Soon some of the waist-hammocks were soaked overboard, and they, with the fire-buckets, were seen passing along the deck with order, regularity, and despatch; and in far less time than I have taken to write these few lines the fire was extinguished.

Here is an instance of the power and commanding influence which an officer, endowed with skill, courage, and discretion, is sure to exercise over the minds and actions of those that are placed under his control and authority. Instead of what he was – brave, cool, and resolute, with that perfect knowledge of his profession, which imparts trust and confidence in one's own skill and resources in the hour of danger – had our First Lieutenant been timid and wavering, weak of purpose and distrustful of himself, the ship was inevitably lost. Without a head to guide and direct them, the men, distracted and confused by the suddenness and activity of the fire, and infected, perhaps, by the cries and terror of the women, would have listened only to the suggestions of their own fears, which, in all probability, would have caused the destruction, not alone of the frigate, but also of many lives.

The fire originated by warming pitch in the galley, where the kettle containing it was left during dinner-time, with a man to watch and guard against accidents. From some inattention on his part, the pitch was suffered to boil over into the fire, which, running up the sides of the kettle, instantly communicated with its contents, and the whole boiling mass was quickly in a blaze. To quench this the man ignorantly threw a bucket of water on it, the consequence of which was, that the flaming pitch flew around in all directions, adhering tenaciously, and setting fire to whatever it touched that was unprotected by lead or sheeted tin. After all, the damage did not prove great: the boom-cloths were consumed, and some of the spars were deeply charred; the beams near the galley were also a good deal burned and blackened, and the aprons of the two guns on either side were melted. This, as well as I remember, was the sum of the injury the ship sustained.

In proceeding to join the fleet at Torbay, soon after this occurrence, the ship was becalmed, and in that state drifted near the Eddystone. The Captain availed himself of so good an opportunity to visit the light-house, and I was so fortunate as to be the youngster that accompanied him in the boat: I say fortunate, for from that day to the present hour I have had no other opportunity of examining its interior.

This very useful and most singular structure measures one hundred feet in height, and twenty-six, I think, in diameter. The basement, and whole of the exterior, is composed of solid blocks of granite dove-tailed into each other. The interior is faced with Portland stone, which is also used for the four or five stories, or apartments, that divide, at equal distances, the whole building; and the slabs which compose the floors of those apartments are likewise dove-tailed into each other. The whole is constructed of stone, and I cannot call to mind that any wood is employed throughout the edifice. Over the door of the lantern, and on the last stone that appears to have been set up, is engraved the date, with the following words of thanksgiving for the completion of so arduous an undertaking:

24 Aug., 1759,
Laus Deo.

Mr Smeaton was the engineer; and he has earned most just and permanent renown by the success which crowned so bold and difficult an enterprise. It is said, that observing the stability and vast powers of resistance which the trunk of an oak presents, first gave him the idea of his plan; and, accordingly, the Eddystone Lighthouse bears an exact resemblance to one in form, being circular, and gradually decreasing in circumference from the base to a certain height, from whence it diminishes more rapidly to the top. The resistance which it has successfully offered for so many years to the buffetings of seas and tempests bears lasting testimony to the judgment and talent of its designer.

The light-house was occupied by three men, who kept alternate watch by night; and whose duty it was to attend diligently to the light, and see that it was kept trimmed and in the most perfect order. They were furnished with provisions and water by the Custom House, which had the care of that duty; and they told us that once, and only once, the supply had nearly failed them, in consequence of a succession of hard gales, which cut off all communication with the shore for three weeks, at the end of which time, and just as their stock was quite exhausted, a boat from Plymouth was with difficulty enabled to reach them.

During the time we remained at Torbay, I do not remember anything remarkable occurring. There was in the bay, at the time I write of, a noble fleet of thirty sail, with the flags of several Admirals renowned in the naval annals of England. This fleet gradually diminished in number as day by day they sailed by twos and threes to the different ports to be paid off. At length it came to the *Diamond*'s turn to move. She was appointed to convey the Commander-in-Chief, who was about to strike his flag, to the eastward.

There was nothing in the outward and visible appearance of Admiral Cornwallis which could lead one to suppose that he was the man who, with such admirable skill, courage, and unshaken resolution, effected the ever-memorable retreat in 1795, braving and baffling with five sail of the line, the French fleet of fifteen; during which, in a short and energetic exhortation to the crew of his flag-ship, he is said to have used these brief but bold and expressive words – 'Remember, men, the *Sovereign*'s flag and ensign are never to be struck to an enemy – she goes down with them flying'; not that it was his judgment and enduring perseverance which first established those long and close blockades that for so large a part of the late war effectually crippled the French maritime commerce, and confined their navy to their own harbours. He seemed quiet and reserved in his deportment – elderly, and rather short and stout in person – and, if habited in a suit of brown and a round hat, instead of blue with a three-cornered one, would have looked more like a sober citizen or simple country gentleman than one of England's naval demi-gods. He was particularly abstemious both in meat and drink, scarcely touching wine, and living for the most part on pulse and vegetables.

After depositing the Admiral and his luggage at his country-seat near Lymington, we passed through the Needles, and anchored at Spithead, where we remained but a few days, and then proceeded with despatches to Lisbon.

Our stay at Lisbon was short, not exceeding three days, on the last of which I accompanied our caterer on shore, who was permitted to visit *terra firma* for the purpose of replenishing our seastock.

As the time we remained in the Tagus was so short, and my excursion on shore limited to an hour or so, it cannot be supposed that I know anything from personal observation of that most interesting city, or retain much remembrance of the surrounding scenery. I have a faint recollection of the appearance of the tall and ship-like burlings as we approached the coast; and of the well-known rock, which has its name from Lisbon, wearing its naked and giant form out of the ocean, whose fury and assaults it has broken and defied since time began. Advancing onwards towards the mouth of the noble river, numerous boats, with their white and picturesque sails, and crossing each other at every instant, danced as it were upon its golden surface. Then came the forts – Belem Castle – and lastly the city itself, rising from the margin of the river, and swelling upwards into a noble amphitheatre of houses, churches, convents, and palaces; whilst, to give animation to the picture, were seen above all, in full-play, the snowy sails of countless windmills. All these have left on my memory a dim and shadowy impression, like objects in a landscape thrown so far into shade and distance by the painter, that their form and colouring is hardly distinguishable.

In returning to Portsmouth we made the land somewhere about St Alban's-head. The Captain seemed anxious to reach Spithead that evening; but as the wind was scant, his object did not appear likely to be fulfilled. On, however, we pressed, and by the time we got abreast of St Helens it was dark night. The Master, feeling confidence in himself, undertook to work the ship in; and everything seemed to promise a speedy termination to a hard day's work, until we reached within one board of our anchorage, when the leadsman called out 'quarter less five'. The helm was instantly put down; but before she came round, or indeed could answer it, the ship was aground, and so fast, that, though the sails were quickly thrown aback, they failed to move her in the least.

Such are the moments that bring to the proof the resources and presence of mind of Captain and officers, and show the order and discipline of a ship's crew.

When we took the ground, the Master had calculated, by some error, that the tide was a few minutes past the flood, whereas it still wanted a quarter of an hour of high-water. As, therefore, there seemed little hope of getting the ship afloat before the next tide, unless the utmost exertions were made, every effort was put forth to lighten her as quickly as possible. All the shot on deck was thrown overboard – the water in the hold was started – boats hoisted out – top-gallant yards and masts, and every top-hamper from aloft got on deck: the maindeck guns were being hove overboard, and an anchor laid out in deep water to heave upon; and, lest all should not do, and the ship might fall over as the tide left her, the spare top-masts were got over the side, and fixed as shores to keep her upright. All this was done (and in the night too) with an order and dispatch that in my subsequent career at sea I never saw surpassed.

Meantime, signal-guns had been fired to give notice of our situation; and, just as we began to heave on the anchor that had been laid out, a pilot from the Isle of Wight, who was passing in his boat at no great distance from where we grounded, and heard our guns, came on board. From him we learned that the shoal we were upon was 'No-man's-land', and that it was still scarcely high-water; so that, lightened as the ship was, and by heaving a taught strain on the cable, in all likelihood she would speedily be afloat. Another 'rally' was given at the capstan, and in a few seconds the ship was hove into deep water, where we remained for the night.

Next day was busily employed in 'sweeping' for the five guns that had been thrown overboard. This operation was easily accomplished with the three that were last ejected from the ship; but not so with the other two. These last were imbedded deep in the sand and ooze, from the force and weight with which I suppose the other guns had fallen upon them, and many hours were fruitlessly spent in trying to recover them. At length it occurred to one of the older midshipmen, who was an expert swimmer and diver, to go down, and try whether he could not scrape away with his hands sufficient of the ooze to admit the line to pass beneath the guns. This he effected with great labour and difficulty, after repeated trials, and by this means they were all finally recovered, so that nothing was lost but the shot which was on deck at the time we got on shore.

The Midshipman alluded to was regarded and esteemed by all in the ship. Happy in his temper and disposition, and blessed with a never-failing fund of anecdote and good humour, his presence was always sure to promote mirth and cordiality amongst his messmates, with the young ones of whom, particularly, he was an especial favourite. Perfectly well acquainted with the various duties of an officer and a seaman, he was ever foremost where intrepidity and skill required his presence. He is now a Captain, reposing, I presume, on his laurels, which, with a wooden-leg, he has gallantly earned in the service of his country.

Soon after our return from Lisbon, Captain Griffith left us, to the general regret of all, both officers and men. He had been in the service about twenty-five years, of which time half that number of months had not been passed on shore. It may well be imagined that he required some repose, and was anxious to avail himself of a moment of peace, to rub off some of the rust which he had contracted by so long a residence upon the waters.

By the Captain's removal from the *Diamond*, the youngsters, about whom he felt interested, were all dispersed. Fresh ships had to be provided for them; no easy matter in the reduced state of the navy during the peace. He was enabled to place me with a friend who had just got the command of a thirty-six-gun frigate, and in a few days after, in the month of June, 1802, I had the good fortune to join the *Immortalité*, commanded by Captain Owen.

There was always to me something melancholy and dispiriting in parting with old friends and making new; and, therefore, although I had been an inmate of the *Diamond* but for the brief space of eight months, it was not without a feeling of regret, bordering on despondency, that I left her. However, as I remarked before, a ship, and particularly that part of one called the Midshipmen's berth, is the worst place imaginable for the indulgence of such feelings. The fun and frolic and never-ending gaiety of the steerage would murder sentiment, if anything resembling such could long exist amidst the bustle and duties of a sailor's life.

My new Captain was a man somewhat turned of thirty, with light hair and a fair complexion; having an open and cheerful countenance, with bright blue eyes that be spoke at once intelligence and good-nature. His figure was tall and commanding, with a frame of vast power and strength, exhibiting in his person the semblance of one of those Saxon Thanes who led his followers to the conquest of Britain.

Captain Owen was the eldest son of Commander William Owen, who lost an arm when a Midshipman, at the attack of Pondicherry, in 1760. Commander Owen, whose family was of high Welsh origin, in the county of Montgomeryshire, was present at the second attack and capture of Pondicherry, in 1778, in command of the *Cormorant*, and being charged with despatches relative to the reduction of that place, he was accidentally killed at Madras, where he had touched on his way to England.

Captain Owen was entered at a very early age on the books of the *Enterprise*, then commanded by Sir Thomas Rich, the intimate friend of his father; but I have reason to know that he did not embark till several years later, for I heard him say in June, 1802, that he was then exactly nineteen years at sea, and that he had embarked as early as youngsters at that time were accustomed to do.

After a service on different stations throughout the peace, which succeeded the American Revolutionary War, Sir Edward Owen, as we may now call him, was made a Lieutenant in 1793, from which time until again promoted, he served principally with the late Sir John Colpoys, who always entertained the highest opinion of his value and abilities.

Soon after Lord Bridport's action off L'Orient, in 1795, in which Sir Edward Owen bore a part as First Lieutenant of the *London*, he was made a Commander. Being unemployed when the mutiny broke out in the fleet at Spithead, he repaired immediately as a volunteer on board the *London*, Admiral Colpoy's flag-ship, where it was known the mutineers were the most violent and determined.

On the suppression of the mutiny he was appointed to command a division of gun-brigs stationed in the river and at the Nore, under the orders of Sir Erasmus Gore, and in that command he remained till April 1798, when he was made Post-Captain.

Sir John Colpoys had just then been appointed naval Commander-in-Chief in the East Indies, and for his prudent but resolute conduct during the mutiny, made a Knight of the Bath by the King. He immediately chose Owen for his Captain, who commissioned the *Northumberland*, which ship had been appointed to receive the flag. But as soon as Sir John was given to understand that a strong though unjust and unreasonable prejudice among seamen existed against him personally, for what had occurred on board the *London* during the mutiny, not wishing that his presence should prevent a perfect oblivion of the past, and a cordial reconciliation between officers and men, forgetful, as he was, of self, and mindful only of his country's interest and advantage, he at once resigned an appointment so every way desirable.

This step on the part of the Admiral placed the subject of this notice again on half-pay, and he remained unemployed till the year 1801, when he was appointed to the *Nemesis*. In that ship he cruised for the most part of the time off the coast of Holland and the mouth of the Scheldt, till the peace in 1802, when he got the command of the *Immortalité*, a larger frigate of thirty-six guns, eighteen pounders.

From the summer of 1802, till the re-commencement of hostilities in May, 1803, Captain Owen was senior officer of a small squadron, whose rendezvous was the Downs, for the double purpose of checking smuggling, and being ready for any other service or emergency for which the squadron might be required.

A brief detail of Captain Owen's services in the *Immortalité*, will be found as these passages proceed, and it only remains for me to give a concise account of his subsequent services, as well as I have been able to collect them, after I ceased to be under his command.

The old *Immortalité*, from hard knocks and rough usage, being fairly worn out, Captain Owen was appointed, in the spring of 1806, to the *Clyde*, a fir frigate of thirty-eight guns. The crew of the *Immortalité* being turned over to the *Clyde*, the latter was soon ready for sea, and he sailed from Sheerness early in April again to resume his station off Boulogne.

His squadron was now much enlarged, and to mark their sense of his activity and services, the Admiralty directed him to hoist a Commodore's pendant. A distinction so honourable, conferred on a Captain whose seniority then did not count more than eight years, proves in what estimation Sir Edward Owen was held at that early period of his career.

The Commodore remained on that service all the summer of 1806, watching the port of Boulogne and the flotilla, with his wonted care and vigilance.

The missile, called Congreve's rockets, had then been newly invented, and the *Clyde* having been supplied with a quantity of them, Commodore Owen was ordered to choose his own time and opportunity for trying their effect upon the flotilla and town of Boulogne. Having assembled his squadron, which consisted of four frigates, including the *Clyde*, seven sloops of war, seven gun-brigs, and three bombs, he sailed from Dungeness early on the 8th of October, 1806, and anchored four miles from Boulogne before noon of that day. The weather proving favourable for a trial of the rockets, the boats of the squadron assembled the same evening, after dark, astern of the *Clyde*, being formed in four divisions of twenty each.

The first division was commanded by Lieutenant Charles F Payne, the senior Lieutenant of the *Clyde*, attended by my old messmate, Tom Clarke, his never-absent aide-de-camp upon such occasions. The three other divisions were each under the charge of a commander, and the whole was directed personally by the Commodore himself.

Sometime before midnight the boats cast off, and pulled for the shore. When sufficiently near they were ranged in front of the pier, and then the work of destruction commenced. The bombardment began before three o'clock in the morning, and continued for more than three hours. Seventy or eighty rockets were distinctly seen at one time in the air by the ships outside. But notwithstanding the severity of the fire, and the length of time for which it was kept up, it did not prove as effective as might have been expected. Possibly the position of the boats was too near the shore, for my friend Clarke has told me that they were not more than their own lengths from the beach – all this time they were unmolested in their work – not a shot was fired from the batteries on shore: nor do I think that this supineness on the part of the enemy is accounted for by what was afterwards learned, namely, that the bombardment of Boulogne was but a feint to mask the disembarkation which was actually taking place on the sands of Etaple, to the west of Boulogne. But if this report had any real foundation, and the French in their turn were alarmed at invasion, does it not prove how denuded the coast of France was at that time of troops; and had the Government of England been aware of that fact, how easy it would have been to have landed a body of troops, and to have inflicted a severe chastisement upon the enemy – if not have destroyed his boasted flotilla.

Upon reconnoitring the town and harbour the next day, it was plainly observed that several houses were much damaged, but it could not be seen that the flotilla in the harbour had received any injury.

On the following night (the night of the 9th and 10th of October, 1806) the Commodore went on board the *Meteor*, and with the other two bombs, bombarded Boulogne for a couple of hours, which must have kept the good people of the town awake, if it did them no more serious mischief.

From that time till the year 1809, Commodore Owen remained, I think all the while, in command of the inshore squadron, watching the flotilla in Boulogne. In that year his frigate formed part of the force which proceeded to the Scheldt, with the avowed object of attacking and destroying the arsenal of Antwerp, and the Franco-Batavian squadron moored below that town. It is not necessary to give an account of all the proceedings of that memorable but unfortunate expedition. Its history has been already written, and the causes and details of its failure were fully sifted by the Parliamentary inquiry which was instituted at the time. Its want of success must not be attributed to a lack of gallantry on the part of the army or navy. When called upon to act, their forwardness and courage were never more conspicuously displayed. One anecdote, however, of Commodore Owen, which shows the bold and ready seaman, though I believe, well known, may here be repeated. The *St Domingo*, Sir Richard Strachan's flag-ship, in passing up the West Scheldt, took the ground on a bank before Flushing, nearly within point-blank range of the batteries. Her situation was most critical, exposed to the fire of the enemy, and being near the time of high-water when she got ashore, it was very doubtful whether she could be got off without prompt and great exertion.

Seeing the dangerous position of his chief, Commodore Owen, without signal and without a moment's hesitation, instantly ran the *Clyde* to his assistance, and dropped the anchor as near as possible to the *St Domingo*'s bow. The *Clyde*'s sheet-cable was then passed from her stern port to the *St Domingo*'s off-shore quarter, while by Commodore Owen's suggestion, the latter ship carried out her stream-anchor and cable from the opposite bow to act as a spring.

While these preparations were going on, the fire from the shore was kept up with great activity – nor was that of the *St Domingo*, whose broadside was exposed to the shore, less idle. Both ships were a good deal cut up. The *Clyde* was hulled several times, and the heads of her fore and main masts were both badly wounded. When all was ready, which, under the circumstances, and considering the work to be done, was accomplished in an exceedingly short time, it being now high-water, a few hearty rallies at the capstan hove the *St Domingo* off the shoal, when she passed the town, and the *Clyde* returned to her former anchorage.

Sir Richard Strachan sensibly felt, and acknowledged the prompt and skilful assistance which he received from the *Clyde*; and when my old messmate, Clarke, went on board the *St Domingo* to deliver some suggestion to Sir Richard from Commodore Owen, 'Thank your Captain from me, Sir,' said he, 'he is a d——d fine fellow, and has placed his ship most gallantly and judiciously – just on the spot I could have wished.'

When Walcheren and Flushing were ordered to be abandoned, Commodore Owen, who had been actively employed with the flotilla under his command in checking the enemy who had advanced into South Beveland, and in preventing him from arming the batteries, which he was enabled to throw up under cover of the night, had charge of the seamen who were on shore co-operating with the engineers in dismantling and destroying the arsenal and public buildings of Flushing; and when all was finished, and he had superintended the embarkation of the last man from the Island, he reported its total evacuation to Sir Richard Strachan, who thanked him a second time for his activity, intelligence, and exertions.

Soon after the termination of their untoward expedition, the *Clyde* being fairly worn out, Commodore Owen was appointed to the

Inconstant, a frigate of thirty-six guns, and his officers and old ship's company a third time turned over with him.

In his new ship the Commodore was sent to Vera Cruz – it is to be presumed to look for money, and to give him the chance of freight, as some recompense for all his hard services. If this were the case, the good intentions of the Admiralty were worse than unsuccessful. Little money was found at Vera Cruz, and soon after leaving the coast of Mexico, the yellow fever broke out on board the *Inconstant*, and carried off many valuable lives – amongst others, John Tapper, the master, a most worthy, excellent man and valuable officer. He was universally regretted in the ship, and by none more than by his captain, whom he had followed from the *Immortalité* and *Clyde* to the *Inconstant* (although by his seniority entitled then to be master of a second-rate), and who, knowing his worth, and appreciating his good qualities, always felt for him a well-deserved esteem and regard.

The *Inconstant* was afterwards stationed chiefly off the Scheldt, where Commodore Owen commanded the in-shore squadron.

His next appointment was to the *Cornwall* a new ship of the line, of seventy-four guns. A recent order of the Admiralty, which directed that first lieutenants of the ships of the line must have served seven years, prevented Captain Owen from taking his first lieutenant with him into the *Cornwall*, because his standing as such was but of six years; and thus by a regulation, which I must characterize as senseless and absurd, my old messmate, Clarke, who had served uninterruptedly the almost unprecedented number of twelve years with the same captain, and who, from a youngster, had risen to the station of First Lieutenant, was separated from his old captain; and Captain Owen had a stranger thrust upon him as his second in command, about whom he knew nothing, instead of an officer who was thoroughly acquainted with his views and mode of discipline, and upon whose efficiency, judgment, and skill he could place implicit reliance.

In the *Cornwall*, Commodore Owen's station was still off the Scheldt, where he continued to command the in-shore squadron, till towards the close of the year 1813, when the successes of the allies in the north of Europe aroused the Dutch to shake off the French yoke also, and he landed in South Beveland with a body of seamen and marines to their assistance.

When, by the overthrow of Bonaparte and the French power, peace was restored to Europe, and our fleets and armies were no longer wanted nearer home, war still continuing in America, Commodore Owen was sent out to take the command of the ships and vessels on the lakes of

Canada. But he had scarcely arrived in that country when hostilities ceased between England and the United States; and as soon as the definitive treaty of peace was signed he returned home.

When the Order of the Bath was remodelled and enlarged, Commodore Owen was nominated a knight commander, and he was afterwards successively made a G.C.H. of the Guelphic Order, and G.C.B. From the early part of the year 1816 till 1822, he held command of the royal yacht, *Royal Sovereign*. But even in that command he could hardly be called idle; for during that time he brought to this country four of the royal dukes and their duchesses, besides the Archduke Michael, and the Duke of Hesse-Homburg.

In the year 1822, the pirates in the West Indies were very troublesome, and had committed many acts of violence and depredation on the shipping of all nations trading to those seas. In consequence of this, our merchants made loud complaints to the Government and Admiralty of the inactivity and supineness of our men-of-war on that station, and of the impunity with which those freebooters committed such desperate outrages, and carried off their prey. Under those circumstances, Sir Edward Owen was selected as a fitting officer, and he was appointed to command on the Windward Island station as a commodore, having a captain under him. The *Gloucester* was named for his pendant, and he sailed as soon as she could be got ready, for his destination. But before he reached Barbadoes, piracy was almost at an end; for, awakened from their lethargy by the boldness of these sea-robbers, and the complaints and remonstrances which were heard on all sides, the officers bestirred themselves, and soon crushed the mischief which had been allowed to grow into so troublesome a nuisance.

The health of Sir Charles Rowley, the Commander-in-Chief at Jamaica, requiring him to go to Europe, he resigned the command; and Sir Edward Owen was appointed to supply his place, till the term for which Sir Charles had been appointed should have expired.

During the time Sir Edward held the command at Jamaica, he gave great satisfaction to the merchants, and the House of Assembly in the island passed an unanimous vote of thanks to him for his prompt and unremitting attention to the interests of commerce, and the varies duties devolving upon him as commander of the naval forces in the West Indies.

Sir Edward became a rear-admiral in May, 1825, soon after which he was chosen Member of Parliament for Sandwich. He was next appointed Surveyor-General of the Ordnance, an office which he held till requested by the Lord High Admiral, the late King William IV, to become a member of his council at the Admiralty.

When the Lord High Admiral resigned his office, in 1828, Sir Edward Owen became one of the Board of Admiralty which was then formed, with Lord Melville at its head; and in December of the same year he was appointed Commander-in-Chief on the East India station. On my return from the West Indies, in the spring of 1829, I found him at Spithead with his flag on board the *Southampton*, on the eve of starting for his destination. I immediately got a boat, and went on board to see my old and valued chief. I found him, as he always was, kind and affable, and glad to see an old shipmate; and I rejoiced to see that though he had grown much stouter, and years had rounded his person, they had not dimmed the luster of his eye, nor damped the ardour of his vigorous and ever-active mind.

During his command, affairs in the East remained peaceable, and did not call forth those qualities and exertions for which Sir Edward Owen was so eminently conspicuous. At the expiration of the term of his command, he returned to England, and upon the formation of Sir Robert Peel's short-lived ministry in 1834–1835, he filled the office of Clerk of the Ordnance. Upon the dissolution of that ministry he went out of office, and remained unemployed till the year 1841, when he was appointed to succeed Sir Robert Stopford in the command of the Mediterranean station.

When he assumed the command of that station, the storm which had just before agitated the Mediterranean had passed away. The little war which we had been waging on the coast of Syria was at an end. The Pacha of Egypt was humbled, and the cloud which looked so angry, and threatened a rupture with France, passed off without more mischief than just disturbing for awhile the *entente cordiale* between that country and England. Sir Edward had little more therefore to occupy him than to attend to the discipline and efficiency of his squadron, and to see that vessels of the right force and description were stationed where they were required, for the protection and advantage of commerce.

On the expiration of the term of his command, which took place in 1845, Sir Edward Owen returned to England, and retiring to his country seat at Windlesham, near Bagshot, enjoyed for the few remaining years of his life that peace and quiet which the period of fifty years of active service (longer by far than any other officer in the navy can boast of) deservedly earned.

Sir Edward Owen died on the 8th of October, 1849, deeply regretted by all who knew him, and by none more sincerely than by the writer of these pages.

For some time after Captain Owen joined the *Immortalité*, he quietly observed the working of the system of discipline which he found established in the ship by his predecessor, seldom interfering except when he deemed it absolutely necessary, and only changing those parts of it which he found might be obviously improved. These alterations were introduced so gradually, and, as it were, silently, that they were almost imperceptible; so that he found, in the course of a very few months, without giving the least offence, or wounding the feelings of anybody by a rash and hasty condemnation of all that he found in operation in the ship when he took the command of her, that his own views and wishes with respect to order and discipline were fully and cheerfully adopted.

Possessed himself of a vast fund of professional knowledge, both practical and theoretical, he was ever ready and happy to impart instruction to those who sought it. To the youngsters of the ship he was of incalculable benefit; and I have never met an officer who took the same pains or possessed the same happy method of instilling a knowledge of their duty into the minds of his young *élèves* as Captain Owen.

One or two of us usually breakfasted with him every morning, and he took that opportunity to question us on subjects relating to the duties of our profession, and the advances we were making in the knowledge of seamanship. These questions were put so judiciously, that they not only drew from us all we knew, without wounding our *amour propre* by an exposure of our ignorance, but our answers likewise afforded him an occasion of discussing and explaining the properties and uses of many things, without which we might have known nothing for years. In his inquiries about our knowledge of those things that are least in view, he was most minute, well-knowing that the younger midshipmen trouble themselves very little about matters that are not before their eyes; and, in order that we might be made acquainted with all that was doing under hatches, as well as on deck, one of us was ordered, by turns, daily to attend the mate of the hold in the performance of his duties.

The ignorance in which some officers are contented to remain, with regard to those things that are not always in sight, may be briefly illustrated by the following anecdote:

A midshipman of my acquaintance, and who subsequently attained the rank of captain, had nearly completed his *six years*, and joined a ship in the Mediterranean, taking with him letters of introduction and recommendation to Lord Collingwood, then commander-in-chief. With these he waited on his Lordship, who found, upon perusing them, that one was from Lord Barham, lately First Lord of the Admiralty, containing the simple and very modest request that the young gentleman, the bearer of the note, might be appointed an acting lieutenant until his time should be completed. Lord Collingwood, who was much teased with similar applications, and was, besides, no bad judge of the cut and fashion of a sailor, generally addressed a few questions to such aspirants for lieutenancies as the one who now stood before him; and according to their answers, he either took them at once into his own ship, that he might be a closer observer of their qualifications and deserts, or left them, for an indefinite time, in the one to which they belonged. After the usual commonplaces of 'how long he had served?' 'and with whom, and upon what station?' – in pursuance of this wholesome plan, he proceeded to put Mr——'s nautical knowledge to the proof; upon which he was soon abundantly satisfied. His very first question proved a puzzler – this candidate for *untimely* promotion being unable to tell how or where the 'bitter (better) ends of the bower-cables are clenched.' He was, therefore, sent back to his ship with an admonition to make himself better acquainted with his profession, which, his Lordship added, he should be glad to hear was the case from the captains, whose duty it would be to examine him, when his six years' service as a midshipman should be completed.

But it was not alone to the manual and practical part of our profession that Captain Owen directed our attention; he was equally careful that our instruction in navigation and astronomy should be as good as he could provide: and, at his request, even the chaplain kindly undertook to see that those who had any knowledge of the classics should not entirely lose it. At this time, indeed, he was unceasing in his endeavours to give us a taste and love for learning whatever could be useful; and I remember his once saying, 'let something new and profitable be added to your stock every day: recollect that no kind of knowledge is beneath the notice of a gentleman – all may be useful to the officer.'

Soon, indeed, more busy times and far higher duties claimed his undivided attention. But, although he could no longer bestow much time on the formation and instruction of the youngsters, our conduct and well-doing were ever the objects of his greatest care and solicitude. He had always a passing word of encouragement and advice for us; and, to crown all, we had continually before our eyes the surpassing advantage of his admirable example.

Our station, after I joined the *Immortalité*, was the Downs, and our occupation that of checking smuggling; for which purpose we cruised, during the remainder of the summer months, between the South Foreland and Beachy Head. To assist in the detection of those defrauders of the revenue, our boats were occasionally sent away for a few days, with instructions to cruise close in-shore during the night, on that part of the coast and in those bays which were considered the favourite haunts of the 'free-traders'. Once I was permitted to accompany a mate in the launch on an excursion of this kind, who, disappointed, I suppose, at his little success against the smugglers, contrived nevertheless that his expedition should not be wholly fruitless.

Our cruising-ground extended from Beachy Head to the high land at Farleigh, including within that range Eastbourne, Pevensey, and Hastings; all of which I had but just time to take a hasty glance at, although I should have been glad to have had a more leisurely view of ground every inch of which is interesting, from being the spot in England first pressed by William the Norman and his conquering bands.

Hastings was not, at that time, so much frequented as it has become since, but sufficiently so to furnish company for an occasional ball, one of which was to be held that very evening, and the officers of the *Immortalité* were requested to attend it. Accordingly, in obedience to this request, a party of the officers and midshipmen left the ship for the shore in the evening, and I amongst the number, furnished with a note from Captain Tudor to the Misses Abrams, inviting them to breakfast on board the *Immortalité* the next morning. The note proved for me one of very agreeable introduction, for I was very cordially received, and requested to join their party to the ball.

There is always some little circumstance, though seemingly trifling and insignificant, that brings to our minds the occurrences of by-gone times; and my accidental and transient acquaintance with the Misses Abrams, together with some cutting reflections on the officers of the *Immortalité* by certain young ladies, may account for my retaining any remembrance of the ball at Hastings.

The ladies in question, who were at the ball, having a quick conception of the ridiculous, or perhaps inspired by a little spice of *malice* at being unnoticed by any of the gay officers of the *Immortalité*, wrote a rather ludicrous account of it to a young cousin, who happened to belong to the ship, concluding their description in these words:

'But we forgot to mention your officers; and yet what can we say of them that can meet your approval? Fain would we speak in their commendation and praise; firstly, because they are sailors, whom we ever wished to esteem and respect; and, secondly, because they are our dear cousin's shipmates and companions: but truth, which has been our guide throughout these some-what tiresome observations, compels us to declare that the lieutenants – alas! for poor human nature! – were both very tipsy; and so redolent of onions were your own messmates, that they were quite unapproachable.'

To the charge of committing so grievous a solecism in good taste, and offending noses delicate and polite, I fear the midshipmen must plead

guilty; for on that particular day, their unlucky stars ordained that a
sea-pie of three-decked dimensions, prepared and cooked with all the
culinary skill that their boy possessed, should grace their board. Nor in his
anxiety to render this effort of this genius and art quite faultless, by a due
admixture of all necessary ingredients, did he omit the important adjunct
of onions, without which the world, at least the nautical world, must be
aware that sea-pie would prove tasteless and insipid. To this dish, then,
always an especial favourite in a middy's berth, did we most seriously
apply ourselves, and with that diligence and cordial good-will which are
enlivened and sustained by sea-air and youthful appetites.

Thus much for the midshipmen. The head and front of their offending appears to be this: that they, listening only to the cravings of empty
stomachs, and forgetting that the scented air of the ball-room in the
evening might betray the homeliness of their noon-day meal, partook too
largely of the forbidden, but savoury and seductive, mess.

I am not sure that so valid an apology can be offered for the other
charge. *One* of the lieutenants certainly carried a heavy press of sail, and
steered so ominously wild, that I am at a loss to conceive how he contrived
to preserve his perpendicular so long. Towards the close of the evening,
however, the heat of the room, with perhaps a little more added to the
canvas he was already reeling under, at last proved too much for him,
and, as he was figuring in the dance, something threw him off his already
uncertain balance, and down he came, measuring a length of no common
dimensions on the boards.

Lieutenant S—— was an Irishman, born, I believe, in Dublin. He had
entered Trinity College, which may account for his choosing the profession of the sea at a much later period of life than is generally the case. His
début was in the *Sans Pareil*, under the auspices of Captain Packenham.
From his age and size he could not be regarded as a youngster; and, not
knowing what else to do with him, the First Lieutenant soon placed him
in charge of the after-cockpit, from whence he only emerged to catch
hasty glimpses of the sky, and breathe a more elevated atmosphere, at
those hours when bats and owls are abroad seeking recreation and amusement in their evening rambles. His nautical knowledge, therefore, was in
exact proportion to his opportunities for gaining it. Although his limbs
and frame were not in proportion to his height, Lieutenant S——'s
stature was almost gigantic, measuring at least six feet three inches, his
breadth decreasing somewhat from his hips to his shoulders, which, for so
tall a man, were unusually narrow.

I think he is now before me – his ponderous day and night-glass
under his arm – pacing, with long and measured strides, the *Immortalité*'s

quarter-deck – his face, habitually rosy, and which after dinner assumed the hue of an unripe mulberry, rendered more so by contrast with a broad white neck-cloth, that displayed to great advantage the more than common length of his attenuated neck, and from its tightness prevented his looking to the right hand or left without turning his whole body – his lower man encased in tight pantaloons, over which were drawn a pair of Hessian boots, that idly flapped against his calveless legs at every step he took.

Such, at the time I write of, were the outward bearing and appearance of Lieutenant S—. Possessed of some humour and native quaintness, and by no means ignorant on subjects not connected with matters relating to the sea, he was considered rather a pleasant fellow, and liked very much by his messmates. Not so, however, with the midshipmen. He saw and *felt* his deficiencies as an officer, and was quite aware of his habits of intemperance, although, like many men of cunning but little minds, he hoped to cloak them under a harsh and unfeeling manner to his inferiors. Conduct such as this had, with us, an effect quite contrary to that he looked for. We began to regard him with dislike and disrespect, and, in fact, almost to deride his authority, which led to numerous remonstrances and complaints on one side and the other. Captain Owen endured him long; indeed, until after the commencement of hostilities in 1803, when he exchanged to the Sea Fencibles. From these he again got afloat, and for his besetting sin found himself under an arrest on board the *Conqueror* on the morning of the ever-memorable Battle of Trafalgar. It is customary to release all prisoners on going into action, and Mr S – benefited by the lucky amnesty.

The First Lieutenant of the *Conqueror* fell in the battle, and my friend, who happened to be the second, succeeding to his place, was consequently promoted. That was the first piece of good fortune resulting from his removal from the *Immortalité*. His next was his speedy appointment, as one of the *distinguished* of Trafalgar, to the command of a sloop-of-war on the Yarmouth station. There our hero soon married the daughter of a rich citizen, who, moreover, had weight in the borough; and thus this man, who used to declare that he was quite content to remain a Lieutenant if people would only allow him to live unmolested, without scrutinizing too curiously into his habits and conduct, by one of those freaks of that whimsical goddess to whom he appears so singularly indebted, soon found himself a Post-Captain. Before long, however, I missed his name from the list of Captains, but I never heard either his subsequent history, or the manner of his death, if indeed he be dead.

The morning after the ball was bright and cloudless, and the water, unruffled by a single breeze, smooth and shining as a mirror, seemed to woo the most timid to its bosom. At ten o'clock in the morning the boats of the *Immortalité* were on shore for the expected guests, and soon after I had the happiness to find myself seated beside my partner of the night before, Miss Eliza A –, and rowing towards the frigate.

This young lady was about sixteen or seventeen, rather below the middle stature, but elegantly formed, and with a countenance which, although not critically beautiful, beamed with intelligence and good nature. A native ingenuousness and frankness of heart laughed in her bright blue eyes, which were arched, and fringed with lashes the colour of her brown luxuriant hair.

The night before, at the ball, her manner to me was civil, I may say, almost kind, far more so than boys of my age generally experience from young ladies dancing and chatting with me, and looking for partners for me whenever I wanted them. No marvel, then, that a boy should be attracted by so much condescension and good-nature. I found myself always near her while she remained on board the *Immortalité*, and very uncomfortable and fidgetty if any one else engrossed a part of her time and attentions. Perhaps she observed the increasing pleasure I took in her society, and felt gratified and amused at the opportunity of thus early exercising her powers, and awakening in one, even so young and unconscious, feelings that some day she hoped to kindle in the breast of a more mature and fitter object. She was merely adjusting an arrow to her bow, which, sometime or other, was to take a higher flight, and bring a nobler quarry to her feet. Whatever the young lady's feelings and motives might have been, it proved an epoch in my life; for, from that day, I felt a charm, an attraction, in the society of women that I never knew before. Again, on board I had the pleasure of dancing with her; but when I heard her sing 'Poor Tom Halyard,' which she did, and with that taste and feeling, without which all music, vocal as well as instrumental, makes no impression on the heart, I felt a tear fill either eye, that I was mortally ashamed of, but could not, for the life of me, repress.

Time, however much we deprecate its flight, will not stand still – the moment of separation was at hand. Four o'clock came, the boats were manned, and the whole party quickly rowed to the shore. A friendly shake by the hand from my Dulcinea and her sisters, with a cordial invitation to call on them at Grosvenor Gate whenever I found myself in London, and we parted never to meet again.

Thus, what on the young lady's side was nothing but a little playful, pardonable coquetry, had the effect of making me very uncomfortable, I may say disconsolate, for at least a week, rendering me absent and inattentive to my duty – dreaming of London and Grosvenor Gate – when my thoughts should be given to swabbing and sweeping the decks, and coiling down ropes. These reveries were generally interrupted by the First Lieutenant, asking, in a voice of thunder, what the d—l I was about, and if that rebuke was not sufficient, a four hours' spell at the mast-head had wondrous efficacy; and at the end of a week or ten days, by the application of such remedies, I was quite restored to my senses.

About the end of autumn we returned to the Downs, where we were directed to remain as guardship for the winter. About the same time the ship's company was regulated according to the then peace establishment. This reduced the number of seamen considerably, whilst it gave us a great increase of midshipmen, all those who had served *five* years being to be provided with ships. Thus our complement was doubled; and as they came to us from all quarters, and were of every shade and character, they proved by no means an acceptable acquisition to our already crowded berths. As no youngsters formed a part of this immigration, and the grown-up midshipmen vastly preponderated, it fared but badly with the juvenile party, to whose comforts and feelings, moral as well as physical, very little attention was shown. I forget now how many we mustered in the berth, but I should think not less than fourteen or sixteen, of which number three only could be properly classed amongst youngsters.

Notwithstanding the berths of the midshipmen were so numerously furnished with inmates, from the reduced state of the ship's crew, the idlers' list could not be conveniently increased; and one wretched boy allotted to each berth had alone to perform the three-fold functions of steward, cook, and attendant. The duty, therefore, was imposed upon us (I mean the three young *gentlemen*) to assist in cleaning out the berth before breakfast, and likewise to wash and clean the cups and saucers, glasses and decanters. All this was performed by the young gentlemen of the morning watch; and however marvellous it may appear to men of modern times, I (egomet) have been, times without number, on my knees scrubbing the *Immortalité's* starboard berth, and, when my turn came, if I neglected to do so, the colt of Mr Young, our venerable and respected caterer, admonished me of my remissness in terms not soon to be forgotten.

All this is now past and gone, and I can look back to the time when I was compelled to those tasks, and only smile at the remembrance that such things were; but I cannot altogether forget that the infliction was, at the moment, a burden most grievous to be borne; and though no advocate for a mistaken indulgence in the management of youngsters bringing up to so rough a profession, yet I think the system bad which could require, or tolerate, the performance of such offices as I have described, by the sons of gentlemen supposed to be in the capacity of officers. It was not of long continuance, however, after I entered the navy. It soon became bettered; and, had we gone no further, but laying aside whatever was objectionable in the old manner of treatment, stopped at simple melioration, all would have been well, and now nothing would be left to complain of. I fear, however, that we have departed from the safe and middle course, and advanced a good way further; for now, instead of one boy being allowed to each midshipman's berth, there are three, sometimes, I believe, four, allotted for that purpose. Now, instead of blacking their own shoes, and performing such offices as I have mentioned, the midshipmen have each a marine to attend them in the quality of valet. Instead of visiting the shore once or twice in a quarter of a year, as was formerly the custom, now they are not satisfied or happy, when the ship is in port, unless they are almost daily there.

These changes have taken place since I embarked in the profession, and herein is certainly reform, but I much doubt whether it will turn out to be an eventual improvement. Instead of noon, five o'clock is now considered a more fashionable hour for the midshipmen to dine at, and silver forks and port-wine being commonly found at their table, is gravely adduced as a proof of the great advances which they are making; but we are not told whether in epicurism, or the knowledge of their profession. Then, in place of learning to turn in a dead-eye, and to reeve the lanyards of the lower rigging, they may now be found in some lady's bower, writing couplets in her album, or taking lessons in weaving a purse; or mounted on splendid hunters, instead of the topsail yard, they are flying over fences, emulous in the chase, instead of that far better ambition of being first at the ear-ring.

Shades of the mighty dead! ye whose deeds have given imperishable fame to the naval glory of England, what would be your horror and astonishment, should you rise from your resting-places and behold such things as these! Midshipmen equipped in leathers and pink (*proh pudor!*) preparing for the hunt! The youth of England, to whom the future conduct of her navy is to be confided, learning their noble profession in such a manner!

This, indeed, is reform for the reefers with a vengeance. We have blindly rushed from one extreme to the other, and, abandoning a wise and middle course, have adopted one that can hardly be called safe, and from which we can now, I fear, never return.

Whilst we lay in the Downs, for want of something better to attend to (for there really was not sufficient employment for such a concourse of midshipmen as we had), the elder bethought them of various modes of amusement, one of which soon eclipsed all the others, and proved to them for some time a source of great entertainment. This was the establishment of courts-martial for the trial of all offences committed against the republic, or rather oligarchy, which they organised in the steerage. These were conducted with all the regularity and precision observable at courts-martial of a graver nature. A President and Judge-Advocate, with the stipulated number of members, always composed them; and the unhappy culprit, if he did not always obtain justice (for prejudice sometimes exercised an influence in those courts, as well as I have know it do in others), was certain, at least, to have all the forms of law observed in his case.

The person elected to the presidential chair was chosen to fill that responsible situation as much from his deep knowledge upon all intricate questions that had reference to the discipline and good government of the steerage, as for his seniority in the service over all his brother midshipmen.

The person elected was a thin, spare little man, Barnard by name, in height about five feet four inches, with a head out of all keeping and proportion with the rest of his body. To this was appended a chin of more than common extension, which, instead of projecting outwards from the person, as long chins generally do, prolonged itself downwards straight to his chest. His mouth, wide and capacious, was in shape exactly like that of a dog-fish, and when he laughed, showed itself armed with two rows of yellow, formidable-looking teeth. His eyes, small and twinkling, were hazel, and expressive more of shrewdness than ill-nature. The colour of his hair and of his whiskers, which he wore enormously large, was reddish, and his complexion, at all times sanguine, assumed after supper a ruddier tint, glowing like the departing sun, when sinking into the bosom of the ocean.

Such was the redoubted Mr Barnard, and dressed in uniform, with blue breeches, shoes and buckles, sword and cocked hat worn athwartships, he had the appearance and bearing of a most imposing and awe-inspiring president.

In addition to his profound knowledge of cockpit and steerage law, written as well as common, Barnard's memory was stored with all kinds of anecdotes of the sea; and having commenced his nautical career under the auspices of the East India Company, he had doubled the Cape more than once, which gave him the privilege of recounting all the wonders, visible and invisible, of the eastern hemisphere. Certainly he must either have seen much, or else placed no restraint upon his inventive genius. Mendez Pinto or Sir John Mandeville himself could not have challenged the credulity, or more astonished the western world by the marvels which they imported from the East, than did Barnard when, after supper, and inspired by the second glass of grog, he related in glowing language to his youthful and admiring audience the wonders and dangers, both by 'blood and field,' which he had witnessed and escaped.

The oligarchy above-mentioned consisted almost exclusively of passed midshipmen, who, valuing themselves upon their standing in the service, and claiming a deference and respect from the rest, which they had no right to exact, exercised a tyranny and dictatorship in the berths really most galling and vexatious, but which it was vain to resist; for if you presumed to dispute their orders or authority, or to make any complaint, you were speedily had before one of their terrible courts-martial, always composed of themselves, escape from which without punishment, was as hopeless as it was from the Venetian oligarchists of old.

Time, however, that modifies and tempers all things, gradually removed these veterans from the ship, and relieved the younger midshipmen from a species of petty despotism infinitely more harassing and oppressive than any that may be practised by legitimate superiors.

During the greater part of the winter of 1802 the weather was remarkably boisterous, and I remember one long easterly gale that caused the loss of several ships and much property, and likewise occasioned great trouble and anxiety or board the *Immortalité*, which were increased from the following circumstance. Captain Tudor had passed several winters in the Downs, when he remarked that westerly winds chiefly prevailed. When he anchored in the Downs to take up our station there for the winter months, he determined to moor the *Immortalite* so as she should ride with an open hawse to the westward. With that intent, therefore, our small bower anchor was laid to the southward, and the best bower to the northward, thus reversing the usual manner of mooring in the Downs. The Captain's anticipations of westerly winds were not fulfilled: we had a succession of easterly gales; one of which lasted so long, and blew so hard, that riding as we did with a cross in the hawse, it required the utmost attention to the service of the cables to guard against their being chafed through; and, during a short and temporary lull, it was only by the utmost exertion and activity of the First Lieutenant, master, and boatswain, that we succeeded in lashing, and then shifting the cables, so as to change the small bower for the best, thereby securing to the ship an open hawse, when she rode with her head to the eastward.

About February, 1803, rumours of a rupture with France, and the speedy renewal of hostilities were so prevalent, that they were generally believed to be true, gladdening the hearts of all that were panting for fame, or promotion; and if a lingering doubt still remained with some of the sceptical, it was soon dissipated by the receipt of an order for the *Immortalité* to proceed forthwith to Sheerness, there to enter or impress as many men as would complete her crew to the war establishment.

Upon a hasty and superficial view of the subject, impressment, or the forced service of seamen in king's ships, seems a blot on the escutcheon of England, an anomaly in our free country, where the laws are supposed to regard and protect the rights and liberties of all its subjects in an equal degree. It appears an arbitrary and tyrannical act directed against seafaring men alone, and from which all others of the King's subject are exempt.

But if we examine the matter more closely, we shall find that the law requires all to arm and serve in defence of their common country, and that it is only upon that element, to which they are accustomed, and in that particular profession in which they have been brought up, and in gaining a knowledge of which they have been guarded and protected by the King's ships, that seafaring men are expected to afford their services. The whole external commerce of the empire is watched over and protected by the military navy of the country, to which, indeed, it owes its very existence. Surely, then, the mercantile navy may well contribute to its maintenance, and, all things considered, if seamen of the merchant's service will not voluntarily enter into that, without the aid and protection of which the privilege of quietly pursuing their profession would speedily be destroyed, there seems to be no remedy; they must be compelled to do so. All admit that impressment is a grievous evil, and one which they would gladly see abolished. But that it has existed so long, and still exists, notwithstanding its general condemnation, is a proof of the hazard of dispensing with it, and the difficulty of providing a suitable remedy. Although I abominate impressment, and would most willingly accept any feasible alternative for it, I trust that England will hesitate long and cautiously before she rashly, and without deep deliberation, relinquishes the power of speedily and efficiently manning her fleets, should a sudden emergency require their equipment. Without such power it is quite manifest that seamen, in numbers sufficient to make a squadron of even eight or ten sail of the line, are not to be procured. Witness the great difficulty and consequent delay to the service, which officers have found during the peace in entering volunteers for the navy; and even of their quality and description, for the most part the refuse of the merchant service, those who have to do with them very generally complain.* Should a

---

* This was written some years ago, when the difficulty of procuring seamen was great, and such as were to be had, were of a very inferior description. Of late, I believe, seamen have entered more willingly, and of a far better kind.

sudden rupture take place between this country and any of the great maritime nations, it is really awful to reflect on the consequences, if we thoughtlessly and inconsiderately part with the only means we possess of quickly and efficiently manning our fleets, and thus anticipating, or, at least, being prepared to meet our enemies at sea.

The insular position of Great Britain, her inferiority in number of inhabitants compared with the great continental nations of Europe, the dislike and jealousy (disguise them as we will) with which they view the surpassing wealth and grandeur of our country, and the vast and growing extent of our foreign possessions; the great probability that, as they did before, so they may again combine for their curtailment or overthrow; if we wish to secure the integrity of the British Empire, and guard its soil from the pollution of a hostile footstep – all call loudly for vigilance and caution, and tell us to beware, in language clear and distinct, how we lightly put to hazard that dominion which we hold (and may we ever hold it!) upon the waters.

Many men have turned their thoughts to the subject, and many plans have been devised for doing away with the necessity of impressment; but I confess that none of those that I have seen have satisfied me, nor do I think that any one of them could be safely substituted for it. Something, certainly, may be done to lighten the evil, and thereby render unnecessary so constant and general an impressment as we were compelled to resort to during the late war.

From the difficulty of procuring seamen to man the King's ships, we may be sure that it partly proceeds, if not in a great degree, from there being no surplus after the merchant vessels are supplied. This being the case, perhaps it would be well to compel by law, and see that law attended to and enforced, all fishing boats and trading vessels of every class and description to be fully and efficiently manned, and also to take additional apprentices, varying in number according to the rigging and tonnage of the different vessels. This measure, if duly enforced, would, in the course of a very few years, give a great increase of sea-faring men to the empire; and if the merchant vessels were at all times fully and adequately manned, in case of emergency a proportion of seamen might be spared for the wants of the King's service, without risking the safety of the trading vessels.

In the French mercantile marine their vessels carry at least a third more than the same description do in the English ships; and their fishing craft are furnished with crews generally fourfold more numerous than those which navigate boats of the same size and tonnage belonging to England. This, together with their well-organized mode of registering all sea-faring people, supplies them with a ready way of manning their men-of-war whenever they stand in need of seamen. Besides attending strictly to the efficient manning of the merchant ships, I would suggest that every ship in commission bear, in addition to the full war complement, which ought never to be diminished, a certain number of extra boys, varying, according to the size of the vessel, from five for a brig or packet, commanded by a Lieutenant, to forty, which might be the *maximum* for a first-rate. This would be a progressively increasing nursery for seamen, and eventually of the best description; for I take it that their early education in a man-of-war where their habits, cleanliness, food, and clothing, are so different, and so much more attended to than they are, or indeed can be, in merchant ships, would attach them to the service, a consideration that ought never to be lost sight of. A small increase of pay for length of service and good conduct, such as is given to soldiers, might likewise be beneficial; but before all things, a scale of pensions, on a far more liberal footing than those granted at present, should be established, so that the man who had served his country long, well, and faithfully, would be certain of a comfortable provision for his old age.

An attention to these objects, I think, would certainly lessen, though they never might entirely do away with the necessity for impressment, particularly should England ever be again involved in such a war, or rather wars, as she unhappily was engaged in from the year 1793 to 1815.

3: The Inshore Squadron

The conclusion of the second chapter of our Reminiscences left the *Immortalité* at Sheerness, she having been ordered to proceed thither to complete her crew to the war establishment. This was in February, 1803; but the time she remained there was not long. In March, the rumours, which had been for some time current, of the probable rupture of the treaty of Amiens, were gaining strength daily; and the King's message to the two Houses of Parliament, asking for means to enable him to increase the naval and military strength of the country, assigning as a reason for such a request the vast preparations going forward in the French and Dutch ports, and the unsettled state of the Continent in general, no longer left any doubt on the subject.

Nearly about the same time, we were ordered to Long Reach, in the Thames, there to enter or impress a new ship's company as quickly as possible; the old one, which had served in the late war, being promised their discharge from the service as soon as the new crew should be completed. All now was eagerness and anxiety to raise men, and get the ship ready to put to sea with the utmost dispatch: the officers urged by those motives that usually animate the breasts of the young, the ambitious, and the daring – the men stimulated by an anxious desire to revisit their long-absent homes, and the prospect of being soon released from a discipline and confinement which a service in time of peace had, I fear, rendered perfectly odious to them.

Considerations such as these made every one most desirous to complete the new ship's company; and all, both officers and men, vied with each other in diligence and exertion. No vessel inward or outward bound escaped a search; and from the Hope to London Bridge, our boats, day and night, according as the tide served, were employed on the same duty.

Some time before we were complete, the ship still wanting perhaps some forty or fifty good hands, the captain learned that two Indiamen, which had just dropped down to Gravesend, had received their crews that morning, preparatory to sailing on the next day. Considering this an excellent opportunity to get the description of men he was still in want of, and, at the same time, complete the crews of two other men-of-war in Long Reach that were under his orders, he directed the boats, manned and armed, of the *Immortalité, Amethyst*, and *Lynx*, to proceed at sunset, in charge of Lieutenant S——, of the *Immortalité*, to Gravesend Reach, to board the two before-named Indiamen, and select from their crews such men as they required, and should be fit for the King's service. The assembled boats, in one of which, under the charge of a mate, I found myself as a volunteer, accordingly proceeded at the appointed time.

The evening was mild and still; and on the crews pulled vigorously, exulting in anticipation of the famous sweep we were about to make, and little anticipating the reception we were to meet with.

The boats had now nearly reached the Indiamen, and were on the point of separating into two divisions – those of the *Amethyst* and *Lynx* to board one (the *Ganges*), while the *Immortalité*'s boats were destined to board the other (the *Woodford*).

At this moment one of them was distinctly heard to hail her comrade, and immediately after the boatswain's call piped all hands to quarters on board them both. The lieutenant of the *Immortalité*, deeming this a piece of mere bravado meant to deter us from persevering, pushed alongside the *Woodford* with his detachment of boats, whilst the others pulled for the *Ganges*.

Here we found the whole crew at quarters, armed with pikes and cutlasses, and every description of missile that the ship could supply.

They warned us off, and seemed determined to resist every attempt at boarding. In vain did the lieutenant remonstrate, and caution them as to their conduct, and the consequences of a blind and vain resistance. The crew stood firm, and only answered by loud threats of defiance and contempt.

Mr S—— now ordered his men to board. But this order was more easily given than accomplished. The sides of the Indiamen were high, and everything which might aid a man in mounting had been carefully hauled in board; besides, she was terribly wall-sided, which rendered the ascent still more difficult. The boats' crews, as they attempted to board, were thrust back by those long pikes with which the Indiamen are supplied, one of which was hurled with great force into the boat I was in, and nailed a poor fellow's foot to the bottom of the boat.

Once more the lieutenant cautioned our stout opponents as to the consequences of conduct so refractory and illegal, ordering the marines in the boats at the same time to load. At length, finding every remonstrance unavailing, and every species of missile, including cold shot hurled into the boats, his patience became exhausted, and he ordered half a dozen muskets to be fired.

This fire, though fatal, wounding two men mortally, had only the effect of exasperating the Indiaman's crew more and more, and rousing them, possible, to a fiercer and still more determined resistance.

Up to this moment no officer had shown himself on board the ship; but immediately on the discharge of fire-arms, the captain, or chief officer, hailed the boats, and informed the lieutenant of the fatal effect of his fire, throwing the whole responsibility upon his shoulders; and when questioned as to the state of his ship, and whether her crew was not in open mutiny, he replied, that he did not consider them to be so, for the men were willing to obey every order of his, save that of suffering a King's officer on board, and they were resolved, one and all, not to permit that. They were still determined to oppose every attempt to force an entrance into the ship, and therefore all further efforts on his part to do so would prove, with his present force, unavailing, and could only be attended with a greater effusion of blood.

The lieutenant now paused, and taking prudence, I suppose, into council, ordered the boats to lie off a little on their oars. He then sent a boat to the *Immortalité*, to acquaint Captain Owen with the state of matters, and to ask further instructions how to act. I am unable to say what were the fresh orders sent to Mr S——.

The boats continued to row guard round the two Indiamen, but I fear not very watchfully; for towards midnight, when they were bailed, and told that they were then at liberty to search the ships, we found only a few men on board the *Woodford*, and those of a sorry description.

Thus terminated this most untoward affair, fatally and unsuccessfully, and at the same time reflecting but little credit upon the men-of-war. The boats of the *Amethyst* and *Lynx*, meeting with the same opposition from the *Ganges*, did not proceed to the same extremities, and were consequently saved from the fatal results of our too long perseverance.

In this affray our *casualities* consisted of – one man having a pike driven through his foot; Lieutenant S——, and some men in his boat, struck with missiles, one heavily with a ballast-bag, which fell on the small of his back, and I fear injured him for life; the mate in our boat was also struck on the side of the head with a wedge, and I received a slight contusion on the knee.

I have, in a previous chapter, noticed some of the evils attending impressment, and pointed out how they might be remedied or alleviated. By many it is viewed as an inroad on, if not a positive breach of our Constitution. This matter should be clearly defined; a doubt should no longer exist upon the subject; and the statute or warrant under which an officer is to act should have such sanction and authority that no mist or cloud could any longer hang about it. In the present state of uncertainty regarding the authority under which warrants for impressment are issued, many consider they have a right to resist them; – and they do so even to the death, and, as far as I know, without ever having been punished, or even prosecuted for such resistance. It is not fair, it is not just, to impose a painful, a hateful duty upon officers – in the execution of which, should wounds or death ensue, they alone, it appears, are liable to be criminally prosecuted and punished.

In the case that I have just now related, the Coroner's jury at Gravesend brought in a verdict of wilful murder against the Lieutenant of the *Immortalité*; and though he escaped the irksomeness of a gaol by being allowed to absent himself furtively from his ship, at the following assizes at Maidstone he had to undergo the ignominy of a trial for his life, and with some difficulty was acquitted.

Our crew completed, and the former ship's company paid off and discharged, on the 18th of May, 1803, we proceeded to the Downs. There we remained, most impatiently expecting our orders, which although dated on the 18th, did not reach us until the 23rd, owing to some neglect or mistake in the Secretary's office at the Admiralty.

During this vexatious and idle time not a day passed that we had not the rather doubtful satisfaction of seeing two or three prizes, French or Dutch, anchor in the Downs; and at length, when our orders did arrive to proceed to sea, we found golden harvests not only reaped, but cleanly gleaned; for not an enemy's vessel did we see, except a few loiterers in the possession of our friends. We cruised for three weeks between the South Foreland and Beachey Head, Fecamp and Calais, without anything remarkable occurring, and then returned to the Downs.

One morning, towards the end of June, when standing across for the French coast, we observed two brigs, the *Jalouse* and *Cruiser*, in pursuit of a brig and schooner, to the westward of Cape Blancnez. We immediately joined in the chase, and just as we closed, the fire of the English brigs compelled the enemy's vessels to run ashore under the Cape. Captain Owen immediately directed the brigs to anchor as near the enemy as the depth of water would permit, and to open their fire upon them, and at the same time gave orders for the boats of the three vessels to be hoisted out, and got ready to board them.

This was soon accomplished. The brigs performed formed their allotted part, and the boats pushed stoutly and rapidly for the stranded vessels, though exposed all the way to a galling fire of grape and musketry from the shore. Nearly at the moment that they touched the vessels upon one side, the crews of the brig and schooner were seen to abandon them on the other, and they soon aided the military on the beach, who continued to keep up a heavy fire of musketry and artillery on the two abandoned vessels and our boats whilst employed in getting them afloat.

Anchors were soon run out, windlasses manned, and, as the tide was still rising, they were soon afloat amidst the loud hurrahs of our fine fellows, which must have reached the ears of the Frenchmen despite the roar of their artillery. The names of the brig and schooner were *L'Inabordable* and *Le Commode*, mounting each eight 24-pounder guns, and intended to form part of the flotilla at Boulogne. Our loss in this affair consisted of but one man killed, I think, on board the *Cruiser* and a few wounded. Such is an account of the first little brush in which I was engaged, and my ears were then first saluted with the music of a shot, with which they were afterwards pretty well familiarized.

At this time preparations were in active progress throughout all the harbours in France and Holland. The flotilla meant for the invasion of England began to assemble at Boulogne – Bonaparte was loud and boastful in his threats of what he should perform – and the whole French nation seemed confident that at length the conquest and humiliation of their hated rival was about to be achieved; all seemed awakened and inspired by the energy and ever-active mind of their chief. From Brest to Boulogne he inspected all that was in progress, and wherever he appeared, his presence inspired new life and animation. Boulogne was the grand rendezvous for the flotilla and army of invasion, and he stopped there a few days to trace the sites of the camps, and to give directions about enlarging and improving the contiguous harbours of Vimereux and Ambleteuse.

It so happened, that, whilst he was thus employed, Captain Owen observed a brig and six luggers in the road. Having viewed them more nearly, and resolved to attack them, he anchored with a spring on the cable as near as the depth of water would permit. For a good half hour and more did we hammer away at them right merrily, and with such good effect, too, that two of the luggers cut and ran aground. All this time we were surprised that none of the enemy's shot reached us, a few shells only going over, or dropping near the ship. At length, however, they seemed to have got our range, the shot from some of the batteries passing between the masts low over the hammocks, and hulling the ship pretty often. In a few minutes more the stream-cable was cut, when all the vessels, except the two that were on shore, being under weigh and making for the harbour, Captain Owen hauled out of gun-shot.

The following anecdote was told a few days after by the master of a French fishing-vessel:* – The morning of our attack upon the gun-vessels, Bonaparte, who was at Boulogne, the moment the firing commenced, repaired to one of the batteries nearest the scene of action. His practised eye soon observed that the shot from the battery fell short of their mark. He became fidgetty – uttered a few *sacrés* – then examined the pointing and elevation of the guns; but upon further inquiry, finding that the cartridges were only filled with the quantity of powder used in saluting, his rage and indignation became quite uncontrollable – he flew towards the unhappy subaltern – upbraided him with his ignorance and neglect, and, with his own hands tearing the epaulettes from his shoulders, told him he was no longer an officer in the French army.

During the summer of 1803, the whole line of coast from Calais to Havre being strengthened, all the old defences were augmented, and new ones sprang up wherever they were found to be useful or necessary.

On our part we gave them all the interruption that we could, and, besides bombarding the towns of Tréport, Dieppe, St Vallery en Caux, Fecamp, and Havre, in company with the *Sulphur* bomb, we were constantly engaged in harassing and annoying the men employed on the new works. These new batteries, or towers, they appeared particularly anxious to complete.** They were intended for the further defence of the bay of

* This anecdote was afterwards confirmed by an English lady, then residing at Boulogne.

** Fort La Crêche, Fort Imperial, or Pile Battery, and Fort L'Heurt.

Boulogne, and were situated, one at the eastern extremity of the bay, one in the centre immediately at the entrance to the harbour, and the third off Point D'Alpreck. On these a number of workmen were actively employed day and night, whilst we lost no opportunity of retarding their operations, and, whenever the state of the wind and tide permitted, scoured the beach from Vimereux to D'Alpreck.

Fort Imperial, the centre of one of the three, was to be erected on piles a little beyond low water-mark, and for this purpose four pile-drivers, with their machinery, had been erected. One night in August, the boats of the *Immortalité* and *Perseus* bomb, under the command of the captain of the latter, proceeded with directions to intercept anything moving along shore, and to destroy, if possible, the before-named machinery. The boats were provided with axes, except that of the first lieutenant of the *Immortalité*, in which was placed a barrel of gunpowder primed and fused, and ready to be slung within the upright beams or supports, down which the driver slides. The night, though calm, was pitchy dark, and the boats rowed along shore, and then crossed the bay once or twice without meeting a vessel, or falling in with the pile-drivers. After rowing about in this manner for a considerable time to no purpose, we found that we had imperceptibly approached to within pistol-shot of the pier-head; and the captain of the *Perseus*, thinking the distance to be rather too near to be pleasant, and judging also that we must have been far within the objects of our search, gave directions to get the boats' heads round, and to pull quietly off shore. The first part of this order was executed; but the oars were scarcely dipped into the water in obedience to the second, when a fire-ball flamed upon the mole, shedding such a glare of bluish light all around for more than a quarter of a mile, as rendered every object distinctly visible.

The boats now gave way manfully, but before the men had bent a second time to their oars, a shower of grape and the musketry of the guard on the mole whistled over our heads, fortunately, however, without doing any mischief; and before they could repeat the salutation many times the boats were beyond the circle of light, which the still burning fire-ball cast upon the water. The first gun fired from the mole seemed the signal for all the batteries within the bay to open, and they continued to fire *salvos* for a considerable time, not rendering the 'night hideous' but with the most harmless and prettiest effect possible.

The boats pulled right out, and in ten minutes stumbled upon what they had been so long seeking with such pains and diligence. The crews immediately fell to work with the axes, and in a very short time three of the pile-drivers floated upon the water, when the sailors' knives cut the gear in pieces. Meantime Mr Payne,* the First Lieutenant of the *Immortalité*, slung his barrel of gunpowder to the fourth, and when all the boats but his own had pulled to a safe distance, he lit the fuse, and then joined us. For some time the port-fire continued to burn brightly, and we were in momentary expectation of seeing the whole mass driven, rocket-like, into the air, and add its novelty to the *feu d'artifice* which still continued to illumine the bay. Soon, however, the light burned less clearly, by degrees it became fainter, and in a few seconds more all was dim. For some time everybody was in suspense, some thinking that the fuse had gone out, whilst others supposed it might be concealed from view, and, without having yet reached the powder, might still be burning within the cask. Lieutenant Payne, however, resolved that our agony should not be long; for with the greatest coolness and intrepidity he rowed back to the pile-driver, when, finding the port-fire quite extinguished, he unslung the powder-barrel, and replaced it in the boat!

In September of this year, we proceeded with the *Perseus* and *Explosion* bombs on a bombarding tour along the coast; and no town from Boulogne to Fecamp, where a vessel was constructing or that sheltered any of the flotilla, escaped our notice.

From eight until half-past ten one morning, Dieppe and the batteries that protect it was furiously cannonaded and bombarded. At that time the weather-tide ceased, which, as the ships kept under weigh, had until then favoured our operations. We did not discontinue, however, before the town appeared on fire in three several places. Considering how long and closely we had been engaged with a formidable line of batteries, our damage was trifling. The bombs did not suffer at all; and on board the *Immortalité* the boatswain and a few men only were wounded, and the spars and rigging a good deal cut. In the afternoon, when the weather-tide made again, we saluted St Vallery en Caux in the same way, and quickly drove every man from the town and battery.

Many years after these occurrences, I was strolling one morning on the quay at Dieppe, when, falling into conversation with a *bourgeois* of the town, who was indulging in the luxury of fresh air and a cigar, amongst other things I asked him if he recollected the bombardment of Dieppe in the late war by an English frigate and bomb? 'Certainly I do,' he replied, 'and warm work we had that morning. There was not a single soldier of the line in the place at the time,' he continued, 'though five companies were forwarded with the utmost despatch from Rouen as soon as they were informed by telegraph of the attack upon Dieppe. The whole duty devolved upon the National Guard. He himself,' he said, 'belonged to

* Now Rear Admiral Payne.

the artillery of that force, and served that morning in the battery at the Mole-head. Their casualties in killed and wounded were but few, and the damage to the town not great. A good many houses were damaged, and three wood yards were set on fire by the explosion of shells; but the fires were soon extinguished without spreading, or doing much mischief. Most of the inhabitants fled from the town as soon as the firing commenced, a circumstance which may account for the loss of life being so small.' He then inquired how we fared on board the ships, and evidently was not a little chagrined at learning that our loss and damage had been so trifling, puffing forth, with every whiff of his cigar for some time after, his vexation and astonishment in muttered *sacrés* and *diables*.

This service over, our next excursion was, I think, off Flushing, whither the *Immortalité*, attended by two cutters, was ordered to convey Captain Bligh (*Bounty*) who was directed to take the soundings of that part of the coast leading to the entrance of the Scheldt. We were occupied with this duty for, I believe, a fortnight, during which we had nothing to diversify the monotony of a very tedious piece of work, except the capture of two Dutch galiots one morning by our boats. We then resumed our station off Boulogne.

One morning early in November we observed a numerous division of the enemy's flotilla get under weigh in the Road of Boulogne, and proceed to enact various evolutions; and as it seemed to be part of our duty to prohibit all such pastimes, or, at least, to restrict them to very narrow limits, we prepared to compel them to resume their former state of quiescence.

Our squadron was comprised, on that morning, of the *Raisonnable* the *Leda* and several smaller vessels, the names of which I forget; the enemy's consisted of eight brigs, fifty-six luggers besides several schuyt-rigged mortar-boats. After an hour's firing, we compelled the whole to desist from manœuvring, and to re-anchor. In this little affair we had one man killed and three wounded; the foremost shot through; and the ship suffered other damage, which obliged her to go to Sheerness for repair.

Some night in January, 1804, when the *Immortalité* was again off Boulogne, and at anchor, her barge, under the command of the first lieutenant, was sent in-shore, towed by the *Archer*, gunbrig. I am not sure that they had any definite object when they left the ship – most likely it was to observe whether anything was moving alongshore, and to pick up whatever they could. They had not been gone an hour when a brisk fire of musketry and the report of a few guns was heard inshore. The firing did not last many minutes, and we remained in darkness and uncertainty as to its cause for some time. In an hour, however, the brig and boat returned, bringing with them a French lugger, a small schuyt laden with gin, and a dogger in ballast. All three had sailed together from Calais early in the day, bound for Boulogne, and were met with farther off-shore than they calculated upon. After an exchange of musketry and a few shot, it being nearly calm, the barge shoved off from the brig, and, boarding the lugger, carried her after a slight resistance, two of her crew only having been wounded; the barge had not a man touched. The lugger was to have formed one of the flotilla, and was commanded by an *enseigne de vaisseau*; she mounted two guns – a twenty-four pounder forward, and one of twelve pounds aft. Besides her crew, she had twenty-five soldiers on board; and there were also a few embarked in the schuyt and dogger; making the number of prisoners amount altogether to fifty.

On the following day the prizes were sent to the Downs; and as the schuyt was confided to my care, proud enough and much gratified I felt at the charge, inasmuch as it was the first of the kind I had been intrusted with. Alas! how vain are often the cherished aspirations and ambitious view of midshipmen, as well as of other men! When they have attained the summit of their wishes, and enwrap themselves in a cloak of pride and self-gratulation, they frequently meet with such a fall as robs them of all their boasted glory, and restores them at once to a sense of their own nothingness. This will be fully exemplified by my subsequent adventures in the schuyt.

The next morning the three prizes arrived safely in the Downs, and I dropped my grapnel (*anchor* I had none) close inshore, at the north end of Deal, and then repaired to the prize-agent. It was determined that the vessel should remain where she was until the following day, when three or four men were to be sent on board to relieve the prize-crew, and to take her into Ramsgate harbour.

These matters being arranged to my satisfaction, I returned to the prize; and at nine o'clock at night, it being then fine, with a moderate breeze from the N.W., I turned in, having first given the man who had the look-out such orders as I thought necessary, with directions to call me if the wind freshened, or anything particular occurred. About one o'clock in the morning I awoke, and perceiving that the vessel rolled a good deal, and that the wind whistled much louder than when I went to lie down, I jumped upon deck, and at first thought, with the stupid fellow who had the watch, that the vessel was tending to the weather-tide, which made her lie broadside to the wind, and roll so much. In a moment, however, when I looked about me, I saw the South Foreland lights, which were quite shut in where we anchored, but which showed by their present bearing that we had drifted as far to the southward as Walmer Roads.

The wind at the time, although fresh, not being very strong, and as we had not a great deal of cable out, I thought that by veering we might possibly hold on where we were until day-light, and then, by the help of the weather-tide, get back to our former anchorage. With this expectation I veered to the clench; but finding that she continued to drive, and not wishing to lose my only grapnel by cutting, I resolved to weigh, and try what the craft could do till daylight, when I hoped be able to fetch either Walmer or Dover Roads. The operation of getting under weigh, however, was neither soon, nor very easily performed. The night was pitch dark. The schuyt, broadside to the sea, was rolling and tumbling like a porpoise presaging a storm; a whole cable was to be hove in, and only four men and a windlass to do it with, so that by the time the grapnel was up, and a sail made on the vessel, we found ourselves completely clear of the Downs. To add to our misfortune the ebb-tide was still running, and before the flood made, the wind had considerably increased, so that at daylight we found ourselves far to leeward, with little hope of recovering our lost ground that day.

Of all the craft it has been my luck to be on board, the schuyt in question was the dullest sailer, and the least manageable; for with lee-board down and every attention paid we could never prevail upon her to stay, or keep her within less than seven points of the wind. Add to this, that we had been victualled for only three days, and this was the third day since we left the *Immortalité*. The wind was freshening, no man-of-war in sight, and no chance of gaining an anchorage; and it may be conjectured that our prospects were none of the pleasantest. The Dutchmen, indeed, left a little biscuit and water behind them, and this, with a modicum of gin, served us for the three mortal days and nights that it pleased the north-west wind to blow, and keep us buffeting the sea between Folkestone and Dover. At length, on the third night, there came a calm; then a light breeze sprang up from the westward, which wafted us safely once more into the Downs, when, crestfallen and mortified, I was glad to resign my charge into the hands of the prize-agent; and, on my return to the *Immortalité* was unmercifully rallied by all my messmates.

In the month of February we were again off Boulogne, when we had several sharp bouts with the batteries and flotilla. On the 8th, I think it was, we were hotly engaged, with short intervals, from noon until half-past five. During the day's work we had a marine killed, two midshipmen,* the captain's clerk, and three or four men wounded. A good many shot hulled the ship, the main-yard was shot through, and the sails and

* The present Commander, Thomas Pickering Clarke, and Rear Admiral Sir Joshua Rowley. The Clerk left the service early.

rigging a good deal cut. Several of the enemy's vessels were on shore; but as they were all flat-bottomed, drawing very little water, and never ventured to move from port to port, except with a leading wind inclining off the land, they were in this, as in almost all other cases, enabled to stop the shot-holes when the tide ebbed sufficiently, and float them again at high water.

In moving alongshore, the Flotilla was invariably accompanied by a brigade of horse-artillery specially organized for that purpose; and as they were all covered and protected by numerous batteries and musketry from the beach, any attempt by the boats to destroy them, or bring them off, must have been attended with a wasteful sacrifice of life, – far greater, indeed, than their capture, or the *éclat* which might have resulted even from the attempt, could have repaid.

Although these expeditions were not often attended with success, they served to foster that spirit of enterprise and daring, which is, if I may to express myself, the very life-blood of the navy. When the ship was at anchor off Boulogne, on dark nights and during calm weather, the first Lieutenant and Clarke frequently went in the *gig* to endeavour to blow to pieces, or, at least, to keep on the *qui vive*, the Flotilla, which lay in the Roads. This was to be effected by means of coffers, or carcasses – a newly-invented engine of murderous contrivance and most destructive force. These engines were made of copper, and, as well as I remember, spherical in form; hollow to receive their charge of powder, which by means of machinery, that worked interiorly, and so secured to be perfectly water-tight, exploded at the precise moment that you chose to set it to. The mode of managing them was in this wise: – Two, attached together by means of a line coiled carefully clear, were placed in the boat ready to be dropped over-board. The line was buoyed by corks, like the roping of a seine, so as to allow the carcasses to sink to a certain depth, and no further. When you had approached near enough to the vessel or vessels against which you meant to direct the carcasses, and saw clearly that you were in such a position that the line could not fail to strike her cable, one carcass was first dropped overboard, and when that had extended the full length of the line from the boat, then the other, both having been carefully primed and set to the time, which would allow of their floating to their destined object before they exploded. Of course it is presumed that wind and tide set in the direction, so as to ensure their not deviating from their course.

These preliminaries being attended to, the carcasses drifted until the line which attached them together struck the cable of the vessel, when it was presumed that the carcasses, one on either side, would swing under her bilge, and, at the fated moment, explode and shatter her to pieces. In order not to be too wasteful, instead of a carcass, Captain Owen frequently attached a breaker, in shape and size like one, with weight sufficient in it to serve as a counterpoise to the other.

Often as this attempt was made we never could ascertain that it was completely successful, although the First Lieutenant, with a determination to effect his object, approached so near the flotilla, and remained so long, in order to see everything in proper train, as to draw upon his boat a heavy fire of musketry from the nearest vessel, which not unfrequently killed or wounded some of his men. Sometimes, after an expedition of the kind, we saw a vessel in the morning with her jib-boom gone, but without any confusion appearing in their line; and if any one sustained greater damage, they took care that we should be none the wiser, by removing her whilst it was dark, and supplying her place with another, so that they always appeared in precisely the same order at daylight, and the same number was counted as had been at sunset on the previous evening.

As a proof, however, that the enemy was kept on the alert, and had a just apprehension of the dangerous powers of those engines, whenever a division of the flotilla was at anchor outside the harbour, they always latterly moored a boat at the buoy right ahead of each vessel, so that she would be sure to bring up anything that might be set adrift for the annoyance of the flotilla.

As we could not report that they made any impression on the enemy, there seemed to be, at one time, a doubt as to the efficacy of the carcasses; and, indeed, so otherwise harmless were those expensive explosions, that Bonaparte called it breaking the windows of the good citizens of Boulogne with English guineas. In order to ascertain the point, an old collier brig was procured and moored in Walmer Roads, and two carcasses placed a couple of feet under water, just beneath the main-channels. They had been set to five minutes, at the expiration of which time they exploded, when the brig, rolling deeply three or four times, sank at her anchors. After this experiment no doubt could be entertained as to their force, and, if the machinery were all in order and they fairly swung under a vessel's bottom, inevitable success.

This species of warfare, unmanly, and I may say assassin-like, I always abhorred. Under cover of the night, to glide with muffled oars beneath the bows of a vessel, and when her crew is least suspicious of impending danger, to affix such an *infernal machine* beneath her bottom, and in a moment hurl them to destruction, in what does it differ from the midnight attack of the burglar, who steals into your house, and robs his sleeping victim at once of money and life?

In a few years afterwards, when similar attempts were made (I believe with more success) by the Americans upon our ships, which were engaged in the blockade of their ports, I well remember what an outcry was raised against such dastardly proceedings, and how much the cowardice and baseness of such a mode of warfare was railed at and condemned by the English journals. Aware, however, that the example had first been set by England, I, for one, could not join in the outcry. On the contrary, conscience-stricken, I felt myself compelled to be silent, or confess with shame and bitterness, that we deserved no less, 'seeing that we ourselves had come into the same condemnation'. Let us hope that in future wars the nation will evince a more chivalric spirit, and abandon for ever a system which, to all generous minds, must ever appear mean as well as dastardly.

By March in this year we observed that the flotilla had much increased, and the enemy was constantly adding to it as fast as the vessels building at the different ports were completed, and the state of the wind and weather gave them courage to creep alongshore.

It was about this time that the notable stone-ships were placed under the charge and management of Captain Owen. Some sapient blockhead, whose name I forget, had contrived to persuade the Lords of the Admiralty that they might be used with effect in blocking the harbour of Boulogne, and preventing the egress of the flotilla. Those vessels, three in number, were old three-masted merchant-ships, in each of whose holds was built a piece of masonry, well cemented, and having the stones cramped together with iron, so as to render the whole mass more solid and durable.

The harbour of Boulogne is dry at low-water, the entrance to it being shoal and narrow, and liable to be choked or obstructed by the accumulation of sand, which the north-west winds are constantly throwing in. To prevent this obstruction, the little river Liane, which flows through the harbour, was carefully kept free, and also, as at Dieppe, dammed up, having a sluice, which, when opened at low-water, suffered the whole river to rush with such force, that it swept everything before it, and kept the harbour and the channel leading to it perfectly clear.

Hence the care and secrecy with which those ships were prepared, and the purpose to which it was intended they should be applied may easily be conceived. Some fine night, when wind, weather, and tide favoured the enterprise, it was meant to take them to the very mouth of the harbour, and there scuttle and set them on fire abreast of each other. This being effected, it was supposed that the stream of the Liane would not be powerful enough to move them, and, from the great weight of the masonry, that they would imbed themselves more and more in the sands, and eventually forming a bar at the entrance of the harbour, effectually close it against either ingress or egress.

Such, I suppose, were the confident expectations of the ingenious projectors of this memorable contrivance. I am not prepared to say what might have been the opinion of Captain Owen with regard to the scheme; but this I know full well, that he spared no pains to put it into execution. The ships were officered and manned from the *Immortalité*, by people in whose judgment and resolution he had the greatest confidence; and they were all made perfectly conversant with what was expected from them, and the whole nature of the service they were going upon. But although our captain could effect much, he could not render the elements propitious, and after several abortive attempts to place the ships in a fitting situation for scuttling, which lasted a full month and was constantly baffled by calms and contrary winds, the whole plan was abandoned.

It is difficult to comprehend how any men, much less men supposed to be capable of managing the affairs of this great nation, unless stunned and bewildered by the projects of the arch-enemy, and his threats of invasion, could incur an expense so considerable, and adopt a scheme which, if practicable in the execution, might be useless and inoperative in a few tides. For what more easy than to place a few barrels of gunpowder under those masses of stone at low-water, and blow them to pieces, when, at the next tide, the little Liane would flow as uninterruptedly as heretofore into the ocean.

In spite of all efforts to prevent it, the enemy's flotilla continued marvellously to increase; and in April and May the number which they anchored in the Roads frequently amounted to two hundred.

About this time, we often found ourselves alone off Boulogne, or only with a gun-brig or two. Captain Owen's plan then was to keep under weigh generally during the day, and anchor again in the evening on the outer edge of the Baas bank, about three miles off shore; the brigs, when with us, being so stationed as to intercept anything coming either from the east or west.

Considering it not impossible that the frigate at anchor so near the shore, and unsupported too, might invite the enemy, albeit unused to enterprises of the kind, to make a dash with the overwhelming force which they had at command, and try to surprise her, Captain Owen took care to be always prepared for their reception. For this purpose the guns, when the ship was at anchor, were always shotted with round and grape, and hung in the tackles, the boarding-nettings triced up, and a hawser was extended round the ship in a manner to prevent boats from getting alongside, and keep them at such a distance, that the guns, when depressed, could fire into them. This latter was effected by means of the guess-warp booms, and spars prepared to be rigged out from the main and mizen-chains, and spritsail-yard, the parrel of which, instead of the ordinary manner, was fitted with a long-leg and thimble, so as to admit of its being easily lowered and swayed up again in a moment. In addition to the marine sentinels, the *look-out* men were placed as at sea, being provided with loaded small-arms, which, soon after daylight, were always discharged at a target; a practice in which the whole crew partook by turns, thereby making them all expert marksmen.

Some part of June and July we were obliged to be at Sheerness, in order to have the ship docked, a great part of which time I passed solitarily, and, of course, miserably enough, in charge of one of the ill-omened stone-ships, which we found lying there not yet dismantled. A mystery was still hanging over those vessels, and the wisdom of the people at head-quarters judged it right to keep their further use and destination still a secret. With this laudable and very discreet purpose in view, they gave directions that whoever was in charge of them should not only as carefully eschew the shore himself as if he were in quarantine, but avoid all contact and intercourse of every kind with that forbidden element. This, to one yearning for the land, and some of the good things that it produces – such as *soft tommy*, milk, butter, &c. (the delights of which are best known to, and appreciated, I do believe, by midshipmen) – was tantalizing enough; but it was nothing when compared to the *ennui*, the dreadful lassitude of the mind, which I endured, without a companion to exchange a thought with. Then the few books that I had were read over and over again in less than a week; and I well remember the delight with which I used to hail the signal to loose sails as something which afforded variety and relief from the depressing state of monotony in which my days were passing.

Early in August we again proceeded off Boulogne, taking with us a gentleman, whom, as his name never transpired, I must still designate by the appellation of 'Mr Nobody', the cognomen by which alone he was known to the midshipmen.

During the fortnight that this gentleman passed on board the *Immortalité* she was kept constantly close in shore, whenever the state of the tide and weather would permit, in order to give him an opportunity of pursuing certain researches upon which he seemed intent, and which, to give him his due praise, he did with the greatest earnestness and coolness, unruffled and undisturbed by the showers of shot and shells that fell around the ship, splashing the water about her at every instant. The object of this scrutiny seemed to be to ascertain, as correctly as he could, the fortifications around Boulogne, and the position and bearings of the different batteries which faced the sea, and also the exact distance at which the flotilla in the roads was anchored from the shore. When these purposes were accomplished, I conclude to his satisfaction, we ran back to the Downs, where he was landed, I confess to my no small satisfaction, and, I suspect, without regret by any one on board, for his presence imposed a load of additional trouble on the ship, besides making her serve every day, whilst he was on board, as a target for our friends to amuse themselves by practising at.

For three successive days, about the middle of August, we were warmly and closely engaged each day with an immense force of the enemy's flotilla. The little squadron that supported us consisted of the *Harpy*, brig of eighteen guns; the *Adder* and *Gallant*, gun-brigs; with the *Constitution*, cutter. Considering the length of time, and closeness and animation of the firing, our own loss was small: four men wounded, a few shot in the hull, and some trifling damage aloft; but a shell fell on board the *Constitution*, which passing right through her, sent her almost instantly to the bottom. Fortunately there was little wind at the time – the sea was as smooth as a mill-pond – and as the squadron had their boats towing astern, the crew, with a few exceptions, were all saved. The *Harpy* was also struck by a shell on the same day, which lodged in her main-beam; happily, however, without mischief, for the fuse was extinguished by the shock, which prevented it from exploding.

The enemy, although he did not venture from under the shelter of his batteries, was unusually bold, and boats, having officers of rank on board them, were seen frequently to pass along their line. From these circumstances it was thought, and not without probability, that Bonaparte was present at the time, and that, under the eye of their newly-elected Emperor, they fought with a resolution and boldness unknown to them before. It is certain indeed that he was at Boulogne on the 15th of August, his own birth-day; for in order to view the preparations in progress for the invasion of England, and to preside at the inauguration of the Legion of Honour recently instituted, he had quitted Paris early in that month, and, accompanied by his brothers, Joseph and Louis, the chief ministers of state, and the great officers of his staff and household, repaired to Boulogne. The institution of such an order of merit as the Legion of Honour he considered as well adapted to consolidate and uphold his newly-acquired throne; and the place, time, and circumstances seem to have been admirably well chosen for the celebration of such a ceremony.

On the morning of the 15th of August, the whole of the army, to the number of one hundred thousand men, encamped in the neighbourhood of Boulogne, was formed in columns, sixty file in front, the cavalry being drawn up in rear of the columns. A knoll, or mound, which rose in the centre of this mass of soldiers, formed a kind of dais, or throne, upon which was placed the ancient chair of King Dagobert, the founder of St Denis, and the originator of the Oriflamme. The standards and colours taken in the battles won by the French in Italy and Egypt, formed an appropriate canopy for such a throne. The decorations, about to be distributed, were placed in the helmet of Du Guesclin, and in the buckler of Bayard, borne by officers of the staff.

When all was arranged, Napoleon left his quarters, and the roll of two thousand drums saluted his appearance on the ground, and yet their sound could not drown the acclamations of his soldiers, raised to a pitch of enthusiasm by the presence of their chief.

As soon as the Emperor had taken his seat upon the throne, the Grand-Chancellor of the Legion of Honour advanced into the midst, and pronounced a discourse in praise of the institution, and pointed out the solemnities which it imposed upon the dignitaries.

When the Grand-Chancellor had done speaking, a roll of the drums drew the general attention, and Napoleon, rising from the imperial seat, pronounced he form of oath which the members of the Legion and to take: 'We swear!' cried they; and with spontaneous movement, the whole army repeated the oath of fidelity and devotion.

The grand officers, the commissioners, the officers, and the simple Legionaries, now approached the throne, when each individually received from he hands of the Emperor the decoration of the region of Honour.

The ceremony concluded by four o'clock in the afternoon, when the Emperor withdrew amidst the same salutes and acclamations that greeted his appearance in the morning. *Fétes*, dances, illuminations, and fireworks, closed this memorable play.

Bonaparte remained some time longer on the coast, from which it may be reasonably inferred that he was a spectator of the actions on the three days before mentioned.

In establishing this Order, which has survived its founder and his empire, and promises to be as durable as France itself, Bonaparte evinced how clearly he had penetrated and understood the character of the people over whom he was called to rule. Vain of themselves individually, still vainer of their nation, and inordinately greedy of military fame and renown, he lost no opportunity of feeding this passion; and in what way could he have more abundantly or cheaply satisfied it than by instituting an order of merit and distinction which should embrace within its circle all classes of the deserving, from the highest to the least elevated of their fellow-citizens? Then the spot chosen for its celebration seems to have been most happily selected. With England full in view, and amidst the mighty host assembled for its invasion – surrounded by the men most eminent in the country for station, for talents, and for military fame – seated in the chair of one of the ancient monarchs of France, and taking the decorations from the helmet and shield of the two heroes most celebrated in her history for purity of conduct and gallantry in the field, the newly-elected Emperor distributed, with his own hands, alike to marshals of the empire and to private soldiers, those marks of honour and distinction, the proud reward of their deserts, which should serve to stimulate their ardour, and excite the emulation of their companions.

An order of merit, which might embrace all classes of her citizens, like the Legion of Honour, seems to be much wanting in England; and it is to be regretted that, when that of the Bath was extended, in 1815, it did not go further, and become accessible to all, whatever profession or class of society they belonged to, whose talents, actions, or inventions, reflected honour and credit on themselves, or conferred benefit on their country. Why, it may be asked, should not the humble in life, as well as the most exalted, meet with reward and distinction, if he deserve it? Or why should not the senator, the man of science, or the author who has really added to the useful literature of the country, be honoured as well as the diplomatist, the soldier, or the sailor?

In instituting an order of the kind, care should be taken, however, to confer it only on the really meritorious. Let other degrees of knighthood be conferred on whom the sovereign or the minister listeth; but let not an order, which should be the distinctive badge of merit alone, be bestowed on the undeserving, thus rendering valueless an object of legitimate ambition to all men of worth, of talent, and of virtue.

We have seen, in these our days, with what lavish hand knighthoods and honours have been showered on the heads of the Lord knows whom, and with what eagerness men, whose actions or merits never distinguished them from the herd, sought to be invested with an *alien* order, which, in my conscience, I think an Englishman, whose services were not deemed worthy of the order of his own country should blush to wear.

In the renovation of the Order of the Bath, or establishing an entirely new one, whatever may be the rank of the individual at the time, would not be just to bestow at once the reward to which his actions entitle him, with permission also to wear all its insignia; for what can be more puerile and contemptible than the distinction which now exists in this respect between the general and field-officer? The one is allowed to array himself in all the trappings and decorations of his order, whilst the other, shorn of his due proportions, is forbidden to display upon his breast the star which distinguished conduct in the field had so nobly won for him, until he attain, by slow gradation in time of peace and inactivity, the rank of general-officer? In youth we have a pride, an honest and heartfelt pride, in displaying such proofs of gallantry and good conduct to parents, relations, and friends – then marks of distinction are valuable and highly prized. But when parents are no more, and relations and early friends gone or dwindled to a few, of what value can a cross or star be in the eyes of an old man, now shrunk into the 'lean and slippered pantaloon', and tottering on the verge of the grave? No. If a man, by superior merit in the senate, the closet, or the field, be distinguished above his fellows, let him at once have all the honours, and *wear* them, too, which he deserves, and not wait until the death of some esteemed friend or former companion in arms leaves room for him to slip into his shoes.

4: Attack on the Boulogne Flotilla

In the month of September, 1804, we were busily occupied with the batteries and flotilla off Boulogne, and upon one occasion were lucky enough to get within grape-shot distance of a detachment of several brigs to the eastward of Ambleteuse, four of which we compelled to run ashore; just, as usual, when the shot-holes were plugged, and the tide rose, they were enabled to get them into harbour. Upon this occasion we had a man killed, and three wounded. Several shells, which upon that day were thrown remarkably well, burst immediately over the ship; and a heavy fragment of one, after breaking through the gangway and main deck, was afterwards found in one of the men's chests between decks.

Whenever the state of the weather permitted, a strong division of the flotilla was constantly anchored outside the harbour, as well to give regular exercise to their crews, as to brave and set the English squadron at defiance. When the tide suited they sometimes got under way, and manoeuvred, but always under the protection of their formidable batteries. A grand attack, which had been maturing for some weeks, against this part of the flotilla was ready to be put into execution in the beginning of

October, the general management and conduct of which was intrusted to Sir Home Popham.

For several days prior to the attack there was a great display of our force before Boulogne, amounting to between fifty and sixty vessels of all kinds, for no object that I can conceive, except to put the enemy on his guard, and give him timely notice of our intentions. Besides the *Monarch*, Lord Keith's flag-ship, this force consisted of two or three ships of fifty and sixty-four guns, four or five frigates, a few sloops of war, and the remainder of bombs, armed ships, and gun-brigs. Besides these there were a few sloop-rigged vessels, prepared as fire, or rather explosion vessels, the number of which I forget, but not exceeding, I think, four or five. These vessels were filled with combustibles and powder, and supplied with explosive machinery similar to that which was fitted to the carcasses or coffers.

Sir Home's arrangements and preparations being completed, on the evening of the 3rd of October the boats of the fleet in three divisions, each division under the charge of a Commander, moved to the attack. As the wind was light, the explosion vessels were taken in tow by the larger boats, the whole being covered by the gun-brigs, which had orders to keep as near the scene of action, during the night, as possible, and be ready to afford assistance and support, whenever it was necessary and practicable to do so. The lighter boats, such as the galleys, were provided with coffers, and were intended to approach so near, and in such positions, that in setting those machines adrift, there would be every likelihood of their taking effect. The larger boats were to protect them and the explosion vessels, and by keeping up a well-sustained fire of guns and musketry, distract the enemy's attention, and prevent their guard-boats from interrupting their manoeuvres. Such, I think, is an outline of the plan of attack. Burning and blowing up seemed alone the order of the night, and I am not aware that an attack *de vive force* on the flotilla was contemplated.

The French (how could they be otherwise?) were perfectly awake to all that was going forward. The flotilla had been moved as near to the beach as it could anchor with safety; and in addition to the precaution of mooring a boat a-head of each vessel to arrest anything floating in its progress towards the flotilla, they had alarm boats, and pinnaces rowing guard round the whole; our leading boats were, therefore, soon descried. The enemy's sentinels hailed and discharged their muskets nearly at the same moment; and long before the carcasses could be set adrift, the whole bay was lit up by vivid flashes of musketry that was soon increased to almost noonday brightness by a blaze of artillery from the flotilla and batteries, which continued to pour heavy, though happily with few exceptions, harmless showers of grape in the direction of our boats. I cannot now call to mind the casualties which they occasioned: none whatever occurred in the boats of the *Immortalité*.

Meanwhile the explosion vessels were advancing under sail to the different points against which they were expected to act; and just before penetrating the line of the flotilla, their officers and crews jumping into the boat, which each vessel towed astern for the purpose, abandoned them to their fate. One by one, in a few minutes, accordingly, as they entered the line, and at the time for which their machinery had been set, they exploded, and shot in columns of flame into the air, adding by the splendour of their meteor-flight to the brilliancy of a scene, which, with one melancholy exception, proved nothing but a grand and expensive, though harmless *feu de joie*. In the morning we observed no change or alteration in the French line, and we counted precisely the same number but one, which composed it on the evening before. It was not until some days afterward that we ascertained the fate of the missing gun-vessel. This vessel was a pinnace, mounting an eight-inch howitzer, with a crew of thirty-six men, commanded by an *enseigne de vaisseau*. This young officer, more enterprising than his companions, observing a cutter-rigged vessel approaching, and advancing steadily for the French line, pulled for her resolutely with the intention of boarding her, and should she prove a fire vessel, which the previous explosions led him to suspect, tow her clear of the line, and then try to extinguish the fire. The English officer and crew had already left the vessel, so that the first part of his intention was easily performed. A few of his crew jumped into a punt which was towing astern of the abandoned craft, whilst he and the remainder ascended her side; but scarcely had the poor fellow ascertained that she was indeed a *brulot*, and was trying to find out whether any trace of fire was to be discovered, than she blew up, and launched him and his devoted crew to instant destruction: the only men, out of thirty-six, that escaped death, were the few who had been ordered into the punt to assist in towing the vessel's head around.

Thus ended this costly *feu d'artifice*, which had been concocted with much thought and ingenuity, and was preparing, with great labour and expense, during several weeks. If it ended in smoke, and served no other purpose, at least its previous show and parade kept our friends in the flotilla on the *qui vive* for several nights; and when at length it did come off treated many thousand spectators, both ashore and afloat, to one of the most splendid fire-works I ever beheld. In a day or two after this attempt the fleet separated, the different squadrons of which it was composed resuming their proper stations.

In the afternoon of the 24th of the same month (October), soon after we left Walmer Roads, we observed three ship praams, seven brigs, and fifteen luggers. They appeared to have left Calais but a short time, and were creeping along shore in the direction of Boulogne, with the wind from the east. All sail was instantly made on the *Immortalité*, and by half-past five o'clock she was enabled to close with them under Cape Blancnez; from hence to the eastern extremity of the Banc De L'aisne we engaged them as closely as the depth of water would permit; sometimes within grapeshot distance, and directing our fire chiefly at the praams. We were then obliged to haul into deeper water; and the enemy, taking the whole sweep of the bay, and keeping as near the shore as possible, was far beyond the range of our shot. The *Immortalité* in the mean time ran along the outer edge of the banc, and waited under Cape Grinez until the flotilla had cleared its western extremity. From that spot to St John's, near Ambleteuse, we kept up a heavy fire of round and grape upon the praams, the *Immortalité* drawing eighteen feet water, being, for most part of the time, in *half three*; nor did we discontinue the action until the darkness of the evening hid them completely from our view, when we hauled off shore and anchored for the night.

It was impossible to ascertain what the enemy's loss was upon this occasion. No vessel was observed outside Ambleteuse the next morning, in which harbour we supposed the enemy had sheltered themselves. The *Immortalité*'s was rather severe: she had four men killed; the third lieutenant and nine men severely, and several others slightly, wounded; she had her bowsprit, fore-topmast, heel of the mizen-mast, and cross-jack-yard wounded; many shot in the hull, and the sails and rigging much cut. These casualties, though severe, cannot be considered extraordinary, if we reflect upon the nature of the batteries with which the whole length of coast, from Calais to Boulogne, is bordered – the heavy armament of the flotilla, and perfectly smooth water in which it fought, and that they were accompanied by brigades of horse-artillery through-out the whole way. One shot, which struck the ship very early in the engagement, was a most wicked one, and caused much mischief: it came in on the main deck near the second port from forward, just after the helm was put up, and the ship paying off to run parallel with the enemy. It tore away nearly the whole side of the port, and with it the breeching and side tackle bolts, which, broken into pieces, flew in all directions, and acted like a shower of grape or canister. The second gun was entirely, and the third partially, unmanned; and the third lieutenant, who I believe was pointing the gun at the time, was so seriously wounded that he suffers to the present day from its effects.

Lieutenant Charles Strong, our third lieutenant, though a young man, had seen much service, and was a perfect seaman; his frame, cast in a mould of great strength and hardihood, seemed formed for endurance. Generous, manly, and brave, he joined to these qualities a ready knowledge of an officer's and a seaman's duties, which he always performed with so much cheerfulness and zeal, as not only to earn the approbation of his captain, but to infuse those feelings into all his subordinates in the ship. A perfect judge himself of all that seamen ought or could perform, Strong never exacted from them more than the occasion or duty which they had in hand seemed to require, nor ever urged them to an useless, ill-timed, or over-wrought exertion.

For qualities and accomplishments such as I have described, he was a great favourite, and exercised a corresponding influence over both midshipmen and men. The latter used to work for him with a willingness and alacrity that no other officer in the ship could command.

Often in the night (I was a long time in his watch), when getting under way, have I known the watch on deck *toss* the anchor up, and run away with the cat, if they heard his voice, with as much apparent ease as the whole ship's company when commanded by another officer. There was a coolness and self-possession, mingled with a sufficient degree of energy in his method of commanding, that seemed to make obedience and exertion a pleasure to all that were subject to his sway.

In Strong the youngsters always found a friend and protector, as well as an instructor in their profession. Frequently at night, when the weather permitted, and the opportunity offered, he ordered the midshipmen of his watch to work the ship by tacking or wearing, in order to render them expert at those manoeuvres, – a practice most useful and beneficial, but very little imitated in any other ship that I have served in.

Many and many a time have Strong* and I cheated the 'lagging hours' of a wintry middle watch in friendly and social conversation, or cheered them with a glass of schiedam, such as Deal or its vicinity alone could furnish.

Long years, with the exception of one or two short glimpses of my friend, have separated us; but no length of time can make me forget his unceasing kindness, nor his invaluable advice and counsel in the days of my youth, and when I most stood in need of them.

As soon as the ship was remasted and repaired at Sheerness, we resumed our station off Boulogne, which we never left, except in strong westerly gales, during which we always lay at single anchor in Walmer

---

* The late Captain Strong, who died an old Captain about two years ago.

Roads, ready to start the moment the wind came at all to the eastward of south, or to such a point as would allow the flotilla to venture outside their harbours.

On the 22nd of December, whilst at anchor off Boulogne, the wind blowing strong from the eastward, a vessel was seen to come round Cape Grinez, which was soon made out to be a wreck. In a short time we discovered that the vessel was bark-rigged, that all the fore part of her was under water, and that the crew were all huddled together close aft by the taffrail, which, with the exception of her masts, was the only part visible. At this time she appeared to be drifting so exactly into our hause, that it was thought she must come in contact with the *Immortalité*, or, at all events, pass so close that a rope might easily be thrown to her, by means of which we could hang her astern of the *Immortalité* for the short time necessary for taking the crew off the wreck. To avoid her coming actually in contact with the ship, men were placed at the wheel to sheer the ship in the direction that should be necessary, whilst others were stationed fore and aft with ropes coiled in their hands, ready to fling to the wreck as soon as she should drift near enough for that purpose. Slowly she dropped down upon us, affording time for much speculation and conjecture; but as she got nearer there was a good deal of anxiety and uncertainty as to whether she would approach near enough to enable a rope to be thrown on board. Soon the poor fellows' signals of distress – handkerchiefs displayed on staves and the waving of hats – are observed and answered by the *Immortalité*.

On, on she comes, and just clears the spritsailyard; and now the man on the cat-head flings his rope – it misses; and one after the other, as she drifts slowly by the ship, they all fall short by a few tantalizing inches. But when the last man flung his coil of rope as unsuccessfully as the others, and the wreck drifted past the ship, who shall paint the look of hopeless agony of the wretched crew, as their shriek of wild despair rose high above the blast that howled amid the rigging of the *Immortalité*. From the condition of the wreck, her taffrail being now scarcely above water, and the roughness of the sea, which washed over them every instant, they now abandoned all hope of rescue, and considered death as inevitable. But the shield of Providence was over them, and succour, which they deemed impossible to reach them, was at hand. The *Immortalité's* boats in a moment were in the water, and before the wreck had drifted three cables' lengths astern, the whole were rescued from their perilous situation; and most fortunate it was that so much despatch had been used, for in ten minutes more not a vestige of her was visible. As it was impossible for the boats to pull up against the wind and sea, the *Immortalité* slipped her cable and ran to leeward to pick them up.

The vessel was a Swedish bark, laden with iron and fir plank, and got ashore the previous night on the Banc De L'aisne, near Cape Grinez. Some time after she struck, the mate and a boy, in endeavouring to carry a rope to the shore, were upset in the boat and drowned. She continued to strike heavily all the night, but towards daylight floated off the banc. By this time she was a complete wreck, and so full of water, that the whole fore part of her was speedily immersed; and had it not been for the quantity of plank which constituted the greater part of her cargo, and being stowed chiefly abaft, kept that part of the ship buoyant, she must have gone down in five minutes. The men saved were the master and six of the crew, the only people lost being the mate and boy. They were all in a most pitiable condition, half frozen and greatly exhausted. Dry and warm clothing, and then a good meal and some grog, soon restored them. Poor fellows! their present gratitude was as lively and boundless as their late despair of safety had been deep and hopeless.

In this month (December), I think on the second, all the batteries along the coast, as well as the flotillas in the harbours and in the roads fired a salute of one hundred and one guns each, at daylight in the morning, which was repeated at noon and at sunset. The camps around Boulogne, and all the batteries displayed their standards, and the whole flotilla was dressed in colours. At night, the town of Boulogne and camps were brilliantly illuminated, and fire-works of the most splendid description only ceased with the dawn of day. It was the day of Bonaparte's coronation.

On the 5th of January, 1805, we had a short but close and warm skirmish with a part of the flotilla, which we soon compelled to re-anchor. Their force outside the harbour on that day exceeded one hundred and twenty.

Some time in this month an officer from the *Immortalité* was sent in with a flag of truce. He was received on board the praam which bore the flag of Rear-Admiral Savary. This praam, whose armament and scantling appeared the same as all the others, mounted twelve long twenty-four-pounders. She was very wide, very deep-waisted, and her bulwarks were immensely thick. The flag of truce was supposed to bear the Minister's answer to Bonaparte's celebrated letter to his *brother*, George III, proposing peace between England and France.

On the 29th of January, we drove a detachment of the flotilla into Etaples, and succeeded in cutting off and capturing a lugger, which had a crew of thirty-two men, including a party of soldiers, and mounted two guns, a twenty-four pounder forward, and a twelve-pounder aft on a field carriage. Upon this occasion the *Archer* gun-brig was with us, and was very active, and of much service.

Two days afterwards we attacked a detachment of the flotilla off Cape Grinez, proceeding in the direction of Boulogne. We forced two brigs and three luggers on shore, after some close and very warm firing. The *Archer* and *Watchful* gun-brigs were with us, and behaved with great spirit and gallantry. Each brig had a shot through her main-mast, and the *Immortalité* had a man killed and four men wounded. In other respects her damages were trifling.

We found that wherever a gun or mortar could be usefully planted, the spot was not long left unfurnished with one by the enemy; for on the 13th of February, on some rising ground immediately in rear of the place where we drove the brigs and luggers on shore on the 31st of January, some excellent shot were fired at us from two heavy guns.

In March, all on board the *Immortalité* were most unexpectedly delighted with receiving orders to proceed off Havre, and having there joined the *Melpomene*, the two frigates were to cruise together for nine or ten weeks to the westward. War had been declared for some months with Spain, and the newspapers teemed with accounts of the Spanish prizes and their riches, which were almost daily arriving in England. It was with joyful hearts and fond anticipations of success that we started upon this cruise. Besides, we began to be weary of the service where nothing was to be got but deuced hard knocks and a very profitless share of honour which we all, at least the greater part of us, would very willingly exchange for a few of the doubloons that were showering so plentifully upon the more fortunate cruisers to the westward.

The day after we got our orders we joined the *Melpomene* off Havre, and Captain Oliver's arrangements being soon completed, the two frigates bade adieu for a time to the north coast of France, and by midnight had passed the Gaskett Lights with a fair wind.

We proceeded to the southward and westward, and somewhere about the latitude of Cape Ortegal captured a small Spanish brig privateer, after an uninteresting chase of a few hours. After this, nothing occurred to render our cruise different from that of a hundred others. The same 'hands up, make sail', when a stranger hove in sight, and the same hopes, fears, and conjectures were indulged in and hazarded, according to her rig and manœuvres, until all anxiety on the subject was put an end to by the certainty of her being a neutral, and with papers so orthodox and regular as to defy scrutiny and challenge detention.

Once I recollect the two frigates chased a ship, which, from the spread and colour of her canvass, length and lowness of her hull, and various manœuvres to effect her escape, we were convinced was a French privateer of a large description. From early 'morn till dewy eve' did this ship keep, at one time our hopes, at another our fears balanced on the very tenter-hooks of doubt and uncertainty, as the faithless wind now enabled us to near her, and again forsaking us altogether, allowed her nearly to double her distance. At length towards sunset the breeze freshened, and became steady. At this time we were close to the Desertas rocky islets, at no great distance from Porto Santo and Madeira, which from their sterility and uninviting appearance well deserve the name they bear. The chase, now seeing that the wind was steady, and that she had no longer anything to hope from its fickleness, pushed for a narrow opening between two of those rocks, trusting that the frigates would not dare to follow her through a passage, the dangers of which were perfectly unknown; and as they would have to go round one of the islets, and darkness was fast coming on, she would have so far the start of them as to ensure her escape altogether. The *Melpomene* was the leading frigate, and Captain Oliver, judging that if there was water enough in the channel for the privateer, a foot or two more would carry him through likewise, resolve to try the passage. Keeping his eye, therefore steadily fixed upon the privateer, to watch her motions and observe how she steered, he boldly followed her, and by the time he had cleared the passage was rewarded by finding himself within gun-shot of the chase, when the latter, seeing it hopeless any longer to attempt to escape, hove-to.

We rounded one of the rocky islands, and in two hours afterwards, when we joined the *Melpomene*, learned that she had boarded a Jersey privateer, who had given us a day's amusement from apprehension of losing some of her men if boarded by a man-of-war. Thus it is plain from the length of time which it occupied the *Immortalité* in rounding the island, that had it not been for the dash of the *Melpomene*, in following the privateer through this unknown and unexplored passage, she would have escaped in the night, and we should have remained in ignorance to the present hour whether we had chased friend or foe.

Towards the end of April, the *Immortalité* anchored in Funchal roads, in the island of Madeira, to get water. The expense attending this process at Madeira, is really very considerable, and some steps should be taken, if possible, to render it less so. The cost per ton is, I think, from one to two dollars. The watering place is at the western gate of the town, and the casks, when filled, are dragged the sledges by bullocks to the water side. They are then floated through the surf, which is always rolling in upon a beach that lies open and exposed to the whole fetch of the ocean, after which they are hoisted into the boats, that are obliged to lie at some distance from the beach at a grapnel.

The town of Funchal is beautifully, I had almost said romantically, situated in the bay of that name. Its neat whitewashed houses have a most cheering and inviting appearance, particularly to those who have been any time upon the waters. Immediately in front of you, as you view it from the sea, is Peak Castle; on the left is the picturesque Love Rock, with its frowning artillery, whilst the back-ground of the picture, in form of an amphitheatre, is dotted high up with the prettiest country-houses imaginable, in the midst of vines and orange trees, and which have all the appearance of being suspended in air, so sheer and precipitous is the ground upon which they are perched. High over all rises the mountain's peak, showing clear and almost imminent, through an atmosphere unacquainted with the fogs and mists of our more northern climate.

As we remained only two days at Funchal, my visit to the shore was of but a few hours' duration. The general appearance of the interior of the town has escaped my recollection. In fact, the only circumstance that has made any impression upon my memory is a walk which I took with one of my messmates, to visit a convent at some little distance; but whether we were seduced to climb the hill which led to it under a broiling sun, from a wish to view something of the country – purchase sweetmeats, for which the convent was then renowned – or have a peep at a pretty nun – I now forget. Perhaps we acted in this matter under the influence of all three. Be it as it may, certain it is that we toiled up the steep ascent, reached the convent, and were allowed to enter the *parloir*, where we were rewarded for our labour, not by the view of youth and loveliness, rendered more interesting and attractive by all the accompaniments of situation and forced seclusion, with which the young imagination is wont to invest the recluse, but by a box of sweetmeats, handed through the grate by the withered fingers of a plain and elderly sister, who civilly refused us admission to the interior of the convent, but made us pay a most extravagant price for our *Whistle*.

At the time we were in Funchal roads we counted one hundred and twenty pieces of cannon mounted on the castle, and in the different batteries looking towards the bay.

After we left Madeira we cruised off the western islands by ourselves, without any success, until the end of May, when we returned to the Downs, and found ourselves again upon the old station, no richer, or very little so, than when we left it two months before.

The *Immortalité* was immediately ordered to Sheerness, and, after refitting, resumed her station off Boulogne towards the end of June. At this time Captain Owen hoisted a broad pendant as Commodore, but without having a captain under him, and the advanced squadron under his command was considerably increased.

On the 18th of July, in company with a small part of our squadron, we had a warm brush with a division of the flotilla which attempted to manœuvere, but were soon compelled to re-anchor.

On the following day, from information received, that a strong detachment of the Dutch flotilla, which some time before had been driven into Calais, and was waiting for a wind to take it to Boulogne, might be expected to sail, Commodore Owen lay-to off Cape Grinez with his little squadron, to be in readiness for their reception. At five in the afternoon the enemy's flotilla was observed coming out of Calais, and formed in line a-head, steering with a fair wind to the westward. It consisted of three ship-praams, which led the line, and were under French colours, and twenty-two schooners under Dutch, the centre one of which bore the flag of the Dutch Admiral Verhuel. They were followed by the *Ariadne* and the little Calais squadron, which kept up as close a fire upon them as the depth of water would allow.

As soon as they appeared, we filled and made sail with our squadron, and, in one board, fetched the western extremity of the Banc De L'aisne. There from her draught of water, the *Immortalité* was obliged to wait, until the flotilla, which, to avid the fire of our ships, rounded the Bay of Ouissant as close to the beach as they could, should emerge from its shelter. The *Arab* and *Watchful* gun-brig, and some more of our squadron, whose names I forget, from their lighter draft of water, were enabled to close the enemy, and behaved in the most gallant style, particularly the two former, which were both a good deal cut up. The *Arab* had several men killed and wounded; and the *Watchful* lost her brave commander, Lieutenant Marshall, who was steering his brig at the time, with the intention of running one of the enemy's schooners on board. Some time before six o'clock they had cleared the shoal, when the *Immortalité* immediately closed with the praams, which kept together, and, covered and supported by the bateries and a formidable flying artillery, which accompanied them all the way, opened upon us heavy and well-sustained fire. These we engaged most part of the way, within grape-shot distance, from Cape Grinez, until they found shelter in Ambleteuse, when our fire was directed at the schooners; and the *Immortalité*'s last shot was not fired until after sunset, by which time the sternmost of the flotilla had gained the entrance of the same harbour.

This proved one of the closest and severest actions we had been engaged in, and lasted considerably over two hours. The *Immortalité*'s loss was rather heavy: four men killed; twelve badly, and several more or less severely, wounded.

At this time I was the Signal-Midshipman, and my quarters had been changed from the main to the quarter-deck. This gave me an opportunity of observing the judgment and admirable coolness of Commodore Owen in time of action. His most common station upon those occasions was just abaft the capstan, whence his tall figure, raised still higher upon a platform of shot-boxes, enabled him to see over the hammock-nettings, and commanding a view all around him, to con the ship in such a manner as to render her fire the most effectual without the hazard of her running aground.

During the action a shot came through the quarter-deck hammocks, immediately over one of the carronades, covering the men that were quartered at it with a cloud of flock and feathers, and, taking an oblique direction, it wounded at the same moment the quartermaster at the con, and the one at the wheel, taking off the arm of the first very high up, and grazing the point of the other's shoulder, who was a very short man; then passing through the arm-chest abaft the mizenmast went through the bulwark on the other side.

The Commodore, hearing the clatter which the shot made amongst the Marines' muskets, turned round, and, seeing a man stretched on the deck, exclaimed: 'Hah! is that poor Mouat? Lift him up, and take him carefully below.' But Mouat was on his legs before the sentence was finished, and, motioning the men who hastened to his assistance to return to their quarters, he coolly walked down the hatchway, his countenance retaining its usual calm expression, not a muscle moving, or giving evidence of the least suffering or pain.

Andrew Mouat belonged to a class of seamen not often met with. Thoroughly versed in every branch of a seaman's duty, he had none of the thoughtless, reckless habits and manners, that usually characterize the profession to which he belonged: on the contrary, his were peculiarly quiet, orderly, and sober: whatever duty he was put to perform, or whatever trust was reposed in him, he never left the one until he had finished it, and never disappointed or betrayed the other. And yet Mouat was a pressed man, with a wife and children, from whom he was unwillingly separated. His former situation, too, had been one of respectability, being mate of a vessel that traded between London and one of the north-eastern ports.

Mouat, however, never thought of deserting, but used to say to the midshipmen, who sometimes in a middle watch, when at anchor, obtained his confidence – that since luck, or Providence, had decreed that he should serve in a man-of-war, he should continue to do so with as much willingness and cheerfulness as possible, until peace, which he always flattered himself was not remote, again restored him to his family, when he had no doubt but the owners of his late brig would always find him employment. Thus he argued – and thus hope, so wisely and beneficently implanted in the breasts of all, enabled him to anticipate an early restoration to his wife and children, and in the meantime to discharge his allotted duties with cheerfulness and unrepining. Since then, how often have I thought of, and envied too, a philosophy which taught to endure evils and privations with such equanimity and contentment!

The dreams and expectations of poor Mouat, however, were not fated to be realized. Peace did not take place as early as his wishes led him to expect – and the unlucky shot which robbed him of his arm, at the same time deprived him of all hope of future employment in the merchant service. But Commodore Owen, who was never unmindful of the deserving, always exerting himself to the utmost in their behalf, procured for him a gunner's warrant as soon as the poor fellow's arm was healed.

Besides our loss in killed and wounded, the ship sustained a good deal of damage. Her foremast, maintop-mast, and spanker boom were shot through; two carronades wounded, and three boats cut to pieces. To repair these defects, it was necessary that the *Immortalité* should go into port; and the morning after the action, before we parted company, the signal was made for an opportunity to send men to the hospital. In closing around us for this purpose, our little squadron successively passed under the *Immortalité*'s stern, and as a mark of respect to the Commodore, and self-gratulation for their conduct on the previous day, each vessel cheered him as she passed. As the *Arab* shot by I noticed, with a throb of exultation more easily felt and conceived than expressed, two noble fellows on the booms, who, holding up the stumps of their amputated arms, joined in the shout of triumph as she passed.

5: Gale off the Elbe

Early in August, 1805, having had our defects repaired at Sheerness, as we were about to sail from the Downs to resume our old station, Lords Spencer and Althorpe, with General Ross, embarked in the *Immortalité* on an amateur excursion off Boulogne. An easterly breeze soon took us across the Channel, when Commodore Owen gave them an excellent opportunity of viewing the coast; for from Cape Grinez to Point d'Alpreck, we ran along, nearer perhaps than was pleasant, saluted the whole way by shot and shell from all the batteries, with a constancy and rapidity that almost told they had divined the noble cargo with which the *Immortalité* was freighted. As we passed before Ambleteuse, we observed a large body of men, amounting, as we judged, to eight thousand or ten thousand, reviewing on the beach. We anchored for the night, during which the wind changed to the westward. In the morning it freshened very much; and, just as we were about to get under weigh, the cable parted, saving us the trouble, when we bore up for the Downs, and in a few hours landed our noble visitors.

As soon as the wind moderated, and came a little to the eastward of south, we proceeded again off Boulogne; and on the 13th of that month, were so fortunate as to fall in with the buoy of the anchor and cable, which we had parted from ten days before.

On that morning there was a very large force of the enemy's flotilla in the roads, amounting in all to one hundred and eighty-nine vessels, including eight ship-rigged praams. The day was beautifully fine, inviting, as it were, the Frenchmen to try some manœuvres, whilst their immense force inspired them with confidence to venture far beyond their customary limits. The ship's company were busily employed in the recovery of the anchor and cable before mentioned, when Commodore Owen, who had been watching the motions of the flotilla all the morning, observed that six praams, one of which bore the flag of a Rear-Admiral, were manœuvring together, distinct from the rest of the flotilla, and considerably out of gun-shot of the batteries. Our squadron at the time consisted, as well as I remember, of the *Vestal*, Captain E Heywood, with the *Adder*, *Bloodhound*, and *Sprightly*, gun-brigs. The *Renommée*, one of the frigates belonging to the Dungeness squadron, and which took no part in our proceedings, was advanced close to us by Rear-Admiral Billy Douglas, then at anchor five or six miles further out.

From the situation of the praams, and the state of the wind and tide, the Commodore considered that he had at last caught those gentry on the hip, and that so favourable an opportunity of bringing them to close action should not be neglected. We immediately slipped; and in a few minutes the *Immortalité*, under sky-sails, with the wind somewhat abaft the beam, was dipping through the water in a most promising manner. The praams, as soon as they perceived our movements, formed in compact line ahead, their Admiral being in the centre, and steered under all sail before the wind, with their heads to westward, nearly parallel with the shore, just having an inclination to near it withal. The tide at the time was running flood, and those heaviest of heavy sailers scarcely stemmed it, whilst the *Immortalité* advanced upon them as if they were at anchor. Everything wore a most propitious appearance: the long-desired moment of bringing them to decisive action, unaided by their batteries and flying artillery, seemed at last within our reach. We were steering right for their admiral's praam, with the certainty of being alongside of her in a few minutes more, when Admiral Douglas, who, from the distance at which he lay, could have formed no correct opinion of the relative positions of the English and French squadrons under the high land of Boulogne, nor of the great advantage for attacking them which Commodore Owen had at length obtained – displayed at his mast-head the large recal, with the *Immortalité*'s, pendants, attention to which was enforced with a gun.

As signal-midshipman, my duty was to report the signal, which I did; but so engrossed was the Commodore with the business in hand, that I am inclined to think he did not hear me; at all events, he took not the least notice of the signal, nor of my report.

On we flew with bounding hearts, such as are felt by men on the point of grappling with an enemy – No. 5, over a red pendant, the signal for close action, still flying on board the *Immortalité* to her little squadron, which was formed in her wake – when, just as we had reached within grape-shot distance of the praams, and had all in readiness to run their Admiral on board, another gun from the flag-ship, which was repeated by the *Renommée*, drew the Commodore's attention. Seeing that our recal was flying on board the latter ship, as well as at the mast-heads of two of the gun-brigs, he judged it most prudent to answer it; when, putting the helm *aport*, without firing a gun, or taking any further notice of the enemy, he hauled to the wind on the starboard tack, and stood towards the *Leopard*, the Admiral's flag-ship.

The *Immortalité*'s stern was no sooner presented to the praams, than they and a cloud of mortar-pinnaces, which had rowed out to their assistance, opened their whole fire upon her, happily without mischief, except to the rigging, which was a good deal cut. Our squadron wore in succession after their Commodore, and in so doing, received and returned the broadsides of the praams.

At this termination to hopes so highly wrought, Commodore Owen's countenance expressed deep mortification, in which I believe everybody throughout the ship participated; for we all felt that we had lost the best, indeed I may say the only, opportunity we ever had of doing anything really brilliant with an enemy that never, but upon this occasion, ventured beyond the protection of his batteries.

In the month of September, Sir John Moore and Sir Sydney Smith came on board the *Immortalité*, from the *Antelope*, when we showed them the coast from St Jean's to Etaples; and in doing so ran the gauntlet of the whole of the batteries, which threw their shot and shells well, though luckily without mischief.

In the months of September and October our boats, with those of some of the squadron, were frequently sent in shore, sometimes with carcasses and always to harass and tease the enemy whilst at anchor in the roads; but we could not discover on the following morning that we caused them any serious mischief by those enterprises. It was about this time, I think, that Commodore Owen went in his gig three or four nights successively to sound in the harbour's mouth of Vimereux, and also behind the forts or towers which had been erected at low-water mark since the commencement of the war (la Crêche, Fort Imperial, or pile battery, and de l'Heurt), in order to ascertain clearly, and at what time of tide, vessels could pass between them and the land.

In reconnoitring, on the 11th of October, a 13 inch shell from one of the batteries fell on one of the forecastle carronades, and, from the great weight of its fall, broke in pieces without exploding. The fragments wounded four or five men that were grouped together on the forecastle just before the watch was called up from dinner; and some of the larger ones, breaking through that and the main-deck, lodged between decks. At first the Commodore was not aware of these results, and, supposing from the quantity of smoke occasioned by the dispersion of the powder with which the shell was charged, that it had exploded below and set the ship on fire, ordered the drum to beat to quarters; but as he was soon made acquainted with the extent of the mischief, the men were again dismissed.

This circumstance brings to my recollection some of Commodore Owen's arrangements in the event of the ship catching fire, which, if my memory serve me right, were as follow: – On an alarm of fire the drum beat to quarters, as when preparing for action. The carpenter, with that part of his crew quartered in the wings, was immediately, without waiting for orders, to turn the cocks and fill the well with water as fast as possible, and then to proceed with axes, &c., and be prepared to scuttle the decks above the spot where the fire was supposed to be, if that should be necessary. Those carpenters quartered on the main-deck abreast the mainmast were to *fetch* the hand pumps, and rig the winches of the chain-pumps, whilst the carpenter's mate and the rest of his men prepared the fire-engine, and laid the hoses fair fore and aft the main-deck. In the mean time the firemen with their buckets, ranged themselves on either gangway; and the fore, main, and mizen-rigging men, taking the hammocks from the waist-nettings, held them in readiness to soak overboard, and then to pass them wherever that should be found necessary. Those men, to whom no other station was assigned, were to range themselves, under their respective officers, in a double line on each side of the main deck, where they were to be prepared to pass the buckets along, give a fair direction to the hoses, and *spell* the pumps; whilst the first lieutenant and boatswain, with the boarders quartered on the quarter-deck and forecastle, should proceed with axes to the spot where the fire was supposed to have originated.

Such, as well as I remember, is an outline of that arrangement which Commodore Owen had established for subduing fire in the event of its breaking out in the ship – an arrangement in which the crew were so well practised, that even if it happened in the night, no mistake as to station could possibly have occurred.

Towards the latter end of October a pinnace, having a small punt in tow, was observed rowing from the shore in the direction of the *Immortalité*, and at the time at anchor in her usual position before Boulogne. When they had reached nearly within gunshot of the ship, the small boat was set adrift, and the larger one pulled back again for the shore. The circumstance was so unusual, and excited so much curiosity, that Commodore Owen, in order to satisfy himself on the subject, sent a boat to pick up the punt, and see whether it contained anything or not. In half an hour the boat returned, having the punt in tow, in which had been found a note from Admiral La Crosse, who then commanded the flotilla, addressed to the English Commodore, and which contained the following words: – 'The Austrian army of one hundred thousand men is no more. General Mack is a prisoner at Ulm, and Prince Ferdinand is put to flight.' An account that seemed so wholly improbable, and which, if true, would have been so ruinous to the allies, was scarcely credible. That an army, which had only quitted the vicinity of Boulogne in the early part of September, should have traversed such an extent of country – crossed rivers – forced defences – fought battles – and, after annihilating an army of one hundred thousand men, and capturing its commander-in-chief, have established itself in Ulm, the key of all the Austrian movements and positions, upon the strengthening and storing of which so much pains had been bestowed, and all in the brief space of six or seven weeks, seemed so far to exceed all that one had ever heard or read of in ancient or modern warfare, that the account was considered a fabrication, and wholly disbelieved.

Putting no faith, therefore, in the courteous and *well-meant* communication, Commodore Owen returned an answer by the same mode of conveyance, the exact words of which I forget; but the purport signified strong doubts as to such great successes attending the operations of the Grand Army, with a hope that Admiral La Crosse had been imposed upon, and that the account would not prove more true than former reports of victories that had been carefully circulated in France, and for which rejoicings took place and *Te Deums* were sung, that in the end turned out to be reverses. With this answer the punt was again towed in-shore, to what may be called the neutral ground; and as soon as she was abandoned, a boat from Boulogne, which seemed to be kept in readiness, pulled out to meet her. After the lapse of about an hour she was once more towed out and turned adrift; but, upon being visited by our boat, she was that time found to contain nothing save Commodore Owen's own note, the seal, indeed, broken, but without comment of any kind; thus silently rebuking his incredulity and want of faith.

In November, Commodore Sir Sidney Smith arrived off Boulogne with his squadron, and assumed the command. The force, when united, consisted of twenty-five sail, which did not include three explosion-boats and a mortar-ketch. Of this number five were bombs; the remainder were vessels of all descriptions. Several fire-vessels joined afterwards, which swelled our force to more than thirty sail, enough to alarm the whole flotilla; and, in truth, our new commander seemed bent on desperate deeds. The force collected before Boulogne, and under the command of an officer of Sir Sidney's character, plainly showed that an attack of no ordinary kind was mediated.

After the vessels had all assembled, few preparations were necessary. The arrangements were soon made, and the officers who were to hold commands in the attack received their instructions. All now depended upon the weather, which, in the course of a few days, seemed to favour the enterprise. For two successive nights the boats of the squadron, bombs, and fire-vessels, under cover of the sloops-of-war, armed ships, and gun-brigs, moved towards their allotted stations; but owing to a fail-ure of wind, and the very heavy sailing of many of the ships, the attack could not be made, and they all returned, the vessels to their anchorage and the boats to their ships. At length, on the evening of the 21st, the boats once more assembled in three divisions, each division under the charge of a commander, when they, with the bombs and fire-vessels, cov-ered as before by the sloops-of-war, armed ships, and gun-brigs, moved towards Boulogne. The *Immortalité* was the westernmost ship of our line, and was anchored within long gun-shot of Fort de l'Heurt. With the exception of her boats, which had been despatched to the rendezvous, it was not intended that she should take part in the attack. Her station was therefore to lie at anchor; but Commodore Owen, seeing that the wind, though moderate at the time, was blowing on the land, with every appearance of freshening, got under weigh in the evening, and steered in the direction of the *Diligence* sloop-of-war, on board which ship Sir Sidney had hoisted his pendant, in order that he might more conveniently direct the operations that were in progress. It was whispered amongst the midshipmen (but how the rumour got afloat I am unable to say), that he anxiously sought Sir Sidney, in order to try and persuade him from persevering in the attack, which, with the wind directly on the land, and every appearance of its coming on to blow, would inevitably prevent the heavy sailing vessels, such as the bombs, armed ships, and fire-vessels, from being able to work out of the bay, and possibly the boats from regaining their ships. Amidst the crowd of ships, Commodore Owen had great difficulty in finding the *Diligence* at night; but when at length he made her out, and went on board, his opinion and advice were at once adopted by the Commodore; the signal of recal was made; and an hour before midnight Commodore Owen had returned to the *Immortalité*, and sail was made to work off the land. Fortunate, indeed, it was that this advice had been so early tendered and followed; for, as had been expected, the wind increased very much in the night, and had the attack been persevered in, I believe that few of the dull-sailing ships or heavy boats would have been able to avoid the shore. As it was, they had great difficulty in doing so. Some of the boats did not regain their ships until the following afternoon, and one or two were stranded. The whole squadron proceeded to Dungeness; and the wind continuing adverse for some days, the expedition against Boulogne was abandoned for the present, and the *Immortalité* was ordered to the Downs.

In twenty-four hours after she had anchored, the *Immortalité* was again ordered to sea. Information had been received that two French frigates were fully equipped at Flushing, ready to put to sea at the first opportunity; and as it was uncertain whether they would go to the northward, or attempt the English Channel, Commodore Owen received instructions to be on the look-out for them.

For ten days we cruised with unabated vigilance between Boulogne and the opposite coast, without being rewarded with the sight of anything even of a suspicious nature.

At length, on the eleventh day, in the evening, some time after dark, a vessel was seen right ahead; which had all the appearance of a large man-of-war. The *Immortalité* at the time was standing for the French coast, having the wind from the eastward; and the stranger, under all sail, was steering in a similar direction.

We immediately gave chase, and made the night-signal as soon as possible. As, however, it remained unnoticed, and no signal was made in return, the drum beat to quarters, and a very few minutes sufficed to have the ship ready for action.

Although the chase, when first seen, was not far from us, and we neared her pretty fast, as she was right ahead, and running from us under all sail as fast as she could, we did not get within hail of her for nearly an hour, affording leisure for serious thought and reflection at such a time. And certainly, after the bustle and excitement attendant upon a sudden call to quarters at night is over – when the guns are all cleared and laid, and everything at quarters is now in its proper place – when expectation and anxiety, by the protracted chase, are raised to a painful degree – and a silence, a stillness almost breathless, only broken at times by a whispered order from a Lieutenant giving some necessary directions – succeeds to hurried preparation, I own I have felt, at such a time, a thrilling solemnity, approaching to awe, which I never knew when the broad clear day gave light to such scenes. Then the dusky figures of the sailors, with arms bared, and heads and loins girded for the strife, or their hats, ornamented with bits of oakum twisted hard for *vents*, appear of larger proportions, seen by the doubtful light, as with folded arms, and bent, determined brows, they pass, from time to time, with silent step, between you and the fighting lanterns, whose feeble rays scarcely serve to penetrate the gloom – the whole offering a picture not unworthy of the painter's art.

But to return. Near and more near drew the flying chase, and anon the Commodore's voice, bidding the men 'stand to their guns' disturbs the transient calm. In an instant the crew start into activity and animation, and every soul on board seems instinct with life, energy, and emulation. We are now close upon the stranger's quarter. The captains of the guns, the lanyards in their hands, bring the dark artillery to bear, and a word, and the iron tempest, with which it is loaded, bursts in fire and thunder upon her decks. Again is heard the Commodore's voice. This time he hails the chase; but, alas! the answer of a friend meets the ear, and disappoints our cherished hopes – hopes that were raised so high of a fair stand-up fight with a ship of our own size, in open sea, untrammelled by land and unannoyed by batteries!

The chase turned out to be one of our armed ships, the captain of which had been warned of the probable departure of the French frigates from Flushing, and as the strange ship which pursued him was end on, and consequently the whole of the lights that formed the signal could not be seen, he thought it wisest, weak as his own force was, to observe a respectful distance until he ascertained whether she were friend or foe.

It was during this cruise that we first heard of the mighty victory of Trafalgar: a victory of such vital importance at the time to England, neutralizing in some degree the consequences of the vast successes of the French upon the continent; and I can well remember how much the pride and exultation, which we should otherwise have felt at our country's success, were saddened and subdued by the irreparable loss of her favourite hero. Instead of shouts and songs of triumph and gratulation, the subject was mentioned in broken whispers, and all seemed to feel, not only that some great national calamity had befallen the land, but as if each individual had lost a friend and leader, with whom it would have been the happiness of his life to serve and follow. Soon after this event, it being ascertained that the frigates, which we were on the look-out for, had made their escape, and gone north-about, the *Immortalité* returned to the Downs.

We had now done for a time with Boulogne. Work enough had been cut out for Bonaparte's Grand Army in Germany: his threat of invasion was suspended *sine die*, and the *Immortalité* could be spared for other service. Accordingly, before Christmas she was ordered to proceed to Harwich, there to receive the Duke of Cambridge, who was nominated to command the German Legion, then serving in Hanover with the British Army, the whole commanded by Lord Cathcart. In anticipation of his royal guest, Commodore Owen had to provide wines, lay in stock, and make alterations in his cabin. (Was he ever reimbursed for those heavy additional expenses?) The account, however, of the signal defeat of the Austrian and Russian armies, in the memorable battle of Austerlitz, having reached England at this time, it was thought probable that the British Army would re-embark, and consequently that the Duke's presence with the Legion was no longer required. Therefore he did not embark.

Here I may pause a moment to ask whether Bonaparte ever seriously meditated the invasion of England? The question has often been asked, and when the threat of invasion passed off, was generally answered in the negative. Indeed many Frenchmen now doubt that such was his motive for assembling such a mighty host at Boulogne.

His reason for collecting together so large an army, and building a flotilla numerous enough for its transport at so vast an expense, is supposed to have been threefold. First, to feed and keep alive the vanity of his countrymen, and by dazzling their imaginations with the splendour and magnitude of such a project, divert their minds from the object upon which he was then intent, namely, to assume, with as little delay as possible, the Imperial purple; next to harass and annoy England, and by so serious a threat of invasion, prevent her from sending her ships and troops from home on foreign conquests, when they were so likely to be required for the protection of her own shores; and thirdly, and chiefly, to keep a large force assembled together perfectly disciplined, and with all its material ready to commence instant operations, should the exigency of the moment, or any unforeseen occurrence on the continent require it to be put in motion. But I cannot think that all these reasons combined, though plausible enough, were of sufficient force to have induced him to make such a display for no other purpose, and at so vast a sacrifice. A flotilla capable of transporting an army of one hundred and sixty thousand men, nine thousand seven hundred horses with fifteen days' provision, and all the material necessary for such a force, was built and assembled. This flotilla, which consisted of two thousand three hundred and sixty-five vessels of various descriptions, cost, in building and equipping, twenty-seven millions of francs. But this is but a small part of the expense, when it is considered that the harbours of Etaples, Boulogne, Vimereux, and Ambleteuse had to be either wholly excavated and constructed, or considerably enlarged and repaired to contain and shelter so great a number. If to this be added the charge for the erection of the hut-barracks, of which the camps were composed, and for fortifying the line of coast from Cherbourg to Ostend, in order more effectually to protect the vessels as they proceeded to the place of general rendezvous, we shall have a sum whose aggregate must have been immense. From Cape Grinez to Point d'Alpreck, a distance of only seven leagues, there were mounted in batteries of different descriptions and sizes, one hundred and thirty heavy guns, and twenty thirteen-inch mortars; and if we reflect upon the sum which it cost England at that time to put part of the coasts of Kent and Sussex in a state of defence, we may form some proximate notion of the expense of the mighty array of force, and all its concomitant adjuncts, assembled on the shores and in the opposite harbours of France. Taking all these circumstances into consideration, I am of opinion that Bonaparte fully intended the invasion of England, which only the rupture with Austria, and the mismanagement of Admiral Villeneuve, in 1805, prevented his attempting. In this opinion I am fortified by what I learned from Admiral Lacrosse, some years ago, at Bordeaux. This Admiral was second in command under Admiral Bruix, at Boulogne, and in consequence of the latter's feeble state of health, had been nominated Director-General of the flotilla. In that situation, he had the entire management and arrangement of the naval force there and in the contiguous harbours; and upon the death of Admiral Bruix, which took place in 1805, he succeeded to the chief command.

The flotilla was formed into six squadrons or divisions. The first, or larboard division, stationed at Etaples, was meant to embark Marshal Ney's corps, encamped at Montreuil. The second and third, called the right and left centre-divisions occupied the Harbour of Boulogne. These were intended to convey the corps of Marshal Soult, and occupied the camps to the right and left of that harbour. The fourth, or starboard division of the flotilla, was stationed in the Harbour of Vimereux, and was appointed for the transport of Marshal Lanne's corps, which consisted of different divisions of infantry, and amongst others of the grenadiers of the advanced guard, and of the reserve. The Batavian or Dutch vessels, in Ambleteuse, formed the fifth squadron, and were to embark the corps commanded by Marshal Davoust; whilst the sixth, called the reserve, and assembled in the harbour of Calais, was destined for the Italian division of infantry, and for different detachments of dragoons, mounted and dismounted.

All the vessels were ranged in tiers along the quays in the different harbours. Each regiment, and company of a regiment, knew the vessel appropriated for its reception; and in order that there should be no mistake in marching to the point of embarkation, guide-posts were fixed upon the quays to direct the officers in command to their proper vessels. In fact, nothing was omitted to obviate error or confusion, and to facilitate the embarkation of the troops whenever that object was desired.

When the vessels composing the flotilla were all assembled in their proper harbours, the Emperor, anxious to ascertain the shortest time in which the operation of embarking could be accomplished, had it twice performed in his presence; and the result exceeded his expectation, for men, horses, and all were on board in one hour and a half after the drums in the various camps beat to arms.

But although everything, so far as it regarded the flotilla, and the army of England, as it was called, seemed to favour the enterprise, Bonaparte, knew that so long as England had the command of the Channel, the flotilla could not force a passage, and effect a disembarkation of the troops, in face of the overwhelming force of ships of the line, and other large vessels with which it would be opposed. But if by any means a plan could be devised for removing the English fleets to a distance, and a French one to have the command of it for even a few days, then, indeed, the flotilla might push across unopposed, and a disembarkation of the army be effected without interruption from the sea.

While, therefore, the flotilla and grand army were preparing and concentrating in and around Boulogne, the utmost activity prevailed in all the harbours of France, and nothing was left undone to increase and equip her fleets and squadrons. In the Texel several Dutch ships were ready for sea; and as war was now (1804) declared between England and Spain, the fleets of the latter nation were also at the disposal of Bonaparte.

At the beginning of the year 1805, by extraordinary exertion he had at his command eighty ships of the line ready for sea, besides a number of frigates, and smaller vessels.

By a skilful combination and direction of this force, he had good ground to hope he might succeed in luring the English fleets to a distance from the Channel, and with his own, of getting command of it for a time sufficient to allow the flotilla to cross without opposition.

With this object in view the Toulon and Rochefort squadrons were ordered to put to sea, and proceed to the West Indies, Admiral Villeneuve, who commanded that of Toulon being directed first to raise the blockade of Cadiz, and when joined by the French and Spanish ships in that port, pursue his course to the West.

These operations, though retarded by the state of the weather that winter, were at length performed, and Admiral Villeneuve reached Martinique in May, where, when all were collected, the united French and Spanish ships formed a fleet of twenty sail of the line.

An abortive attempt upon the island of Dominique, and the capture of the Diamond Rock, a singular insulated precipice, close to Martinique, occupied by a party of sailors, and commanded by a lieutenant of the navy, who defended his post with great gallantry for several days, were the only feats accomplished by this large force, during the time it remained in the West Indies; and Admiral Villeneuve, as soon as he heard of Nelson's arrival in those seas, in pursuance of his instructions, instantly sailed for Europe. His further instructions were to make Ferrol, and being joined by the French and Spanish ships in that port to the number of fifteen sail of the line, he was to proceed off Brest, when his fleet being added to the ships in that harbour would form a force so superior in number to the blockading fleet, that it was to be supposed no attempt would be made to impede its progress to the Channel; and once in command of it, the flotilla, which could clear the harbours in two tides were immediately to push across the Straits.

But Villeneuve's encounter with Sir Robert Calder and, when he succeeded in forming a junction with the ships in Ferrol, his subsequent retreat to Cadiz, instead of showing himself off Brest, together with the rupture with Austria, all combined to defeat this well-planned scheme; and England was relieved from present apprehension of having her shores polluted by the footsteps of a foreign enemy.

But that the idea of invasion has not been relinquished by France may well be supposed from the great attention which that country has payed for a number of years to her marine, and the extraordinary care which she has bestowed in making her harbours, and naval arsenals as perfect and secure as possible.

No form of government in France, be it monarchical, or republican, ever loses sight of this object; and whatever opposition is made in the Chamber of Deputies to other expenses of the State, none is ever offered to those which relate to the army or navy.

The consequence is, that at this moment the ships of France, both sailing and steam, are in a most efficient state. Of these, a considerable number are in commission, and they are allowed, in all points, to be in excellent order and condition, while her mode of registration, and laws relating to mariners, give her the power and facility of speedily and effectually manning all the others.

Neither for the protection of her own shores, nor for her foreign possessions, of which she has but few, does France require such a force; and therefore to increase it each year, and continue preparations at so vast an expense, has evidently more an aggressive than a defensive character.

The power, wealth, and extensive possessions of England are the envy of every country, and of none more than France, which cannot forgive the part she played in the long revolutionary war, nor forget that it was by the valour of her fleets and armies, and her great persevering exertions that she was often thwarted, and checked, and finally humbled and subdued.

These painful remembrances are still rankling in their hearts, and therefore to revenge former reverses, and crush the pride of the haughty islanders, are the cherished objects of nine out of ten Frenchmen.

And what blow could be more damaging and humiliating to England than to see her shores trodden by a foreign enemy, and her fair towns and villages ravaged, and given to the flames? To speak of the conquest of our country is absurd: but with the assistance of railroads and steam, such a force of troops and ships could quickly be assembled – say at Cherbourg, distant but a few hours' run from England, with a basin capacious enough to hold more than fifty sail of the line – with all the steam navy of France, and landed on our shores, as would cause incalculable mischief, to say nothing of the disgrace and deep humiliation which so mortifying an occurrence would inflict upon the nation. But neither the Government, nor the people of England seem awake to the danger. The army and navy are reduced to the lowest standard, and if the Minister sometimes start from his lethargy, and make a proposition to increase the force, the fierce opposition and threatening cries of the economists, check his purpose and fright him into silence.

Hence the country is bare of troops; nor is the militia, in case of need, prepared to be called out and embodied for its defence. Our coasts, vulnerable on many points, almost invite attack, and there seems nothing to prevent the easy descent of an invading force whenever our neighbours may decide upon such a step.

On the 15th of January, 1806, the *Immortalité*, having received two pilots from the Trinity House, proceeded for the Elbe, in conformity with Commodore Owen's instructions to take charge of the transports in that river and the Weser, where they had been assembled for the reception of Lord Cathcart's army, in the event of its being compelled to retire and re-embark.

The evening we sailed from Harwich the wind was blowing strong from the south-west, with thick and gloomy weather; and as not a soul in the ship, except the pilots, who did not inspire much confidence, had ever been on the coast to which we were steering, a general depression, not to be accounted for, and quite unusual, foreboding something disastrous, weighed upon the spirits of all on board. We were running with the wind, which increased in the night on the quarter, at the rate of ten knots, under close-reefed maintop-sail and fore-sail. The course was shaped to round the Texel point, avoiding the shoals on that dangerous coast.

Some time in the night, about two or three o'clock, one of the pilots informed the Commodore that the ship had run far enough to clear the Texel shoal, and that it was time to haul further to the southward. After consulting the chart and logboard, to see how far the ship had run, the Commodore was of a different opinion, and we continued to steer the same course until five o'clock in the morning, at which time it was altered something to the southward of east. And fortunate it was that he did not attend to the pilot's first suggestions; had we sooner hauled up the ship must inevitably have been on shore; for, as was subsequently proved, she was at the time considerably to the southward of the Texel. As it was, indeed, she escaped very narrowly. Immediately after breakfast I went upon deck (I was still signal midshipman), and thinking that the sea broke in a different manner on the lee-bow from what it did close to the ship, and that the water all around had assumed a muddier colour from what it had half an hour before, I mentioned the circumstances to the lieutenant of the watch. He, however, probably from being longer on deck, and the change in these appearances having taken place gradually, could not at first perceive what was so obvious to my eyes. Upon this I went forward upon the forecastle, and called the gunner's attention to what I observed, who was instantly struck with the same appearances, and ran aft, and again pointed them out to the officer.

The lieutenant seemed now to awake all at once from his apathy; the helm was ordered to be put up, a midshipman despatched below to acquaint the Commodore, and before the sails were trimmed, with the ship's head to the north-west, we had shoaled the water suddenly from twelve fathoms, in which we had been running for some hours, to a quarter less seven, and the sea was plainly observed to break close to us, in the direction in which we had been steering.

The shoal, which we had so providentially avoided, was the Hakes, not far from the Texel, a shoal that has proved so often fatal to our cruisers, and, indeed, to mariners of all nations. Blowing so hard, and going at the rate she was running, had the *Immortalité* touched the ground, she must speedily have gone to pieces, and nothing but the will of an all-wise Providence could have saved a soul in the ship.

The weather continuing very thick, and the wind increasing, sail was still further reduced, and the ship's head kept to the northward for about thirty hours, when the wind becoming more moderate, we stood once more for the Elbe.

About noon on the eighteenth some steeples and beacons were seen, which showed that the land could not be far distant; but as no observation had been had since we left Harwich, and all objects were rendered indistinct by the haze, we were uncertain as to the exact part of the coast we had hit upon. In half an hour more three ships were observed running into what at first we supposed to be the entrance of the Elbe, but which afterwards turned out to be the river Jade. For some time longer we continued to run to the southward and eastward, until, by mismanagement and blundering, the pilot contrived to get the ship to leeward of the fair way into the Elbe. When they observed their error, they proposed to anchor the ship until the following morning to the southward and eastward of the Vogal, a most dangerous shoal, of horse-shoe form, convexing to the southward. The weather continued remarkably hazy, and the few objects which rose above the flat shore were but dimly visible. Commodore Owen, therefore, who, as I said before, had never been on the coast, closely questioned the pilots, and asked them repeatedly if they were quite confident as to the ship's situation, and if they were sure she was to the southward and eastward of the shoal. To this they replied that they were perfectly satisfied as to the ship's position, and when she had run a little further they wished to anchor.

We were now in ten fathoms, in the act of clewing up the topsails, when the water suddenly shoaled to half six, and the anchor was instantly let go. This was about three o'clock in the afternoon; the weather gloomy; the wind freshening fast, with every appearance of an approaching gale. We prepared to meet its force: veered to a cable and a half, sent the top-gallant-masts on deck, and made everything snug. The gale hourly increased, with heavy squalls, one of which, about nine o'clock, momentarily blew aside the veil of mist in which we were shrouded, disclosing at the same time the lights upon the nieuwork in the Elbe, and that upon the island of Heligoland, by the bearings of which we were first enabled to have a conception of the awful situation in which the ignorance of the pilots had placed us. Instead of being to the southward of the Vogal, we now found that we had anchored deep within its bight, and should the wind veer to the north-west, which, from the squally nature of the weather, there was every likelihood of its doing, the ship would ride with the horns of the crescent projecting on both sides before her beam.

At midnight, the wind having greatly increased, with a heavy fall of sleet, the topmasts were struck. Before daylight, as was expected, the wind shifted to the north-west, and brought with it a very heavy sea. A second anchor was then let go, and two cables were veered upon the one, and half a cable on the other. The situation of the ship was now awfully critical. Anchored within the bay of an extensive and most dangerous shoal, the wind blowing a gale in the direction most adverse for her working out, and bringing with it a sea so heavy as to render it nearly hopeless to think that anchors and cables could withstand its weight and fury, and if they failed, no human means or skill could save her or her devoted crew. So desperate, indeed, did Commodore Owen think our situation, and so improbable that the ship could ride out such a gale, accompanied, as it was, with such a sea, that he wrote a letter to the Admiralty, and another to his wife, which he had corked and sealed in a bottle, that, should it be found after her destruction, the fate of the old ship and her unfortunate crew might at least be known.

For thirty hours and more the same weather and sea continued: our safety dependent upon a few strands of a hempen cable. The ship behaved nobly; and although she might be deficient in some properties requisite to make her a perfect frigate, she possessed one quality, and that a very important one, of riding easy at her anchors, which under Providence, at that time, I am persuaded saved her from wreck.

During all the time, a subdued tone seemed to pervade the ship's company. A strong anxiety was visible in their countenances, and plainly showed that they had a just notion of the imminent danger in which they stood. This feeling, however, did not in the least paralyze their energies; on the contrary, they moved to the performance of every duty, noiselessly indeed, but with a zeal and alacrity that almost anticipated the orders of their officers; whilst all, both officers and men, looked to the Commodore as to one with whose abilities they were long acquainted, and whose thorough seamanship and resources would be sure to extricate them, if human skill could do so, in a time of such fearful peril.

In the afternoon of the second day, while the officers were below to snatch a hasty meal, I happened to be on deck, standing near the Commodore, who had the moment before sent the lieutenant of the watch to examine the service of the cables in the hawse – just then an enormous sea, whose dark and ominous bulk was crowned with foam, that shone and glistened like the light which sometimes presages the mountain's disruption, was observed to roll, in swift and menacing convolutions, towards the ship, and, striking her obliquely on the bow, it burst with a terrific crash upon her decks, deluging the forecastle and waist in water. For a moment the ship, yielding to the mightily pressure, lay almost broadside to the sea, stunned and writhing as it were, beneath the blow.

In an instant every soul rushed on deck from below, and it was easy to see by their expressive features that all hope from anchors and cables had passed from their minds. Every eye was turned in mute expectation towards the Commodore. He, however, stood unmoved, simply giving directions to observe how the cable grew, and whether it hung slack, and ordering the man in the chains to keep his lead on the ground, and report the moment he thought the ship drifted. Our agony, however, lasted but a few seconds: the ship gradually recovered, and righted herself, and again rode head to wind. Soon after this it was perceptible that the force of the galo was broken, and in the course of the night it moderated considerably.

6: A Visit Home

The early part of the morning of the 20th of January was devoted to putting the ship to rights, and preparing to be ready to weigh, as soon as the tide should serve. By a man-of-war cutter, which arrived the same morning from England, and was bound to Cuxhaven with despatches, we were first made acquainted with the death of Mr Pitt, and the consequent change of ministry.

As soon as the ebb-tide had done, we got under weigh, and, preceded by the cutter, which was to report by signal if the buoys were in their places, we steered for the Elbe. The ship was anchored for the night somewhere above Nieuwork, and the next morning, having got a river pilot, we proceeded to Cuxhaven, and moored in the afternoon about two miles from the town.

From its entrance to Cuxhaven nothing can be more triste and dreary than the appearance of the Elbe and its neighbouring shores in the winter. Nothing to cheer the heart, or gratify the eye; but a broad, rapid, and muddy stream, whose numerous buoys and beacons point out to the navigator its frequent shoals and treacherous sands, whilst its flat, sandy, and barren shores are often only to be guessed at by the spires and towers, which, rising, as it were, out of its oozy waters, serve as land-marks to the stranger.

We found several men-of-war, and more than one hundred sail of transports in the Elbe, the whole under the charge of Captain Bland of the *Flora*. The river in front of Cuxhaven seemed to be blocked with vessels, without any order as to their mode of anchoring, or any disposition made for the more convenient and speedy reception of troops.

Commodore Owen's first care, upon assuming the command, was to rectify this state of things. The transports were classed and disposed in divisions, and anchored in the clearest and most convenient positions for embarking the army, and all its *matériel*, whenever they should arrive for that purpose, a man-of-war having charge of each separate division.

Captain Heywood, of the *Vestal*, an officer upon whose judgment and ability the Commodore could rely, was sent to the Weser, there to take the command, and superintend all that related to the transports and embarkation of the troops. Meantime an officer had been sent to the head-quarters of the army, with dispatches from Commodore Owen: and as it was not yet known that Lord Cathcart had decided upon withdrawing the troops from Hanover, two six-pounder field-pieces, which we had on board, were prepared, and a lieutenant, two midshipmen, and a party of seamen to man them, ordered to be in readiness to land, should they be required. I happened to be the elder of the midshipmen ordered for this service, and upon me chiefly devolved the superintendence of everything necessary for our landing, and also training the men to the management of the field-pieces. Little, however, beyond what they already knew of *boxing* an eighteen-pounder ship gun about could I instruct them in; but the service was new, and its novelty had an attraction for sailors – we were all in high glee – and we felt confident that the *Immortalité*'s men and field-pieces would do more execution among the enemy than all the artillery in the army.

Our hopes of military fame, however, were fated soon to be extinguished. The officer who had been despatched to head-quarters brought back word that the army was preparing to fall back upon Bremen and Cuxhaven, and Commodore Owen was requested to have the transports ready for the reception of the troops. It had been ascertained that immediately after the battle of Austerlitz, Marshal Augereau, whose corps of the Grand Army had remained in observation on the frontiers of Bavaria and Suabia, received orders to move down into Hanover, and drive the British to their ships. These directions were more easily effected than, perhaps, Napoleon or the Marshal had calculated upon; for before the latter could have made many marches, the English army was already in the act of embarking.

In those days of doubt and indecision, before any important movement or plan of operation was determined upon, it was not unusual, I believe, to hear the opinions of all the general officers of an army assembled in council of war. Upon the present occasion, before Lord Cathcart finally decided to retreat, and withdraw the army from the continent, such a council was held, at which the subject was discussed, and where, as was commonly reported afterwards, the whole assembled officers, with one exception, were unanimously of opinion that the army ought to be re-embarked. It was agreed that it would be impossible to contend with the force which Augereau was preparing to march against them. In such a case resistance would be worse than useless, exposing Hanover to the brutality and horrors of a licentious and infuriated soldiery, and the British Army to hazard and destruction.

The officer who differed upon this occasion form the rest of the council was said to be Sir Arthur Wellesley, then recently returned from India, and serving as the junior major-general in the army of Lord Cathcart. The following were said to be some of the reasons which he gave for differing from the opinion of his brother officers:

'That the British Army, including the German Leg on amounted to thirty thousand men, besides a small force at Stadt of six thousand or eight thousand Swedes, with which it was in communication. That the troops were in a state of the most perfect health, spirits and organization. That, moreover, they had a friendly country in which to act, with the command of the *embouchures* of all the rivers, by means of which reinforcements of men and munitions could always be received, and where our men-of-war and transports could lie securely, in readiness to embark the troops whenever they should be driven to such a necessity. On the other hand, the corps which was to act against them, was said not to exceed forty thousand men, a number that might be greatly exaggerated, and which, at all events, was sure to be much reduced before it reached Hanover, from the various casualties to which an army is exposed during long and hurried marches through a hostile country, and in an inclement season of the year. Then the moral blow which the retreat and withdrawal of the British Army, without an effort for the cause, must inflict upon the Allies, ought to be taken into consideration, and how completely prostrate at the feet of Bonaparte such a desertion, at such a time, would leave all Germany. Should our army, on the contrary, maintain its ground, and gain a battle, the position of Augereau would be critical in the extreme, removed to such a distance from succours and support, isolated, and in a manner cut off in the heart of an enemy's country. Austria would have breathing time, and might again raise her head; and the smaller States of Germany, if not completely crushed, and reconciled to a state of bondage, would have a rallying-point, and might make an effort to throw off the yoke.'

Some such reasons as these were said to have been advanced by Sir Arthur, in order to induce the council to await the approach of Marshal Augereau. His judgment and opinion were disregarded, however, by veterans, who considered him as a hot-headed young man, unacquainted with European warfare, fresh from India, where he had been accustomed to see a host of Asiatics sometimes routed by a handful of European soldiers.

Whatever may have been the opinion and suggestions of Sir Arthur Wellesley, at the time, as to the management of the force entrusted to Lord Cathcart, certain it is that the latter did not await the approach of the French, but, as soon as he heard of Augereau's making a march or two in advance, he moved the army towards the Elbe and Weser, and began to embark it by divisions early in February. By the 15th of that month, the last division of transports had left the Elbe, and on the 17th the *Immortalité*, having on board General Don, the second in command, and Major-General Finch, with the officers of their staff sailed for England.

Whilst we were in the Elbe, my occupation as signal midshipman, particularly with so large a fleet of men-of-war and transports under the command of the Commodore, necessarily confined me to the ship; and, indeed, in those days – at least in the *Immortalité* – the duty of a midshipman afforded ample employment and amusement, without indulging him with too many visits to the shore. I landed but once at Cuxhaven, and then only for a few hours. The impression which its appearance might then have made upon me is nearly effaced by the lapse of thirty years. I have a dim and faint recollection that the houses struck me as low and flat-roofed – the streets unpaved and muddy, like the margin of the turbid Elbe, and that it presented altogether a very dirty, trite, and uncomfortable aspect. That length of time, however, has not sufficed to blot from my memory the impression left there by the sinister and cunning features of a scoundrel Jew, who, taking advantage of my hurry and ignorance of the town, cheated me most unmercifully in the purchase of some shawls, and the cashing of a bill of exchange.

Our passage back to England was retarded by light and contrary winds to the 23rd, when having weighed from Margate Roads, where we had anchored the night before, we proceeded in the morning for the Downs, with a light wind from the westward. In less than an hour after we weighed, there came on a fog so thick that we could not see twenty yards from the ship. As there were pilots on board, however, who professed to be perfectly well acquainted with the soundings, and we could depend upon our leadsmen, no uneasiness or apprehension was felt on that account. Just, however, as it was supposed that the ship had entered the Gull Stream, having shoaled the water a little, and being then on the starboard tack, the helm was put down; but before the ship came head to wind she was fast on the North-sand Head. Fortunately at the time there was very little wind; the sea was as smooth as glass, and the ship lay still and motionless. The Trinity House pilots had now wound up the catalogue of their blunders. Twice before they had nearly wrecked the ship; a catastrophe from which she escaped, as it were, by a miracle.

When we got ashore it was not low water. We had, consequently, to wait some hours before there was any prospect of the ship floating. Meantime the stream-anchor was run out and hove upon, and as she only hung forward, the guns and other weight were moved from her bows.

The fog did not last long, and as soon as it was dissipated a gun was fired, to draw the attention of the *Devastation* bomb, and some boats, that were seen coming out of Ramsgate. Commodore Owen determined to trust no longer to the Trinity House pilots, and got the pilot of the *Devastation* to take charge of the ship to the Downs. The Ramsgate boats, with the sagacity peculiar to the boatmen that dwell between the Forehands, judging how matters stood, were soon alongside the *Immortalité*, into one of which General Don and the officers of his staff put themselves, without waiting for the luggage; and long before the tide rose high enough to float the *Immortalité*, they were safe within the pier of Ramsgate. Late in the afternoon we anchored in the Downs, where the *Immortalité* remained but a few days, and was then ordered to Sheerness, Commander Owen having been appointed to the *Clyde*, a fir-built frigate of thirty-eight guns, the old ship being fairly worn out.

We found the *Clyde* at the Little Nore, rigged, but not manned, it being intended that the officer and crew of the *Immortalité* should be turned over to her. She had been fitted out at Woolwich by the riggers of the Dockyard, and as those gentlemen, in the days I write of, were not renowned for the neatness and perfection with which they turned matters out of hand, her masts had to be stripped and re-rigged, and her holds cleared and stowed afresh. At the same time, the *Immortalité* was being prepared to be paid off into ordinary, and as both duties had to be attended to by the crew of the *Immortalité* alone, they necessarily occupied some time.

A fortnight, however, saw the *Clyde* in the Downs, whence we sailed in a day or two to resume our station once more off Boulogne, and the command of the advanced squadron. About the middle of April, a boat, with a flag of truce, came off to the ship, for some purpose with which I am unacquainted. While the French officer was on board, the *Clyde* lay to, with her head in shore. During this time she gradually forged in, approaching the land nearer than the enemy liked. They, therefore, very soon warned us, with shot and shell, to preserve a more respectful distance. One of the latter, I remember, fell within a foot or two of the French boat, before she was well clear of the ship; so that the officer, when he returned to the shore, could make a favourable report of the excellent practice of their mortar batteries.

We found the *Clyde* a remarkably fast frigate, but awfully crank, to remedy which defect we twice took in a considerable quantity of iron ballast.

This brought us to the end of May, when my time as midshipman was completed; and it was with no small delight that, on the 31st of that month, I got permission to go to London, to pass my examination for lieutenant. On that occasion, as, indeed, upon all others, I experienced the greatest kindness from Commodore Owen. Besides the usual certificate given to midshipmen, when they have their captain's permission to be examined, he gave me one written in his own hand, in which he spoke of me in terms far handsomer I fear than I deserved.

On the morning of the 1st of June, 1806, I landed, for the first time, in the metropolis, and hastened to find out my brother R – , who had been a lieutenant in the navy for some time, and was then in London for his health, which had suffered much from long service in a tropical climate.

The day of examination is, I do believe, the most momentous in the career of a naval officer and the 4th of June, 1806, the day on which I passed mine, stands at the head of the memorabilia of my sea-life. An awful thing it is to stand in the presence of three stern, grave-looking officers, whose fiat is fame or disgrace, happiness or misery, holding, as it were, your future destiny in their hands. On my departure from the ship, I fancied myself not ill-prepared for the searching ordeal, and in practical seamanship, at least, felt pretty confident that I should pass muster. No sooner, however, did I feel the keen, scrutinizing eyes of my judges fixed upon me, than my self-confidence, like Acres' courage, fast ebbed away: trembling and bewildered I stood fascinated before them, and literally '*vox faucibus hæsit.*'

To various questions in seamanship and navigation, I blundered and stammered out answers, mechanically I believe, but to which my examiners, in compassion for my extreme shyness and nervousness, I conclude, made no objection; and at length, when I was dismissed from their presence, my mind would at once have been relieved from all anxiety and apprehension on the dreaded subject, had it not been for certain doubts which they hazarded, as to my having attained the proper age, and which doubts had the effect of nourishing and keeping alive rather uncomfortable sensations for the remainder of the day. On the following morning, however, when I again called at the Admiralty, all doubts and misgivings were removed; and no future occurrence of my life afforded me more unmingled satisfaction and delight, than did the receipt of the all-important document, which testified to my competency for the charge and duties of a lieutenant.

Although pleased and gratified with London, which possesses so much to fascinate youth, particularly on a first visit, I left it at the end of a fortnight without a sigh; for my steps were turned towards home, from which I had been absent five long years – (and what an eternity do five years comprise for youth before the age of twenty!) – a home to which all my yearnings and aspirations were directed, almost from the moment that I first left it.

There were no steamers in those days, and the little trading sloop in which I took my passage from Bristol to Cork, her creeping progress still more retarded by light and baffling winds, ill kept pace with my boiling impatience. On the fourth morning, finding her becalmed off Youghal, I jumped into a fishing-boat alongside; and after a row of two hours, once more stepped upon my native earth with a thrill of rapture, such only as those can imagine, who, like me, had been long and early separated from kindred and from country. My breast swelled with emotion – tears of joy filled my eyes – and my heart giving vent to its overwrought feelings in some such apostrophe as burst so naturally, and yet so beautifully and pathetically from the lips of the returned exile, 'O patria! dolce ed amata

patria! alfin a te ritorno!' I could have almost knelt and worshipped the
ground upon which I trod.

After a hasty breakfast, I procured a horse, hoping to traverse the
cross-country mountain road, that divided Youghal from Lismore, before
dinner. It happened to be market-day, and as I *backed* and *filled* through
the long narrow street of Youghal, encumbered with pigs, poultry, cattle,
and crowds of country people, at every step I advanced, my ear and eye
were struck with the well-remembered accent and characteristic costume
of the peasantry. The long, flowing blue mantles of the females, some
hooded, some uncapped and unbonnetted; the grey frieze cloaks of the
men, thrown loosely and carelessly around them, after the fashion of
Spain, and meant to guard them from summer's sun and winter's cold,
with hats broad-brimmed and slouched, gave them a wild and foreign
appearance, which, though not so neat and trim as the dress of the people
of the other island, was far more interesting and picturesque.

Having at length *worked* my way through the crowded street, I
stopped not until I passed the little town of Tallow, when I paused on the
brow of the hill which separates it from Lismore, arrested for a moment
by the view of the fine range of mountains that from so remarkable and
so beautiful a feature in the landscape to the north of the latter. From that
spot they are seen to great advantage, from base to summit. Their heath-
covered sides had then put on their summer's dress, which at the distance
appeared of purple and gold, save when a cloud, chased by the breeze,
flung its shadow across their outline. To me those mountains were old
and cherished friends: I loved them with a fondness, I may say enthusiasm, rarely felt in maturer years, and hailed them, at the time, as beacons
that should guide me to 'the haven where I would be'.

During the brief space for which I paused upon the hill-side, what a
multitude of remembrances and sensations crowded upon my memory!
In a moment of time I lived over again the years that were fled. Each
occurrence of my past life, painted in colours distinct and vivid, like figures in the magician's lantern, glided swiftly through my mind. But a few
minutes were given to this meditative luxury. I again pressed forward,
and soon found myself at home, greeted and welcomed in smiles and
tears by my affectionate sisters, and no less warmly and cordially by my
excellent father.

Various were the questions asked and answered, and numerous the
topics discussed during that happy evening. Separated as we had been for
five long years, a thousand little anecdotes and circumstances, trivial in
themselves, but possessing a lively interest for such dear friends, had to
be rehearsed; and, except the occasional interruption of two or three

urchins, that came into the world during my absence, and called me uncle, tugging at my boot-tassel (*tights* and *Hessians* were worn in those primeval days), twelve o'clock found us, with spirits unflagged, and curiosity still unsated, in the same delightful interchange of thoughts and feelings. We then parted for the night; and it was with mingled sensations of overflowing happiness and fervent thankfulness to the Giver of all good, that I found myself in the same room, and soon stretched in the same bed, in which I had nestled when a little boy.

Next morning I arose early, and sallied forth before breakfast to visit some of my old and favourite haunts. My steps were first directed to a spot, where, in summer time, many of my holiday hours used to be passed, sometimes in reading, often in that kind of dreamy musing in which boys love to indulge. This place lies a short mile to the east of the village, and is commonly known as the *Round Hill*. It is evidently one, and a very perfect one, of those raths or Danish forts, which are not uncommon in either island. The form of the one in question is conical, and surrounded by an inner and outer ditch of very distinct formation. At that time, the whole circumference, from base to summit, was clothed with tall furze, whose yellow blossoms shone like burnished gold in the morning sun. A narrow footpath, that wound through the furze, which rose above my head, rose to a circular platform of about the third of an acre, smooth and even as a bowling-green, and covered with a beautiful green-sward. Thence, every object that met my eye was as dear and familiar to me as household gods.

Almost at my feet glided the classic Blackwater, upon whose clear and placid bosom reposed, as it were, two verdant islands, dotted with a few peaceful sheep, while a flock of noisy geese preened themselves and luxuriated at their margins. Before me, on the other side of the river, sloped upwards the grounds and woods of Ballygalane, Saltibridge, and Belmont; and if I turned my eye to the right hand or to the left, it rested on the ruins of the Preceptory of Kilbree, and the picturesque villages of Cappoquin and Lismore, or the dark, mysterious entrance to the glen of the fairies, the softer beauties of Ballyinne, the noble bridge and the commanding and majestic castle of Lismore.

For an hour and more I continued to view with increasing admiration scenes amidst which my childhood had been passed. Years had fled since last I looked upon them, during which I had wandered far, and seen much. I found, on my return, all unchanged – or if anything was changed, changed for the better. A sister married and a mother, and three others, whom I had left growing girls, ripened into the form and bloom of womanhood. But the mountains, the woods, the rivers, the troops of ruddy ragged children that issued from the cabin-doors – the wilding or aged thorn that sheltered the humble thatch – even the very pigs that rolled and wallowed in the stagnant pools, in none of these could I note a change; all seemed the same as I had left them five years before. Filled with pleasing thoughts and reflections, such as the scenes which I had been viewing were calculated to inspire, I returned to the house, and found the family assembled at the breakfast-table, where the meal was prolonged almost until noon in conversation, such as the lateness of the hour the night before alone had been able to interrupt.

Upon this my first return to Lismore, three weeks, three little weeks fled with the rapidity and the sunshine of a summer's day. In times of activity and war, a sailor was a description of animal, a sort of lion, that seldom visited an inland town, and an opportunity now presented itself to the lieges of inspecting and examining the properties of the genus. In consequence of this, I was much sought after and *fêted*. Even to the village folk I found I had become an object of some interest; and the lads who, in days of yore, for want of others, had often been my playmates and companions, approached me now with very unwonted deference. One of them, Jack Nugent by name, after sundry twitches and wriggles of the shoulders, and scrapes of the feet, ventured to accost me with: 'You are welcome home, Master Abraham' (with the humbler classes in Ireland all are *masters* from the third or fourth generation upwards, except the patriarch of the family, who alone is distinguished with the title of *mister*, as amongst themselves all are boys even to the age of fifty, so long as the father continues to hold on existence) "tis myself that's heartily glad to see your honour.' Your honour to a midshipman! I was at a loss to know whether I ought to feel flattered, or to laugh at an appellation so egregiously misapplied. 'Are you come now to stay with us, Sir, or are you going to *say* agin? Ya thin, Master Abraham! what a dale you've thravelled, and all the grand sights and places you've seen. Have they any rivers, I wonder, like the Oun-a-Shad and the Blackwater in England? and do there be any trout or salmon in 'em? Aiye! Master Abraham, and 'twas you that was fond of fishing! and yourself just bign'ning to throw a pale fly whin you went away from us! – and there was not a purtier ball-player in Lismore than your honour – I mane for your years. You didn't play a dale of ball at *say* to be sure, Master Abraham; did your honour?' This was said with a glance of the eye, that left it doubtful whether Jack was quite so simple as to suppose that people played ball at sea. 'Not once, ashore or on board,' I replied. 'I never had an opportunity of playing since I left Lismore.' 'Ya thin! think o'that! may be, if I might make so bold, your honour would like to thry a game this morning – the old alley, you know, Sir, is quite handy.' 'With all my heart, Jack, come along; but I fear you will find me a very indifferent player, for want of practice.'

Whilst we are proceeding to the ball-alley, I may as well give a short account and description of the appearance of my interlocutor. He was some three or four years older than myself, with a frame wiry and extremely hardy, but spare, and short of stature. His features, regular and pleasing, had derived an expression of what might have been either cunning or sagacity from a pair of deep-set, keen grey eyes, which were generally shaded by a quantity of long thick hair falling in matted locks low over his brows, and which, all unconscious of even a crownless caubeen (hat) would have been brown had it not been marred and tarnished by the bleaching and scorching effects of summer's sun and winter's rain. From long exposure to the weather, his face and bare neck were tanned to the colour of mahogany. His body was enveloped in a 'looped and windowed' garment much too long and wide for his person, whilst a pair of sheepskin shorts, as usual unbuttoned at the knee, left exposed his naked sinewy legs, which were marbled red and white, from too close an acquaintance with the cabin's turf-supplied hearth. Jack excelled in most kinds of games, and at fives, hurling, and foot-ball, few, if any, were his superiors. He was also a sportsman in his way, and could beat a cover, break dogs, and in winter track a hare upon the mountain's snowy side. But it was as a fisherman that Jack acknowledged no superior, or if he did acknowledge one, that superior was his own father, in whose footsteps he had walked from infancy, and whose mantle was now about to fall upon him. Each pool and stream, where a fish was wont to lie, were more familiar to Jack than the paternal cabin. He also could read the signs of the times, and, by the motion of the clouds and direction of the wind, tell whether the day would prove propitious to his favourite amusement. He knew with an accuracy that outstripped the science of the naturalist, every fly that furnished food to the inhabitants of the Blackwater and the Oun-a-Shad, and could imitate their hues and forms with unrivalled neatness and skill. Marvellous were the stories told of his performances, and vast the quantities of fish he used to slaughter in a day, – so vast indeed, that I fear to mention what I have heard and seen, lest the world should think I deal in hyperbole.

Arrived at the ball-alley, Jack's many-coloured robe was laid aside, when he very soon had an opportunity of seeing how sadly fallen off was his former pupil, in whose proficiency he once took so much pride.

'Och! Master Abraham,' he would exclaim, as his regret and displeasure were excited by my bad play; 'what ails you, sir? sure that's not the way at all at all to knock 'em out. Strike the ball low and sharp – that's better. Turn your hand to the left, sir. Aiye! don't you remember where to put the ball? My heart's kilt wid you; sure here's the very stone where your honour used to drop it – and the div'l a rise was in it after it tiched that same. – That's better: a hand out. Now sir, mind the left hand. Och! the dickens a ball at all at all, you can take. – What a murther! and your honour that used to be so handy! Be gar that's better. Och! death alive boys! did ye see that? The kith-oge (left hand) for ever! Be gonnies, sir, you'll do yet – that's a tiche of ould times.'

And so my friend Jack, after some more drilling, pronounced that with practice, I might in time recover lost ground.

Before we parted, Jack drew from a deep pocket, concealed in the folds of his multitudinous garment, a round tin case, rusty from the blood, and spangled with the scales of whole hecatombs of fish. The case contained flies of all sorts and sizes for every season of the year, from the minutest gnat for summer trout-fishing, to the largest-sized winter salmon-fly. These he tendered for my choice and acceptance, and at the same time proposed that we should have a day's fishing together.

'There's been a dale of rain out in the west, and the water is too dark and high now; but no matter, 'twill bring up the pale in plenty, and if there's no more rain, after to-morrow the river 'll be a fine beer colour, and thin, your honour, I'll be bail, 'tis ourselves will have the day's diversion.'

But Jack's day of diversion, as well as many others, which I had vainly promised myself to pass at Lismore, was not written in the book of fate. The very morning after our fishing excursion had been planned, a letter from my first patron, Captain Griffith, was put into my hand, which told me, that, upon repairing to Plymouth, I should there find letters of introduction and recommendation to Lord Collingwood, who then commanded in the Mediterranean, and also to Sir John Duckworth, whose flag was flying at Plymouth in the *Royal George*, which was on the eve of starting to join Lord Collingwood's fleet; and that no time was to be lost, as it was uncertain the moment she might be ordered to sea.

There were blank faces at the breakfast table that morning. After perusing the letter, my father, in whose face disappointment and sorrow were visibly depicted, asked me how I meant to act; and upon my saying that I thought the better way would be to follow Captain Griffith's instructions, he applauded my resolution, bestowing great credit upon what he was pleased to call my courage upon the occasion, whilst his countenance all the time gave contradiction to his assertions. And in truth, it required no small effort to tear myself away so soon and so unexpectedly from a happy home – a home, where I was so loved and so caressed, and again to go and drudge as a midshipman: for, disguise it as we may, still the life of a midshipman is, or perhaps more properly speaking, was a fearful slavery. Moreover, there was a certain Mary O'B——, whose father had lately come to reside in the neighbourhood of Lismore, who had imperceptibly thrown around me a net of slight and filmy meshes indeed, but through which I found it not a little difficult to break.

Before strangers Mary was almost shrinkingly retiring; but in her own family, or with intimate friends, she was joyous and animated, and the life of the circle. When released from her morning tasks of music or of drawing, delightful it was to watch her, as I have done, fly, unencumbered by shawl or bonnet, through the woods of Tureen; the intricacies of which she threaded as swiftly and unerringly as does the young Indian the mazes of her native forests; whilst her little brothers and sisters panted after her in vain. She would then return towards the house, carolling one of her native songs: her dark-brown glossy hair floating unrestrained in natural ringlets over her neck and shoulders – her naturally clear pale cheek mantled with the blush of exercise and health – her soft dark-blue eyes beaming with happiness and good-nature; and her lips, which Moore would say a bulbul might mistake for a rose-bud, and fly to for its morning draught of honied dew, just apart so as to afford a glimpse of the pearly treasures that lay enshrined within.

For her years, which scarcely numbered sixteen, she was tall and womanly, and her form was cast in nature's happiest mould. Joy and sunshine seemed to gild her path, and all things promised her happiness and length of years. At that very time, however, her days were numbered. The winter after I left Lismore, she was at a crowded ball, the first I believe she had ever appeared at in her life. There she danced all night with her usual animation, and shone 'the admired of all admirers'. The night was bitterly cold; and, the ball being over, as she stood for some time in the hall waiting for her carriage, feverish from excitement, and heated with dancing, a keen and searching east wind smote her to the heart, blighting in the bud this young and lovely flower. I never saw Mary again. Fever and inflammation of the lungs hurried her in a fortnight to the grave.

On the fourth day after receiving Captain Griffith's letter, I landed at Bristol, and proceeded to Plymouth with all the speed that the six inside *heavy* of that day would permit, viz, thirty hours from the time of starting, until it deposited me at Gowde's Hotel in Plymouth Dock. My first care was to get my letters, and to ascertain the state of forwardness of the *Royal George*, and whether she was likely soon to go to sea. Upon inquiry, I found that she was in Cawsand Bay, fully equipped, but wanting one hundred men to complete her complement, and that it was quite uncertain when she might proceed to her destination. Having ascertained thus far, I lost no further time in repairing to the house of Sir John Duckworth, whom I was anxious to see as soon as possible to present my letters to him, and learn if I could be received into the *Royal George*, and if so, to obtain his sanction to my going for a few days into Cornwall, whither my heart was bent upon going to visit my eldest sister, before I should leave England, I did not know for how long a time, and whom I had not seen for seven long years.

Upon calling at Sir John Duckworth's house, I found that he was absent, and that he was not expected home for two or three days. What was to be done? If I awaited his return, by that time his orders might have arrived, or he might consider the uncertainty of the moment of their arrival a sufficient reason for not permitting me to be absent from Plymouth at such a time. These thoughts shot quickly through my mind, and without further consideration I resolved to leave the letters for him, and to start the following morning for Truro, trusting that the chapter of accidents would bring me back in time to secure my passage in the *Royal George*; and that the cause and nature of my flight would plead my excuse with the Admiral for any apparent disrespect to himself. In thus deciding, I did not attend to certain inward suggestions which told me I was about to do what I ought not to do, nor reflect that an unfavourable impression once made upon minds of a certain structure, is scarcely, if every, effaced. I mention these circumstances, that in the event of these pages ever being seen by young men; they may serve as a warning always to reflect before they take any step that requires deliberation, and where duty is concerned, never to neglect the whisperings of conscience – that honest counsellor, so wisely and beneficially implanted in our breasts, but whose advice we are all too apt to disguise and disregard.

7: The *Royal George*

I pass over the few incidents that occurred during my two days' sojourn, all that I permitted myself in Cornwall; and, on my return to Plymouth, I called immediately on Sir John Duckworth. Upon being ushered into his presence, I was at once given to understand that, to say the least of it, I had taken a very injudicious step in departing for Cornwall without his previous knowledge and consent. His reception of me was far from gracious; and he expressed a decided disapprobation at my leaving Plymouth without first seeing him and obtaining his sanction. No excuse that I could offer seemed to convince him that I had not done what was very disrespectful and very thoughtless. It was plain that this proceeding had, in the outset impressed him very unfavourably in my behalf, and that it behoved me to be very circumspect in my future conduct, if I hoped to remove the prejudice, and stand well in his opinion.

After inflicting upon me a pretty considerable jobation, he relaxed somewhat from the austerity of his manner, and, inquiring for the gentleman to whose kindness I was indebted for my introduction and recommendation to him, he bade me go on board the *Royal George*, where directions had been given that I should be received; upon which he bowed, and I withdrew.

The *Royal George* was in Cawsand Bay when I joined her – still short of men, but in other respects fully equipped. The captain, as well as most of the lieutenants, were acting, until the arrival of the *Acasta* frigate, whose captain and officers were destined to replace them.

The midshipmen seemed to have been collected from the four winds of heaven, and were comprised of characters as various as were their ages, and the different parts of the world that gave them birth. Ireland and Scotland – Devonshire and London – Norfolk and Cornwall – the Isle of Man and the Orkneys – Jamaica and Madras – Calcutta and Barbadoes – all furnished their quota, and all were distinguished by something peculiar to the region of their nativity. Their ages, too, varied from the child of twelve or thirteen to the ripe old stager of thirty-six. Then their conversation and general deportment (I speak of those grown up) at once denoted the *school* to which they belonged. Those who had served chiefly in ships of the line, or passed much of their lives in guard ships, I remarked were well skilled in slang, and even their ordinary conversation was garnished and interlarded with a superabundance of oaths and obscenity. The collection from sloops of war and gun-brigs might be known by an absence of good breeding, and a certain slouching vulgarity and slovenliness of appearance; while those of the frigate-school differed widely from both. Of this they seemed themselves aware, avoiding as much as they could an intimacy with the others, and forming, as much as possible, a society apart. But on shipboard, and more especially in a midshipman's berth, it is impossible always to close the eyes and ears to what is hourly taking place; so that the very familiarity with what at first is odious and distasteful, makes it at length endurable, finally, perhaps, agreeable.

On first joining the *Royal George*, crowded though a three-decker be with human beings, I felt myself, as it were, in a vast solitude, without a friend or acquaintance with whom I could familiarly converse, or to whom I could impart my thoughts or feelings. Perhaps I felt all this the more, fresh as I was from *home*, and from the affectionate kindness of my sister in Cornwall. For hours and hours I used to pace the middle deck in a most dolorous and woe-begone frame of mind, contrasting my present abode and situation with that which I had just left; and bitterly, oh! how bitterly, did I lament leaving my old ship and commander, and the officers and messmates who knew me so well, and whom I valued and esteemed so much.

Nor was this feeling lessened when I came to do duty in the ship. In the *Clyde* I felt myself to be an officer of some *little* consequence. I frequently was placed in charge of the deck, and never was ordered to perform any duty but such as comported with my years and standing in the service. In my new ship, on the contrary, I was but one, and I believe the youngest one of a host of passed midshipmen, who were no more regarded, nor their feelings consulted, as to the duty they were required to perform, than if they had entered the service the day before. They were commonly ordered on the most trifling service, which I had been accustomed to see allotted to the veriest tyros in the ship; and oftentimes have I been cooling myself, from nine o'clock at night till past midnight, in a boat near the beach of Cawsand, but with orders not to touch the shore until hailed by the captain, who usually passed his evenings, with the surgeon and captain of marines, in playing at billiards, at the little inn, for egg-wine – a pleasant beverage, for the judicious concoction of which its worthy hostess, the good Mrs Elliott, was renowned.

Since those days something has been done to improve the condition of the midshipman. He cannot now be disrated, and turned before the mast, at the caprice of his captain; nor is it any longer permitted to send even youngsters to the masthead by way of punishment.

Their situation is, however, still sufficiently harassing and annoying. They may be sent on the most trifling and humiliating duties, and teazed and degraded in a thousand ways. What, for instance, can be more wounding to the feelings of a young man, who has passed his examination, and is qualified in all respects – by birth, by years, and by experience – to fill the situation, and do the duty, of a lieutenant, than to be ordered, as I have been, to attend with a boat upon the captain's pleasure, lacqueying him like the menial who stands behind your chair, or opens your carriage-door at the opera?

Although the ship was now complete in men, several weeks dragged heavily along, without any appearance of her being ordered to sea. At length it was rumoured that the *Royal George* was to convoy a fleet of transports to the Mediterranean, having a large body of troops on board, destined to reinforce the army in Sicily. Already had the convoy begun to assemble in Catwater and the Sound, and we were in joyful anticipation of being soon released from the dull and tiresome routine of port duty.

From the day I joined the *Royal George* I had not been absent from her a moment, except on duty; but now there were two visits I was anxious to pay before our departure: one to an old mess-mate, who I had just learnt was lieutenant of the *Rosario*, the other to a lady, whose name and story had awakened a good deal of interest, and whom I had known long and well, when quite a little boy. At the time I write of she was married to an officer of the army, and embarked in a transport forming part of the convoy collected in the Sound. Having obtained leave, I went on board the *Rosario*, where I passed some hours with my shipmate in discussing various matters of by-gone times, and then got a boat and proceeded to the transport.

I found my female friend in the cabin of a wretched little brig, full to overflowing with officers, whilst she was the only lady on board. Several years had passed since we met – time enough for me to have grown out of her recollection. She appeared pale and thin, and already looked older than her age by any means warranted. Upon recognising me, which she did not for a moment or two, her eyes lighted up for a time with their wonted brilliancy, and her countenance, now 'sicklied o'er with the pale cast of thought,' assumed the pleased and animated expression that I so well remembered. She spoke of old times and old friends with the liveliest interest, and asked many questions about my father, who was always a great favourite with her, as, indeed, she was with him. Of Lismore she spoke with the deepest emotion, and dwelt with pleased recollection on the many years of peaceful happiness which she had passed there. After a time, however, other thoughts and other remembrances would intrude – the contrast, perhaps, which forced itself upon her of those days, unclouded by a single care or sorrow, 'with that world of woe' with which her heart had since become familiar – the melancholy despondency that now habitually overcast her intellectual features, and almost quenched the lustre of her large expressive eyes, would settle on her face, and she would again become silent.

The story of Sarah C—— is too well known for me to dwell long upon it here. More than one version of it has appeared in prose, and the poet, *par excellence*, of her own country, has touched upon the most melancholy part of it in verse. A few circumstances, however, of her early history, and subsequent to the fatal catastrophe which has excited so much sympathy and interest, may not be considered altogether out of place.

Sarah C—— was the third daughter of Mr C—— , a celebrated Irish barrister and judge, whose extreme political opinions, uniformly and vehemently expressed in Parliament, and strenuous, and often successful, advocacy and defence of persons prosecuted for treasonable or seditious offences, during the stormy period from 1793 to 1800, attracted the notice of all parties in Ireland, while they drew upon him the hatred, and even excited a suspicion of his loyalty, in the breasts of his political opponents.

Several years before I went to sea, Sarah C—— passed some time with my father's family. Her father and mine had been fellow-collegians, and a friendship, which only terminated with their lives, ever afterwards subsisted between them; and Mr C—— was very glad to accept the offer, and intrust a child, in whom he took a peculiar pride, to the roof and protection of his earliest friend.

At that time Sarah C—— might be about fifteen years old; and was, for that age, womanly in appearance. Her form and figure were remarkably good – her neck, throat, and shoulders were dazzlingly white, and classically shaped and set on. Her features, if taken separately, had nothing in them to notice, except her eyes, which were large, lustrous, and dark as the Pyrenean izard's, and fringed and softened by the longest lashes I ever saw; but when animated by conversation, or lit by reflection, from a mind that teemed with imagery and information, you forgot that they were not perfect, so much were you captivated with the graceful mobility of their expression, and fascinated by the charms of an unrivalled wit.

Many a time have I, with my younger sisters, listened delighted, as she related, for our amusement, with the grace and fertility of invention of Scheherazade, that queen of story-tellers, tale after tale of a winter's evening, by the dubious light of the fire, in a parlour, ominously denominated red; or seated, of a summer's day, on the Warren, beneath a projecting crag overhanging the Blackwater (the very spot is now present to my mind's eye), beguiling me of my favourite amusement, fishing – she would read to us portions of some volume adapted both to instruct and entertain children. Often, too, would she keep our family party in 'a roar', by flashes of drollery and wit, which came from a mine that, at times, seemed inexhaustible; or, by a word, a gesture, playfully, and without malice, evoke the semblance of some absent friend or acquaintance, in whom some peculiarity of manner or phraseology was observable.

Sarah C—— 's education had been carefully attended to. Her intellect was of that order, and her apprehension so quick, that she seized, as by intuition, whatever she was put to learn, and being blessed with a most happy memory, she retained what she had read. Besides my father's library, she had also the advantage of Mr Jessop's, which was extensive and well-chosen: and while at Lismore she gladly availed herself of both, for her mind was ever thirsting after fresh acquisitions of useful knowledge. But it was music that seemed to call forth, in an especial degree, all her fine taste and genius. In her it was a passion; and, if it be not profane to say so, in music she seemed to 'live, and move, and have her being'. And well had the muse of song repaid such deep, such fervent devotion! Though an admirable instrumental performer, it was in vocal music that she most delighted.

As an amateur, I never heard her equal; and when seated at the instrument, entranced, as it were, with her subject, and regardless of all around her, she poured forth her whole soul in strains of the richest melody. Her voice was not remarkably powerful – it was rather soft and sweet, but of extraordinary compass and flexibility. Every syllable was distinctly audible, and uttered with that depth of true feeling and expression, which lend such a charm to music, and without which the most elaborate and finely executed cannot reach the heart. When she sung a Scotch or Irish ballad, such as 'Auld Robin Gray', – 'Gramachree' – 'Oh! open the door,' – or her father's plaintive lines of 'The Deserter's Meditation' every busy hum and whisper in the room were hushed in an instant, and the most indifferent and apathetic turned to listen in wonder and delight.

But although her audience were charmed and fascinated with whatever kind of music she touched, profane or otherwise, her own taste led her to prefer sacred; and the divine compositions of Haydn and Mozart, drew forth all her powers, filling her with a rapture and enthusiasm that seemed to lift her above this lower world. Often, of a summer evening, would she steal from the company, though rendered more attractive, one would suppose, for girls of her age, by the addition of several gay young officers, attached to the party of military stationed then at Lismore (for in those troublesome times the roll of the drum and clang of arms frequently disturbed the quiet of even the most peaceful and secluded villages in Ireland), and beckoning some of us young ones to follow, stroll to the church, and then coax the old verger to admit her within its silent walls. There, ascending to the organ she would pour out her whole soul in song, dwelling with a fervour of devotion on the finest passages of her favourite composers.

Since those days what varied scenes have chequered a life, the greater part of which has been passed in wandering from country to country, and from clime to clime! Nor time, nor change, however, have effaced from my mind the remembrance of those days. Yes! after the lapse of so many years, I see poor Sarah now, by the light of memory, as plainly and distinctly as I did then by the level rays of the departing sun, as they streamed through the western window, and partially illumined her expressive features! – her eloquent face, from its position, necessarily foreshortened, – while not a feature, a muscle, was strained or distorted by exertion, – her fine dark eye raised towards heaven, imploring, it might be, that inspiration so bountifully accorded, and poured again, from lips just parted, in floods of the most thrilling, the most touching melody, – she looked the St Cecilia painted by Rafaelle, which reminded me so forcibly of her, as I once stood gazing upon it in the Academia delle Belle Arti at Bologna. Yes! (to borrow a beautiful idea from a poem by her father),

> Memory, that, with more than Egypt's art,
> Embalming ev'ry grief that wounds the heart

is not less powerful to preserve and consecrate those moments of blissful enjoyment which Providence grants us in our journey through life.

Like her father, this child of genius and imagination was subject to great alternations of spirits. These appeared to be constitutional, and to proceed from some peculiar organization of the nerves, being quite independent of the will, and altogether beyond her control. At times a melancholy and depression, amounting almost to despondency, would possess her so entirely, that no soothing or endearment could win her or relieve her from it. Frequently would she shut herself in her room, or saunter out alone, and pass hours in solitude, when sometimes she would be found in tears, which the tendernesses and caresses of friendship seemed only to augment.

Some time before I became a sailor, Sarah C——— had gone to reside with her father in Dublin; and, except an occasional letter to my father, or one of my sisters, little was heard or known of her at Lismore, until the explosion of Robert Emmett's foolish and wicked conspiracy brought her name too prominently before the public.

Young Emmett had recently returned from the continent, where, I believe, he had resided ever since the Rebellion of 1798, in which his elder brother was involved so deeply as to forfeit his life – a punishment commuted into perpetual exile.

This young man had very early imbibed all the wild and visionary theories about liberty and the rights of man entertained by his brother, and which, towards the close of the eighteenth century, agitated and shook, not only Ireland, but all Europe, to its centre.

During his residence abroad, an intercourse with the most fiery of the French and Swiss republicans had strengthened and increased those theories, so that they became a deep-seated passion; and the object dearest to his soul was, what *he considered*, the regeneration of Ireland, and the emancipation of his native land from the thraldom of England. In these views, however fanciful and mistaken, it is supposed he was perfectly honest and single-minded, and that no selfish or unworthy motive influenced his conduct and actions.

Glowing, therefore, with what he felt to be patriotic enthusiasm, and deeming the moment most propitious to make one mighty effort to attain these objects, he landed in his native country, just as England was again plunged, single-handed, in war, and the mighty preparations of now colossal France for her invasion, kept every part of the kingdom in a state of the most watchful and feverish anxiety.

Robert Emmett's connexions and profession as a barrister procured him, in Dublin, an easy access to society; and he very early became acquainted with Mr C——. His fine taste, extensive reading, and agreeable manners and conversation, made him always a welcome guest at the Priory, Mr C——'s country house, where he usually resided; and a similarity of feeling and judgment upon matters of politics and government soon rendered his society more and more pleasing and attractive, so that he early became an almost daily visitor at the house.

Enthusiast as he was, Emmett was cautious, upon a first acquaintance, of touching upon extreme measures; and he soon perceived that, however liberal were the views of Mr C——, and however extensive the reforms and ameliorations that he mediated for Ireland, they fell immeasurably short of the revolutionary schemes that filled and agitated his own breast. During all his subsequent intercourse, therefore, with Mr C——, he continued to observe the same caution; and always taking the initiative from him, when conversing upon themes so deeply interesting to both, he never ventured to exceed the limits beyond which he clearly saw it was not the intention of Mr C—— to advance.

A character like Emmett's, – young, ardent, and enthusiastic, – with a mind singularly endowed and richly stored with various information, enlarged and improved by travel, could not fail of attracting the notice and fixing the regard of such a being as Sarah C——. On his side he was early won by that union of genius, simplicity, and imagination, which added such a charm and *naïve* grace to her rare and numerous accomplishments. Reciprocal esteem and affection soon bound their hearts in one; but a less cloudy atmosphere and more propitious season were necessary to complete the union of their hands. Sarah C—— had always been an ardent admirer of the liberal politics of her father; and she now listened, not only without alarm, but with mingled sensations of pleasure and admiration, as her lover gradually unfolded to her his plans for the separation of the two countries, and the future independence of Ireland.

Meantime, he was deeply engaged in organizing and furthering the treasonable conspiracy, upon the success of which, fame, fortune, and life itself, were staked, and which issued in the abortive but wicked and sanguinary outbreak of 1803.

To effect an object so vast as that which he contemplated, Emmett's means seem to have been miserably deficient. No proper organization or discipline had been effected among his wretched and half-armed followers. They appear to have had no leaders or chiefs to guide and direct such a body except himself, who is said to have comported himself upon the occasion as a brave and humane man. But how could a single head, and that not a military one, rule such a rabble in the heart of a large city? He could not show himself everywhere. His orders for an immediate movement upon the castle and other points of attack had not been attended to; and the insurgents having entered Dublin, and finding themselves without leaders of authority, broke their ranks and commenced plundering, and, upon the first appearance of a body of military, fled in the utmost trepidation and dismay, without even the show of resistance.

When Emmett saw that the rout and dispersion of his miserable followers was complete and irretrievable, he withdrew from Dublin, and concealed himself somewhere in the vicinity of the Priory. He had prepared, in some measure, for such a termination to his attempt, and engaged a passage in a vessel bound to America, which was to sail the day but one after his attack upon Dublin. All this had been explained to Sarah C—— ; and, after much persuasion on his part, and hesitation on hers, she consented to be the partner of his flight, should adverse fortune compel him to seek for safety on the other side of the Atlantic.

The night succeeding his failure, Emmett found means to obtain an interview with his beloved. He informed her that all was lost, and explained to her his hopeless and desperate situation: a price was set upon his head, the officers of justice were even then upon his track, and it was vain to hope to escape their vigilance if he remained many hours longer in the kingdom. He told her that all was ready for their departure, and urged her by every soothing and persuasive argument he could think of, to sustain her drooping courage. He painted, in the most forcible language, the danger of delay; and adjured her, by their mutual affection and vows, and her promise, so lately given, not to forsake him at such a moment.

It has been said elsewhere, that hers was a most timid and nervous temperament, upon which even the 'skyey influences', exerted a power that no reasoning or mental effort could subdue or control; how much more, then, must she have felt herself perplexed and shaken by a thousand doubts and fears, when called upon to separate herself for ever from country and from friends, and commit herself – weak, and wavering, and helpless – to unknown perils, magnified a hundredfold by her ever-active imagination! It will not be wondered at, therefore, that he found her irresolute, nor that all his arguments, urged in the most imploring and passionate language, failed to arouse her sinking spirits. Her constitutional nervousness completely mastered her faculties, leaving her no power to act with the firmness and decision that such a crisis required.

She begged, she entreated Emmett to leave her, and seek his own safety in flight, when at some future day, perhaps, they might find some means of meeting again. Thus passed the night, and thus many precious hours were wasted in fruitless endeavours to revive and reassure her. Morning dawned, and found him in the same imploring attitude, and using every topic he could think of to sustain her wavering purpose, and prevail upon her to fulfil her promise, and share his exile. Day was now so far advanced that it would be madness for him to stay longer at the house. At length he tore himself away; but still lingered near the spot in the vain hope of finding a last opportunity to see her once more, and again to urge her to be the sharer of his fortunes, fondly hoping that a few hours of calm and undisturbed reflection would tranquillize and brace her nerves, and that he might find her in a more firm and happy frame of mind. Alas! unhappy man! at that moment his hours were numbered! His place of concealment had been discovered, or betrayed. From thence he was tracked in the direction of Mr C——'s house, and in less than two hours after he had parted with Miss C——, he was a prisoner in the hands of justice.

As Emmett was taken in the vicinity of Mr C——'s house, and as it was known that he was a frequent guest there, the Irish Government, not without some show of reason, conjectured that Mr C—— was aware of, if not a participator in, the treason of Emmett. The prominent part which he took in politics towards the close of the last century, together with his energetic and often successful advocacy of traitors, or suspected traitors, and decided and openly avowed ultra-liberal opinions and views upon questions of state and government, gave a colourable pretext to those suspicions; and accordingly a warrant was issued to search his house, and examine all papers that should be found there.

Aware that he was still regarded with aversion and distrust, and conscious of his own innocence and integrity, Mr C—— was indignant at this proceeding of the government, considering it as meant to impugn his loyalty, and degrade and humiliate himself. As to the result, he felt no uneasiness or discomposure. He was convinced that it would establish his own and his family's perfect exoneration from any knowledge or participation in Emmett's schemes; and he anticipated, with a kind of grim satisfaction, the discomfiture of his enemies, and how this attempt to injure and insult a political adversary, would rebound to their own obloquy and disgrace.

As far as he was personally concerned, not the remotest trace of any connexion with the conspirators was discovered; and so far his anticipations of triumph over his adversaries were justified. But, when letters were found in his daughter's desk, which showed not only that an attachment existed between her and Emmett, but also a knowledge of his designs, imagination is unable to conceive the mixture of rage and mortification that boiled within his breast. His was a wrath, deep, concentrated, and silent; and so much the more enduring and unmitigable, as it found no vent in words.

Mr C—— had never been a tender father, his conduct towards his children being often marked by austerity and harshness, that happily distinguished him from most other parents. His door was now relentlessly closed against his unhappy daughter, who was cast off and abandoned by her natural guardian and protector, without resources of any kind, and, as far as he knew, without a friend in the world. Her sad story and forlorn situation, however, no sooner became known, than it awoke the sympathy of a family in the south of Ireland, esteemed as well for refinement of taste and elegance of mind, as for kindness of heart and unbounded hospitality and benevolence.

Mr P——, whose charming residence was situated about two miles below Cork, on the banks of its beautiful river, immediately commissioned his daughters to write and offer the poor outcast a home at W——, where she should find, not only kindness and sympathy, but friends that were prepared to love her as a child and sister. This commission was joyfully executed with all the feeling and delicacy of minds which join to refined and cultivated tastes an innate grace and goodness of heart. Sarah C—— thankfully accepted the generous kindness of friends, whom Providence had so unexpectedly and so beneficently raised up for her in an hour of such extreme need; and before many weeks had elapsed after she was driven from the roof of her father, she found herself sheltered beneath that of the hospitable and generous Mr P——, where the unobtrusive study of all the family was to make her forget her sorrows, and feel that she had a home. But though sensibly alive to their kindness, for a long time nothing seemed capable of diverting her mind from the contemplation of those dreadful events which had so recently taken place, nor rouse her from that depth of woe in which they had steeped her.

For several months subsequent to her arrival at W——, she scarcely ever left her room; and it was only by the gentlest and kindest attention on the part of the Misses P——, that she was at length a little weaned from dwelling so entirely upon her sorrows, when she occasionally joined the family circle. From time to time, however, she would relapse, and shutting herself up, indulge for days in a passion of grief, when she would refuse all comfort even from her kind and considerate friends. Gradually these fits of utter despondency became of less frequent recurrence, and of shorter duration. She began to mingle a little in society, and resume in part her usual occupations, and at times even to venture upon music. Her story was too public not to be universally known; and as her unparalleled misfortunes were viewed as the result of attachment and devotion to the man to whom she had plighted her faith, not as sharing and abetting his wild schemes and treasonable acts, general sympathy and interest were excited in her favour amongst Mr P——'s friends. Among the visitors at W——, was an officer of the Staff Corps, at that time quartered in Cork. He was a young man of distinguished acquirements, and gentlemanly and agreeable manners, and was always a welcome and favoured guest.

The story of Sarah C——, and the melancholy that generally shaded her expressive features, almost at first sight attracted his attention, and the information with which her mind was so richly stored, and the various graces of her conversation, soon chained him to her side. Captain S—— was a passionate lover of music, of which he was a tolerable proficient himself; and it is little wonderful therefore that the first time he heard the tones of Sarah C——'s unequalled voice, his whole soul thrilled with rapture; and from that moment he became her ardent, her most devoted admirer. But the knowledge of her so recent love for another, and the dreadful, the tragical manner in which that love was severed, forbade all idea of speaking to her on such a subject. His admiration was therefore confined to the most assiduous but delicate attentions, not calculated to awaken alarm or wound a mind, still suffering from the effects of so fearful a blow. Meantime her mind was becoming more and more composed, and she began to take some little interest in the every-day concerns of life.

The admiration of Captain S—— for their interesting friend was not long unperceived by the young ladies of W——. In fact, it was evident to all eyes but those of its object. At length, observing his reluctance to declare himself, and with that delicacy of tact and feeling so natural to the female mind, rightly conjecturing the cause from whence it sprang, one of them took the opportunity one morning of a stroll through the grounds to sound him on the subject; when, by a union of warm encomium on her friend – warm and eloquent as it was sincere – with a little judicious and well-timed flattery of himself (an unction by no means disagreeable to the rougher sex, and which ladies know so well how to administer), she quite established herself in his confidence. Finding that she approved and sympathized in his attachment, and glad to have gained a friend to whom he could disclose all that his heart had been labouring with for months, he at once laid it bare before her, and then anxiously sought her advice and assistance to further his suit. Miss P——, who saw in Captain S—— a young man of excellent character and principles, united to talents and acquirements of no ordinary kind, willingly undertook to aid him with both.

Knowing the state of Miss C——'s mind, and how cruelly her feelings had been crushed and wounded, she advised him as yet to make no disclosure of his sentiments to herself, but to wait until time should have exerted its tranquillizing influence, and calmed and soothed her many sorrows. She promised, in the meantime, to be on the watch, and to seize every favourable opportunity of speaking of him as he deserved, and gradually to pave the way, so that hereafter she should not feel alarmed or shocked at the avowal of his sentiments.

For some time longer things remained pretty much in the same state at W——. Miss C—— was evidently becoming tranquil and more herself. Once more she listened with seeming pleasure to the sound of music – was again sometimes found seated at the piano-forte, and even warbling some of her favourite airs.

It was about this time that a fancy ball took place in Cork, given, I do not know upon what occasion, but to which all the *élite* of the vicinage were invited. The P——'s were all going to it; and after a week's entreaty, the girls succeeded in prevailing on Miss C—— to go likewise. Everybody was to appear in character; and the one selected for Miss C—— by herself and her friends, was that of a flower-girl. Her dress was white, trimmed and ornamented with flowers. Her raven hair fell in natural curls over her alabaster neck and shoulders. On her head she wore a broad-leaved, low-crowned straw hat, encircled with a wreath of flowers, peculiar to the peasant girls of the canton of Underwald, and on her arm, to complete her costume, was hung a basket of flowers. Her whole appearance, so well adapted to the part she was to sustain, was striking, and the *naïve* manner mixed with a little, a very little archness, with which she recommended her flowers, attracted the general admiration.

After making the circuit of the rooms two or three times with the Misses P——, she stood in the door-way that communicated with the card-room. When she had stood there some time, after much entreaty, she was prevailed upon by her friends to sing a little ballad, appropriate to the character she represented, and in commendation of the beauty of her flowers. In an instant a crowd was gathered around the warbler, who continued to sing several stanzas, her voice gaining strength and firmness as she proceeded. While her auditory, however, were enraptured, and scarcely dared to breathe, lest they should lose a word or a note, her voice suddenly ceased, stopped by some stroke or impulse as swift and powerful as the lightning's bolt. Her arms dropped to her sides – her face assumed the hue of death – her features became fixed and inanimate as marble, and has whole figure stark and rigid as a statue. Terrified and alarmed beyond measure at a change so awful and unexpected, her friends took each a hand, and begged and implored her to say if she felt unwell – if anything was the matter. Finding that she made no answer, and took no notice of what was said, they gently led her to a sofa in the card-room, when she as suddenly went into the most violent and distressing hysterics, falling from one fit into another, until the carriage arrived and conveyed her to W——. Something in the song – a word, a note, an intonation it might be, of her own voice, had touched a chord, that vibrated to her heart's core, and froze the current of her blood, which nothing but successive floods of tears could release, or again set in motion. Whatever was the cause of it, many weeks elapsed before she recovered from the shock, and again became calm and composed.

It was long after this occurrence that Captain S—— hazarded a declaration of his love; and his constancy and patience were further tried for more than a year before Sarah C—— could be brought to listen to his pretensions, and finally accept him for her husband. It is needless to say how the delicate assiduity and fervent and disinterested love of Captain S——, seconded by the friendly remonstrances and representations of the Misses P——, finally silenced, if they did not entirely overcome, her scruples and objections. They were married in the pretty little church of Glanmire; and when I saw her on board the transport in August, 1806, she had been a wife six months.

After a long and disagreeable voyage, she reached Sicily in safety, where she remained three years with her husband. At the end of that time, he was ordered to England; and they embarked on their return in the autumn of 1809. The homeward passage was rough and tedious; and in crossing the bay they encountered a heavy gale, in the midst of which Mrs S—— was confined of her only child, no medical man being on board. Though the infant died, she lived to touch the shores of England; but her frame, which had been wasted and shattered, more perhaps by mental than bodily suffering, was too feeble to resist such a trial as the last; and in two months after she landed, her spirit was released, and returned to God who gave it. Before her death, she expressed a desire that her remains should be laid beside those of her sister Gertrude, which had been interred in the garden of the Priory, her father's country residence; and her wishes were most religiously fulfilled.

8: In the Mediterranean

In a few weeks after my visit to the *Rosario* and the transport in Cawsand Bay, our crew being now complete, the *Royal George* sailed with a large convoy of transports which carried a considerable body of troops for the reinforcement of the army in Sicily, having the *Atlas* of seventy-four guns and *Gannet* brig of sixteen guns in company. Sir Hugh Dalrymple and General Edward Paget, with their aides-de-camp, and several staff-officers, were embarked in the *Royal George*. It was the month of October, and the voyage was rough and tedious, so much so, that before we crossed the Bay, the *Atlas* had sprung her foremast, and was compelled to return to England. We found the *Gannet* very useful in keeping the convoy together, Captain Bateman, her commander, moving from flank to flank with wonderful celerity; and like an experienced whipper-in, who always has the dogs so that a sheet might cover them, by his great diligence and watchfulness he prevented straggling, and kept the fleet in compact order. Soon after Captain Bateman joined the fleet off Cadiz, he had an opportunity of distinguishing himself in a very conspicuous manner by the skill and gallantry which he displayed in attacking and cutting off some Spanish gun-boats, which were close in shore, and protected by the heavy guns of the sea-batteries. But although Captain Bateman had been promoted before this brilliant affair could be known in England, whither he soon returned, he was never again employed afloat; and courage, zeal, and skill, such as his, were ever after allowed to languish in useless inactivity, to his own great injustice, and the manifest loss and injury of the country.

The frequent neglect, and shelving of brave and skilful officers has been the besetting sin of every Board of Admiralty, so long as I have known the service; and some of their regulations, so far from lessening the mischief, have a tendency to increase it. To select one example from a multitude, what can be more unfair than to say that an officer must complete a given number of years in command of a rated ship, and not abate a day of the time, and all the while deny him the opportunity of fulfilling the regulation? If he decline to serve, or be incapacitated by mental or bodily infirmity, not contracted in the service, there is an honest and legitimate cause for setting him aside. But if his conduct have been correct, his efficiency and ability unquestioned, and his perfect willingness to serve at all times apparent and expressed, then it seems most unjust and cruel to say to that officer:

'Sir, we know that you served long and meritoriously, and that you have always shown a zealous and anxious wish to be employed. Your character and ability as an officer are highly esteemed at the Board, and your conduct has procured for you an honorary distinction from your sovereign; but you want three months, or six weeks, or three days as the case may be, of the regulated time in command, and therefore you are not entitled to your flag.'

But to return from this digression. I said that our progress, retarded by blowing and contrary winds, was slow; and it was the end of October before we joined the fleet off Cadiz. Being provided with a letter of recommendation to Lord Collingwood, the commander-in-chief, I took an early opportunity to wait upon his Lordship. At the time I write of, Lord Collingwood was between fifty and sixty, thin and spare in person, which was then slightly bent, and in height about five feet ten inches. His head was small, with a pale, smooth round face, the features of which would pass without notice, were it not for the eyes, which were blue, clear, and penetrating; and the mouth, the lips of which were thin and compressed, indicating firmness and decision of character. He wore his hair powdered, and tied in a queue, in the style of officers of his age at that time; and his clothes were squared and fashioned after the strictest rules of the good old sea school. To his very ample coat, which had a stiff, stand-up collar, were appended broad and very long skirts – the deep flaps of his single-breasted white waistcoat, descending far below his middle, covered a portion of his thighs; and blue knee-breeches, with white stockings, and buckles to his shoes, completed his attire.

My interview with the chief was short. On entering his presence, he took a rapid and searching survey of me from head to foot; then asking kindly for Sir John Colpoys, the gentleman to whom I was indebted for the letter to his Lordship, in a quiet tone, amounting almost to gentleness, he put a few questions to me in nautics, which, I believe, I answered to his satisfaction. He then inquired in what ship I came out; and learning her name, he simply added: 'Very well, for the present you will remain in the *Royal George.*' Thus ended my five minutes' audience; and as my stay in the Mediterranean was at that time brief, it is all that I ever heard from his Lordship upon the subject of the letter.

Upon the following day we proceeded with the convoy towards the Straits, the *Sophie* sloop of war replacing the little *Gannet* as whipper-in. A strong easterly wind detained us ten days or a fortnight off Cape Spartel; for although the men-of-war might have beat through, it would have been very hazardous to have allowed the transports to attempt it in face of the Spanish gun-boats, which were bold and daring, and very formidable to merchant ships, which they frequently succeeded in cutting off and capturing, and seldom lost an opportunity of cannonading even men-of-war, whenever they caught them becalmed, or otherwise rendered unmanageable by flaws and light baffling winds, which often happens, on entering the Bay of Gibraltar.* At length, the wind shifted to the westward, and as the whole of the convoy was bound up the Mediterranean, we proceeded to Tetuan Bay, to complete the water of the transports, now nearly exhausted by so long a passage.

On the evening of the second day after the fleet had anchored, one of those sudden and violent squalls so common in the Mediterranean, particularly under high land, surprised the boats in the midst of their occupation, endangering the safety of those that were rafting the casks between the ships and the shore, and obliging several to remain all night on the beach. Happily no loss of life, or serious accident occurred; and the following morning, which proved moderate and beautiful, showed the fleet as it appeared the day before, with the exception of two transports, which had been driven from their anchors, but which, it was afterwards found, had reached Gibraltar in safety.

It was on the afternoon of this squally day, that one of the mates, who had strayed to some distance from the beach, suddenly disappeared, and the next morning was nowhere to be found; nor did we recover him until energetic remonstrances were made by the British Consul about his suspicious disappearance, to the Moorish authorities at Tetuan. On his return to the ship, he gave the following account of his rather curious adventure. It seems, the first lieutenant, who entertained a well-founded opinion of his trust-worthiness, and whose right eye or right arm he sometimes proved himself, as mates often do to first lieutenants, had

---

* An instance of their boldness occurred at this very time. The convoy having been observed from Gibraltar, a gun-boat, manned by a lieutenant, and, I believe, twenty-five or thirty men from the *Queen*, was sent out to assist in covering its passage through the Gut. This gun-boat was chased, overtaken, boarded, and captured by two Spanish boats of superior force, before the convoy's escort could come to her assistance.

desired him to look out for some spot, not far from the watering parties, where brooms might be procured. In his rambles to execute this duty, Jock (for that was his prenomen) found himself suddenly confronted and seized by two huge, fierce-looking Moors, who had been squatted under a bush, whence, unseen themselves, they commanded a view of the bay and beach, and had their eyes fixed upon him the whole way as he ascended from the shore, until he walked unconsciously into the lair of those wild, ferocious-looking animals. They made him comprehend by signs that he was to accompany them; and when he hesitated, and showed symptoms of disobedience, they soon gave him to understand, by the manner in which they flourished their long muskets, that they were not to be trifled with; and upon his still moving slowly and unwilling, casting many a wistful look towards the beach, one of them whipped out his dagger, and applying the point of it to poor Jock's seat of honour, urged him in the tenderest and most persuasive manner to freshen his way.

Ascending the mountain for about fifteen or twenty minutes, they arrived where the body of the Moorish guard was bivouacked. This party consisted of a dozen men, one of whom appeared the chief, – the whole dressed and armed in the Moorish fashion, viz. close brown cloth vest, with white sleeves, which displayed their bronzed and brawny throats and chests, loose white linen drawers or breeches drawn in a little below the knee, bare legs, with yellow slippers, or tanned leather sandals on their feet; a red sash, which held their daggers and pistols, girt their waists; and all but the chief or captain, who was turbaned, wore red worsted caps on their heads, similar to the French *bonnet rouge*, and which, I believe, are very general among the Moorish Arabs.

This savage-looking gang had selected a very convenient, as well as picturesque spot, for their bivouac. It was a natural platform in the side of the mountain, raised considerably above the beach, whence it might be distant about three parts of a mile. Its form was circular, and covered with a short, springy greensward – a thick underwood, principally composed of myrtle and algarroba, or locust-tree, with here and there the orange and a stunted fig-tree, enclosed the whole arena, screening the company within its circumference effectually from view, whilst a few openings, natural or designed, enabled them to see what was going forward on the beach, and likewise any change or movement among the shipping in the bay; – a tiny stream had worked a deep channel more than half-way around this area, and as it hastened to join the rivulet that supplied the water for the parties on the beach, its low and refreshing murmur well harmonised with the quiet and seclusion of the whole scene.

Old Jock,* or, as he was more commonly called by his youthful messmates, 'Old sand and holy stones' from his occupation of dry rubbing the cockpit and orlop deck, was then between thirty and forty, and a rough and tough sailor of the old school. His stature was short, but his frame was wiry, and firmly knit, and hirsute, shaggy and enduring as the ponies of his native Isle of Skye: his face had been deeply imprinted with the small-pox, which the hand of time was slowly effacing, and his features all bore the stamp of his Celtic origin, with high cheek-bones, and small light grey eyes, wide apart and deeply set.

On his release from Moorish captivity, many a jest had Jock to endure from his younger messmates, who used to condole with him with mock gravity, upon his return to the humble station of orlop mate, when by following his good fortune, turning Turk, and getting duly docked, trimmed, and rigged, he might have fitted himself for the berth, and been chosen Kislar Aga, or keeper of the harem, to his Moorish majesty.

When the transports had completed their water, they sailed for Sicily with a fair wind; and the *Royal George*, after stopping for a few hours at Gibraltar, proceeded to join the fleet before Cadiz.

At that time, Lord Collingwood's fleet consisted of about fourteen or fifteen sail of the line; and the combined squadrons blockaded in Cadiz, of six sail French and eight Spanish, the remains of the once formidable fleet which fought at Trafalgar, reinforced by a few sail which subsequently slipped in.

Life on board a ship forming one of a blockading fleet, offers little variety, and no opportunity for remarks the least interesting or amusing. If a strange sail heave in sight, it may afford room for speculation and conjecture, until suspense is put to flight by the display of her number, which indicates the quarter from whence she comes. Should she prove from merry, happy England, the hope of news from friends at home lightens in the eyes and beams on the countenances of all on board; for nothing more cheers the spirits, or gladdens the heart, than a letter from distant and long-absent friends.

In this way passed several leaden and very monotonous weeks, until at length, to our great joy, a small vessel, whose name I forget, joined from

* John Lindsay. He was made a lieutenant about three years after this, and at the peace in 1815, returned to his native island. There he purchased a small sloop, in which he was in the habit of making two annual voyages to London, whence he brought goods for the supply of the inhabitants and shop-keepers of the island. Four or five years ago, I was shocked at reading in the *Times*, that my old messmate had been waylaid, robbed, and murdered one night, in returning from a friend's house.

England. Shortly after her junction, the signal was seen flying for our Admiral to repair on board the *Ocean*, the flag-ship of Lord Collingwood – an unusual circumstance, which set us all on the *qui vive* to divine what the chief could want with his second. In an hour Sir John returned, when he immediately ordered the signal to be made for the captains of the *Windsor Castle* and *Repulse*, and for those ships to close round and follow the motions of the *Royal George*. We now guessed that something more than common was in *the wind* – that perhaps we were about to be detached – and those conjectures were confirmed, when, soon after dusk, followed by the two before-named ships, we left the fleet and steered for Gibraltar. I do not know whether it was the intention to keep the destination of the squadron a secret. If it was, the attempt was a failure; for it somehow leaked out in a very few hours that we were bound to Constantinople to coerce the Turk, and compel him, *nolens volens*, to surrender his fleet to the safe keeping of England, lest it should fall into the hands of Bonaparte, whose eye was then fixed upon the East, and whose influence with the Porte, through the able and adroit management of his Ambassador Sebastiani, was paramount.

The following day we anchored at Gibraltar, where we remained a few hours, to get some necessary stores, and then proceeded with our squadron to Sicily, whither a stiff gale from the westward wafted us in five days. Our only object there seemed to be to communicate with the *Pompée*, bearing the flag of Sir Sydney Smith, lying, with her mizen-mast out, within the mole of Palermo, which we did by telegraph, and then immediately proceeded to Malta, where we anchored on the following day. I was so fortunate as to get leave to visit the shore for a few hours on one of the three days, to which time our stay at Malta was limited, and in that brief space I managed to see as much as people, who have more time, commonly do in three weeks. Having landed at the well-known Nix Mangiare Stairs, we (for we were many) strolled through La Valetta, peeped into and admired the grandeur and magnificence of St John's, and others of the most celebrated churches; ordered a dinner to be ready for us by six o'clock, at the Croce di Malta; and then mounted such cavalry as we could procure, intending to have a gallop right across the island.

Reader (if these pages ever find such) did you ever see a party of royal reefers just *broke loose* from ship-board – emancipated for a few short hours, after six or eight months' close confinement – released, like school-boys, for a moment, from their daily task – like them casting every care and grievance to the winds, and, with unalloyed, unrestrained happiness and glee, revelling in all the joy and gladness of youthful hearts? Just such a party might you have seen on the 3rd of February, 1807, mounted on barb, or mule, or Egyptian ass, sally forth from the quarter of La Valetta, and take the road that leads to Citta Vecchia. The daily toil and nightly watch – the stern forbidding aspect of the captain – the lieutenant's sharp rebuke, and terrors of the masthead – the 'whips and scorns' of every Jack-in-office – all, all are forgotten in an hour like this. Even the remembrance of the coarse, and sometimes scanty fare of a middy's berth is buried in anticipations of the glorious 'blow-out' that awaited our return to the Croce di Malta. After all, such moments of unmingled gaiety and happiness are felt and enjoyed perhaps by no class of individuals with the same intensity of delight, and perfect oblivion of all past annoyances and grievances, as they are by sailors. On our way we stopped to view a beautiful little retreat of the Governor, called, I think, St Antonio, or Il Boschetto. After the palaces of La Valetta the house appeared small, and scarcely worth noticing; but we found the gardens green, cool, and refreshing, forming a delicious contrast to the parched aridity and barrenness which seemed the general characteristic of the island. Shrubs and flowers were growing in wild luxuriance, and the orange, bearing its exquisite fruit and flowers at the same time, regaled the senses at every turn.

A ride of about two hours took us to Citta Vecchia, and after *freshening hause*, we proceeded to view the famous catacombs, the chief object of our excursion. They are situated near the village, and excavated in the rock of which the whole island is composed, resembling Portland stone, but softer and more porous, and, on examination, did not excite as much admiration or astonishment as I expected. After an easy descent of some little way they branch off into numerous passages and chambers, whose seemingly endless mazes and turnings might well puzzle a stranger, if he trusted himself among them without a guide. Apertures, opened at top from distance to distance, gave admission to a current of pure air, which kept them dry, and prevented any close or disagreeable odour. The only relics of mortality which I observed in those 'low-browed caverns of the dead' were five men, dressed in the habiliments of Capuchin friars, and placed upright in one of the numerous recesses in the passages. Their hands and faces were shrunk and withered to the appearance of dust-coloured parchment, and their glassy eyes stood open with vacant, unmeaning stare. At six we returned to Valetta, dined, went to the opera, which was far from contemptible, and then on board. And thus ended the day's amusement, and the only visit I ever paid to *terra firma* at Malta.

The watering and provisioning of the squadron being complete, and the *Pompée* and *Ajax* having joined from Sicily, we sailed in the afternoon of the 4th of February. Lord Burghersh,* then a fine young man, attached to the staff of the army in the Mediterranean, embarked in the *Royal George*, as a guest of the Admiral, anxious to partake of the fun, and glad to exchange a life of idleness for the bustle and activity promised by the expedition.

Again the wind favoured us, and on the fourth day from our departure the *Ajax* was despatched a-head, to procure pilots for the squadron at Milo. On the evening of that day I think it was that we made Cape Matapan, and for the first time I beheld the land of Greece, the birthplace of heroes and demigods. We passed Cerigo and Cape Malio, and then the Ægean Sea was spread before us, studded with its countless isles, the least important of which possessed its story of stirring interest, and produced men whose names shall live as long as arts and arms, philosophy and song, shall find a place in the admiration of mankind.

In sailing rapidly past the land, neither the main nor the islands offered any object or landscape of a peculiar or attractive nature. Now and then, indeed, as we rounded some point, and opened a little cove or bay, I was charmed by the unexpected disclosure of a secluded fishing village, whose snow-white houses seemed to bathe themselves in the calm unruffled water, so distinctly were they reflected from its glassy surface, while their brightness contrasted not unpleasingly with the deep green of the land, which rose almost abruptly behind them. A few fishing-vessels lay motionless in the bay, and here and there a fisherman spreading his nets, or following some business of his craft, might be seen on the beach, the only sign of animation to break the stillness of that seemingly peaceful scene. With few exceptions, the islands bear the form of steep conical hills, or knolls, broad at the base, and varying in size, height, and outline, but universally clothed in dark green; like our own heath-covered mountains in spring, before they are embrowned by the heat of summer, and when distance and atmospheric changes do not, chameleon-like, at every instant, vary their hues.

We anchored off Tenedos on the evening of the 10th of February, where we found the *Canopus*, bearing the flag of Rear-Admiral Sir Thomas Louis, with the *Thunderer*, and *Glatton*, and *Active*, and *Endymion*, frigates, *Lucifer* and *Meteor* bombs. The following morning the squadron shifted to the northward of the island, and nearer to the mouth of the Dardanelles.

Mr Arbuthnot, our Ambassador to the Porte, had found it necessary to withdraw from Constantinople, and was on board the *Canopus* when we arrived at Tenedos. The day after our arrival he changed to the *Royal*

* Now Earl of Westmoreland.

George, to be at hand, and concert measures with the commander of the squadron as to future operations.

Soon after we anchored, a Turk of some eminence, who was said to have come from Constantinople, communicated with the chiefs; but the purport of his visit did not transpire. Had the intention been to proceed without further delay, and force the passage of the Dardanelles, after this first attempt at a diplomatic arrangement of differences, a fresh wind from the N.N.E., which set in the following morning, would have prevented it.

What might have been the Ambassador's opinion of the ultimate success of the expedition, upon cool reflection, during the time it was detained off Tenedos by the weather, it is impossible to conjecture. It was planned by his wisdom, and undertaken, I believe, entirely at his recommendation and suggestion. It is, therefore, to be supposed, that he was still confident as to the result. With the Admiral, however, it was very different. Upon him rested the whole charge and responsibility of the expedition, and upon his head its failure was certain to be visited. He, therefore, had cause for deep and serious anxiety; particularly when he reflected on the smallness of his squadron, the strait he had to pass, and the batteries he had to contend with the force, before he could reach the point of attack, – batteries which a hostile fleet had never before dared to pass, and whose real strength was magnified, perhaps, by the ignorance which concealed their true character and condition. And here it may be remarked, that the Admiralty, and indeed the Government, seemed to have been dazzled and blinded by the unparalleled and almost uniform successes of the navy, and to have entertained an exaggerated opinion of its invincibility and power; else, how are we to account for the infatuation which led them to risk the execution of so daring and hazardous an attempt as the threatening and, if necessary, coercing a great and haughty power, like the Turk, with eight sail of the line, two frigates, and two bombs – a force so wholly disproportioned to the magnitude of the undertaking, and calculated from its very smallness to rouse resistance and excite contempt? Small and insufficient as this force was, it was still further reduced, before the squadron weighed from Tenedos, by one of the most appalling and awful catastrophes I ever witnessed, some account of which may be seen further on.

But if Mr Arbuthnot and the Admiral had any misgivings as to the issue of the coming enterprise, certain I am, that they were not shared by the inferior officers and men; not a doubt of the sufficiency of the force, or of its complete success, ever crossed their minds. Their wonted eagerness and zeal were awakened from the inactivity in which they had slumbered ever since the victory of Trafalgar had confined the enemy's ships to port, and the hope of soon being in action seemed to breathe into them fresh animation and life. Upon no former occasion of the same kind have I observed a more confident or fearless demeanour; whilst in the middy's berths we had already chalked out the different Turkish ships, whose names we had learned or guessed at, to which we *intended* to be appointed *acting* lieutenants. Very good intentions, but, alas! not fated to be realized.

As the squadron lay at anchor off this classic coast, how many recollections of early years floated through my brain! – freshly and vividly recalling my schoolboy days, and renewing all those feelings of enthusiasm and delight with which the soul-stirring story of those countries is wont to inspire the youthful mind! Scarcely could I bring myself to believe that I beheld, indeed, the battle-field of the contending hosts of Ilion and Greece! – the arena where fought the heroes, fabulous or real, of the master-bard! – that I was in the very waters that bathed the shores of immortal Troy! How anxiously did my eyes strain to discover its site! And who can describe the pride and pleasure that I felt, when, in a silvery thread, margined by a gravelly border, I thought that I made out the ancient course of famed Simoïs or Scamander! Short and disturbed, however, are the visions that middies are permitted to indulge in; but now, if constant and various duties did not interrupt all mental abstraction, an occurrence so overwhelming and astounding, and of consequences so calamitous and unfortunate, absorbed, for the time, every others feeling and sensation. I allude to the destruction of the *Ajax* by fire.

On the night of the 14th, soon after I had turned in, I was suddenly roused by an alarm of fire. Jumping out of my hammock, I learned from the sentry in the cockpit that it was not the *Royal George*, but one of the squadron. I was dressed and on deck in a moment, when I saw volumes of dense smoke, illumined by occasional flashes of lurid flame, issuing from the stern-ports of the *Ajax*. The *Royal George* was the nearest ship to the *Ajax* which was distant from her about two or three cables, and as many points on the starboard bow. It was blowing moderately fresh at the time from the N.N.E., and the squadron rode head to wind. As soon as he knew the critical situation of his ship, Captain Blackwood sent a midshipman in the jolly-boat to apprise the Admiral of his danger, and to request that the boats of the squadron might be sent, in readiness to take off the crew, should it be found necessary to abandon the ship. It was soon seen that the fire was making fearful progress – the flames now issuing in a stream from the after-part of the ship, and ascending towards the poop. The night signal had been made for assistance upon the first alarm of fire, and every exertion was making to get our own boats into the water. It was plain that the hope of saving the *Ajax* was fast decreasing: every instant the flames were gathering head, and, from our proximity to the burning ship, it became a question whether, in the event of the fire reaching the magazine and exploding, there was not danger of some of the burning mass falling on board the *Royal George*. Some such idea, no doubt, influenced the admiral and captain; for, before the boats could be got out, orders were given to cut the cable, and in a few minutes the *Royal George* was running to leeward under jib and staysails. This step, which many people in command, and who are keenly sensible of the great weight and responsibility that are always inseparable from it, would perhaps have adopted under the circumstances, struck me at the time as being rather precipitate; for before the boats could be got away, we had run more than a mile to leeward, to recover which distance they had to pull against a rather fresh breeze and lee current. When the ship had dropped to a distance thought sufficiently safe and clear, she was again brought up. From the manner in which the fire was gaining head, it was now evident that the safety of the crew must depend upon the exertions and assistance of the boats of the squadron; by ten o'clock the flames had burst through the stern, wrapping the whole of the after-part of the ship in fire; owing, however, to the direction of the wind, and, no doubt, to the great and untiring efforts of the stout-hearted crew to subdue them, their progress forward was not rapid. Still they advanced, and before midnight presented one of the most terribly-sublime pictures I ever beheld – beautiful, it might be described, could the mind divest itself of its fears and anxiety for the gallant crew.

The wind had sunk almost to a calm, and the dense, black smoke, hung like a pall or canopy around the devoted ship, whilst the fire that glowed and raged within, showed every spar, shroud, and rope, as distinctly painted as if traced by an artist's pencil. Heated by the intenseness of the fire, the ordnance are discharged one by one, knelling the death of the noble ship, like minute-guns at the funeral of some deceased officer. Fiercer and fiercer glows and hisses the now resistless fire; higher and higher mount the aspiring flames; soon the tough, strong cordage feels their withering touch, dissolving like flax before the breath of the destroyer. No longer sustained aloft, the yards cant on end, and sink into the yawning, fiery gulf, which seems to roar and hunger for their reception. The lofty masts, which stood proudly erect to the last, nor yielded till the relentless fire had pierced their inmost core, at length fall prone into the sea; like the warrior who, though the steel have reached his heart, still faces and frowns defiance on his foe, nor blenches nor falls till the life-blood gushes from the wound. After the fall of the masts, the smouldering hull long remained unmoved, nor did it drift until two o'clock in the morning, when, the light wind having veered a little more to the eastward, it was slowly borne towards the island of Tenedos, upon which it struck; and at five o'clock, a partial explosion of the magazine shattered to pieces what the fire had not consumed.

Thus miserably perished the noble but ill-starred *Ajax*! – a most inauspicious omen for the success of our enterprise, and an irreparable loss, considering its magnitude, and the smallness of the force with which it was to be attempted. Our boats returned soon after two o'clock in the morning, having saved a good many of the crew. The following day, it was ascertained that the Captain and half the officers and crew had been rescued – all the rest had miserably perished.

It is probable that many more men would have been saved, had the same intrepidity, coolness, and attention to orders, been observed by the whole of the crew, after all hope of saving the ship had been abandoned, that marked their conduct up to that time. But who dare say that he will preserve his self-possession at such a moment, and, keeping all his faculties so clear and undisturbed as to form a calm and deliberate judgment, follow with precision and obedience the orders of his superiors – at a moment when, no longer cheered by hope, or sustained by the excitement of exertion, a miserable death from fire or flood stares him in the face – and as he tries to escape the still advancing flames, or shun the blazing rigging as it falls from aloft, in momentary expectation of being launched, with the whole burning mass, into the air?

On this dreadful, this trying night, nothing, I have been assured, could exceed the fortitude, coolness, and exertions of Captain Blackwood: all his orders were given with a distinctness, judgment, and absence of hesitation, that inspired his crew with confidence, whilst his voice, conduct, and demeanour, excited them to still renewed exertions. As long as the remotest chance of saving the ship remained, those exertions were not relaxed: inch by inch, and foot by foot, he retreated before his powerful adversary, until forced to the forecastle, where, with a few officers and men, he strove to shelter himself. At length, driven to the spritsail-yard, which the fire had not yet reached, and seeing that every soul had now left the ship, he finally plunged into the sea, where he struggled for a considerable time, until picked up by a boat from the *Canopus*.

It was never clearly ascertained from what cause the fire originated – not even at the court-martial, which acquitted the surviving officers and men of all blame; but smoke was first seen to issue from the bread-room, and it was generally supposed that the fire was caused by the negligence of the purser's steward, who must have left a lighted candle in his cabin, which adjoined the bread-room.

9: The Dardanelles

The wind continued adverse until the 19th (Feb, 1807), when it shifted to the south-west, and, early on the morning of that day, the squadron weighed, and formed line; then, leaving the *Glatton* to watch the wreck of the *Ajax* and the entrance of the strait, steered for the Dardanelles. As well as I remember, our order of sailing was thus – the *Canopus*, with the flag of Sir Thomas Louis, led, followed by the *Repulse*, *Royal George*, *Windsor Castle*, *Thunderer*, *Pompée*, *Standard*, *Endymion*, and *Active* frigates, and *Lucifer* and *Meteor* bombs.

As soon as the leading ship was supposed to be within gunshot, the Turks opened their fire upon her from the Castles of the Dardanelles, situated on Capes Greco and Janizary, and supposed to command its entrance; but we found that few of the shot crossed each other – none of the large stone shot, I should say. No notice was, therefore taken of them, and the squadron passed on without firing a gun.

To me, the Dardanelles, or Hellespont, bore the appearance of a broad river, quietly flowing between banks of a yellowish-grey colour, the European side being considerably the more elevated and precipitate of the two. Sometimes those banks opened into bays, often the sites of villages, and, being furnished with trees, and other signs of life and cultivation, presented a pleasing contrast to the nakedness and aridity of the surrounding scenery. An occasional shot from a battery placed on some projecting eminence, as it whistled over our heads, would recall, from time to time, our attention from the contemplation of such objects.

A strong adverse current, and but little wind to stem it, made our progress slow, so that it was nine o'clock before a bend in the course of the channel gave us the first view of the fortresses of Sestos and Abydos. For some time, these fortresses appeared to touch each other, and to be thrown across the channel so as to completely block it. No opening seemed left by which the ships could pass, until another gradual bend in the stream displayed an opening three-quarters of a mile wide, and, nearly at the same instant, both batteries opened their fire on the leading ship.

In advancing upwards, my station on the poop as signal-midshipman enabled me to have a good view of both shores; but as soon as the firing commenced, the smoke, which the light wind could not disperse, hung around the ships, and prevented me from having a clear sight of the fortresses with which we were engaged. As well as I could see, these fortresses, presented a triple tier of guns, the heaviest and lowest being nearly on a level with the water, and flanked by towers of great solidity and strength. As soon as her guns would bear, the *Royal George* opened her fire from both sides; and as the light wind fell lighter when the firing became general, the ships did little more than stem the current, and it took more than half an hour to pass the forts. During this time, and amid all the roar and din, the coolness and perfect self-possession of the Greek pilot were admirable, his only thought and anxiety seeming to be to conduct his charge in safety; no easy matter, considering the obscurity of every object, enveloped as we were in a dense smoke.

The enemy's fire was far from rapid, while his guns were pointed so low, evidently with the design of hitting the ships between wind and water, that generally the shot, after striking the water in the bound flew harmless over the ships. That from the squadron was vigorous and well-sustained; but whether any execution was effected by it, could never be ascertained. Having passed the Castles of Sestos and Abydos, we opened the Bay of Nogera, in which was anchored a Turkish squadron in form of a crescent. This squadron consisted of one ship of sixty-four guns, four frigates, and four ship-corvettes, two brigs, and two gun-boats, their position and force being greatly strengthened by a battery *en barbette*, of thirty heavy guns, on Point Pesquies, the north-eastern boundary of the bay.

The Admiral was aware that this squadron had been anchored in the position above described and had given the necessary orders for its attack and destruction, should it have the temerity to await his arrival. Without altering their course the four leading ships gave this squadron their broadsides in passing, which was feebly and ineffectually returned by the Turks ashore and afloat. These ships, retarded for some time by the still feeble wind and strength of the current, having at length rounded Point Pesquies, immediately anchored.

Meantime, Sir Sidney Smith, in the *Pompée*, followed by the *Thunderer*, *Standard*, and two frigates, had hauled in for the Turkish squadron, which, after a show of resistance, all but one frigate cut their cables, ran ashore, and were immediately deserted by their crews. The frigate, having contrived to set her topsails and foresail, steered for the opposite shore, closely followed by the *Active*, which stuck to her quarter, pouring into her a most destructive fire, which was only returned by a gun now and then from the Turk. On reaching the European side, the Turkish frigate took the ground, when she was immediately abandoned by the crew, and taken possession of by the *Active*, whose men were ascending one side before the last of the Turks had left the ship on the opposite.

As men could not be spared from the squadron to man the prizes, an order was given immediately to blow them up; and in this work of demolition Sir Sidney was assisted by the boats of all the squadron, when Lord Burghersh and Captain Blackwood were zealous volunteers.

The destruction of the Turkish ships being complete, with the exception of one corvette, a strong party of seamen and marines was landed, which, advancing at once to the battery on Point Pesquies, found it likewise deserted, when the guns were spiked, and otherwise rendered unserviceable.

All was finished by half an hour after four in the afternoon – boats hoisted in, and the squadron under weigh; when, leaving the *Active* with the prize corvette, to watch proceedings in the channel, we steered for the Sea of Marmora.

In the day's operations, the *Royal George* had four seamen and marines killed, and one midshipman, and twenty-five seamen wounded. As well as I remember, the rest of the ships suffered in rather a less proportion, and none had her rigging damaged to any extent.

In our progress upwards there was no more work to be done. The channel widened every mile we advanced; and as the day closed in soon after we made sail, we had little opportunity of observing its appearance, or the features of the scenery which spread along its banks.

On the following day, the squadron passed within sight of the Island of Marmora; and in the evening anchored seven or eight miles to the south-east of Constantinople, off the small island of Prota, one of the group called 'Prince's Islands'. The *Endymion* was ordered to anchor a couple of miles from the town, as well to watch and report the Turk's preparations for our reception, as to serve as a medium of communication between the Admiral and the shore.

On the morning of the 21st, the wind was too light, I think, to enable the ships to stem the current, which, coming from the Bosphorus, ran past them at the rate of two knots and a half per hour.

Early in the morning, a lieutenant from the *Royal George* was sent to Constantinople with a flag of truce; but the purport of the message or letters with which he was charged, this historian is unable to say. He returned about noon, and I am alike ignorant of the rejoinder which he brought back. It was evasive and temporizing, or mayhap smacked of war and defiance; for on the morning of the 22nd, much to the joy of ambitious passed midshipmen, and expectant first lieutenants, whose left shoulders had long yearned for additional weight, the squadron exhibited undoubted symptoms of pugnacity.

Soon after breakfast, there being no appearance of anything coming from Constantinople, the decks were cleared, an additional quantity of shot got upon deck, the cable shortened in; and at eleven o'clock the ship's companies of the squadron dined by signal.

There was now a commanding breeze from the southward, everything looked as it ought, and as if we were going at it in right earnest. But, alas! for all human hopes – all human expectations! It proved no go; for before the men had dined, a signal from the *Endymion* announced that a boat had left the harbour, and was pulling in the direction of the squadron.

The truth of this sad announcement we could soon verify with our own eyes. And soon after noon, an elderly gentleman, 'hight Isaac Bey', with a grave and solemn aspect, and a more than common length of grizzled beard, shawled and turbaned as became a functionary of his rank and importance, slowly ascended the *Royal George*'s side, followed by his dragoman or interpreter. These worthies were received by the Admiral with all due honour and ceremony, and then ushered to his cabin, where, with Mr Arbuthnot, the Ambassador (who, by the way, had been sick from the day he embarked in the *Royal George*, and confined to his bed the greater part of the time), they remained in conference for an hour and a half; at the expiration of which time the Turks departed with the same ceremony with which they had been received.

The nature of their communication, or the discussions and deliberations thereupon, did not transpire; their effect, however, was soon visible. Our warlike preparations were stayed – guns secured – decks cleared, and we once more veered to a whole cable.

Meantime our friends on shore were not idle; every moment's delay on our part was a gain to them, and they were not slow to take advantage of it. For once the proverbial tardiness of the Othman was laid aside. The old sea defences were repaired and strengthened, and new ones in the most eligible situations thrown up under the able and indefatigable direction of General Sebastiani, the French Ambassador.

Equally active was the stir among the shipping. On the morning of the 23rd, two ships of the line, and two frigates, came from the Bosphorus, and joining themselves to the squadron already outside the harbour, anchored in a position to give their support to the defences on shore.

Seeing that it was not a difficult matter to mystify the British Ambassador, and deeming their preparations not yet sufficiently advanced, Isaac Bey, attended as before, again made his appearance on board, on the 23rd. The British and Turkish chiefs remained in deliberation for a couple of hours, when Isaac Bey again took his departure, but now no more to return.

After letting slip the opportunity of the steady, commanding breeze of the 22nd and 23rd, had we been so minded, it would have been impossible to move the squadron towards the town. For several successive days afterwards, the wind proved so variable and light, that it would have been vain to think of making head against the current. All this time, the Turks did not relax their preparations for defence. Their fleet, moved outside the harbour, already considerably outnumbered ours. Every salient point and available situation bristle with cannon; and they became so far emboldence as to throw a party of soldiers, with some field guns, across from Point Fener on the Asiatic shore to the island of Prota, in the night of the 26th and 27th. In the morning, as soon as the boats busy upon this service, were descried passing to and fro between the island and the main, those of the squadron were sent in pursuit; but they succeeded in capturing only one,* which, retarded by the weight of two brass field-pieces, was unable to effect her escape, which the others, from their extraordinary swiftness in rowing, were enabled to do.

At noon, the boats returned to their ships. Later in the day, Sir Thomas Louis having observed some men on the island busy in throwing up a field-work, sent the boats of the *Canopus* to interrupt their labours and dislodge them. Upon seeing the boats approach the shore, the Turks quitted their employment, and betook themselves to a Greek convent, that crowned one of the highest points of the island. The party from the *Canopus* landed; and, seeing the newly-begun work forsaken, ascended the hill, and advanced towards the convent unsuspectingly, and without precaution it would appear; for no sooner were their heads seen on a level with the platform upon which the building stood, than a volley from its walls brought several to the ground, killing the captain of marines and two or three seamen outright, and wounding several others. A rush was instantly made towards the gate by the rest of the party; but its strength and solidity were such, that, unprovided with implements fit for the purpose, it was found impossible to force it. Several attempts were then made to set fire to the gate, which proving also ineffectual, the officer in command at length drew off his men; and placing them under shelter, sent a boat with the killed and wounded men to the *Canopus*.

* By Lieutenant Willoughby, the late Rear-Admiral Sir N J Willoughby. After the prisoners were removed to his boat, a Turk, in the act of firing a pistol at a seaman, was shot dead by Mr C Tullock, but too late to prevent the discharge of the pistol, which wounded the seaman.

This statement was communicated to Sir John Duckworth, when the signal was immediately made for the ships nearest the shore to send boats manned and armed to the island. Those from the *Royal George*, under the command of the third lieutenant, Willoughby, now Captain Sir Nisbett Willoughby, were, in a few minutes, all stretching out for the shore, with the exception of the launch, of which Jock Russel, another of the lieutenants, had the charge. With the calculation and forethought, which long experience and much service of a somewhat similar nature had given him, he judged that a carronade might be required on shore, and very useful in opening a way into such a building as the convent, and therefore that materials for its transport up so steep an ascent would be necessary.

Before these indispensable addenda to his equipment could be procured, some little delay took place, at which the Captain, not knowing I presume the cause, flew into a most towering rage; but while he was fuming and stamping at the boat's detention, Jock, heedless of the storm, continued lustily to sing out for a couple of capstan bars, and two pair of bale slings, to enable his men to shoulder the iron pot, as he facetiously called the thirty-two pounder carronade. Scarcely were they in the launch, when she was toiling after the lighter boats, which now nearly touched the shore. Willoughby, but partially informed of the enemy's position, and not at all apprized of the necessity of approaching it with caution, as soon as he landed, advanced quickly up the hill; and the first intimation he had, when he gained its crest, was from a fatal discharge of musketry from the convent, by which he received two balls in the face; Lieutenant Belli, next in command, and the chief boatswain's mate, were killed, and two midshipmen, and several men wounded. The rest of the men now sheltered themselves from this murderous fire; and when Russel, soon after, joined the party, a single glance showed him that the only way to gain an entrance to the building was by means of the carronade.

Orders were, therefore, instantly given for its transport up the steep, which was accomplished with much labour and difficulty, and a spot two or three hundred yards in front of the gate offered the convenience of a natural embrasure to plant it on. Before this could be completed it was getting dusk. The wounded officers and men had been removed to their ships, and the Admiral, not wishing to risk the further loss of life in an enterprise of such little moment, and also unacquainted, I must conclude, with Russel's proceedings for the speedy reduction of the little Turkish garrison, gave orders to withdraw the men from the island for the night.

These orders reached Jock just as he had brought the 'iron pot' to bear upon the gate, when, after a low growl, and a 'blessing not loud but deep', and one shot to say farewell, he gave directions to move the carronade, with all its furniture, back to the launch. This was effected happily without further loss; by eight o'clock at night the boats and men had returned to their respective ships. On landing again, next morning, it was found that the insignificant party of Turks had made good its retreat from the island, though boats from the squadron rowed guard all night to prevent such an occurrence. As the look-out was chiefly directed towards that part of the island which faced the main, most probably it escaped from some other part, and so effected its retreat in safety.

Thus terminated this ill-arranged and ill-fated affair, the result of which reflected so little credit upon the squadron, causing it a greater loss in officers and men than forcing the redoutable Dardanelles themselves.

A report, I know not by what means, or through what channel, had reached the squadron that a number of rafts and fire-vessels were preparing in the harbour, with the intention of being launched against the English ships, to which was added another on the 28th, that ten thousand of the Faithful had sworn by the beard of their Prophet to destroy the Christian dogs and their ships, or win Paradise in the attempt; and sufficient credit and importance seemed to be attached to those rumours to cause an order to be issued, that each ship should keep a guard-boat ahead during the night in the direction of the town, and that the utmost vigilance should be observed throughout the squadron.

The morning of the 1st of March was dark and lowering, and the wind, which for several days had been light and variable, sprang up fresh from the north-east. On that day, before noon, the squadron was under sail, and having formed line, stood in a warlike attitude towards Constantinople.

This celebrated city, and the extraordinary beauty of its situation have been so well and so often described by others, that, if I were competent to the task of doing justice to their surpassing majesty and loveliness, the attempt, even then, might be thought a work of supererogation: and, besides that many years have rolled over my head since I beheld them, causing their images to wax fainter and fainter on my memory, numerous objects around and in the back-ground were on that day shrouded in clouds and vapour, which, if seen, would have lent an additional charm to the picture. Still, I can call to mind that Constantinople, embracing a wide sweep of its matchless bay, swells gradually upwards from the margin, expanding as it rises, and offering to the eye of him who views it from the sea, a succession of white shining houses, amid which domes, and kiosks, and slender minarets rear their glittering heads; the whole diversified and relieved by the dark green foliage of innumerable cypress-trees, that seem to impart shade and freshness to all quarters of the city. But it is not by the unrivalled beauty of its site, or the charm of its surrounding scenery, that Constantinople chiefly recommends itself to our notice. Possessing the advantage of a most serene and happy climate, and seated on the confines of the two most important and civilized quarters of the globe, in a region teeming with all the necessaries and most of the luxuries of life, having the keys which open and shut the entrance to two vast inland seas, it ought, one would suppose, to be the emporium of the world's commerce, – the mistress of a mightly empire – the queen of cities, – where arts, and arms, and all that gives grace and dignity to man, might flourish, and find a secure and fostering abode. Such was the noble destiny which its great founder beheld for it in perspective; and such, no doubt, was the lofty eminence to which it would have attained, had Constantine's successors been as wise, and brave, and politic as himself, and its inhabitants an enterprising, industrious, and energetic race. No wonder, then, that a city combining such rare advantages should excite the cupidity of an ambitious neighbour, that other Powers should continue to prop its crumbling and decaying strength, and guard such a prize with jealous care from a keen, crafty, and grasping rival.

The threatening and bellicose attitude which the squadron assumed, and maintained throughout the day, was but a feint: for, soon after dusk, the ship's sterns were presented to the Golden Horn. Urged by a fresh northerly wind, the squadron was soon many leagues distant, and on the eve of the 2nd of March anchored at Gallipoli, where we found the *Active* with the prize corvette.

Early on the following morning, the squadron was once more under weigh, being formed in the same order of sailing in which it had entered the Dardanelles something less than a fortnight before. A fresh wind and favouring current hurried the ships along; and, when sufficiently near to Point Pesquies, the *Canopus* had orders to try how far a salute would have the effect of keeping the batteries quiet, and lull them into the belief that matters were all peaceably arranged again between the two countries. But the Turk was not so easily to be cajoled; for the moment his guns would bear, a sharp ringing shot was the answer to the *Canopus*'s friendly salutation. Passing rapidly Point Pesquies and Bay of Nogera, the ships were soon in the channel that divides Sestos and Abydos. We now found that the enemy fired with much more precision than upon our ascent; for, though we were borne along with great velocity, the squadron was struck more frequently, and suffered more than it did upon its upward passage. By noon it had cleared the Dardanelles, and soon after anchored between Tenedos and the main.

The *Royal George* had three men killed, her first lieutenant and twenty-seven men wounded, in the descent of the passage. These casualties were chiefly caused by a huge stone-shot, that struck the upper sill of the third quarter deck port from forward, and with the surmounting hammocks, swept every man from the gun, and tearing away in its course the whole of the bulwark between the two opposite guns, expended its remaining force in the water. I watched this monster-shot almost from the cannon's mouth till it struck the ship; and, so little swift was its flight that, had it come in the direction in which I stood, I should have had time to avoid it. Indeed, the whole scene on shore more resembled the bursting of some mountain's side, which, vexed and torn by the throes of a laboring volcano, vomits forth, in fire and smoke, fragments of rock and iron, than the sharp, quick fire of a well-served battery. No very enormous shot was found, after the action on board the *Royal George*, – the largest one, of stone, weighing not more than five hundred pounds, and one of iron, ninety-eight pounds. The *Windsor Castle* was struck by one which weighed eight hundred and fifty pounds, and measured in diameter twenty-seven inches and a half. It entered between the middle and main decks, and, glancing upwards, dismounted a gun, and cut two-thirds through the main-mast. The *Active* likewise received a shot in one of the bows that weighed between seven hundred and eight hundred pounds.

On the 7th, a Russian squadron, of six or seven sail of the line, arrived, under a rear-admiral, whose unpronounceable name I cannot even attempt to spell. (Why did not they arrive sooner, and whose was the fault that the junction was so late and so ill-timed?) At first they would scarcely credit our having passed and repassed the Dardanelles, without exhibiting more appearance of damage, the *Windsor Castle* being the only ship that showed any. When, however, it was found to be no joke, and that this formidable strait had been forced without much loss, the Russ waxed valiant, and proposed that the combined squadrons should proceed once more against Constantinople. But such an attempt was considered now rather late in the day. The proposal was declined, and four or five days passed in mutual civilities between the chiefs of the friendly squadrons, which were humbly imitated by their subordinates.

At length a brig arrived from the southward, when, leaving the Russian squadron to look after matters at the mouth of the Dardanelles, the *Windsor Castle* having been previously sent to Malta for a new mainmast, Sir John Duckworth proceeded with the remainder of the squadron on the 13th, for Egypt.

For two days after our departure from Tenedos the wind proved light and variable, and our progress among the islands was slow; but on the morning of the 15th it freshened up from the southward, with an angry and hazy atmosphere. To beat against such a wind with a squadron was useless, and, as the pilot said that the anchorage in the Bay of Patmos, then under our lee, was secure and good, the Admiral bore up for it, resolved to ride out the gale there.

The Bay of Patmos is protected from southerly winds, the only winds that can affect it, by a small flat island and numerous rocky shoals. Two passages conduct to the anchorage – one to the southward, amidst the before-named shoals, the other to the N.W. of the flat island. The former was the one by which we steered, and as we led in, trusting alone to the knowledge and fidelity of our Greek pilot, it was rather nervous to observe how closely we brushed the rocks, and how small appeared the distance which separated the ship's keel from the bottom, that glittered clear and distinct through the medium of the bright blue waters. Patmos, in appearance, differs little from the numerous small islands that spring up and gem the bosom of the Ægean. It is a lone and solitary spot, whence the jarring interests and countless busy cares that distract the world, seem for ever excluded; but where the pious thoughts and heavenly communings of a holy man may find undisturbed exercise and constant aliment.

Around the little bay, not deeply indented, were scattered a few low-roofed white cottages, seemingly the abode of fishermen or sailors, whose boats and small vessels were drawn up on the beach; while high upon a crag, overhanging the village, was reared a strong square building, that served the double purpose of an abode for Caloyers, or Greek monks, and a place of strength and security in the event of invasion and attack by an enemy. During the night the wind increased so much that by twelve o'clock the ships were riding with two cables on end and topmasts struck. In the morning it was observed that the little brig, the *Hirondelle*, had dragged her anchors and gone ashore. By the 17th the gale had moderated, and on that day the *Hirondelle* was hove off into deep water by the aid of our men and boats, without any damage. On the following day the squadron proceeded for Alexandria, where it arrived on the afternoon of the 22nd. We found the *Tigre*, Captain Hallowell, and the *Apollo* frigate, outside the harbour, which was occupied by a large fleet of English transports. When Sir John Duckworth was despatched to batter Constantinople, and awe the Sultan into the surrender of his fleet, Captain Hallowell was sent to Messina, to superintend the embarkation of a division of troops under the command of Major-General Frazer, and after convoying them to Alexandria, with the assistance of the *Apollo*, co-operate in an attack upon that town.

All this had been happily and successfully accomplished, and two days before we made our appearance Alexandria had surrendered to the British forces. Thus, of three feeble expeditions – though meant to fulfil great ends – directed at the same time against three separate divisions of the globe, viz., Constantinople, Egypt, and Buenos Ayres, one only in the outset promised success, ending, like the other two, in failure and defeat. Our troops held Alexandria, it is true, for some months. Further however, they never penetrated; and after the disastrous attempt upon Rosetta, followed by the rout and capture of poor Colonel M'Leod's detachment, the British general was fain to evacuate Egypt, – a step which would have been attended with little credit had it not been for the firm interposition and salutary counsel of Captain Hallowell.

We now remained in a state of inaction for several days. No one, except an officer sent from time to time to communicate with the general, was suffered to visit the shore. Thus we had ample leisure to ruminate upon those occurrences of which Egypt, at different epochs of her eventful history, had been the busy theatre. This state of inactivity lasted until the 29th, when we were once more under weigh, and leaving the *Canopus, Tigre, Apollo*, and a brig, in charge of Sir Thomas Louis, who was in future to direct the operations of the naval part of the expedition, bade adieu to the parched and barren sands of the desolate-looking coast of Egypt. This charge Sir Thomas Louis was not destined long to hold: in a few weeks after we sailed an inflammatory illness consigned him suddenly to the grave, when the command once more devolved upon Captain Hallowell.

A passage of ten days, during which nothing worthy of note took place, bore the squadron to Syracuse, where it anchored on the 8th of April. The Admiral's object in visiting Sicily was the more speedily to obtain pratique, which could not be procured at Malta in less than twenty days.

The entrance to the harbour of Syracuse is narrow; but once in, it presents a noble sheet of water, capable of holding several sail of the line, circular, and completely land-locked. All around the shore is fringed to the margin with vines and olive-trees. Once the chief of Sicilian cities, embracing within its walls a circuit, I believe, of twelve miles, Syracuse, miserably shorn of its vast proportions, has dwindled to a paltry town, limited to the quarter formerly called Ortygia. Until you cross the drawbridge, which connects modern Syracuse with the main, nothing now exists, save the poetic fountain of Arethusa, to recal the memory of classic days. Beyond are the remains of a theatre and amphitheatre, with some fragments of buildings, and faint but sufficiently-visible traces of walls may be seen, which mark the extent to which they formerly reached.

One short and hurried visit of eight or ten hours to the shore, besides a glance at these objects, and listening to the surprising echo in 'Dionysius's ear', which is oft-repeated and deafening, though it may well be doubted whether it ever had the faculty of conveying a whisper to a concealed person, enabled me likewise to descend into the catacombs, and view this subterranean city of the dead. They differ little from others of the kind that are found in various parts of Italy and Sicily. Perhaps the galleries and alleys, which are numerous, are loftier and better ventilated, – a circumstance that may account for the rude paintings, all of scriptural subjects, with which they are profusely decorated, being fresher, and in better preservation, than others that I have seen.

We left Syracuse on the 14th of April, and anchored in Malta harbour on the afternoon of the following day.

10: To Cadiz

Sir John Duckworth found despatches awaiting his arrival at Malta, which contained orders for him to proceed forthwith to England, and take upon him the command of the fleet then preparing for the memorable expedition against Copenhagen. When these orders were written, it is to be presumed that the failure of the attempt upon Constantinople was unknown to the Ministers in England. They seemed to argue, that by them its complete success was fully anticipated; for as soon as the unfortunate result was ascertained, Sir John's new and flattering appointment was cancelled, and Admiral Gambier named in his stead.

We left Malta on the 16th of April, the day after our arrival. Several passengers, male and female, embarked in the *Royal George* for a passage to England. Amongst the number were the late Ambassador to Constantinople, and the Secretary of Legation, whose boast I remember it was that he never had been able to accomplish the mechanical task of learning to write.

Our voyage down the Mediterranean was lengthened to several weeks, perhaps because we hugged the African shore, where light and variable winds usually prevail at that season of the year, to avoid a Spanish squadron of six or seven sail of the line, then lying in Carthagena Harbour, whose national indolence might for once have given way at the prospect of so easy a capture as a single ship, should the *Royal George* have approached too near the Spanish coast.

The tedium of a long passage was now and then relieved by the performance of plays, enacted upon alternate nights, by three distinct companies, furnished by the wardroom, cockpit, and lower deck. The inmates of the wardroom, as the more dignified, chose the upper walk of the drama for themselves, the Mids exhibited in genteel comedy while Jack shone, with a lustre all his own, in broad farce. And, truth to say, 'Henry IV', 'The Poor Gentleman', and 'Mayor of Garret', have been worse represented on more pretending boards than those of the *Royal George*.

We joined the fleet off Cadiz on the 12th of May, and, after the admirals had held a brief communication, again parted company in the afternoon, when, shaping our course for merry England, we arrived safely at Spithead on the 26th. In a few days we were admitted to pratique, and had got rid of our passengers, when we sailed for Plymouth, where we arrived on the 3rd of June, and soon after went up the harbour.

When the bustle and activity required in stripping a ship, and preparing her for the shipwright's hands are over, the duties of a midshipman's life in harbour cease to be exciting, and soon become tame and wearisome – one eternal round of visits to the dockyard – returning or drawing stores – overseeing a party of men at the sail or rigging-loft, boat-house, or mast-house, fills the measure of almost each day's employment. It is very irksome, although I must confess very necessary and very expedient. To be sure, the monotony of such an existence is sometimes relieved, if the first lieutenant is particularly well pleased with you, by permission to pass a day amid the lovely scenery of a Cotile, a Saltram, or Mount Edgecombe, or a gallop to Ivy Bridge. Still I sighed, oh! how I sighed to be released from such drudgery! until my complaints and remonstrances, continually and urgently repeated, at the supineness of friends in not pressing for my promotion, at length brought upon me, and very justly, the reproach of querulousness.

After passing the summer and greater part of the autumn in Hamoaze, the *Royal George* moved into Cawsand Bay, whence she soon after sailed to join the Channel fleet, then under the command of Lord Gardner, and cruising off Ushant.

Even employed in blockade alone, life on board ship is then far to be preferred to a lengthened continuance in harbour. The mere operations of veering and tacking, making and shortening sail, reefing, &c, with all the other duties of a ship at sea, keep the attention alive, and prevent that total stagnation of the mind and spirits, with which they are apt to be oppressed, when there is nothing to rouse or excite them. The emulation in the fleet arising from the celerity and skill with which these various manœuvres are required to be performed, with occasional trials of rate of sailing, create a deep interest in sailors, who are as jealous of the reputation and qualities of their respective ships, as ever lover was of the charms and perfections of an adored mistress. Then ever and anon comes a vessel from England, the bearer of letters from distant friends, or news of some kind or other from our beloved country, diffusing joy to some, and furnishing matter for thought and conversation to all.

Some such arrival as this was announced one morning in the early part of December, 1807; and though I had hopes of hearing from distant friends, I little expected that the stranger could be the bearer of such glad tidings as I that day received. I was seated in the berth, my thoughts fixed upon home, when the midshipman who had been sent to the commander-in-chief's ship for the despatches, rushed into the berth, and putting an Admiralty letter into my hand, wished me joy of my appointment as a lieutenant. For a moment I thought I had not heard aright, and doubted the distinctness of my vision, as my eyes rested upon the superscription of the letter. But when I broke the seal, and read the following words, plainly and legibly written: 'My Lords Commissioners of the Admiralty having been pleased to appoint you a Lieutenant of H.M.'s ship the *Sultan*,' &c, words are, indeed, but feeble things to express the joy, the boundless rapture which at that moment filled my breast.

A multitude of pleased and happy thoughts and sensations came crowding thick and fast upon me, amidst which was the exultation of being at length raised from the humble post of midshipman to that of a Lieutenant – from the depth of the candlelit cockpit to the more elevated and purer atmosphere of the wardroom; no more to be brow-beat, bullied and mast-headed, but henceforth to be regarded and treated as an officer and a gentleman. No! except perhaps by the apprentice released from the servitude of a hard task-master, or the slave whose shackles have been newly stricken off, can it be imagined what a thrill of happiness I felt at this, my first commission as Lieutenant.

Several days elapsed after the receipt of the Admiralty letter before I had an opportunity of proceeding to England, and wearily and anxiously did I count the lengthened minutes. At last a signal from the *Ville de Paris* announced the early departure of a vessel for Plymouth, into which I was discharged for a passage. Strange, however, notwithstanding my more than delight, my ecstacy at leaving the *Royal George*, and particularly for the cause of it, – a ship, too, in which I never felt myself perfectly at home, nor comfortable, when the moment of separation arrived I could not part without a feeling of regret from messmates with whom I had lived for more than a year, if not on terms of great intimacy, at least in social intercourse and good fellowship; – and, shaking them all by the hand, I sincerely, and from my heart wished them the same good fortune that had just befallen myself. I landed at Plymouth on the following day, and proceeded to London with the least possible delay, to receive my commission.

The first thing after I arrived in town, was to repair to the Admiralty, the next to order the necessary equipments, when I hoped to have a week's leisure, to view the marvels of London. In that I was mistaken: for calling upon Sir John Colpoys, he told me that the *Sultan* was short of officers, and that Captain Griffith, who commanded her, was anxious that they all should join as soon as possible; and should he learn that I made any unnecessary delay in town, he would be exceedingly displeased. Whereupon I got my traps together as speedily as I could, and then started for 'Long Reach', where the *Sultan* was lying, only waiting for sufficient men to take her to the Nore.

I found the ship less than half-manned and half-officered, with guns on board, sails bent, and all ataunto; but slovenly rigged, and in a sad mess, as all new ships are, fresh from the hands of dockyard riggers. But good-will, a little trouble, and blue water, put all matters ship-shape and to rights in a very short time. In nine or ten days, having got a few more men, the ship dropped down to the Nore, where she remained some time waiting for the last draught to complete her complement. Meantime the measles, introduced by some children belonging to the sailors' wives, made their appearance on board the *Sultan*. Several of the crew were attacked, though none fatally; amongst the rest, I was a sufferer, and so virulent was the disease, that my life was despaired of for many days. Youth, and a constitution not prone to inflammation, at length got the better of it; but left me reduced to the feebleness of infancy, and I did not recover my strength for several months afterwards.

The *Sultan* was paid advance of wages about the middle of January, 1808, and then proceeded to Portsmouth, there to wait for further orders.

When these arrived, they contained instructions to proceed off Cadiz, and join the fleet blockading that port; and it was with light and merry hearts that the anchors were tossed up and sail made round St Helen's, – for Cadiz and the Mediterranean have always been favourite stations with both officers and men. Owing to the prevalence of strong westerly winds, our passage, marked by no incident worth recording, was long and tedious; and we did not join Admiral Purvis, who, in the absence of Lord Collingwood, commanded the fleet off Cadiz, till the middle of March. The enemy's fleet in that harbour consisted at that time of five sail of the line and one frigate, French, under Admiral Rosilly, and six Spanish, two of which were three-deckers.

At this time, those intrigues and cabals were in full activity which terminated in the memorable treaty of Bayonne, and by which the ancient kingdom of Spain was transferred from the hands of the feeble Charles, and his still weaker and more vacillating son, to those of the then dictator of Continental Europe. At first, everything seemed to favour the projects of Bonaparte. Every pass and fortress extending along the line of the Pyrenees, from Roncesvalles to Figueras, were in possession of his soldiers. His legions were pouring into the country; and the addition of that fine kingdom, with its transmarine empire, to his grasping rule, seemed of no more difficulty than had been that of the republic of Genoa, or the electorate of Hanover. But the pride of the Spaniard was fired: the blood of their Gothic sires still flowed in their veins; and the spirit that awoke resistance to and enabled them to burst the bonds of their Moorish conquerors now filled the breasts and stirred the hearts of their descendants. Spain arose as one man; and from north to south, from east to west, amid the din and preparation for war, nought was heard but 'Guerra a la muerte! – Guerra al cuchilo! – Mueran los Franceses traidores!'

Much censure and obloquy have been cast – unjustly, I think – upon the Spanish nation by some historians of the Peninsular War, for a want of firmness and energy during the struggle that followed the invasion of their territory. Her armies, it is true, were almost invariably beaten in pitched battles, and her generals and officers frequently displayed a deplorable want of tact and knowledge of the art of war. But although often vanquished, and sometimes betrayed, the Spanish people never succumbed to the invader; and it is even marvellous to think with what speed an army was got together, after it had, to all appearance, been dispersed and destroyed. The nature of the country, in many parts traversed by mountains and intersected by deep and rapid rivers, was favourable for resistance; and the Spaniards were neither slow nor inactive in availing themselves of such advantages. Their Guerillas, composed for the most part of hardy mountaineers, and led by chiefs of foresight, enterprise, and resolution, hovered on the flanks and rear of the French armies, or occupying the passes, intercepted their communications, and cut off their convoys and detachments: so that the French could not be said to possess a rood of ground which was not occupied by a strong force; and they found it, consequently, much more difficult to make 'the war feed the war' in Spain than they had in other countries. If to this be added the firmness and endurance with which many sieges were supported, and the great length to which they were protracted, thereby causing an incalculable loss in men and treasure to the enemy, it may be safely presumed, contrary to the opinion of the before-named writers, that British valour, unaided and alone, did not save Spain from subjugation, nor eject her invaders from the soil. Nor can it be supposed that an army, at no time, I believe, exceeding forty thousand bayonets – unrivalled though that army was by any in the world for courage, discipline, and valour – could expect to resist, much less to vanquish, the myriads which France kept pouring into Spain, unsustained by the Spanish nation. Without such support, albeit not as efficient as might be expected from a people once second to none for warlike deeds, British valour and British skill must have yielded to the mighty torrent which swept over the country. On the other hand, it is equally true, that, had it not been for the aid of England, and her band of iron-warriors, which for seven years stood a tower of strength in the land, around which her scattered and discomfited armies might always recruit and rally, Spain must have fallen before her persevering and relentless foe, and finally ceased to be a nation.

Towards the middle of May, the enthusiasm of the inhabitants of Cadiz was at its height: not a Frenchman dared show his face in the town. The officers and men belonging to the French squadron were strictly confined to their ships, which had been moved further up the harbour into the channel of the Caracas, as much out of the range of the Spanish batteries as possible; or probably with the hope that, by being nearer to the Isla de Leon, it might be rescued from its perilous situation by the French army, then said to be not far from Seville, should it make its way down to the vicinity of Cadiz. Friendly communications had been opened between Sir Hugh Dalrymple, the Governor of Gibraltar, and General Castanos, who commanded the Spanish troops in the vicinity of that fortress; and, soon afterwards, General Spencer was dispatched from thence with three thousand or four thousand men, which were freely offered to the Governor of Cadiz to assist in the reduction of the French squadron, or for any service in which they might be usefully employed. A courteous answer, declining the proffered assistance, was returned by the Governor, Don Thomas de Morla, confident in his own strength, or perhaps from a feeling of jealousy and distrust of the English, not yet forgiven for the attack and capture of the treasure-ships and victory of Trafalgar, and with whom friendly relations were not yet re-established and formally recognised by their respective governments.

Propositions, considered inadmissible, had been made by the French admiral, and preparations to compel their unconditional surrender on the part of the Spaniards, by the construction of fresh batteries, which commanded a nearer range, and bore more directly upon the new anchorage which the enemy's ships had taken up. When all was prepared, the batteries opened a not very spirited or mischievous fire upon the French squadron, which was continued at intervals during the 8th and 9th of June. A truce of four days followed, at the end of which time Admiral Rosilly, considering his resistance sufficiently respectable, agreed to surrender, and struck his colours. Prior to this event Lord Collingwood had arrived from before Toulon, and assumed the command of the fleet off Cadiz. By reason of the cessation of hostilities between Spain and England, and the new aspect which matters had assumed at Cadiz, his Lordship was enabled to release some of the ships which formed the blockade of that port, and send them into the Mediterranean, whither the increasing strength of the French fleet in Toulon and other important services imperiously called them.

One of the first ships detached for this purpose was the *Sultan* and the day prior to our separating from the fleet, Captain Griffith asked and obtained permission from the Admiral for his officers to land and visit Cadiz, a proof of consideration and kindness, for which we were not unthankful. Accordingly, as many as could be spared from the duties of the ship started next morning for the shore. The day was bright and cloudless – such a day as usually lightens the sunny shores of Southern Spain in the month of June. On landing we strolled through the streets and plazas of the clean and pretty little city of Cadiz. We visited its ramparts and Alameda, thronged with 'Grey friars and white, white friars and grey', and then entered several of the churches, which, like all Roman Catholic places of worship, were redolent of frankincense and wax tapers; the walls for the most part hung with indifferent paintings; their various little chapels glittered with tinsel and brocade; while the high altars of many were decorated in a more solid fashion, with gold and silver and precious stones. In one of these, a church attached to the Capuchin monastery, we found a friar, a pale slender young man, whose province it seemed to be to guard the sanctuary from any profane or unhallowed touch, and act the part of cicerone to strangers like ourselves, who might be curious to examine its treasures.

One of our party, who had formerly served in the Mediterranean, and gathered along its shores a few stray words of Spanish and Italian, which, with the help of his vernacular, he had woven into a lingua Franca of strange texture, peculiarly his own, undertook the office of interpreter, and tried to make our questions intelligible to the youthful friar, who seemed to have great difficulty in comprehending our comrade's 'unknown tongue', and also to restrain the laugh that twinkled in his keen bright eye, and curled the corners of his mouth into an expression of indescribable drollery. At length he could command himself no longer, but, yielding to his natural humour, exclaimed, in an accent about which there could be no mistake, 'Don't trouble yourselves, jintlemen, with trying to make yourselves understood in that hard-crampt Spanish. Sure 'tis myself has been larning it these two blessed years and more, and little good it's done me. If you'd try English, may be I'd understand you better; though belike you're not countrymen at all – you come, I'm thinking, from the other side.' And our new friend stood confessed a native of the shores of Dingle. He told us that being partly educated for the priesthood, and having a relation in Spain, he had left Ireland two years before, and through his means was introduced to the fraternity, with whom he had nearly completed his novitiate, and hoped soon to be ordained a deacon. He professed to like his situation, and the friends among whom his lot had been cast.

When he found that I was a countryman, he became more communicative and confidential, and from what he said, and his enthusiasm when he spoke of home, I suspect he would have greatly preferred his own dear land, ranging at will in the exercise of his pastoral office, over some wild extensive parish of his native mountains, where, to use his own words, he would be hailed by his flock, as the coadjutor of his parish used to be by his own mother, after a short absence, with 'Your Riverence is kindly welcome this morning. 'Tis long since we had a sight of you, Father Mick, dear! 'Twas only yesterday I was saying to Biddy; "Biddy," says I, "what's come to Father Mick? 'Tis a month," says I, "this blessed morning – God be good to us – since we sot eyes on him here. May be 'tis sick his Reverence is – the Lord be his keeper. I'm sartin sure he wouldn't pass our door any how without a God save you!" Sit down, Father Mick aghra. Biddy, reach a chair to his Riverence. Bad manners to the girl, why don't you wipe it for his honour's Riverence? The honest man and the boys are above in the field – but they'll be home agin the praties are biled. You'll break your fast with us this morning, Father Mick. There's a nice fresh egg jist laid, and I'll have a rasher ready in a jiffy, and (with a smile) something hot and comfortable for your Riverence agin the road this raw cowld morning. You'll be going further, I'm thinking, Father Mick – to the Cross, any how, to see Norry Doolan. Poor woman! 'tis she have the bad time of it. Twins! Father Mick; and she with seven of 'em to the fore!'

On taking leave of our new friend, I could not help reflecting that he was now not likely ever to experience the quiet pleasures of a life he seemed to value, and had so well described, and that a longing, lingering desire to be once more amid the scenes of his early days would sometimes painfully obtrude itself, and cloud the otherwise serene and tranquil tenor of the young priest's life.

After this hurried glance at the marvels of Cadiz, we dined at a kind of *table-d'hôte*, kept by an old American lady, at which was an 'olla', curiously compounded of sea-lieutenants, midshipmen, Yankee skippers, and merchants' clerks. At sunset we returned to our ship.

The following morning we left the fleet, and having taken in a supply of bullocks at Tangiers, and completed our water at Gibraltar, we proceeded to join Admiral Martin, who, with the *Canopus* (his flag-ship), and the *Magnificent*, was off Port Mahon, and had opened a communication with the authorities of the island, and the admiral commanding the Spanish squadron, which had moved from Carthagena to Mahon, for greater security in the then posture of affairs. Matters were not yet re-established upon so friendly a footing as to admit the British ships into the harbour; but we obtained all kinds of refreshments in abundance, and were allowed to water at an excellent watering-place outside the harbour, but considerably within Cape Mola, its north-eastern point of entrance.

The officers of the *Sultan* had now been five or six months together, and the more we knew each other, the greater became our cordiality and friendship. In the ward-room we were like brothers – and so truly comfortable and contented did every individual feel himself on board, that the ship was known throughout the fleet as the 'Happy Sultan'.

Although distant and reserved in manner, Captain Griffith was considerate and just, and in conduct and deportment a perfect gentleman. His outward appearance, and ordinary speech and tone of conversation, exhibited none of those technicalities which so often distinguish the rough and ready sailor; but I never knew a man that, when necessity required it, handled a ship better under any circumstances, or evinced more nerve, self-possession, and skill, in a trying or perilous situation, than Captain Griffith. But these qualities he never put forth unless he thought the occasion demanded it – ever placing that proper confidence in his officers which their abilities and conduct deserved. To his judgment we were indebted for a storm-topsail, better known by the name of the 'monkey topsail'. He first used it in the *Dragon* in the Channel, and afterwards in the *Sultan*, when it soon became general with the ships off Toulon; and very useful the fleet found it during a winter's cruise in that gulf, where the northern blasts come rushing as through a funnel, and with a violence and fury unsurpassed in any quarter of the globe. Perhaps it may be as well to let the present generation know, that this storm-topsail is formed by simply goring the spritsail at the clews to give the foot more spread. The standing part of the topsail-sheets being secured a fathom or so in form the yardarms to confine the clews closer to the yard, the sail is then brought to the yard by long ropebands passed over the furled main-topsail.

Captain Griffith was always anxious to promote the real comforts and innocent amusement and recreation of his crew. An observation of his, and one that, from its humane consideration, made a lasting impression on my mind, was, that he 'considered it as unjust as it was unwise and impolitic, to confine the men to their ships, and refuse them that indulgence of leave to visit the shore whenever the duties of the service admitted it, which was freely enjoyed by himself and his officers, whenever they happened to be in port'.

In consonance with those sentiments, his general orders were, that so soon as the ship was perfectly ready for sea in all her equipments, a certain number of the crew were always to have leave to go on shore: if in one of our own harbours, this leave extended to twenty-four hours; but only till sunset, if in one belonging to another power. The men very rarely abused this indulgence; and its effect, combined with other salutary and judicious regulations, made the men happy and contented with their situation – so much so, that we never lost a man by desertion, whilst it was a common occurrence for the men of other ships, in which a similar indulgence was denied, to run from the boats whenever a fair prospect of escape presented itself.

The lieutenants of the *Sultan* were all young officers – the senior, John Popham Baker, not numbering more than five years in that rank, while that of the others varied from two years to scarcely as many months – the writer of these pages being the junior. In age as well as rank we were likewise all young, if I except Tom Gill, who might well have figured as the father of his messmates. Tom was a man considerably above the common height, and of proportions almost herculean, with broad rounded shoulders, prodigious length of arms, and calves to his legs which a coalwhipper or drayman would have envied: a head of the bullet order, small compared with his huge frame, with close-cut bristly hair, somewhat grizzled by time, and a shrewd, but good-natured, honest expression of countenance, completed the outward man of our second lieutenant.

Tom's had been a chequered life: he had not always followed the occupation of the sea: part of his youth and manhood had been passed in the West Indies; but how employed, or what situation he filled there, I am unable to say: like St Paul, thrice had he suffered shipwreck – twice in returning from the West Indies, before he adopted the navy as a profession, and the third time in the *Anson*, when that ship was lost in the Bay of Helston in 1807. Upon each of these occasions the waters engulfed his all, and poor Tom was flung upon the shore almost as naked as if he had been sea-born.

Vicissitudes like these enabled him to regard great evils with calmness and equanimity: not so the lesser ones, however; for when, in a gale of wind, the ship by an unlucky lurch had fractured some needful piece of crockery in his cabin, Tom would stalk forth, and rail in no measured terms at what he called the freaks of Fortune, exclaiming that he defied her heaviest blows to move his philosophy or shake his fortitude, but (holding up to view the remains of the shattered vase) her minor ills – her 'quips and quillets' – teazed, worried, and unhinged him quite.

He had seen and read a good deal, and he had a greater store of information than usually falls to the lot of us children of the sea: his favourite author was Dr Samuel Johnson, from whom he would frequently quote, and often very happily. Indeed, to judge from his conversation and sentiments, his whole mind and thoughts seemed tinged with the hues and impregnated with the leaven of that great man's dicta and opinions.

Tom was likewise known to be guilty of poetry, and his effusions in that way, though concealed beneath the cloak of 'Anon', could sometimes be detected in a corner of the Hampshire Chronicle; and a correct summary of our proceedings, and an occasional anecdote of the Mediterranean fleet, furnished by the same authority, would figure from time to time in the columns of that useful paper.

From what has been said, it may be supposed that Tom was, in character and feeling, a thorough John Bull. For everything not English he had a very laudable and hearty contempt; and in politics he presented the *beau idéal* of a rabid Tory. To praise the patriotism of Sir Francis Burdett, or the ability and politics of Cobbett, or extol the genius and invincibility of Bonaparte, always stirred the loyal indignation of his inmost soul. Our doctor, a most worthy, excellent, fellow as ever breathed, and one that loved a little quizzing in his heart of hearts, generally led the assault upon his patience and equanimity, and he never failed in getting a 'rise' out of old Tom, as he called it, and arousing his ire, which the other tried to assuage by pouring down half a dozen bumpers, hand-over-hand, of what he called r–t–g–t stuff, 'not worth a single bumper of honest English port'.

11: At Port Mahon

Not many days after our arrival off Minorca, it was known at Mahon that hostilities had ceased between the two countries, and that deputies from the Junta of Seville had proceeded to England for the purpose of adjusting and concluding a definitive peace; whereupon the Governor politely informed Admiral Martin that he was at liberty to enter the harbour with his squadron, and that the island and all it contained were, in Spanish parlance, 'Muy a su disposicion', entirely at his disposal.

The following morning the *Canopus, Magnificent*, and *Sultan* entered the harbour, amid the cheers and vivas of the inhabitants, who thronged the shore; and before the ships were well at anchor, they were surrounded with boats, some laden with fruit, vegetables and all kind of comestibles grateful to the eyes and senses of hungry tars, while others contained visitors anxious and curious once more to behold a British man-of-war, and the wonders and animals it held. Visits of friendly civility were exchanged between the officers of the British and Spanish squadrons. Amongst the latter we found some names, such as Bray, Butler, O'Connock, which showed that Spain was an adopted country, not that from whence they originally sprang. Before many days had passed, we had a number of our new friends to dine with us, when the healths of 'Jorge Tercero', and 'Fernando Septimo', with many other loyal patriotic toasts, were drank. The strength of the wine, to which foreigners are little accustomed – the quick and continuous call to 'fill glasses', a call unrelentingly enforced – the hip! hip! hurrah! that followed each bumper, all united, soon told with fatal effect upon Spanish heads. At one part of the table might be heard snatches of patriotic airs, and amatory seguidillas; while at another, the speech of an orator, full of the prophetic god, 'his eye in frenzy rolling', foreshadowing the heroic deeds and future victories of the united nations, was cut short in the midst by a couple of waltzers (your Spaniard and Frenchman are fond of capering in their cups), who in their enthusiasm and glee had spun themselves into the speaker's lap. Soon the abrazo, or Spanish fraternal hug, declared the triumph of English hospitality achieved, and that our friends were gloriously and right royally drunk. So helpless indeed had most of them become, that we were obliged to sling them, and parbuckle them into the boats that awaited alongside to convey them to their ships. As they had no good mess of their own on board, they invited the officers of the *Sultan* in a few days to a banquet at the only posada or inn that Mahon could then boast of, when they tried their best to serve us in the same hospitable manner that we had served them. But they were soon convinced, to their cost, that Minorca did not furnish artillery heavy enough to make much impression upon the thick skull of an Englishman. The same friendly feeling existed while the squadrons remained together at Mahon; and among other visible signs of this union and cordiality, may be mentioned, that English and Spanish officers wore the black and red cockade, which distinguished the two nations, interwoven and blended together in their hats.

The harbour of Mahon is one of the securest, and, in many respects, most convenient in Europe. From its entrance to its furthest or western extremity, it extends in a somewhat irregular form about two miles, being in breadth about one-sixth of that distance; but as its whole extent is interrupted by few shoals, it is capable of holding a large fleet. There are three small islands in the harbour. On the first is the lazaretto, a fine building, raised at considerable expense, in the hope that the whole Levant trade bound down the Mediterranean, would gladly avail itself of such an establishment to perform quarantine, and get clean bills of health, which would have amply reimbursed the cost of construction, and have also attracted much wealth to the island. In this expectation, however, the Spanish Government was disappointed, and I never heard that the quarantine establishment of Minorca had been much resorted to.

Nearly in the centre of the harbour is the Isla del Rey, or King's Island, upon which is an hospital capable of holding comfortably a good many patients; and close by is a round rock, which went by the name of Rat Island, from the multitudes of those vermin that were found upon it. Three or four coves, each capable of holding a ship of the line or frigate, indent the shore at either side which is moderately elevated, but brown and sterile like most parts of the island. On the right side of the harbour as you enter, is Fort Phillipet; and on the opposite side the extensive ruins of Fort St Philip, once a work of great strength, but which was never restored after its destruction, when it fell into the hands of Marshal Richelieu, in 1756, after General Blakeney's memorable defence. If these two forts, hardly the third of a mile apart, were in proper order, and rightly served, it would be extremely hazardous, if not impossible, to force an entrance into the harbour.

A short distance within Fort St Philip, and about two miles from the town of Mahon, is Arrabal, or George's Town, as it was named by the English, when they held possession of Minorca. It is a considerable village, and probably owes its origin and respectability to the neighbouring forts and barracks, which latter are very fine, and large enough to hold from four thousand to five thousand men. Mahon itself is a respectable little city, clean with no appearance of poverty or meanness about it, with a population, including that of George's Town, in 1808, of sixteen thousand souls, half that of the whole island. This harbour, although too remote and liable to the serious objection of difficulty of egress with the wind fresh from the eastward, proved, notwithstanding, of the greatest convenience and utility to the fleet, whilst blockading Toulon. It was a point of union and refuge to the ships, when buffeted and driven from their stations by the furious gales of the Gulf of Lyons, where they might refit and repair their damages, even to heaving down, if that should be found necessary. There also the store and provision transports might securely lie, ready to supply all their wants, with the advantage of an hospital for the sick, most convenient watering-places, and an abundance of vegetables and other refreshments.

The language and costume of the Mahonese differ but little from those of the people of Catalonia, except the coiffure of the females, which is very peculiar, and not at all becoming. The hair is drawn smoothly back, so as to display the forehead and temples, and tied behind in a stout long cue, very similar to that worn by 'Jack' when I first went to sea, and for some years after. A three-cornered kerchief, called in Minorquin, a 'robasilla', of scarlet woollen cloth, is placed over the centre of the head, and looped or pinned beneath the chin, so as to allow two ends to hang down in front, while the third falls behind concealing part of the cue. The ladies likewise sport the cue; but with them the robasilla is made of finer materials, such as muslin, or black or white lace, and the hair is braided or worn in ringlets in front.

As the ships had nothing to do except the daily routine of duty, and to keep the water complete, the four or five weeks which we passed at Mahon flew idly, and to young men agreeably enough away – the morning in playing at rackets at an excellent racket court at George's Town, built by the English officers when stationed in the island; the evenings at some 'tertulla' or reunion, but more frequently either at the house of Don Pedro Motta, or at that of his brother Don José. Each of these families consisted of a son and two daughters. The son of the elder brother Don José, was a sensible, quiet young man, with much of the gravity that is *supposed* to distinguish the Spaniard, and all the modesty and sobriety of demeanour which often characterize the youth of England. His eldest sister, Antonia, might have been about twenty-four years of age, and had her figure which was short and full corresponded with her features, she would have been a remarkably fine woman. The contour of her face was oval; her small, full mouth inclosed teeth beautifully shaped and of pearly whiteness; her nose, neither small nor large, was classically Roman. The usual expression of her eyes, which were large, black, and somewhat elongated, was thoughtful and pensive, except when excited by music or conversation, and then they spoke, with an eloquence not to be misunderstood, the various emotions passing through her breast. Upon her smooth and open forehead were pencilled brows slightly arched, that, like her hair, were dark as is the raven's wing. Her sister Mariquita was six or eight years younger: with eyes dark, wild, and piercing, and a form as light and agile as the mountain roe's, she would be thought an extremely pretty girl in any country. Both sisters moved and danced as the females of Spain only move and dance; and Antonia, whose voice was rich, full, and sweet, sang numerous seguidillas and other airs to the guitar, with great taste and feeling. The Consul's son, whose name was Geronimo, or Jerry, as he was more familiarly named by the officers of the fleet, had once been a midshipman in the British service, and retained all the recklessness of character that too often attaches to those children of the sea – without a thought, apparently, for anything or anybody save amusement or cigars: in other respects, he was harmless and good-natured. His younger sister Rita had not yet emerged from childhood. Catalina, the elder, might have been about nineteen or twenty years old, and of a complexion totally different from that of her cousins, both of whom were decided *brunes*. Catalina, on the contrary, was as fair as if born on the shores of England or Germany, with light-brown hair, and laughing 'eyes of heavenly blue', her features were all good, and her 'wee bit mou' and teeth perfection: her figure, below the middle height, was rather too much disposed to *embonpoint*, but still agile and elastic; and her whole appearance that of an engaging and exceedingly pretty girl, with an expression of radiant happiness and good-nature that nothing seemed likely to disturb or alloy.

In her childhood, the office of British Consul, which her father held, gave Catalina an opportunity of learning English, and also of seeing so many Englishmen, that it is not to be wondered at if she acquired a preference for everything belonging to our country. This taste she did not attempt to disguise, and in her merry moods was often heard to declare that she would be the bride of an Englishman or none. Poor Catalina! she did wed an Englishman; but I fear her marriage brought no addition to her happiness. Subsequently to this time, Mahon became the general rendezvous where the fleet always wintered, until the end of the war. Of the numerous admirers whom the charms and attractive qualities of Catalina drew around her, one officer, a very elegant young man, by unremitting attentions and a show of sincerity, won her esteem and regard. An offer of his hand was soon made and accepted; but as he was entirely dependent upon his father, and neither party had any fortune, it was arranged that they should wait until he could get advanced in his profession, or obtain his father's consent to the match. He was now received and acknowledged by the family as her accepted suitor, and every thing seemed to promise a bright and happy future. But, alas! 'the course of true love seldom doth run smooth'; either from maliciousness, or prompted by a far different motive – a sincere desire to save a friend from doing what might well be considered a rash and ill-advised act by uniting himself to a foreigner without fortune or connexion – some person wrote to the father of the young man, and informed him of the piece of folly which his son was about to commit. On the receipt of this information, a letter was despatched to his son, couched in language of the strongest reprehension, and declaring, in terms the most explicit, that such an engagement should never have his sanction or approval.

On making known the substance of this letter to Catalina's father, it was deemed prudent to suspend the match, if not break the engagement; and the lover's ship sailing soon after for England, seemed to put an end to it altogether. And well would it have been had it ended thus: but in about a year he returned to the Mediterranean. Again he found himself in the neighbourhood of strong attraction, and all his former attentions were renewed. Poor Catalina was but too happy to recover a lover whom she thought lost to her for ever; and, in a short time, everything was re-established upon the same footing that it was before the late interruption. The engagement was once more renewed, and they now only waited till he should be promoted to put the seal to their union and happiness by marriage.

In about a year after his second return to the Mediterranean, the lover of Catalina was promoted; but the vessel to which he was appointed was ordered up the Mediterranean, from off Toulon, without touching at Mahon. Nothing more was heard of him for six or eight months during which the fleet remained at sea, until a vessel arrived from Malta, when, amongst other *on dits* and fragments of news, we learnt that he had been recently married to one of the numerous daughters of an *employé* in that island. To those who knew the circumstances of his engagement at Mahon, this report caused a feeling of unmingled astonishment and regret. But upon poor Catalina, who was attached to him with an affection as sincere and warm as ever glowed in the breast of woman, it fell with a force as stunning and overwhelming as it was wholly unexpected and undeserved.

When this report reached Mahon, the fleet was at sea, and some months elapsed before I had an opportunity of seeing Catalina. By the time I met her again, she had, in a measure, recovered her composure. But it was evident to the most indifferent observer that the bolt had struck home: a shade of deep melancholy, wholly foreign to her countenance, would now often cloud her brow, and dim the light of those eyes that were wont to shine with so much sprightliness and vivacity. She had resumed her different occupations as before; but, as she passed from room to room, her once cheerful voice was no longer heard humming some lively air, or breaking out into snatches of a favourite song: now, she glided through the house as it were mechanically; and, when her needful task was ended, she resumed her needlework in the parlour, where it was truly pitiable to see her, who, a few months before, was all joy and animation, now sit silent and dejected, taking no part and showing no interest in the conversation, but if addressed, answering with a faint smile or only in monosyllables. The rest of Catalina's story is soon told. Some years after the time we now speak of, being repeatedly and strongly urged to do so by her parents, she reluctantly consented to marry an English gentleman, who acted as storekeeper in the temporary dockyard established at Mahon. At the peace in 1815, she went with her husband to Malta, where his permanent occupation was fixed.

Two or three years after their removal, our worthy Doctor* of the *Sultan* – always a favourite in the family of the Mottas – happening to be at Malta, called on his old friend Catalina, who received him with her usual cordiality and kindness, and took no pains to disguise the pleasure which his visit gave her, although its exhibition was anything but gratifying to her husband. Catalina was much changed – her round, plump figure had become quite attenuated; and the Doctor was shocked to observe that her eyes were sunken, her cheeks hollow and hectic, and that an incessant, teasing cough gave evident symptoms of fast-approaching, if not confirmed, consumption. He called once or twice afterwards to see Catalina, but observing that his visits were by no means agreeable to the gentleman, whose conduct was always sullen and morose to his wife, and almost rude to himself, he did not repeat them.

Poor Catalina, did not long survive. Her married life had been the reverse of happy. Her husband – a gloomy, unfeeling, and ill-tempered man – having heard of her former attachment, and knowing the strong repugnance she had to a marriage with himself, had always treated her with harshness and unkindness; and any manifestation of pleasure on her part in society, particularly in that of gentleman with whom she happened to be acquainted in her unmarried days, was sure to excite his jealousy and ill-humour. Even now, however, while I grieve over the hapless fate and early death of poor Catalina, busy imagination carries me back to the time of my first visit to Minorca, dwelling, with melancholy satisfaction, on the many thoughtless, happy hours I passed there in her company and that of her cousins. Many an evening did a party of us from the *Sultan* spend, from seven o'clock till ten, in the little garden attached to Don Pedro's house. There, seated in an arbour composed of the jasmin, the

---

* The late Dr John Somers Down, whose recent death is universally regretted by all his friends, and by none more so than by the writer of these pages

myrtle, and the vine, with the three cousins, and sometimes Geronimo, we enjoyed the balmy freshness of the evening, after the oppressive heat of a sultry day, and formed as merry and happy a group as ever assembled for amusement. We laughed, and chatted, and made horrid attempts at Minorquin. Some breathed an havanna, – some quaffed 'vino de Alayor', drawn up from a well at hand, one hundred feet deep, into which it had been plunged for the purpose, and made icy cool by immersion, – while the gentle Antonia would sing, from time to time, some soft seguidilla to the guitar, or, joined by Geronimo, give some stanzas of 'Una muchacha inocente', &c. Finding it difficult to pronounce our harsh northern names, the ladies had bestowed upon us such sobriquets as they thought corresponded with our manners and appearance. One was named 'Clemencia', another, 'Loque mas aprecio'; a third, 'Cosita, color de rosa'; and a fourth, 'Mortification'. With such instructors, we began to make some progress in Minorquin, and, like Don Juan,

> Learned our alpha beta better
> From Beauty's eye than any graven letter.

Thus flew the first days and weeks that I passed at Mahon – the idlest, but, I must confess, some of the most agreeable that I have spent in the navy; and, when time brought round the moment of departure, we were surprised at the quickness of its flight, and not a little grieved at parting from friends, who, by that time, had taught us to call them 'Hermanitas'.

We joined the fleet off Toulon about the middle of August. It then consisted of eleven sail of the line, under the command of Admiral Thornborough, in the absence of Lord Collingwood; while the French fleet in the outer harbour, and ready for sea, numbered thirteen of the line and four frigates. This my first cruise off Toulon lasted many weeks, without being marked by any circumstance well worth recording.

Most parts of the Mediterranean are subject to be visited by thundersqualls, in which the lightning frequently causes considerable mischief; and it was remarked that the atmosphere was more than commonly charged with electric matter in the autumn of 1808 – scarcely an evening passing, during several weeks, without a display of fireworks in the heavens. These squalls happening at night, are often attended with danger; and it requires some coolness, attention, and skill, on the part of the officer on the watch, to guard against accidents, and, when in heavy gusts and sudden shifts of wind, the fleet is taken aback, and the whole order of sailing is deranged, to extricate his own ship from the confusion, and place her in a clear and safe position, until the squall be passed, and the wind assume once more a true and steady direction. Sometimes it is curious, and not a little interesting, to mark the gathering and approach of these squalls.

One night I went on deck to keep the first watch, and found the weather beautifully serene and fine. The fleet was standing off the land, with a light breeze from the eastward. There was no moon, but the stars shone clear and bright, and not a cloud was visible, save one dark line that marked the verge of the western horizon, along which was playing, in fitful flashes, the summer lightning. By nine o'clock, my attention was called by what seemed the report of a gun, or the rumbling sound of distant thunder. The dark line, or bank, to the westward, had risen higher out of the water, extending itself gradually to the right and left, and the lightning came from it now in distinct flashes, followed, at long intervals, by the deep growl of the still distant thunder. All this time the sky remained clear and cloudless to the eastward, and the breeze still filled the sails, and kept the ship well under command. At first the motion of the cloud, whose direction was always to windward, was gradual and slow; but in its progress, as it gathered weight and size, it advanced with greater rapidity.

By eleven o'clock, a pall of 'dunnest night' had spread over and quite obscured the one half of heaven, each flash of lightning now revealing all its threatening blackness only to leave the gloom still deeper and more intense. It now fell calm, and for a brief space there was a pause – a struggle it seemed aloft which wind should have the mastery. The topsails were lowered on the cap – the braces and buntlines set taught – the watch kept on the alert – and the ship, under fore-topmast and mizen-staysails, awaited the coming squall. Our suspense was short: soon the storm burst, and with a crash that shook and seemed to rend the ship to her kelson. Such an elemental strife I never witnessed! The very heavens seemed on fire: the lightning flamed, not in fitful flashes, but with one continued blaze of blinding light: uninterrupted deafening thunder, which whole salvoes of artillery could but poorly imitate, tore the air: the wind blew in heavy, shifting gusts, and the rain came down with the weight and volume of a cataract, making it almost impossible for the men to stand its force and keep their legs. In a moment the whole fleet was in confusion. Our second ahead, being taken aback, came round on her heel, with her head pointed for our bows: our next astern, her topsails still at the mastheads, had her flying jib-boom nearly over our taffrail; while a third was coming up to leeward, stemming for our larboard beam; – so that to avoid collision was not a little difficult, in such weather, and in such a situation. Fortunately, the *Sultan* was forewarned, and a good deal prepared for what might occur.

When the squall came, the wind first struck the ship on the starboard beam, and found the topsails on the cap and the yards squared; so that a pull of the larboard braces, and shifting the staysail sheets over, at once filled the sails, and kept the ship under command. An opening was observed on our weather-bow; and, by luffing, we were enabled to draw out clear of our neighbours ahead and astern, and to place the ship in such a position that we might avoid any others that should be thrown out by the suddenness and violence of the squall. In less than an hour, the fury of the tempest began to moderate. Gradually it passed away to the east, a flash of lightning from time to time showed that it still lingered in that quarter. Again our topsails assumed their positions at the mast-heads, and the different ships were seen pushing up to regain their stations. Such nights as those, passed in a fleet, try men's nerves and resources, and assist in forming the quick and ready officer. A few topsails split, and a few spars sprung, was the only damage which the fleet suffered from the squall; upon which occasion the *Sultan* escaped altogether scathless. But this really awful storm reminds me of another time when she was not so fortunate, and when that mysterious and Almighty Being, who rules the storm, and wields and directs the lightning's force – sometimes for weal, sometimes for woe – suffered it to be felt in all its destructive power and strength.

In October the *Sultan* was sent to Mahon to water, and during one of the few days we remained there she experienced one of those fearful visitations that are calculated to arrest the attention of the most thoughtless and unreflecting, and strike every beholder with wonder and with awe. The early part of the morning had been wet, but the rain ceased in the course of the forenoon, and the sails were loosed to dry. The boats had returned from watering, and the ship's company were at dinner, when heavy clouds to the south-east warned the first lieutenant to furl. My station was the poop, and the more than common blackness of the cloud which was right ahead, and its threatening aspect, rivetted my attention.

The men had been a short time on the yards, and were on the point of laying in, when from it came one bright and dazzling flash, followed, as quickly as the report follows the discharge of a gun, by a loud and deafening peal of thunder, reverberating from shore to shore, so that the ship actually shook and trembled beneath the concussion. Attracted by the head-spars, the lightning followed the direction of the jib-booms and bow-sprit, without touching them, exhausting its force in the head and forecastle. But though it left the spars uninjured, its flight was marked in other respects, with the most heart-rending and appalling consequence. Not one of the men that were furling the head-sails escaped without a wound. In an instant of time the living spirit of nine human beings was quenched for ever, and more than that number were seriously injured. Four of the killed dropped without a struggle into the water, and the remaining five, that a moment before were fraught with life and animated exertion, now lay black and stiffened corses, their feet resting on the horses, and their chests pressed against the jib-booms, as if still in the act of furling the sails. For one instant, the twinkling of an eye it might be, a spot, the size of a large metal button, burned on the breast of one of the unhappy suffers, with white-heat intensity, and then became extinct.

When the bodies of the men that were killed were brought upon deck, they were found discoloured almost to blackness, and swollen to double their ordinary size. Those which fell into the water rose to the surface on the following morning – so soon had decomposition set in. They were all interred in the Protestant burial-ground, inclosed by the English when the island was in our possession; not, however, without considerable opposition on the part of the Spanish authorities, instigated, no doubt, by the clergy, who would gladly deny the right of sepulture to all 'heretics', and consign them, with their sins all thick and blossoming upon them, to the safe custody of him who rules below.

Independent of this grievous visitation, and the awful, the startling suddenness with which nine human beings were hurried into eternity, the loss to the ship of so many able seamen was a serious misfortune, and one that could not be replaced on the Mediterranean station; and several others were so maimed or badly injured that they were obliged to be invalided and sent home.

Finding his presence no longer necessary at Cadiz, where, by his advice and assistance, he had put things in the best train he could, Lord Collingwood rejoined the fleet off Toulon about the beginning of October.

His was no ordinary charge at this period. The aspect of the times, and the unsettled, feverish state of affairs all around the shores of the Mediterranean, from Gibraltar to Constantinople, and from the Gulf of Lyons to Egypt, demanded unremitting care and vigilance, in the management of which the utmost forethought, delicacy, and firmness were required. The States of Barbary had to be kept in friendship and good humour, as upon them Gibraltar mainly, and the fleet in great measure, depended for various indispensable supplies.

Our relations with Turkey were not re-established upon an amicable footing, and it was of moment, and required great tact and discretion, to preserve friendly relations with the ruler of Albania, and awaken his jealousy of the designs of Bonaparte, whose acquisition of the Seven Islands, and along the northern shore of the Adriatic, might serve as a lure to the cupidity, and also as a step to the further encroachments of his insatiate ambition. Besides all which he had to detach from a fleet, which, if all united, was barely sufficient to watch the port of Toulon, to Sicily, menaced with invasion by Murat, to the coast of Italy, and to Catalonia, where the bold and energetic co-operation of one of his ships of the line long retarded the fall of Rosas, at that time besieged and hotly pressed by the French. These unavoidable detachments reduced our weak fleet at one time to ten sail of the line, and as one out of that number was always at Mahon completing her water, it left Lord Collingwood with but nine to cope with fourteen of the enemy's ships, should they venture out of port. These are a few, and only a few, of the many cares and responsibilities, obvious to every one in the fleet possessed of the least reflection, which claimed the attention and pressed upon the mind of the Commander-in-Chief.

A correspondence which embraced every quarter of his station, to say nothing of that which the management of a widely-dispersed fleet demands, confined him to his desk, and wasted a frame never, perhaps, the most robust, by that ceaseless, anxious toil of the head, often more fatal to health than the greatest exertion and fatigue of the body. But Lord Collingwood was not the man either to neglect or shrink from duty when his country required his services. Though languishing and pining for home, and told by his medical adviser that total rest of mind and body, and entire relaxation from care and duty, were absolutely necessary for the restoration of his health, he could not be prevailed upon to quit his post. To his urgent request to be released from his charge, and have a successor appointed to the command, the First Lord of the Admiralty had replied that, 'if he left the Mediterranean he did not know how adequately to supply his place' – and that was enough. If his country required it, he was content to sacrifice the remnant of a life which was already nearly worn out in its service.

Bred to the sea, where the greater part of his active and useful life had been passed, Nature seems to have designed Lord Collingwood for the tranquil pursuits and quiet enjoyments of the domestic circle, rather than for those of stormy scenes, and that busy stretch of mind and body which make such inroads upon the days and nights of the sailor and the statesman. Of him it may truly be said that he sacrificed to his country, and to a rigid sense of duty, not only the tastes and pleasures which he most dearly valued, but that the same feelings bore him to a somewhat untimely grave – and that, too, by a kind of death which demands more fortitude to face, and claims a nation's sympathy and gratitude ten times more than had he fallen in battle. And yet posterity will hardly believe that to this truly noble-minded man, one who had achieved so much, and was so attached, so devoted a servant to his King and country – whose health had long languished, until it finally gave way, under the pressure of overwrought exertion of mind and body in their service – that the Government of the day denied to a man like this the only boon he ever asked, viz., that, 'as he had daughters, but no son, his well-earned honours might descend in the female line'. Still less will they credit that a similar favour was conferred a short time before on a nobleman, to compare whose merits and services with those of Lord Collingwood would be a mockery to all acquainted with the history of the great men of their country. So that, while the peerage is graced with the name of Barham,* that of Collingwood is blotted from its pages for ever!!!

12: In the Gulf of Genoa

The *Sultan* lost no time in rejoining the fleet off Toulon, from whence, in the beginning of November, she was detached on a cruise in the Gulf of Genoa, to the no small delight of the whole crew; for besides varying the scene from the tameness and insipidity of blockade, we were cheered with the hope of some active boat service, always agreeable to sailors, and what is hardly less acceptable, a little prize-money – its customary reward.

In detaching a ship of the line from a fleet which could so ill spare one at the time, the Commander-in-Chief's object was to harass and interrupt the coasting trade, the only one the enemy ventured to carry on – to beat up that part of the coast of Italy, keeping its inhabitants on the '*qui vive*', and to get all the information that could be obtained touching the feeling and disposition of the Italians, showing them, if they were weary of French dominion, that there were friends at hand ready and willing to assist them in shaking it off.

For some time Bonaparte had felt anxious and uneasy as to the movements and intentions of Austria. That Power had of late greatly augmented her armies, and assumed a warlike attitude; and to all his remonstrances on the subject, had returned evasive and unsatisfactory answers. Italy was therefore drained of French troops, as well to maintain the efficiency of the corps in Germany, should a rupture break out in that quarter, as to supply the enormous waste of soldiers, which the service and losses

* His grandson in the female line is now Earl of Gainsborough.

in Spain continually required. If the Italians were dissatisfied with French rule, it was reasonable to suppose that they would gladly seize upon such a moment to arise and make an effort to throw it off. But to obtain information, that could be relied upon, as to their real feelings and intentions, was a matter of extreme difficulty, indeed, I may say, impossible.

Aware that there was a strong party always opposed to his authority in Italy, and that a time so favourable for tampering with his subjects in that country would not be overlooked by his enemies, the French Emperor had given the strictest injunctions to all authorities, under the severest penalties, to use twofold vigilance and caution in preventing all intercourse with foreigners, particularly the English. All fishermen on the coast were forbid, under pain of forty days' quarantine for a first, and imprisonment, with forfeiture of the boat, for a second offence, to hold any communication with strangers, or to suffer their boats to be boarded at sea under any circumstances or pretence whatever. If known to transgress, this punishment was rigidly inflicted; but as they never ventured far from the land, and used every effort to escape when chased, they never incurred it, unless surprised at night, – a thing of rare occurrence.

During our cruise of two months, we had much to amuse and keep the attention alive, and both mind and body employed, reconnoitring or chasing by day, and the boats frequently away by night. Upon the latter service, the lieutenants took it in turn to command night and night about in succession; and in this manner we contrived, like the Scotsman, to pick up a few 'wee things alang shore'. Sometimes in sweeping the shore by night with the boats, we surprised a luckless wight in an open roadstead; or creeping along under cover of the darkness, when not a shot was fired, or trigger drawn, but more frequently we had to bring them off from situations more difficult to get at them. When chased by day, and unable to gain an anchorage where they could have the protection of soldiers and batteries, their usual plan was to shove the vessel into some little cove, scooped out of that steep, iron-bound coast, and dropping an anchor, veer till she nearly touched the rocks; a hawser fast to the stern-post or rudder beneath the water-line, and one from the mainmast-head, was then taken ashore, and there secured. That done, the crew all landed, and each armed with a musket, manned every bush and projecting crag that served to cover their persons, and then quietly awaited the approach of the cruiser's boats.

One morning two settee-rigged vessels of large size, were seen to come out of Spezzia, and steer to the westward. Chase was immediately given; but as the wind was off the land, and very light, it took us a long time to close with them, and we only succeeded by dark in compelling them to seek refuge in a small bay near Sestri, where the shore is rugged and precipitous, and the water deep close to the base of the rocks. Here, at sundown, we saw them anchor; and as soon as it was dark, the boats were sent to try and bring them out. The distance from the shore was not more than five or six miles; and as the position in which the vessels had anchored was accurately set by compass before dark, they were soon found. When the men boarded, they found the vessels were laden with charcoal, which was piled high upon deck; but they were completely abandoned, not a soul was to be seen, and all was perfectly still and quiet. The night was clear and bright, and the moon, which rose above the land, cast a stream of light far out to sea, but left the shore and little bay in which the vessels were moored, dark and undefined, The cables were soon in the men's hands; but when they were hauled upon, the vessels did not move.

It was perceived at once that they must be secured to the shore, and the men moved aft, two going over the stern to look for, and cut the fastenings. Then, and not till then, the shore gave signs of life. Every bush, and craggy projection on the face of the cliff, where men could find a footing, sparkled at once, with a sudden flash, and a shower of hissing balls came pattering against the sides, masts, and decks of the vessels. Little mischief was done by this opening fire, and the men were got under shelter. After the lapse of a considerable time, and much trouble in groping, the hawser of one of the vessels which bound her to the shore was found and cut. Still when the cable was hove upon, she stirred not. All this time the fellows on shore did not relax their fire, though happily without any harm. As the vessel was all afloat, and the stern hawser severed, everybody was puzzled to conjecture what could now hold her. At length, in casting his eyes aloft, one of the men, more clear-sighted than the others, thought he saw a line extending from the mainmast-head to the shore; and although the moon shone with great brilliancy, displaying every object above the hulls of the vessels so distinctly, that the man who ventured into the rigging would become a target, against which every musket on shore was sure to be levelled, he volunteered to go aloft and cut it.

Taking his open knife in his mouth, to be used when he got aloft, the stout-hearted sailor was soon in the rigging, and had 'shinned' two-thirds of the way up (there were no rattlings), when a ball struck his left arm; and although it did not bring him down by the run, it compelled him to let himself down without accomplishing his object. Another volunteer took his place; but scarcely did his head appear above the pile of charcoal, which hid the lower part of the rigging from view, than he was wounded severely, the ball penetrating between the shoulders, and coming out under his right breast, without however touching anything that was vital. There was now a pause for a few minutes. The Lieutenant was unwilling to expose any more men to a fire, which seemed so unerring, and yet he did not like to return to his ship foiled in his object by the crews of a couple of merchantmen. After considering a short time, he bethought him of a stratagem, which, without much risk to his men, appeared likely to prove successful. A boat-hook staff was procured, and a short spar, in length about the breadth of a man's shoulders, rigged athwart it, so as to form a latin cross. Upon this was hung a man's jacket, beneath which dangled a pair of trousers, and a hat surmounted the whole. When complete, the figure made no bad representation of the 'human form divine', and might easily have deceived in a light less dubious than the moon's.

As soon as all was ready, the man of wood and wool was shown in the rigging, being made to imitate the jerking motion of a man in the act of 'shinning' aloft. The men on shore had been for some time anxiously straining their eyes in the direction of the vessels for an object to fire at, so that as soon as the image was visible every musket was discharged simultaneously, and the figure made to disappear as if brought down by the volley.

An active, resolute fellow, Bill Turnbull by name, was held in readiness for this event, and the flash of the muskets was no sooner seen than he sprang into the rigging, and before the men on shore had time to reload and have another shot, he had mounted aloft, cut the rope, and was on deck again, amid the cheers and hurrahs of his admiring comrades. To haul the vessel off to her anchor was now the work of a moment; and, although the fellows on shore plied their muskets quick and well, one man more only was touched in getting under weigh. They had not been successful in discovering the mast-head fastening in the other craft; the midshipman was therefore hailed and desired to abandon her, and the boats with the prize returned to the ship about midnight.

The captured vessel, a large settee, as has been said, laden with charcoal, poorly compensated for the loss sustained in bringing her out, viz., one man killed, and five badly wounded, in the two boats. But Clemencia* (to call him by his Minorquin name), our third lieutenant, who commanded the boats, although placid in temper and manner, was a very determined fellow, and was stimulated to a little more obstinacy on

* The present Captain Archibald Tisdall, made a Rear-Admiral while this was going through the press.

that night than was judicious, by the difficulties he met, and the casualties the men sustained.

Such is an account of one of a multitude of pieces of service that naval men are engaged in during war, but which are never reported, and consequently never find their way into the gazette, or to the ears of the public.

It was during this cruise that I first set foot upon the classic shore of Italy. The boats, four in number, were sent in shore one fine night, having no definite object in view, but with orders to sweep the coast, and gather up whatever might be found at anchor, or moving along shore under cover of the night. Two midshipmen had charge of two of the boats, I was in a third; the whole being under the command of the first lieutenant.

After closely examining Sestri, and two or three other bays, the names of which I forget, we rowed along shore to the eastward, without falling in with anything. When the boats had proceeded thus a good many miles, and the night was now far advanced, we came to a part of the coast which, generally sheer, rocky, and precipitous, is there a little indented, breaking the uniformity of the line, and, by means of a detached rock, which stands in the centre of the curve, affords tolerable shelter to boats. There the lieutenant in command stopped, having determined to land as soon as it should be light, and then try to gain some eminence, whence he should be able to have a bird's-eye view, and see whatever might be stirring along the shore, and by concealing the men, and keeping the boats hid behind the rock, he could push out if anything approached, and so surprise them before they could be aware of our vicinity.

As soon as morning dawned, leaving two boatkeepers in each boat, the party landed, and, led by the first lieutenant, followed a rill, which had scooped a channel for itself out of the living rock, bringing with it, in its downward course, sufficient soil to nourish a little herbage and a few stunted bushes of myrtle, arbutus, and wild olive, by the aid of which we hoisted ourselves up the steep ascent. After clambering some one hundred and fifty feet, it might be, the most difficult part was surmounted. The remainder of the way, about the same distance, was far less steep, and led to a platform, where the party breathed, and examined the contents of haversacks and canteens. Having refreshed with salt pork and a biscuit, washed down, and levelled by the aid of a little grog, we had leisure to indulge in speculations and conjectures upon what might betide us in the morning.

In about an hour the grey tints of early dawn were visible in the east, and showed us that we had stumbled in the dark upon a most convenient bivouac. The spot where we found ourselves was a kind of flat table-land, of semicircular form, open to the sea, but inland scarped by nature nearly all round, in such a manner as to conceal the party from view of the surrounding country, unless a person approached the very edge of the scarp or precipice, and so looked down. Behind, as far as the eye could see, the ground sloped upwards into vast downs, dotted here and there with low stunted trees, over which browsed and wandered at will a number of animals, the nature of which we could not make out from the distance. Not a hamlet, house, or even signal-station was visible, at the same time, that the line of coast to a considerable extent to the right and left was seen.

As the daylight advanced, and objects became more distinct, the *Sultan* was seen in the offing, her topsails and topgallant-sails idly flapping against the masts, for want of wind to fill them. The mists gathered by the night, and which always hang longer about the shores than they do in the open sea, still hid the coast from our view, and it was not until the land-wind sprang up, and the sun was some degrees above the horizon, that they were sufficiently dispelled to allow us to see things clearly along shore.

Though the breeze gradually freshened, it had not yet reached the *Sultan*, and before her appearance could startle anything, we were in expectation of seeing some craft take advantage of it. In this expectation we were not disappointed, and before many minutes our eyes were gladdened by the sight of a fine polacca ship, and three settees, steering apparently into the jaws of the hungry animals which, cat-like, lay crouched only till they should be near enough to spring upon them. On they came without any suspicion for a full half-hour, when, unfortunately for our plans, the breeze reached the *Sultan*, and, from her making all sail upon a wind, it was evident that she saw the strangers in-shore. The latter, as soon as they saw they were chased by an enemy, tacked, and laid their heads in-shore – a manœuvre that increased, instead of lessening, the distance from the point where the boats lay in ambuscade. It was now evident that the quarry had been scared by the *Sultan*, and were using every effort to gain the shore. So we slid down in the best way we could from our perch, and jumping into the boats with all expedition, stretched out in the direction of the strangers. But, although the crews pulled manfully, and the sails set to assist the rowers, as soon as the boats were discovered, in spite of every exertion, the settees rounded the eastern point of a small bay, the bottom of which was filled up by a town of considerable extent, flanked at either extremity by a battery of three heavy guns. A loud hurrah of encouragement to each other was now given by the men, and they bent to the oars till the boats flew through the water, to try and cut them off before they reached the protection of the guns and musketry of the place. But, although we succeeded in capturing one, the other two ran upon the beach by the time the boats were within range of grape, with which they were plied pretty sharply, but, happily, to very little purpose.

It being evident, from the enemy's force and preparations on shore, that an attempt to bring the grounded vessels off, even if attended with success, must be followed with greater loss than they were worth, the lieutenant in command showed his stern to the shore, and made sail out of the bay with his prize, a three-masted settee, laden with wine for Genoa.

Meantime the polacca, not being able to round the point in time, dropped her anchor a couple of miles to the eastward, and let the cable run out till the swell hove her on the rocks of that iron-bound coast. When we pulled to her we found her abandoned by the crew, with her sails at the mast-heads, and fast upon the rocks, which had already pierced her bottom, and half filled her with water. Her cargo consisted entirely of rags, intended for the paper-mills at Marseilles.

To move her from her position was impracticable; nor, had we succeeded in doing so, would it have been possible to keep her afloat, so effectually had the rocks bored her bottom. We proceeded, therefore, to strip her of her sails, running rigging, and any other ship's furniture likely to prove useful, and afterwards set fire to the hull. This work was not effected without an attempt at interruption from the shore, for the crew of the polacca, aided by a party of the national guard from the neighbouring town, kept up the whole time a random fire of musketry, rendered harmless and unsteady by the grape of the barge's and yawl's carronades, which fired in whatever direction the smoke and flash came from.

Not many days after this occurrence we fitted up a tender, the command of which was given to me, in reward, I believe, for having been successful in bringing out, one night, three vessels from Port Maurice. One, though very small, was valuable for her size, being laden with oil, bales of cloth, and twelve hundred dollars in money. The other two were settees in ballast, one of which was a stout vessel, armed with four light guns, and a crew of twenty men, each provided with a musket and cutlass, which they were only able to discharge once before the barge's crew were up the side, when they fled below without further resistance. The small vessel was cleared of her cargo and then to conciliate the Italians, permitted to return to the shore with the crews of all three. The smaller of the other two was the one selected for a tender, as from her appearance and build, she promised to be the better sailer. She was a two-masted settee, of about fifty or sixty tons, and when fitted with two 4-pounders and a crew of twenty-one, including a midshipman, surgeon's assistant, and myself, cut a very respectable appearance, and was a command that I felt not a little proud of. It was six o'clock in the afternoon when I took charge of the tender, at which time it blew fresh from the S.S.W., with an appearance of an increase of wind and dirty weather. The *Sultan* placed herself under low canvass, took the other prize in tow, and stood to the S.E. on the starboard tack. We followed her example in reefing, and stood off also on the same tack. By nine, the wind had freshened to a gale, knocking up a good deal of sea, and for the first time, since my noviciate at sea, did I feel again what it was to be sea-sick. Never in my life did I pass a more wretched night! With head and stomach racked by that most distressing and subduing of all maladies, '*le mal de mer*', I could not leave the deck during the whole night; first close-reefing the sails, then, when the gale increased, bending and setting the storm-sails, – no easy job in a dark, blowing, and rainy night, on board so small a craft, knocked about with a motion as rapid as that of a light collier riding weather tide in the rolling ground at Harwich.

When this change was accomplished, however, and the heavy main-yard no longer swagged aloft, the little vessel experienced all the benefit of it, rising lightly over the waves like a sea-bird, without shipping a drop of water. As the wind still seemed to increase, and the sea to get up, I thought it better, about two o'clock in the morning, to try the other tack – particularly, as I knew that gales in the gulfs and bays of the Mediterranean are often local and partial. We soon found the advantage of this, for in less than two hours after her head had been put to the W.N.W., the wind had sensibly decreased, and by daylight we had run quite out of the gale. The *Sultan*, on the contrary, by standing on, found, as she approached Corsica, the wind increased to a hurricane; so that, as she drew near the land, she was glad to put the helm up, and shelter herself under Cape Corse. Early in the night the prize in tow broke adrift, and whether the vessel sprung a leak, or had her sails blown away and drifted ashore, I know not; but we afterwards learned that she was wrecked near Leghorn, when the crew were saved, but became prisoners of war.

The following morning, the gale had entirely ceased, and we found ourselves in the tender midway between Corsica and Genoa. My object was to get in with the land in the gulf as quickly as possible; but the wind continuing light from the northward, I was not able to do so for some days. At length a moderate breeze sprang up at west, and by daylight on the following morning, we were not far from the land between Rapallo and Sestri. For some time the mists which hang about the land, and fill up the bays in the early part of the morning, prevented us from discerning objects near the shore very clearly; but, when the rising sun helped to withdraw this veil from before our eyes, a convoy of several vessels under the protection of two armed feluccas, were seen taking advantage of the breeze, and steering to the eastward. The armed vessels were stout, saucy-looking gentlemen, and seemed large enough either of them to hoist the little tender in; therefore an open attempt upon their charge could not be justified in any way by prudence. But, as I observed that two settees lagged a good way astern of the body of the convoy, several of which were rigged like the tender, I hoped we might escape notice, and pass for one of themselves, and thus be able to cut off one if not both of the stragglers. With this object in view, we kept nearly parallel to the course they steered, just edging in a little, so as to near them without exciting their attention.

To take away all semblance of the vessel being armed, tarpaulins, or men's jackets, concealed our little pop-guns, – no unusual number of men appeared on deck at a time, and the few that remained, with the man at the helm, had their waists girt with sashes, and *bonnets rouges* on their heads, after the fashion most in vogue with Mediterranean sailors. But all our wariness and precaution did not lull their suspicion. They had been too well accustomed to the sight of Maltese privateers, – one of which they took us for, I have no doubt.

Before we got very near them, they hauled right in-shore, one firing a gun to alarm the rest of the convoy, and draw the attention of the Commodore; and the wind having by this time fallen very light, they got their sweeps out, and pulled vigorously for the land. It was evident, from these proceedings, that our real character was suspected; and, as the feebleness of the breeze held out no hope of coming up with the tender, our skiff was launched over the side, and six men and the midshipman sent in pursuit. This was a heavy clumsy boat, built for burden, not for speed, with long unwieldy oars; and, therefore, in spite of every exertion, the vessels were secured in the usual way for defence, and their crews on shore, before she got within musket-shot of them. The whole convoy had now taken the alarm, many having repeated the signal-gun, to call the attention of the armed vessels; and the latter, which might be about six or eight miles distant, put their heads round, and, as it was nearly calm, swept in our direction. If our boat succeeded in bringing one of the vessels out, it must be attended with the sacrifice of time now precious to us, – probably with that of life; I therefore judged it prudent to recall her, as we should want all our men together and intact, should the feluccas come up with us, which there was every likelihood of their doing, if a breeze did not spring up.

As we were near the shore, the boat was not long in returning; and, when once more on deck, the tender's head, by the help of her two only sweeps, was kept to the westward. I next bethought me of how to make the most respectable defence, in case the enemy came up with us. The spare sails and hammocks were stowed round the quarters and stern, as a protection against grape and musketry, room being left abaft for one of the little four-pounders, in case of need. Spare ammunition was got on deck, the men's cutlasses were buckled on, and the muskets examined and loaded. Still, when all was done, and we had leisure to mark how sensibly the distance between us and our pursuers was diminishing, our cogitations were anything but pleasant.

Visions of French prisons and gens-d'armes flitted before the imagination; and though the men passed their jokes about 'bed and board without work', they whistled very strenuously for the breeze that mocked their invitation. The calm continued until the chasing vessels were within two miles of us, when a light breeze sprang up from the northward, filling and keeping steady the sails, which for two hours before had been flapping against the masts. The little craft now felt her helm, and began to move through the water. But still the enemy's sweeps helped them, giving them greatly the advantage of us; and by noon the headmost was so much advanced, that she tried a shot at us. Another and another followed, but all fell rather short.

The breeze continued to freshen, and in half-an-hour more the feluccas laid in their sweeps. They now gained very little upon us; and taking the angle with a quadrant, there was little or no perceptible difference in half-an-hour. Of this they soon became aware themselves; for not choosing, perhaps, to separate too far from their convoy, which was now more than hull-down, they gave up the chase, and hauled their wind again to close it. And, to confess the truth, I was not sorry to find they did not persevere. Their near neighbourhood, for the last couple of hours had been anything but agreeable, presenting images of a very uninviting nature to the mind; for I had heard of such things as prisoners being driven through France with a bayonet at their backs to persuade them to greater exertion should they flag, or treated to a 'promenade à cheval', strapped to a surly, fierce looking gens-d'arme.

Giving Rapallo and Genoa, at which there generally lay a man of war brig, a wide berth, I got off Port Maurice by daylight on the following morning, between which place and Villa Franca I cruised for four or five days, without seeing a single sail. Then as the tender was victualled but for three weeks, rather more than two of which had expired, I steered for Mahon, where we arrived in a few days, without anything particular occurring.

My short experience in a tender has satisfied me, that, to be of service, a vessel employed as such should sail well, and, if assailed by anything more than her match, be capable of at least a stout resistance, and also be provided with a fast-rowing boat, or boats (if large enough to stow two). With a vessel of that description, something might be done: but the one I commanded was small, and weakly armed, and sailed no better than the common class of merchant-vessels, of her rig, in the Mediterranean. Then she had nothing but clumsy tub of a boat, large and strong enough to take out or purchase an anchor, if required, but perfectly useless if wanted to chase.

The *Sultan* had not yet arrived; but I found a part of the fleet in Mahon harbour, under the command of Admiral Thornborough. The Commander in Chief, it seemed, kept the sea that winter as long as he could, persevering with great determination during a succession of gales, until one, more violent and lasting than the others drove the fleet to the south-west of Minorca, when it became literally dispersed, after which, when it moderated, the ships straggled by ones and twos, into Mahon, where six or seven had assembled, when we arrived in the tender. Not a ship escaped without loss of sails and spars; and a few were so strained in their hulls, that they were compelled to go to Malta or Gibraltar to refit, and amongst the number, the *Ocean*, Lord Collingwood's flag-ship.

To account for this apparent obstinacy of his Lordship, it is but fair to mention, that Barcelona and Monjui were closely blockaded by the Spanish army, under General Vives, and that he was aware that a squadron was held in readiness at Toulon, to slip out the first favourable opportunity, and throw supplies into those places, the garrisons of which were much pressed at the time for stores and provisions. To defeat an object of such moment, which involved, according to its success or failure, the relief or fall of two such important fortresses, Lord Collingwood resolved to keep the sea; though by so doing, in that tempestuous gulf, and in the winter season, he hazarded the efficiency of his fleet, and his own hard-earned reputation: for, had anything untoward or disastrous resulted from its incomplete and shattered state – no matter the cause, or how strong soever the motive which urged him to risk its falling into such a condition – no excuse would have been listened to; all his former services would have been forgotten, and the name of Collingwood, once so honoured and respected, would have been vituperated and vilified throughout the length and breadth of England. With us, courage, endurance, devotion – nay, self-immolation in our country's cause – are esteemed as nothing: rewards, honours, and applause, await the successful commander alone.

In order to show how partial the gales are in the Mediterranean, and how restricted are their force and direction, I may say, that at the time the fleet off Toulon, which was separated from us by so small a distance, was buffeted about in so furious a manner, the *Sultan*, with the exception of one or two short-lived breezes, experienced in the Gulf of Genoa weather so fine, that there were few nights during her cruise in which her boats might not have been safely sent away upon service.

That winter's cruise was not, however, without its salutary consequence. It convinced Lord Collingwood how impossible it was to keep his station off Toulon, and how useless, in that season of the year, to contend against the storms of the Gulf of Lyons. In future, therefore, he, as well as his successors in the command, very wisely gave up the contest, taking shelter from their fury every winter in Mahon, where the fleet was kept in perfect readiness to put to sea at a moment's notice, whilst a ship of the line and a frigate were left to watch Toulon, and give information of any change or movement which they might observe in the enemy's fleet. The *Sultan* and the remainder of the scattered fleet, except three that had gone to Gibraltar and Malta, arrived at Mahon two or three days after we did in the tender; and a very few more were only necessary to set things once more to rights, and have the ships in condition to put to sea the moment they were required.

13: Blockading Toulon

In a few days after the *Sultan* arrived in Mahon, I delivered over my charge into the hands of the prize-agent, when I returned to my ship. I found that during my absence she had been more successful than the tender, having taken a brig off Nice, with a somewhat valuable cargo from Marseilles bound to Genoa. Part of her lading consisted of several cases of a variety of 'vins de dessert', of exquisite quality, which were disposed of to the officers of the ship at the same price that wines of a similar description would fetch at Gibraltar.

And a very pleasant addition did we find those said wines to be, whenever it fell to our turn in the *Sultan* to give a dinner to our friends in the fleet, and one that seldom failed to allure to our board three sons of Apollo, known in the Mediterranean by the name of the 'three jolly warblers', or the 'generous Nips', whose glees and catches imparted a new charm and zest to those delightful and still well-remembered meetings.

As soon as the prize brig was lightened of the aforesaid cases, she was sent to Gibraltar in charge of Tom Gill, who was chosen for that duty. When arrived there he was to act as part agent, and attend to the condemnation of our various prizes – a matter which could not be done at Minorca, where there was no English Admiralty Court. These duties were well adapted to the business-like habits of Tom Gill, besides which the captain was glad of an opportunity to put a few dollars into his pocket, which the poor fellow's numerous shipwrecks and losses had left very empty.

As soon as he anchored in Mahon harbour, and found himself in the temporary command, Admiral Thornborough gave an order little calculated to reconcile men to restriction and privation, or nourish that contentment, cheerful obedience, and zeal for the service, so necessary to the efficiency and well-being of either fleet or army. By this order, the seamen of the fleet were prohibited from going on shore at all on leave, and all officers under the rank of captain were required to be on board their respective ships at gun-fire.

It was early in the month of January, 1809, when the fleet sought refuge in Mahon from the tempestuous weather of that stormy winter. Carnival, that most joyous season of the year in Roman Catholic countries, was about to commence, and the officers of the fleet consequently felt the hardship of being confined to their ships at such a time the more grievous, being prevented from sharing in the gaieties and festivities in progress, and that from the whim or caprice of an officer who finds himself accidentally in command, and thinks proper to give an order which Lords Nelson and Collingwood never found it necessary to issue.

We of the *Sultan*, however, were but little affected by it. Captain Griffith's sentiments and opinions, with regard to the relaxation to be allowed to officers and men when in port, were known to us all. We knew that he wished us to have every fair indulgence which the well-being of the service admitted; and so long as the duties of the ship were well and efficiently performed, that he would not be too curious to ascertain that the late order was complied with to the very letter.

As soon as the ship was refitted and completely ready for sea, as many of the officers as were not required for duty generally paid a visit to the shore every evening; and as a masked ball took place each night of the Carnival at the 'Posada Alexandrina', that was our chief point of attraction. It was at those balls that we took our first lessons in the waltz and *contradansa Española*, in despite of sundry *carambas*, and other Spanish expletives, forced from the patient dancers against whom we blundered, and upon whose toes we trod, in our many awkwardnesses; ay, and persevered to, with a constancy so untiring, that we mastered their difficulties and intricacies, so as at last to pass muster with the most fastidious *ballador* of them all.

But our amusements were not confined to the evenings: we made excursions into the country; we climbed Monte Toro, and dined with the sleek and jovial brethren of the Augustine monastery at its summit.

As spring advanced, we had pic-nic parties in various chosen spots of the island; the most favourite of which was an orange-grove at Alayor, where bunches of fragrant silvery blossoms contrasted on the same trees with the green and golden fruit.

Occasionally too, to vary the thing, we had our *petits dîners* at a kind of restaurant in George Town, kept by a Frenchman, who was miraculously saved from the wreck of *L'Orient*, when that ship blew up at the battle of the Nile. At that time he was filling the important office of *chef de cuisine* to Admiral Brueys, the commander-in-chief of the French fleet; and well did the talents and acquirements of Pierre Brissat merit a situation of such trust and responsibility. When dressed in a linen jacket of spotless purity, from whose too strict embrace his portly person seemed struggling to be free – a cotton cap, varied at times for one of paper, on his head – his ample waist girt with an apron, that 'badge of all his tribe', which turned up at an angle allowed his well-knit limbs, clothed in nankeen smalls and snow-white stockings, to be seen to much advantage, with some implement of his art in his hand; and thus arrayed, Pierre presented in his person the beau ideal of a *professeur*. What, though Minorca could not boast the same variety and profusion of delicacies which the markets of Paris supplied, still Pierre always contrived that his *petits plats* should be found exquisite, and his pâtés de bécassines, his salmis d'alouettes, and côtelettes à la Provençale, would have done no discredit to the artistes of Abbeville, Very's, or the Trois Frères.

Before we left port this time, the officers of the *Sultan* gave a ball, to which all the *élite* of the Mahoneses, and our friends in the fleet, were invited. And an admirable suite of rooms for such a purpose may be arranged on ship-board. The mizen-stay is cast off below, and the *legs* made fast round the mainmast-head. From the centre of this support, a spare maintop-sail drops in form of a lofty dome, and embraces in its folds the whole quarter-deck. The carronades are dismounted, and when the slides are slued fore and aft, cushioned and covered with flags, you have as luxurious seats and sofas as were ever fashioned by the most expert upholsterer – at least, I thought so at the time. The architect next tries his hand at decoration, and shows his taste in the arrangement of flags, flowers, and green boughs, with which the interior should be ornamented; and then, if lit with variegated lamps (ours were procured from the churches at Mahon), and the hanging stanchions under the half-deck knocked up to give play and elasticity to the planks above, the whole forms a most pleasing *coup d'œil*, and an enviable ball-room. The fore-part of the poop is very well adapted for the orchestra, while the afterpart, now lone and deserted, may serve as a retreat to some solitary couple, who, fatigued with the dance and heat of the ball-room, prefer its fresh-ness and quiet, and to look out upon the sober light of the moon and stars, to the glare and heat below, and the oftentimes troublesome and too-curi-ous gaze of the gay and giddy crowd. The Captain's cabin answers the purpose of a cardroom, and the supper tables may be spread under the half deck, and prolonged as far forward as necessary. Hence it may be seen that sailors, in spite of the confinement, manage to enjoy and amuse themselves, whether at sea or in harbour; and although the splenetic Dr Johnson may have likened a ship to a prison, assigning to its inmates the very consolatory alternative of being drowned or blown up, they contrive to render it far from intolerable, dreaming little all the while of the fear-ful casualties and dangers to which the worthy Doctor said they were hourly exposed.

During the time the fleet remained in harbour, 'Tisdall' and I, in company with a gentleman of Mahon, rode across the island to Ciudadella. Except Monte Toro, and one or two other little elevations of little note, the whole of Minorca is flat, bare of tree, and its general aspect brown and arid. The road passes through the villages of Alayor, Mercadel, and Ferrarias, which are small and mean-looking, but the ground has a greener and more cultivated appearance in their neighbour-hoods. Alayor, indeed, is rather celebrated for the goodness and flavour of its light red wine, and also for the firmness and delicacy of its pork, from which a delicious kind of sausage, called 'Sobresada', is manufactured.

Although the capital of the island, and a walled town, Ciudadella, when we saw it was fast crumbling to decay. Its streets were deserted; many of its houses unoccupied; its walls and towers ruinous; and the har-bour, empty of vessels, fast filling up: in short, the whole impressed one with the idea when we arrived, of decrepitude and old age. It was late in the day, but there was still sufficient light to allow us to ramble through the town and down to the habour, which having done, we betook our-selves to the wretched Posada la Cruz de Malta, a favourite sign in the islands and parts adjacent of Spain.

We had made the acquaintance of a certain Frayle, who managed to pass most of his time at Mahon, though his convent was at Ciudadella. Neither the disposition, temperament, nor tastes of Padre Bru (the name of our friend), meant him for a recluse. His tall, robust, full figure, – sanguine complexion, deepening to a more purple shade as years advanced, – his arch blue eye, and somewhat voluptuous mouth, plainly spoke the contrary. He was by no means averse to the good things of the table; and as his gregarious propensities led him to court the society of his kind, *le beau sexe* included, it was natural that he should prefer Mahon, where he had 'troops of friends', and where his frank, jovial character, and agreeable manners and accomplishments, always made him a welcome guest, to the solitude and insipidity of his dreary convent. This preference seduced him into numerous scrapes. Divers were the excuses that he made to get permission to visit Mahon, and when they failed, and further leave was denied him by reason of his invariably outstaying the time for which it had been granted, sundry were the escapades that he made from thraldom, eluding the vigilance of the porters, under various devices and disguises, by which he incurred the scandal of the whole convent, as well as the sharp rebuke, and it was whispered, sometimes even the castigation, of the superiors.

To many other attractive acquirements, Padre Bru added a considerable knowledge of music. He was a finished guitarist, and in a fine 'Lablache' voice, sang with infinite humour and expression every bacchanalian and anacreontic song, I believe, that the languages of Spain and Italy could furnish. From what has been said, it will be readily inferred that solitude and retirement were gall and wormwood to a disposition such as Padre Bru's: and truth to say, to hear him after dinner, with a volume of voice that would fill St Paul's, sing one of his songs, or see him striding along between Ciudadella and Mahon with a Spanish cloak thrown over one shoulder, while the opposite hand grasped his heavy orange-tree walking staff, few would take the stalwart figure before them for a monk of the strict and austere order of the Holy St Francis. He had been made acquainted with our intention to visit Ciudadella, and we found him at the inn door ready to receive us. Submitting ourselves to him with all docility as to an accomplished guide, we sallied forth to take a cursory glance at the town, its harbour and battlements, and then returned to discuss such things as the Posada had provided for our entertainment. When we had dined and heard a few of the Frayle's choice songs, and no less amusing stories, we betook ourselves to our apartments, but not rest: for we found our bed peopled with myriads of *petites bêtes* which stung and worried us all the night, setting the power of the sleep-compelling god completely at defiance, aided though it was by the exercises and fatigue of the day's ride from Mahon. At dawn we sprang from our uneasy beds, leaving our relentless and persevering enemies in undisputed possession of the field; and rejoiced to be rid of them at any sacrifice, we descended to the Sala, when we found that our friend was already arrived, and busy in the kitchen, preparing what he called 'chocolate de los Frayles', 'cosa excelente', he said 'para expeler el viento del estomago', a kind of beverage, half honey, half brandy, warmed so as to render the honey fluid, and which upon trial we did not think so palatable as the worthy friar.

Having dispatched our 'morning', we proceeded under his guidance to view a natural cave, which lies about three miles to the S.E. of the town. This cavern does not sink to any great depth below the surface of the ground, which is flat all around: but it branches into numerous chambers or compartments of various proportions and dimensions, some much loftier than others. One of the latter is named 'la Catedral', from its resembling very much the interior of a church, with its transept and nave, separated from the side aisles by a range of columns on either hand. Many of the chambers sparkled and glittered with spar and stalactites, emitting a variety of brilliant and dazzling hues with the changing position of the torches as we moved from room to room. Reminded at length, despite the friar's chocolate, by certain monitory pangs in the region which the learned call epigastric, that we had not breakfasted, we emerged from the caverns and wended our way back to the inn. A walk of some six or seven miles, with the brisk morning air, and a dip beneath the surface of the earth, imparted a wonderful relish to as rude a breakfast as ever I sat down to, after which we took a hasty glance at Padre Bru's convent, and then mounted our steeds and returned to Mahon.

Early in March, Lord Collingwood rejoined the fleet, soon after which, we sailed to resume our station off Toulon. We found the French fleet in much the same state as it was in the last December: thirteen sail of the line and five frigates, in a forward state to put to sea when required. The weather was still almost as unsettled and boisterous as in the winter. Leaving therefore the *Sultan* and *Pomone* frigate, to watch the port of Toulon, his Lordship bore up with the remainder of the fleet for Minorca, under the lea of which the ships would be sheltered, and at the same time ready to proceed in whatever direction they might be required.

Nothing could exceed the fury of the gales during the three weeks that we remained out. After having been driven perhaps eight or ten leagues to the southward, by which time old Boreas from his exertions had blown himself out of breath, and by taking advantage of his exhaustion, just as we had recovered our station, and ascertained that the enemy's ships were all safe in harbour, without the least warning, without a frown or angry look on the face of heaven, whiff! would come one blast from his re-invigorated lungs, and compel us to reduce the canvass in ten minutes from royals to storm staysails, with top-gallant masts on deck. Once, in one of these squalls, such was the strength of the wind, that it blew the storm staysails to ribands, pressing upon the ship with such a weight that she lay with her lee lower deck ports under water. There was no sea on, but all around the water was as white and yeasty as if scourged by the fury of an African tornado. The eddy wind under her lee drenched the decks with spray, and flung it in showers over the mast heads. The atmosphere all the time was perfectly clear and dry, and the evaporation in consequence was so rapid, that the rigging became incrusted with salt, insomuch, that ballast baskets full which had fallen from aloft were swept from the decks the following morning. I allude to these trifling circumstance merely to show the kind of weather which may be expected to be met with off Toulon, and the extreme difficulty which even a single ship will find in preserving her station, at certain seasons of the year, off that port.

After a most stormy cruise of four or five weeks, in which we lost some spars and sails, and which strained the ship a good deal, we rejoined the fleet off Minorca. We found Lord Collingwood's flag in the *Ville de Paris*, which ship had been sent from England to relieve the *Ocean*, rendered quite unserviceable by the gales of last winter. Some other ships had likewise joined, which rendered the fleet respectable, and now strong enough to give a good account of the enemy's, should it ever be met with at sea. Several circumstances conduced to detain the Admiral in the neighbourhood of Minorca. Besides that the continued inclemency of the weather was of itself sufficient to make him choose a more sheltered position for the fleet, he had received information that a strong squadron of the enemy's ships had escaped from Brest, and as he thought their destination was probably the Mediterranean, he was unwilling to quit the vicinity of the island, lest in his absence the French should, in passing up, make a descent upon it, when from its defenceless state, every soldier having been withdrawn to reinforce the army in Catalonia, its capture was inevitable. And to add to his perplexity, while he was in suspense as to the fate of this squadron, the Junta of Seville, the then Supreme Government in Spain, sent up a division of the French army taken at Baylen, amounting to five thousand men, to be lodged at Mahon, where there were just eighty militia men to look after them. The arrival of this body of men, who only wanted arms to make them an army at once, threw the whole island into consternation. But the Admiral kept them on board the transports, not suffering them to land until he represented the danger of such a step in the unprotected state of Minorca to the proper quarter, when it was arranged that they should be disembarked on the uninhabited island of Cabrera, where there was not a single shed to shelter them, and where very likely the whole would very speedily have perished from want, had not Lord Collingwood supplied them with rations all the time they were upon the island, which, as well as I can remember, exceeded a year.

Towards the end of April, the fleet, which had gone into Mahon to water and revictual, had just cleared the harbour, when intelligence reached the Admiral that a squadron of the enemy had been seen off Barcelona three days before. There was every probability, that by using despatch, we might intercept them on their return to port. No time was therefore lost in making sail, and the Admiral steered a course which was thought the best to effect that object. The following day the leading frigate took two transports with invalid soldiers from Barcelona, and from them it was learned that the French squadron, after supplying that garrison with provisions, had returned to Toulon, where we had the mortification to see them safely anchored the next morning. We found, afterwards, that we crossed their route just ten hours after they had passed.

Nothing that I can call to mind occurred off Toulon during the remainder of the spring and summer; at the end of which, the *Sultan* was again despatched upon a short cruise into the Gulf of Genoa. But this time she was not so successful in making captures as she had been in the previous winter. This was owing, partly to the greater caution observed by the enemy's vessels in venturing out of port during the long days in summer, and partly to the absence of two of our boats, which unfortunately separated from the ship not many days after we got into the Gulf, and which we did not again recover during the remainder of the cruise.

Three boats, victualled for three days, had been sent in-shore under the command of the first lieutenant, who had discretionary power to remain out a second day and night should he think it advisable to do so, a rendezvous having been fixed upon, where the ship was to pick up the boats. The next day the *Sultan* ran along shore to the eastward, under easy sail, until she reached the appointed station, when she hove to; but although nothing was seen of the boats for that day or night, no apprehensions were entertained for their safety, as the officer who had charge of them had authority to prolong his cruise another day if he pleased. The following day, about noon, the yawl came alongside; but nothing was seen of the other boats, though a gun was fired every half hour throughout the day, to draw their attention and point out the ship's position, should they be within hearing. The account given by the midshipman of the yawl, was this: the three boats had chased a felucca to the eastward the evening before. The wind was light, and they used their oars as well as sails; but the yawl was a dull sailer, and the other boats soon outstripped her, leaving her far behind. By sunset the boats, as well as chase, were out of sight, but the flash of musketry was seen, and the report of a gun heard from time to time. The musketry might have lasted ten minutes or a quarter of an hour, and the report of the gun sometime longer, when they ceased, and all was still. The yawl continued to pull in the direction they were last seen and heard until midnight, when, recollecting that they were considerably to the eastward of the point off which the ship was to pick them up, the midshipman put the boat's head round, and pulled leisurely back to the westward, expecting to be rejoined by his comrades in the morning. He waited some hours after daylight, but nothing was to be seen of them, when, observing the *Sultan* in the offing, he pulled out from under the land, and reached the ship, as has already been said, about noon.

The *Sultan* remained upon the rendezvous firing guns every half hour in the day; and when night came on, burning blue lights, and throwing up rockets from time to time, by way of pointing out the ship's position to them. But we waited there in vain – no boats came near us; and when many days had passed, and still they came not, and when answers were returned to the flags of truce which had been sent into Genoa and Leghorn, that 'nothing was known or had been heard of the missing boats', the Captain and everybody in the ship became seriously alarmed. It threw a damp upon the spirits of the whole crew; and while it curtailed the power, it checked all ardour for enterprise during the rest of the cruise. Indeed, we were glad when it was at an end, and the time for leaving the Gulf arrived, for we clung to the hope that something might be learned of our absent shipmates, when we returned to the fleet.

We rejoined the fleet off Toulon towards the end of September, where, in a few minutes after we hove to, all our anxieties were relieved, and we had the happiness of finding our long-missing friends in health and safety.

It seems, that the evening they chased the felucca, they gained upon her so far by sunset as to exchange musketry with her; but with all their efforts they could not get alongside. The wind, which had been light, was gradually increasing, and the boats for some time just held their own. Soon, however, it freshened so much, that their oars were no longer of any use, and it was evident that the chase was stealing away from them.

In a few minutes the musketry ceased on both sides; and as darkness rapidly came on, it was only as long as the felucca continued to fire her stern chasers, that the flash revealed her position to those in the boats. When she discontinued firing, the night hid her completely from view. Still the Lieutenant stood on, hoping that the wind would again die away, and that they should have another chance of getting hold of her. But though he persevered till after midnight the breeze continued steady, and nothing more was seen of the chase. He therefore reluctantly gave up the pursuit, and put the boats' heads to the westward, expecting to reach the place fixed upon as the rendezvous by the morning. In this, however, he was mistaken: he had either miscalculated the distance the chase had led him to the eastward, or he was deceived in the appearance of the land.

All the following day he looked in vain for the *Sultan*, nor could they see from the boats in the night any signal by which they could judge of her position. The next morning, the fourth since their leaving the ship, which was still nowhere to be seen, the officer in command decided upon pushing for the Magdalene Islands, which he hoped to reach in a couple of days, for which time their remaining provisions, with great economy might last them; whereas, if they delayed another day, and did not fall in with the ship, they would be reduced to so low an ebb, that it would be extremely hazardous to undertake so long a trajet with so scanty a supply. This resolution being taken, the men were put upon an allowance, and the boats urged with oars and sails across the Gulf. Fortunately the weather continued very fine. In passing Capraja the next morning, they landed to replenish their water, which was getting very short. Happily they hit at once upon a spring, at which they filled all the breakers, and got off again, unperceived by the garrison, or any of the inhabitants.

The following day, without another occurrence, they reached the Magdalenes, not a little pleased to be able to stretch their limbs, after having had them cramped for so many days in the boats, and to return once more to full allowance. After having refreshed his men, the Lieutenant, finding at the end of a couple of days, that no English ship touched at the anchorage, determined to proceed to Minorca in the boats.

Accordingly, having procured as much provisions as was thought sufficient for the passage, through the intervention of the British Vice-Consul, who had treated them all with much civility and hospitality as long as they remained at the islands, he again launched forth, and shaped his course for Minorca, where they arrived without further adventure, on the sixth day, in perfect health and safety.

We cruised with the fleet off Toulon, where thirteen sail of the line, and seven frigates, deep in the water, and fully equipped, lay ready for sea in the outer roads, until October, when Lord Collingwood took advantage of a strong northerly gale to run for Minorca, and water and revictual his ships. We might have been there about a week, when a frigate arrived from off Toulon, having on board a French spy. This person, who was a retired officer of the French navy, was in the practice of coming off occasionally with information, which now and then turned out to be correct as far as it went. Lord Collingwood, however, always distrusted this man, having satisfied himself that his movements were guided by the French police, and that his visits to the British fleet were more with the view of ascertaining, if possible, their condition and the Admiral's intentions, than to communicate any intelligence with respect to their own affairs, from which any practicable advantage could be gained. His reason at this time for seeking an interview with the Admiral, was ostensibly to communicate the information that a convoy with provisions was preparing at Toulon for the garrison of Barcelona (a circumstance of which the Admiral was already aware) – that it would be ready to put to sea in about a fortnight or three weeks, and that it was to be escorted by a strong squadron of men-of-war, or possibly by the whole fleet.

His true motive the Admiral conjectured might be to see the exact position of the British fleet, and to judge, or, if possible, to ascertain how long it was likely to lay in port. Its condition, however, when he arrived at Mahon, was well calculated to mislead a better judge than the Frenchman as to the probable time of its being ready for sea. Some of the ships, with sails unbent, were blacking yards and rigging; some with scaffolding over the sides, were caulking; some painting; while a few, with yards and topmasts struck, seemed almost dismantled. In fact, it looked as if the fleet had gone into harbour for the purpose of refitting, and that the time of its again sailing was quite indefinite.

In an hour or so after his arrival, the Frenchman was dismissed, and the frigate which brought him again made sail for Toulon. Scarcely, however, had she left Cape Mola a league astern, when the signal was flying on board the *Ville de Paris* for all Captains, and immediately after for the fleet to prepare for sea. Then might be seen what British men of war are capable of doing when their services are required, particularly if spurred to additional exertion by the stimulus of emulation. The boatswain's pipe is heard, and in an instant the men's occupations are changed. Tar, paint, and blacking brushes are laid aside. Caulkers are 'knocked off', and scaffolding and stages got in board. Top and top-gallant masts are swayed aloft, yards crossed and sails bent, in an incredible short space of time; and, before sunset, the studding-sail gear is rove, boats are upon the booms, everything in its place, the decks clean swept, and the men at their grog; and the whole fleet, which a few hours before seemed half dismantled, and all bustle and confusion, is now in perfect order, and only waits the land-breeze in the morning to lift their anchors and proceed to sea.

The following morning the fleet unmoored by signal, and before eight o'clock was steering in the order of sailing for St Sebastian, whither the

senior officer, watching the enemy's fleet, had instructions to repair, conveyed by the frigate which took the spy back to Toulon, should he have
any important communication to make to the Admiral.

These particulars, with regard to the Commander-in-Chief's opinion
of the French spy, which induced him to sail so suddenly and unexpectedly from Mahon, and to fix upon Cape St Sebastian for the station of
the fleet, instead of Cape Sicie as heretofore, I learned afterwards from
an officer,* the intimate friend of Lords Nelson and Collingwood, and
much in the confidence of those two great men; and I mention them
now, when it is no longer necessary to keep the secret, as a proof of
the sagacity and penetration which so much distinguished Lord
Collingwood.

14: The French Convoy

The fleet reached its cruising ground off Cape St Sebastian somewhere
about the 17th of October, and on the 22d of that month, about nine
o'clock at night, our attention was aroused by the flash and report of a
gun to windward. Every eye was immediately directed to that quarter,
and presently a strange sail, with the night signal displayed for an enemy's
fleet at sea, was discerned coming down before the wind. The signal was
made to prepare for battle, and as we lay all night at quarters with beating
hearts and anxious looks, not knowing the moment when the strangers
might show themselves, we could not help acknowledging, and at the
same time rejoicing at the judicious position in which the fleet had been
placed; for as the relief of Barcelona was plainly their object, it lay in the
very track to intercept the enemy, whom Lord Collingwood, by withdrawing from before Toulon, and keeping his whereabouts a secret, had
at length induced to put to sea.

The fleet stood to the southward under easy sail, watchful and anxious, it may be supposed, but nothing further occurred to alarm or arouse
its activity for the rest of the night.

The next morning was gloomy, with the wind moderate from the
eastward. The ship which made the signals and joined the fleet over
night, was the *Pomone*, Captain Barrie, who had the charge of watching
the enemy in Toulon, and to whom the frigate, which took back the
French spy from Mahon to the coast of France, conveyed instructions to

* The late Sir Benjamin Hallowell Carew.

be particularly vigilant, and the moment he observed any movement in the harbour of Toulon, which indicated on the part of the enemy's fleet an intention to put to sea, to use the utmost diligence in communicating the information to the Commander-in-Chief, whom he would find off Cape St Sebastian.

Soon after daylight the *Volontaire*, which was the weathermost frigate, made the signal for a fleet in the east, and immediately afterwards, that the ships seen were enemies. All eyes were instantly turned to that quarter, and we were gratified with the sight of a numerous fleet of vessels, of various rigs and sizes, coming down before the wind, led and flanked by five large ships, their sails swelled out by the favouring breeze, and shewing like a navy of cygnets under charge of the parent birds. Down they continued to come, seemingly unconscious of any danger, until we made them out to be three sail of the line and two frigates, with a convoy of seventeen or eighteen vessels of various descriptions, from the square-rigged ship to the xebec and felucca.

No change was made at first in the English fleet, except to advance the *Tigre* and *Bulwark*, two of the fastest sailing ships. Afterwards, the signal was made successively to the *Canopus*, Rear-Admiral Martin, *Terrible*, *Sultan*, *Leviathan*, *Renown*, and *Cumberland*, to chase E.N.E. About noon, the enemy having clearly made us out, hauled their wind, the ships of the line and frigates standing on the larboard tack to the S.S.E., while the whole of the smaller vessels stood in for the land in the direction of Cape Creux. The *Pomone* and *Volontaire* were sent in pursuit of the convoy, five or six of which they captured and burned before night; the remaining vessels effected their escape, as was afterwards ascertained, into the Bay of Rosas.

At first, the ships of the line detached in chase, as the signal had been made to each ship separately, acted independently one of the other, and according to the judgment of each individual Captain; but in the afternoon, when the French ships tacked to the northward, five of them followed the motions of Admiral Martin, and closed the *Canopus*, which ship had also tacked to the northward, while the *Terrible* and *Bulwark*, for some reason known only to their Captains, continued to stand to the S.S.E., and we saw no more of them for ten days. By this manœuvre those two ships widened instead of lessening the distance between them and the enemy, and it is a maxim in chasing to windward always to preserve that tack which draws you nearest to the object of pursuit. When the French ships tacked, half their topsails were visible from the deck. The wind, which in the morning was moderate, freshened considerably, causing a good deal of swell, and the atmosphere became so thick and hazy that we soon lost sight of the enemy's ships. As the day advanced, the wind increased so that it was with difficulty we carried three reefs out of the topsails and top-gallant sails; but with attention we were enabled to carry that sail throughout the chase. The wind remained steady at E. by S., and all that day and night, in the language of the old song,

> Not a sheet, nor a tack,
> Nor a brace did we slack

but stood on to the northward, cheered with the hope that the weather might clear, and again let us see the enemy.

Morning dawned, but no enemy appeared. The same thick weather continued, while the wind freshened if anything. The six ships were all compact together, and on they pressed, their crews animated with some such eager, anxious feeling as swells the breast of the gallant sportsman man what time the scent lies well, and the dogs, with noses breast high, are going a pace that tries the speed and bottom of the real good ones.

Towards noon, the *Canopus* had the misfortune to spring her main topmast, soon after which, Admiral Martin telegraphed the *Renown* that he thought it useless to persevere longer in the chase. As such a signal seemed to ask an opinion, Captain Durham of the *Renown*, and afterwards Captain Hallowell, of the *Tigre*, answered to the following purport: 'That as the wind had been since the chase commenced, the French ships could not have fetched any port where they could find shelter. That it was not probable they had tacked to the southward, as such a course would draw them from their own coast, which must now be their object to keep on board, and that in all likelihood they had not been able to weather the Bouches du Rhone, for which the squadron was then looking up, and where they must make the land about five or six o'clock in the evening'. For these reasons, they advised that 'the squadron should stand on until it made the land, or until it was warned off by the shoalness of the water.'

This opinion of the two senior Captains in the squadron, officers, too, of such established name and reputation, as Captains Durham and Hallowell, I suppose decided the Admiral, for we made no alteration in the course, but continued to stand in for the land. The wind continued fresh, and the atmosphere thick and hazy, so that objects could not be discerned at any considerable distance from the ships. It was now four o'clock in the afternoon, and when the discoloured appearance of the water plainly showed that we were fast approaching the low land, where the Rhone discharges its muddy waters into the Mediterranean, and still no enemy was visible, I confess I began to fear that they had escaped us, and to despair getting another view of them save in the harbour of Toulon.

Some such thoughts were perhaps passing through the mind of the Admiral, for, just at that moment, the signal was made to sound, and when that was answered, to prepare to wear in succession. But before it could be replied to, the signal was made by the *Renown* for a strange sail ahead, and the squadron continued to stand on. Every eye was now turned in the direction indicated by the *Renown*, but to no purpose.

Nothing but the now muddy water and the gloomy atmosphere could be seen, and it was afterwards whispered that nothing had in fact been seen by the *Renown* at the time, and that the signal was a 'ruse' of Captain Durham to prevail upon the Admiral to stand on as long as daylight and the depth of water permitted. Whether there was any truth in this conjecture, or that the people in the *Renown* were really endowed with keener sight than others in the squadron, certain it is that it was hoisted at a most opportune moment, for in less than ten minutes from the time, the *Tigre* made the signal for four sail north north-east, and before the signal was hauled down they were visible to the whole squadron.

The strangers were under topsails, feeling their way apparently for the land, which, from the thick state of the weather was still hid from view. When they showed themselves they were two or three points on the lee bow, and as the wind had drawn to the southward, by keeping away we were enabled to set starboard studding sails, which brought us rapidly up with them, when they were seen to be three sail of the line and a frigate. Shortly afterwards they anchored, and as it was becoming dark, the water shoal, with the wind blowing fresh on the land, while no one in the squadron was well acquainted with that part of the coast, the Admiral thought it prudent to haul off, keeping as near the shore during the night as could be done with safety, and so as to prevent the enemy slipping and effecting their escape under cover of the darkness.

We passed the night in watchful anxiety, wearing several times to preserve the necessary distance from the shore. As soon as it was sufficiently light the following morning to render objects visible, the French ships were again seen under weigh, and under topsails and foresails, standing for the land. The wind was blowing pretty fresh from the south-east, and our ships under a press of sail, had some expectation of closing them before they sheltered themselves behind the numerous sand-banks which crowd the entrance of the mouths of the Rhone.

In this we were destined to be disappointed; for, after standing a short time right for the land, the French ships bore round up with their heads to the north-west, when two of the ships of the line, one bearing the flag of a rear-admiral, shortly clewed up their sails, and without shifting their helms, quietly ran themselves aground with their broadsides to the sea, the one not more than a couple of cables' lengths ahead of the other. Meanwhile, the other ship of the line, and frigate, which had kept considerably outside their consorts, had set their top-gallant sails, and steered for the harbour of Cette, then about six or seven miles to the north-north-west. The *Tigre* and *Leviathan* were dispatched in pursuit of them; but the former was only able to get a few shots at them before they reached the entrance of the harbour, where, it was supposed, there was hardly depth of water sufficient to float the frigate, but into which a heavy press of sail likewise forced the line-of-battle ship.

Admiral Martin, with the other four ships, stood in until the *Cumberland*, which led, was in quarter less five, when he wore round, the enemy being even then out of range of shot. The squadron lay to, with their heads off shore, and as soon as the *Tigre* and *Leviathan* rejoined, the Captains repaired on board the *Canopus* by signal. They remained some time on board the Admiral, and then returned to their ships, soon after which a boat from the *Tigre* pulled in the direction of the enemy.

This boat, in charge of the present Captain E Boxer, then one of the lieutenants of the *Tigre*, sounded close up to the French ships, making the signal for the depth of water as she advanced. In doing this, she was exposed to the guns of the stranded ships; but when it was seen that their shot had not the effect of deterring the English boat from her occupation, they started four large boats, manned and armed, in chase of her. Boxer, seeing such odds against him, gave way for the squadron; and the Frenchmen, satisfied with having driven off the English boat, did not long continue the chase, but soon returned to their ships.

The boat from the *Tigre* had ascertained that the squadron could hardly approach within long gun shot of the enemy, who seemed fixed in a kind of dock between two banks, one of which they rounded, and interposed between themselves and the British squadron. In the course of the afternoon, boats were observed passing to and fro between the French ships and the shore, apparently landing stores; and as the mizen masts of the two ships went over the sides before dark, it was now evident that they must become wrecks without any effort on the part of our ships to aid in their destruction. We stood off, therefore, for the night, with the intention of not quitting the vicinity until we saw the end of them.

It fell calm before morning, with a thick haze around the atmosphere, so that it was late in the afternoon of the 26th, before we again got sight of them, and then they were seen to be almost entirely dismantled, one of them only having her foremast standing. In the evening, the squadron lay almost becalmed, unable to approach the land nearer than six or seven miles. About seven or eight o'clock, our attention was called to a brilliant light, which burst out suddenly in the direction of the shore. Upon looking more closely, this light was found to proceed from one of the stranded ships. Presently, afterwards, a dense smoke, followed by a flickering light, was seen on board her comrade, and in less than ten minutes both ships were in flames fore and aft.

The haze, which prevailed all day, had now dispersed, and the night was beautifully fine, with just wind enough to blow aside the smoke, and fan the fire, which rapidly spread to every part of the upper works, and raged and burned with the fierceness and intensity of a furnace. It was a grand and sublime spectacle, the sight of those two burning ships, and one which might be viewed without fear or anxiety for the fate of the crews, who, we had reason to suppose, had their eyes fixed upon the same objects, if not with as much satisfaction, at all events inasmuch security as ourselves.

We had been gazing – it might be about twenty minutes, or half-an-hour – at the grandeur of this sight, not altogether without a certain feeling of awe, which fire, in its unrestrained destructive force, is sure to inspire, when all at once a broad sheet of light, of intense and dazzling brilliancy, flashed from one of the ships, and, in her place, left a shroud of lurid smoke, which, in a second, was rent and torn, and blown aside by the blast and roar of thunder, filling the air with fragments of blazing wreck, that flamed and sparkled a moment in the sky, and then fell, like shooting stars of fearful omen, into the gulf which entombed the remains of the devoted ship.

We had but a moment turned from beholding the termination of this mighty bonfire, when our attention was called to a repetition of the features that marked the circumstance which I have just described. The same intense and brilliant flash – the cloud of smoke that replaced the gallant ship – the thunder's loud and deafening roar – the fragments of flaming wreck that meteor-like glared and shot athwart the affrighted sky – the plash into the water – and all was dark and still, as if the spot had not a moment before witnessed the fiery destruction of two noble ships.

Being thus enabled to give so good an account of two of the enemy, Admiral Martin remained till the following morning to look into Cette, and ascertain if possible, the situation of the other two ships, which had effected their escape into the port. The frigate, with masts and yards all ataunto, seemed afloat; but the ship of the line was evidently aground, heeling very much to one side. Her topmasts were struck close down to the caps, and her mainyard secured, with a purchase up, seemingly for getting out her guns; and although by great exertion, they afterwards succeeded in floating her and getting safe into Toulon, her situation in Cette seemed to us extremely critical. Having completed our reconnaissance, the squadron made sail in the direction of Cape St Sebastian, and rejoined Lord Collingwood, on the morning of the 30th.

The next day, Captain Hallowell of the *Tigre*, having under his orders the *Cumberland* 74, *Volontaire*, *Apollo*, and *Topaze*, frigates, – and the *Scout*, *Philomel*, and *Tuscan*, brigs, was sent in to destroy the rest of the convoy, which had taken shelter in the Bay of Rosas. This service was performed most gallantly and completely by the boats of the detached ships on the same night, under the immediate command of the First Lieutenant (John Tailour) of the *Tigre*, every vessel in the bay, amounting to eleven, being either burnt or brought out.

Among them were four stout armed vessels, which were fully prepared for the attack, and which defended themselves, aided by the batteries on shore, with considerable resolution, particularly the *Lamproie*, under whose charge the convoy remained, after the defection of the other men-of-war, a frigate-built store-ship, armed with sixteen eight-pounders, and a crew of one hundred and sixteen men. This service was not accomplished without loss; a Lieutenant and Master's Mate were killed; the officer who commanded the boats, four Lieutenants and three Midshipmen, wounded, with a proportionate number of seamen and marines.

Lord Collingwood had every reason to be gratified with the zeal and exertion of his ships, by which a convoy of twenty-two vessels, including the escort, were every one destroyed, except one ship of the line, and two frigates, and the enemy's plan for revictualling Barcelona frustrated. We learned, subsequently, that this convoy was under the charge of Rear-Admiral Baudin, and escorted by the *Robuste*, of eighty guns, the Rear-Admiral's flag-ship, with the *Borée* and *Lion*, of seventy-four guns, and *Pauline* and *Pomone*, frigates. Of these, the *Robuste*, and *Lion* were set fire to by their crews off the Bouches du Rhone – the *Borée* and *Pauline* got into Cette; and the *Pomone* which had parted company before we came up with them on the coast of France, reached Marseilles in safety.

The rest of our cruise off Cape St Sebastian was unmarked by any thing worth recording, unless I mention that the *Royal Sovereign* and *Tigre* were both struck by lightning. The former had two men killed and four or five wounded, and the mainmast of the latter was so badly injured, that she was compelled to go to Gibraltar for a new one. It was now the end of November, the weather had become very unsettled and boisterous, and the fleet repaired to Mahon for the winter. Soon after this the *Sultan* was ordered to Palermo for the purpose of allowing Captain Griffith to arrange an exchange of ships with Captain West of the *Excellent*, which ship was soon to return to England: as Captain West was desirous of continuing in the Mediterranean, while business of a pressing nature required Captain Griffith's presence in England, an exchange would accommodate both, and the service would be none the worse for it.

Our passage to Palermo was slow, but agreeable; our society being enlivened by the addition of a Spanish officer, and his young and pretty Sicilian wife, both very nice people, whom we obliged with a passage at the request of a friend at Mahon. This little piece of civility on our parts had its reward; for the lady had a very fine voice, and it was a great treat to listen to her as she touched the strings of her guitar, and breathed one of the wild airs of her native island; or, accompanied by her husband, sang some of those patriotic verses, the creation of the day, that were so well calculated to kindle and inflame the hatred and resistance of her adopted countrymen to the aggressions and tyranny of the invaders of Spain.

When we arrived, we found the *Canopus* and *Excellent* lying in the bay; and while the two Captains were arranging the business of their exchange, we passed a very pleasant time in the company, and under the guidance of the officers of those ships, who, from being 'old stationers', had become, as it were, free of the city. Palermo was then a gay and brilliant town. Driven from Naples, and followed by all the nobility and gentry of property that remained faithful to the royal cause, the King had sought refuge in Sicily, and established his court and government in its principal city.

As is the case in most countries, the court soon attracted within its magic circle all that was gay, and idle, and rich in the island; so that in addition to the beauty of its situation, and its many advantages and attractions, Palermo, when we visited it, had all the characteristics of a fashionable, luxurious and brilliant metropolis. Many foreigners, particularly English flocked there. Besides wealthy mercantile men of the latter nation, it was seldom without a host of tourists; for as they were excluded from the continent of Europe, the greater part of which was under the control or dictation of Bonaparte, the Mediterranean, and its islands, were almost the only places to which the rambling disposition of our countrymen could be prudently directed. Palermo, therefore, seldom wanted a good supply of what was then known by the name of 'T G – 's'

The marina, a noble public promenade, extending two or three miles in front of the town, on one side flanked by magnificent palaces, and on the other washed by the waters of the beautiful bay, used to be thronged in the afternoons with fashionably dressed, well-mounted equestrians, and gay and handsome equipages filled with the belles of Palermo. Though fair and passing innocent to look upon, there were few of the latter, about whom rumour, with her many tongues, had not some tale of scandal to rehearse.

'Who is the lady in that handsome carriage just passed by?' I said to an officer of the *Canopus*, who piqued himself upon his knowledge of fashionable life at Palermo. 'That one, I mean, in the rose-coloured bonnet, which sets off her fine features to such advantage. She is a little too stout; but her eyes are magnificent – full of intelligence and expression – and she wears her dark glossy hair parted upon her smooth and finely formed forehead, where intellect and candour seem united.'

'Don't you know,' said he; 'that is the Principessa B–t–o, whose easy, good-natured husband is little inquisitive as to the manner in which his wife passes her time, provided his own amusements meet with no interruption, and he have money always sufficient for his *menus plaisirs*, a matter that depends a good deal upon the will of his *cara sposa*, who was a widow when she married the prince, and who managed that the control of her ample fortune should still continue in her own power.'

'And the lady now passing us in that dark-coloured carriage with the grays, who is she?'

'That,' continued he, 'is the Principessa L–d–a, a great favourite with the English, whose language she understands and speaks fluently. Her years are not quite so few as you perhaps suppose; and that exceedingly delicate tint, that imparts such a youthful charm to her really beautiful face, is not, I fear, the gift of nature. At least, envious people say that it is borrowed. She has the character of being capricious, and inconstant in her preferences and attachments, changing her *cavalieri serventi*, generally foreigners, English, French, or German, with as little remorse, and almost as often, as the colour of a ribbon. Her favourite this week is a young German, just arrived in Sicily, recommended by a member of the royal family in England to the English Ambassador, and the commander of the English forces in Sicily, for a commission in one of the foreign corps in our pay in the Mediterranean.'

Thus did my friend draw upon his stores of information, and furnish me with a little history or anecdote of every male, or female, whose equipage or appearance attracted particular regard.

Palermo, in point of size and population, may be classed with the second-rate cities of France and England; having more the air of a metropolis, but with that mixture of squalor and splendour, meanness and magnificence, which characterize all great towns – those of the south of Europe, perhaps, more than others.

Its situation is singularly felicitous, in the bottom of a deep bay, surrounded on all sides, but that towards the sea, with a plain of such luxuriance and fertility, as to procure for it from the natives the name of 'Val di conchiglia d'oro', the Vale of the Golden Shell. This happy valley is backed by a chain of rugged mountains, which seem to bar all access to it from the other parts of the island.

One of our excursions took us to Monreale, a neat, small town, to the south of Palermo about four or five miles; where, among other objects worthy of notice, is a gorgeous Saracenic duomo, built, it is said, in the twelfth century, by one of the Norman kings of Sicily.

Two miles of good road, and a gentle ascent from Monreale, took us to the foot of the mountain, whence another mile or two of a steep and rugged pass led to the Benedictine Monastery of San Martino.

This is a noble pile of building. Vast, but simple in its structure, without architectural ornament, and reposing in peaceful loneliness in the heart of mountains, it seemed, from its character and situation, well suited to inspire and cherish holy and devotional feelings in the breasts of men who had renounced the world, and dedicated themselves ever after to the service of religion.

The interior of the building corresponds with its outward appearance. The chapel is of considerable size; but had, with the exception of a few good pictures, less of ornament than is generally met with in places of Roman Catholic worship. The library is a finely proportioned room, and was clean, ventilated, and free from damp when we visited it; and the shelves well furnished with books and manuscripts, which were kept clear of dust and cobwebs.

Although all around is wild, naked, and sterile, the little valley in which San Martino lies embosomed teems with fertility and luxuriance. Corn, wine, and oil, and fruits of every kind that the happiest climate of Europe can supply, were there in abundance, as if an Eden had been scooped out in the mountains, and, like their brethren of Paraclete, the Benedictines had 'opened another paradise in the wild'.

A few weeks before our arrival at Palermo, the Duke of Orleans, late King of the French, was married to the eldest daughter of the King of Naples, a marriage, by the way, which caused no little marvel at the time; for it was thought passing strange that His Majesty of Naples should bestow the hand of one of his daughters upon a man whose fortunes were not only ruinous and broken, but which seemed so completely hopeless and irretrievable. But who can penetrate the mysteries of fate, or look with prophetic eye into the womb of futurity?

This union, which was considered as a very humble one for a princess of the house of Naples, placed her in the end upon the throne of one of the most powerful monarchies in Europe.

Poetry or romance, indeed, in their wildest and most extravagant imaginings, never conceived a story more replete with extraordinary and improbable vicissitudes than are to be found in the eventful history of the late Duke of Orleans' life.

Of the blood royal of France, and born to a princely inheritance, at an early age he saw his country deluged with blood, and a prey to the wildest anarchy and confusion; – his family and kindred massacred, or fled to escape assassination – his own wide domains plundered and confiscated – and himself, banished and proscribed, an alien in foreign lands, where he was fain to earn a scanty subsistence by teaching to others those sciences and accomplishments which he had acquired in the days of his prosperity, as the necessary finish to the education of a gentleman.

After wandering through Switzerland, England, and America, chance at length flung him on the shores of Sicily at which time he was indebted to England for a small pension. His rank, and the name of Bourbon, obtained for him a friendly reception at the Court of Palermo, which speedily paved the way for a nearer and more intimate connection. At that very time, the power and government of Bonaparte seemed more firmly established than ever, and there did not appear the most distant chance of the Duke's being ever restored to his country or his fortunes. Yet it might be said that, from the moment of his landing in Sicily, fortune frowned less angrily upon him.

After his marriage, he continued to reside at Palermo until, in a few years, the downfall of Bonaparte led to the restoration of the Bourbons; and when he returned to France, the Duke found that none, or scarcely any, of his immense possessions had passed into the hands of others, and the head of the house of Orleans was still the richest subject in Europe.

For several subsequent years he was only heard of as a prince of vast and increasing wealth, considerable taste in the fine arts, of which he was the liberal patron and protector; but better still as a kind, judicious, and affectionate husband and father. But notwithstanding the quiet and un-ostentatious manner in which he lived, and his seeming indifference to politics and state affairs, he was always viewed with distrust by the elder branch of the house of Bourbon, and looked upon by many as the head of that party in France, which stood between ultra-royalism on the one hand, and the the designs and intrigues of Bonapartists and Republicans on the other. This party included within its ranks most of the wealthy commercial men, and men of talent, with nearly all the really industrious classes in France; so that, when the revolution of July, 1830, took place, the weight and influence of such a party found it an easy matter to seat the man of their choice upon the throne vacated by the injudicious, weak-minded, and unfortunate Charles X.

Thus, we see the man, who some years ago was a fugitive from his country, and indebted to the generosity of a foreign nation for the means of living in the unpretending station of a private gentleman, first unexpectedly and almost miraculously restored to his country and his fortunes, and not many years afterwards chosen for their king, and placed upon the throne by the same people, who once, thirsting for his blood, had banished and proscribed him; and we are at a loss which to admire the most, – the fortitude, resources, equanimity, and good sense of the one, conspicuous alike in prosperous or adverse fortune, – or the madness, wickedness, reckless folly, and ever vacillating character and conduct of the other.*

Thus, between parties and the opera in the evenings, with an occasional visit to the conversazione, where much of the Società Palermitana assembled each night after the opera was over; – some for a little gossip, and to see and be seen, but more to try their fortunes at Rouge et Noir and Faro; and seeing sights and excursions around the lovely environs of Palermo in the daytime, we passed two or three weeks most agreeably. But our holiday was drawing to a close. The two captains had arranged their matters. Some other exchanges took place, and we lost our third lieutenant Tisdall, whose place was ill-supplied, in the opinion of his messmates, by the man who came to us from the *Excellent*. All arrangements were perfected about the 20th of December, when we sailed with our new captain from Palermo, and joined the fleet at Mahon towards the end of that month.

When Captain Griffith found it necessary for him to go to England, he thought it would be more for my advantage to sail with an officer of such established character as Captain Hallowell, than to remain in the *Sultan*. He therefore spoke to him on the subject before we sailed for Palermo, requesting him, should he have no other person in view, to apply for me as one of his lieutenants, whenever a vacancy for one should occur in the *Tigre*; and as some of my messmates were already gone, and others were soon to follow, I was not sorry at the prospect of quitting a ship, in which some of the happiest days of my life had been passed, and where a new captain and new messmates were but too likely to remind me, by painful contrast, of all that I had lost by the exchange.

* This was written before the Revolution of 1848, which dethroned and banished Louis-Philippe, and compelled him to fly again for safety to a foreign land.

Towards the beginning of January, 1810, the *Tigre* returned from Gibraltar, whither she had gone to replace her shivered mainmast; soon after which the whole assembled fleet sailed to resume its station before Toulon.

We had not been many days at sea, when a vessel from England brought a commander's commission for the first lieutenant of the *Tigre*, the officer who commanded the brilliant and successful attack upon the enemy's convoy in the Bay of Rosas. This created the desired vacancy into which I was immediately removed.

15: Captain Hallowell and the *Tigre*

I joined the *Tigre* in January, 1810, off Toulon. Several of her officers were previously known to me: with a few I was on terms of intimacy, and they were glad to welcome me among them as a messmate, so that I did not feel so entirely isolated and alone as one usually does in removing to a strange ship. In spite of such favourable circumstances, however, I felt a want of ease and confidence in myself for several days after I joined my new ship; for, although there be a general similarity in the management and discipline of men-of-war, yet the details, the mode of carrying on duty, even the hours of its performance, with many minor points too minute to mention, but to which much importance is attached, and the neglect or ignorance of which is seldom overlooked; all these frequently vary with the varying caprices of different captains in different ships, and, until I made myself thoroughly acquainted with the whole, I could not feel myself at home.

So far as to the qualities of the ship, her captain and officers were concerned, I found the *Tigre* what every British man-of-war ought to be – clean – in good fighting order – handy to work – sailing well – and an admirable sea-boat. The only thing in which she was deficient was a good crew; but that she did not possess. The proportion of able seamen to the rest of the ship's company was scantier than ever I knew to be in any other ship.

The *Tigre* had been commissioned in 1804, at Plymouth, which port, as well as every other in England, had been drained of seamen to man the ships that had been fitted out in the previous year; and, as Captain Hallowell was most anxious to be at sea, and join his old friend and commander, Lord Nelson, in the Mediterranean, with as little delay as possible, he was obliged to be content with such men as he could get, and to take an unusually large number of Irishmen to complete his crew, with whom the guard-ship was thronged, and of whom the greater part had never seen a ship before in their lives.

Now, it is generally admitted that Irishmen for the most part exhibit no impenetrability of skull except sometimes when engaged in a bit of a skrimmage at a wake or fair; then, indeed, they seem hard and unyielding enough: but, put them to learn any profession or trade, and they will be found to acquire it with as much, if not more facility than their brethren of the sister island; and it is well known that they make intelligent and expert soldiers in an incredibly short time. But I have never been able to discover that my countrymen possess a genius for salt water. Occasionally, no doubt, an Irish seaman, and a really good one, is to be met with; still, it is my belief, that if the heads of all Irishmen were phrenologically examined, the bump of philo-maritimeness (is that the word?) would not be found in one out of every hundred; therefore I look upon a thorough seaman from that island as an accident of rare occurrence.

With a crew formed of such materials, I found it at first somewhat trying to carry on the duty, and it was not until I began to know them, and could call the best men by name, that I felt myself quite at ease in the night watches. But, at the time I write of, and up to the close of the war, it was too much the custom to send ships to sea, some short of complement, and others very inefficiently manned.

Much difficulty no doubt existed in procuring a sufficiency of able seamen for fleets of the magnitude of those which England was then obliged to maintain, and at the same time supply her vast commercial marine; but this difficulty, great as it unquestionably was, might have been much lessened, if not entirely remedied, by more thought and attention to the subject on the part of those authorities to whom the direction and control of such matters is confided. Some ships had often an undue and unnecessary number of able seamen, while others were at times so destitute of that indispensable part of a ship's crew, that it was dangerous to trust them to sea.

This inequality might have been rectified, and a more even distribution of the crews made by a careful inspection of each ship's company by the admirals; but this important part of their duty was too often neglected, if, indeed, it was ever attended to in time of war. It would be very mortifying, no doubt, to captains to have some of their best men taken from them, and not the less so, if they were conscious of having used great trouble and pains in collecting them together, and to have their places supplied by landsmen, or the refuse, perhaps, of another ship. But, if the completeness and efficiency of a whole fleet require it, the wishes and feelings of individuals must not stand in the way of the general good.

One mode of recruiting for the navy, recommended by Lord Collingwood, always to have an additional number of boys supplied to each ship, was admirable, and, had it been acted upon, would no doubt have been attended with the most beneficial effects. But, although he reiterated his requests to the Admiralty, and tried to impress his own wholesome views upon the subject on that Board, I cannot call to mind that more than one batch of boys for general distribution throughout the fleet, ever reached the Mediterranean during the eight years that I was upon that station, and then not as an addition to the crews, as he requested, but merely to fill up the vacancies caused by death, removals, or other casualties. But had boys been constantly supplied to the ships on foreign stations, according to his Lordship's views and suggestions, each would have had a nursery on board, which would furnish her at need with expert and active topmen.

Young men, likewise, who embark as landsmen, might be made efficient seamen in a short time by due attention on the part of the captains and officers; for, if instead of placing them all in the waist, or afterguard (the general practice), the most intelligent and active were chosen and divided between the tops, forecastle, and gunner's crew, they would soon acquire the knowledge and habits of seamen. By such management, and the great attention he paid to the subject, there was not a man in the *Immortalité* or *Clyde*, when Captain Owen commanded those ships, that could not take the helm and lead, and very few who were not competent to all the duties of practical seamen.

Lord Collingwood's health, long visibly declining, was now completely broken down. Constant confinement to his ship (for even in harbour he allowed himself no relaxation), and that perpetual stooping over his desk, which a wide-spread and multifarious correspondence demanded, and in the conduct of which he gave himself no assistance, at last produced the most injurious effects upon his digestion, ending in a total inactivity and stoppage of the bowels, and a rejection of all food. The surgeon of the *Ville de Paris* represented to him that nothing but an entire cessation from all labour, mental and physical, could now save his life, and to that end that it was absolutely necessary he should leave the fleet, and retire to Mahon, where his mind might be released from the cares and toils of duty, and where he could have the power of taking such exercise as his strength would enable him to support. Yielding at length to the urgency of those representations, he reluctantly consented to resign the charge of the fleet into the hands of Rear-Admiral Martin, and retired to Mahon.

At Lord Collingwood's particular desire, Captain Hallowell accompanied his friend to Minorca, and during his absence, Captain Abel Ferris was appointed to act in the *Tigre*.

We remained but a few days with the fleet off Toulon, and then followed the *Ville de Paris* to Mahon. On our arrival we found that the change to harbour had brought no relief to the Commander-in-Chief. He was now reduced to such extreme bodily feebleness as to prevent his taking any kind of exercise, and his mind, even to the day of his dissolution, was too intent upon his country's interests and service to allow itself that perfect freedom from thought and care, which was so essential to the restoration of his health. Finding that he was daily growing weaker and weaker, Lord Collingwood at length, by the advice, and at the earnest entreaties of his physician and friends, made up his mind to resign his command, and proceed at once to England without waiting for his successor. When this decision was come to, the wind, which blew fresh into the harbour, prevented its being put into execution for several days. At last, after several ineffectual attempts, a lull one morning allowed them to warp and tow the *Ville de Paris* out to a sufficient distance to enable her to get to sea, soon after which Captain Hallowell took a final leave of his excellent and cherished friend, with no hope that his valued life would be prolonged till he reached England. These anticipations proved but too true, and that great and truly good man died a martyr to his love of country, and severe sense of duty, in thirty-six hours after he sailed from Minorca.

After attending to some matters which required his supervision, and providing for the safe custody of a number of French prisoners confined in the Lazaretto at Mahon, Captain Hallowell proceeded to sea, and we joined the fleet off Toulon in ten days or a fortnight after the departure of the *Ville de Paris* for England.

The French had already two ships on the stocks to replace the ones destroyed towards the end of last year off the Rhone, which were sufficiently advanced to enable us to make out that one was of three decks, and the other of two.

Here, perhaps, I may be permitted to say a little of my new Captain, with whom I continued to sail for five years, and for whose memory I feel the greatest respect and regard.

When I joined the *Tigre* in January, 1810, Captain Hallowell was just fifty years of age. In person he was the exact cut of a sailor, five feet eight or nine inches high, stout and muscular, but not at all corpulent. His countenance was open, manly, and benevolent, with bright, clear grey eyes, which, if turned inquiringly upon you, seemed to read your most secret thoughts. His mouth was pleasing and remarkably handsome, but indicative of decision and strength of character; and his thinly scattered hair, powdered, and tied in a cue after the old fashion, displayed, in all its breadth, his high and massive forehead, upon which unflinching probity and sterling good sense seemed to have taken their stand. Such in outward guise was Captain Hallowell, when I first became acquainted with him. His usual manner was thoughtful and reserved; but that was often laid aside, when his conversation became lively and entertaining, mixed with anecdotes of old times and old scenes, and occasionally even sportive and playful.

As an officer and a seaman, few, if any, surpassed him in the service, to which every faculty of his mind seemed entirely devoted. His life had been passed at sea, and from the moment that he first embarked to the period that I joined the *Tigre*, I do not suppose he had been two years on shore. He had served all the first American War as Midshipman, and as Lieutenant on the coast of Africa and in the West Indies during the peace that followed. At the time of the armament in 1790, he was Lord Hood's First Lieutenant, and when the fleet was dismantled upon an arrangement of the dispute which called for its equipment, Captain Hallowell was promoted to the rank of Commander. When the Revolutionary War broke out in 1793, he was appointed to command the *Camilla* storeship, and very soon followed his patron, Lord Hood, to the Mediterranean, and in a few months he was removed to act as Captain of the *Robust*, seventy-four.

In command of that ship he was actively engaged ashore and afloat during all the operations at Toulon, and upon its evacuation by the Allied Forces, bore a conspicuous share in the destruction of the French ships: indeed, I have reason to know that he was the last officer who left the Arsenal on that eventful night, when his boat was crowded almost to sinking by the unhappy Royalists flying to escape the vengeance of the remorseless Republicans. The decks of the *Robust* were thronged with those unhappy beings, in so much that, from her crowded state, when she got under weigh, there was hardly room to work the ship. Captain Hallowell was afterwards present at the sieges of Calvi and Bastia, when he took turn and turn with Lord Nelson to command in the batteries manned by the seamen.

Not long after Sir John Jervis assumed the command of the Mediterranean Fleet, some symptoms of insubordination manifested themselves in a few of the ships; and Captain Hallowell, upon whose firmness and discretion the Commander-in-Chief placed the utmost reliance, was removed to the *Courageux*, whose crew was thought to be more tainted than any other in the fleet.

Towards the end of the year 1796, while Captain Hallowell was attending a court-martial at Gibraltar, a sudden and violent squall blew the *Courageux* out of the bay; and the wind in no way abating, she was wrecked the same night under Ape's Hill, on the coast of Barbary. No blame was attributable to anybody, and after the court-martial, Captain Hallowell remained as Sir John Jervis's guest on board the *Victory*, until an opportunity should offer of allowing him to proceed to England.

Meantime, the action and defeat of the Spanish fleet off Cape St Vincent took place; and so sensible was Sir John Jervis of Captain Hallowell's advice and services on that memorable day, that as soon as the battle was over, he could not forbear telling him so, publicly on the quarter-deck, embracing him at the same time, in testimony of the grateful emotions which he felt. So high an opinion indeed, had Sir John formed of his judgment and abilities, that when Captain Calder was about to proceed to England with the despatches, it not being intended that he was to return and resume his post again, he offered the situation of Captain of the Fleet to Captain Hallowell, although a Captain of little more than four years' standing at the time.

Few men in Captain Hallowell's position would have declined an offer so flattering, and so every way tempting to a young officer's ambition. But a feeling of modesty and delicacy, which ever accompanies true merit and ability, with a strong sense of justice and propriety, made him forego an appointment so every way desirable; and thanking the Commander-in-Chief for his very kind offer, and the flattering opinion of him, which had prompted him to make it, he told him at once that he did not think it would be decorous in him, so young a Captain, to undertake the duties of an office, to which so many older officers in the fleet were, from long service and experience, better entitled as well as better calculated to fill. The Admiral acquiesced in the truth and force of these reasons, and did not urge the matter further.

Upon Captain Hallowell's arrival in England he was immediately appointed to the *Lively*, a frigate of thirty-six guns, and soon returned to his old station – the Mediterranean. In a few weeks afterwards, the *Lively* was sent on a cruise to the westward, when her boats, in company with those of the *Minerve*, cut out the *Mutine*, a French brig of sixteen guns, from under the batteries of Vera Cruz, in the Island of Teneriffe. Captain Hallowell intrusted the conduct of this enterprise to Mr Hardy, first lieutenant of the *Minerve* (Sir Thomas Hardy), who was rewarded with promotion and the command of the captured brig, for his gallantry and success on the occasion. This judicious selection led to his further advancement, and in all likelihood to Lord Nelson's subsequent notice and friendship for him, by which means the services of an officer of such distinguished merit and ability were obtained for the navy and his country.

Captain Hallowell was not permitted to retain the command of the *Lively* for many months. The *Swiftsure*, seventy-four, wanted a captain, and who so fit to command a ship of the line as he? And although there were older captains in command of frigates on the station, Captain Hallowell was the one selected to command the *Swiftsure*.

Soon after he took the command of her, the *Swiftsure* was despatched from before Cadiz, with other ships, to reinforce Lord Nelson's squadron off Toulon. From the moment it was known that the French armament had quitted Toulon, he shared in the fatiguing and harassing search, and in all the anxieties of his commander, until the day that the enemy's fleet was descried at anchor in the Bay of Aboukir. An occurrence may here be mentioned highly characteristic of Captain Hallowell's promptness, decision, and indefatigable watchfulness, and which probably led to the discovery of the French fleet.

When Nelson, after his first search for the enemy's fleet along the coast of Syria and Egypt, was returning the second time up the Mediterranean, the fleet being in extended line abreast, in order to command a wider range of view, the man at the *Swiftsure's* mast-head reported something floating upon the waters. This object was soon made out to be a life-buoy, with the tricolour flying upon it. The *Swiftsure*, being the outer ship of the line, was immediately steered towards it, and when picked up, the name *L'Artemise*, one of the frigates known to be with the enemy's fleet, was found carved upon it, while its appearance shewed that it could not have been long in the water. In a moment up went the signal on board the *Swiftsure*, 'Intelligence to communicate', followed from the *Vanguard* by the signal for the fleet to close. On nearing the flag-ship, Captain Hallowell was lowered down in the quarter-boat with his prize, and as he went alongside, Nelson, looking over the gangway, cried out, – 'Hallowell, what have you got?' The reply was, – 'They are not far off. Here is the life-buoy of one of their frigates.' It was soon on the *Vanguard's* deck, and the gallant chief at once decided to push on a second time to Egypt, confident that now he should find the fleet he had been so long in search of. And thus a circumstance seemingly trifling in itself, but which the quick perception of Captain Hallowell felt to be of such moment, was mainly instrumental in deciding Lord Nelson to try Egypt again, and which led to results so glorious and so important.

The prompt decision with which the mode of attack was planned, the skill and gallantry with which it was executed, and all the glorious results of the battle are matters of history; and it is no further necessary to particularize the share which the *Swiftsure* had in the engagement, than to mention, that as she was a dull sailer, she got late into action; but, although it was dark when she anchored, her position, whether by accident or design, was so admirably chosen on the quarter of the *L'Orient*, that she contributed materially to the destruction of that ship.

Subsequent to these events, the *Swiftsure* was one of the ships which accompanied Lord Nelson to Sicily, where she remained some time, and was then sent to Gibraltar to refit.

I must not omit to mention the singular, though very characteristic and appropriate gift, presented by Captain Hallowell to Lord Nelson before they separated, – a gift which will ever associate the names of those two great men, and make them live together in the memory of their country as long as the history of Lord Nelson shall be read – the coffin made of the mainmast of *L'Orient*, and in which his Lordship was buried.

As soon as the *Swiftsure* had refitted, she first joined the squadron under Commodore Duckworth, off Cadiz, where she assisted in capturing the 'Lima' convoy, the day after it left port for South America; and then proceeded to Egypt, where, in conjunction with the *Zealous*, Captain Hood, she continued to maintain a close and rigorous blockade off Alexandria for several months. She remained on that service until her stores and provisions were quite exhausted, and the ship herself in such a crazy condition, and her bottom so foul, that it was impossible to keep her longer at sea without examination and repairs. Captain Hallowell was therefore ordered to proceed to Malta, having under his charge a small convoy of light store-ships and merchantmen. On the passage down the Mediterranean, he had the misfortune to fall in with a French squadron of five or six sail of the line, under Rear-Admiral Gantheaume, which had entered the Straits a short time before, with the object of throwing supplies of men and stores into Egypt, should they be able to elude the vigilance of the English blockade.

On discovering the French ships, Captain Hallowell immediately made the signal to the convoy not to attend to his motions, but to make the best of their way to the appointed rendezvous. This was followed, and the convoy escaped, the efforts of the French ships being all directed to secure the man-of-war. When they were observed, two of the enemy's ships were on the lee-quarter; and the Admiral, with the remainder of his squadron, right astern. All that knowledge and good seamanship suggested, was tried to make the old ship sail, but to no purpose. The ships in her wake overhauled her as if she had been at anchor, whilst the two on her lee-quarter neared her almost as fast.

Under these circumstances. Captain Hallowell thought it vain to expect to escape; but he resolved to leave nothing undone to effect it: and for that purpose he bore up and set every stitch of sail, steering with the wind abaft the beam, so as, if possible, to cross the bows of the ships on his quarter, and then try what the *Swiftsure* could do before the wind; but should he fail in doing so without coming to action, he would, at all events have but two ships to contend with for some time, which by some lucky chance might be crippled before the body of the French squadron closed and rendered further resistance ineffectual. But this manœuvre was observed, and instantly met by the two ships to lee-ward, who like-wise kept away, and steered in such a manner that the opposing vessels only neared each other with greater rapidity. To add to his mortification, Captain Hallowell soon perceived that his ship made a worse hand of it off the wind than close-hauled.

An immediate action was now unavoidable. It commenced in ten minutes afterwards, and was maintained with great vivacity and spirit against two ships* for three-quarters of an hour, their great superiority in sailing enabling them to maintain a position all the time with their fore sails in the brails – the one on the bow, the other on the quarter of the *Swiftsure*. The other French ships were now drawing up, the head-most beginning to take a part in the action, when Captain Hallowell, see-ing that to continue so unequal a contest any longer, would be productive of nothing but a useless sacrifice of men's lives, after assembling his offi-cers, who gave it as their opinion that nothing further could be done, either for the honour of the flag, or the safety of the ship, was forced to surrender.

The *Swiftsure's* sails and rigging were much cut up; but, considering the length of the combat, and the inequality of the force she had to con-tend with, her loss in men was not great. That of the enemy was supposed to have been far more considerable, although the exact number could not be clearly ascertained.

Admiral Gantheaume got safe into Toulon with his prize, where Captain Hallowell remained a prisoner until the peace of Amiens, which took place shortly after his capture.

After his return to England, Captain Hallowell remained but a short time with his family, when he was appointed to the *Argo*, a ship of 44 guns on two decks, and to the command on the coast of Africa.

On the rupture of the peace in the following year, 1803, he found him-self opportunely in the West Indies, where his services and those of the *Argo* were actively and usefully employed in reducing several of the

---

* *L'Indomitable* and *Dix Août*.

West Indian islands. When this service was accomplished, the *Argo* was ordered to England, and Captain Hallowell, after first taking Ali Bey to Tunis, was soon after appointed to the *Tigre*. But so completely drained of seamen were all the English ports at that moment, that, notwithstanding his utmost exertions, he could not man his ship and get to sea before the latter end of the year 1804. By this time hostilities had recommenced between England and Spain; but, although he met several vessels of that nation in his passage up the Mediterranean, so great was his anxiety to join Lord Nelson, and with his crew complete in numbers, that he would not take possession of them, or even spare time sufficient to destroy them.

He found the English fleet at anchor in Agincourt Sound; and in a few days after his junction, towards the evening, a report reached the Admiral that the French fleet had sailed from Toulon; and although there was great risk in taking a fleet of large ships at night, blowing fresh, through a narrow intricate passage, Lord Nelson did not lose an instant in getting under weigh, and going in pursuit of the enemy. All cleared the channel fortunately without accident; but the *Tigre*, with her raw ship's company, found it difficult to purchase her anchor; and Captain Hallowell had the mortification to see that his ship was the last that cleared the anchorage. From that time, Captain Hallowell never was a day absent from the fleet commanded by his friend, sharing in all his toils and anxieties, and accompanying him throughout his long and arduous search and pursuit of Villeneuve, first all over the Mediterranean, and then to the West Indies, and back again.

When Lord Nelson arrived off Cadiz, and assumed the command of the fleet, a short time prior to the great battle of Trafalgar, three of his old ships, the *Canopus*, *Spencer*, and *Tigre*, formed part of the in-shore squadron. They had maintained that position so long that their provisions and water were nearly exhausted; upon learning which, Lord Nelson, not thinking that the allied fleet would put to sea as soon as it did, and being greatly desirous that his old comrades should take a part in the battle, which sooner or later he felt convinced must take place, and to prevent the necessity of detaching them from the fleet at a later period, despatched those three ships immediately to Gibraltar, where a considerable convoy, bound up the Mediterranean, was waiting an escort.

Captain Louis, in the *Canopus*, having under his orders the *Spencer*, *Tigre*, *Queen*, and *Zealous*, was directed first to see that convoy safe beyond Carthagena, where the Spaniards had a strong squadron, and then complete his water and provisions at Tetuan and Gibraltar, and rejoin the fleet off Cadiz with all the expedition he could use.

By this arrangement the commander-in-chief thought to secure the presence of those ships before anything of moment should take place. But the consequence of it was such as he did not anticipate; for the very circumstance of detaching five sail of the line hastened Villeneuve's departure from port, who expected, in the event of being obliged to fight the British fleet, to have found it weakened by that number of ships; and thus the battle took place before Captain Louis could fulfil his instructions, and the very steps which Lord Nelson took to insure, in his opinion, the presence of three officers in the action, Captain Louis, Captain Stopford, and Captain Hallowell, whose assistance he desired more perhaps, than that of any other officers in the fleet, were the means of excluding those distinguished men from the glories of that memorable day.

When the rupture between England and the Porte took place in 1807, the *Tigre* still formed one of the blockading ships off Cadiz – and when the expeditions against Constantinople and Alexandria were planned, the naval part of the armament directed against the latter place was confided to Captain Hallowell.

At this time there were three rear-admirals attached to the Mediterranean fleet, and, therefore, to intrust the conduct and management of such an expedition to an officer so much their junior, proves the great confidence which Lord Collingwood, the commander-in-chief, reposed in Captain Hallowell's judgment and capacity.

Nor was this confidence misplaced. Transports were to be collected and the troops embarked at Messina in Sicily; and such were the secrecy and despatch with which it was conducted, that the armament appeared off Alexandria before a rumour had reached the place that any such attack was in contemplation; the consequence of which was, that the garrison being weak, and ill-prepared for defence, was taken by surprise, and compelled to surrender after a short and feeble resistance.

During all the operations attending the disembarkation of the troops, investment and attack of Alexandria, occupation of the town, and securing the posts around, Captain Hallowell's local knowledge, counsel, and foresight were eminently useful; and so indefatigable were his exertions, that I have heard his officers say that he was nine days and nights without ever having been in bed, or even undressing himself.

I cannot follow Captain Hallowell, or detail all his useful services during the time we occupied Alexandria; but after the unsuccessful and disastrous attempt upon Rosetta, when the general commanding mediated re-embarking the troops and quitting Egypt at once, Captain Hallowell did all he could to dissuade him from such a course – or, at all events, not in a hurried manner and without weighing well the consequences – to reflect that by so doing he would abandon nearly a thousand Englishmen who were prisoners in the hands of the Turks; and it was only by strong and energetic remonstrances that the army was not withdrawn before a stipulation was made for their immediate release.

After the termination of these affairs the *Tigre* rejoined Lord Collingwood, who had entered the Mediterranean in pursuit of a French squadron which had escaped from Rochefort, and was known to have passed the Straits. When the search after this squadron, which eluded Lord Collingwood's vigilance and got safe into Toulon, was over, the *Tigre*, having been more than three years on a foreign station, and in want of repairs, was ordered to England, where she arrived in the early part of 1808. Captain Hallowell's health having suffered much from anxiety and fatigue of mind and body, consequent upon his arduous exertions during a very trying period of service, he obtained leave for a few months to recruit, and another Captain was appointed to act in his place during his absence. When his health was somewhat re-established he returned to his ship, and having served a short time off the Texel with the North Sea fleet, was ordered again to the Mediterranean, where he arrived in the early part of 1809.

The conspicuous share which he had in the chase of Admiral Baudin's squadron, ending in the destruction of two line-of-battle ships off Cette, and the masterly manner in which the destruction of the convoy that escaped into Rosas was completed under his superintendence, have already been described; and in closing this brief statement of a part of Captain Hallowell's career, it only remains for me to mention that, in my experience I never knew an officer embued with a more fervent and untiring zeal for his profession and his country's service. His whole soul, indeed, and every faculty of his mind seemed to be directed to the single object of best advancing their interests. He was a man of the nicest honour, and strictest probity and truth, and his indifference – I had almost said contempt – for money, could only be equalled by his love for his country's glory and happiness, and an honourable thirst for well-earned fame.

In proof of his utter disregard of wealth, when placed in competition with his duty and nice sense of justice and proper feeling, I may mention that, besides what has already been related of his passing several Spanish ships without stopping to take possession of them, in his zeal and eagerness to join Lord Nelson, with his ship in as complete a state as to crew, and with as little delay as possible, when serving afterwards as flag-officer in the Mediterranean, he never could be prevailed upon to accept a share of freight-money, although every other admiral upon the station did so; and his reason for declining was, that he did not think that they were legally entitled to it; for, when the subject was once discussed at table, in the presence of a rear-admiral, I heard him say that, although he had himself paid freight-money to admirals, he was satisfied that they were not legally entitled to demand it; that when the right was disputed, and brought into a court of law, the decision was always against their claim. Such being the case, so far from demanding it, he would not even accept it, should it ever be his fortune to hoist his flag, until an order in Council, authorizing a new distribution, and apportioning a share to admirals, should be issued. In exact conformity with these words and sentiments was his subsequent conduct when he did hoist his flag; for whenever the Commander-in-Chief's secretary in the Mediterranean, who was also his prize-agent, sent him a rear-admiral's proportion of the freight-money, he invariably sent it back, declining to accept that which he believed neither the rules of the service, nor the laws of England authorized him to demand.*

Our cruise in 1810 was long, lasting from March till the end of October, and not diversified by many incidents which have left an impression on my mind. Sir Charles Cotton arrived from England, and took the command of the fleet in April or May, and soon after a succession of strong north-westerly gales forced the body of the fleet to the eastward. By carrying a press of sail, the in-shore squadron, consisting of the *Warspite*, *Conqueror*, and *Ajax*, of the line, with the *Euryalus* frigate, and *Shearwater* brig, maintained its position off Cape Sepet. As soon as the weather became more moderate the French fleet, as was now frequently the custom, got under weigh and left the Roadstead off Toulon for the purpose of exercising and manœuvring. At this time the *Euryalus* and brig were well to windward of the *Warspite*, for the purpose of looking into the harbour over the low neck of land to the westward of the point of Sepet.

This position they maintained too long; for as soon as the first four or five French ships had cleared the harbour, and observed them so far separated from the ships of the line, they made all sail, and steered evidently with the hope and intent of cutting them off. The moment this manœuvre was observed by Captain Blackwood, he recalled the frigate and brig

* On the change and augmentation of the Order of the Bath, Admiral Hallowell was included among the Knights Commanders, and since the war, he held the commands at Cork and Chatham. A few years before his death, he succeeded, by will of a cousin, to the fine old estates of Beddington and Orpington, the property of the Carews, upon which he took the name of that family.

by signal, at the same time making sail with the ships of the line to cover their retreat, the *Ajax* leading. Whether it was judicious, under the circumstances, to recal them may well be questioned; for although the Commodore assumed a determined front, and stood boldly in to draw the enemy upon himself, yet, from the position of the respective squadrons, it was extremely doubtful whether the frigate and brig could cross the French ships without coming into contact with them, or, at all events, without being exposed to the broadsides of five or six sail of the line. On the contrary, had they been permitted to keep their windward station, it was not probable that the French ships would be able to weather on them so much as to endanger their capture before the time came for their returning into port; for it was very unlikely that they would persevere so long in the chase as to run any risk of excluding themselves a whole night from harbour, when the body of the English fleet was not many miles distant, and which a change of wind might bring upon them in a few hours.

The signal, however, was made, and they had no choice in the frigate and brig but to obey. The *Euryalus* crossed ahead of the French squadron, fortunately without being exposed to more than a few broadsides from the leading ships, which did little or no damage. But the little *Shearwater* had a narrower escape. Being further to windward when the signal was made to close, and not sailing so well as the *Euryalus*, she fell considerably astern of the latter, and as she came down before the wind and neared the French ships, which were standing across her hawse, she became exposed to the foremost guns of the leading ships. The shot flew thick, and beat the waters all around her, but they did not appear to affect her, or to make her yaw or swerve in the least from her course, which appeared to her friends to leeward as if it would scarcely clear the leading French ship's flying jib-boom.

For some minutes, indeed, her situation appeared so critical, that either capture or destruction seemed inevitable. At length, however, there appeared a glimmering of hope. The little brig's head-sails became visible, and in a moment or two afterwards her hull showed itself to leeward of her giant pursuers. A burst of unrepressed exultation testified the joy which was felt throughout the English ships, and as she passed under the stern of the *Ajax*, three hearty cheers greeted the safety, and proclaimed their comrades' admiration at the gallant and seamanlike conduct of the little vessel.

The French Commodore, seeing that the frigate and brig had effected their escape, bethought him of his own safety, and for that purpose tacked to rejoin the body of the fleet. This gave the *Ajax* an opportunity of exchanging several broadsides with the sternmost of the French ships, which we subsequently learned bore the same name as her English opponent, and also that she had suffered in no inconsiderable degree in men and spars. Although a good deal cut in sails and rigging, the *Shearwater* was untouched in hull and spars, and she had not a man scratched.

16: Return to England

Instead of taking his turn to go to Mahon and complete the ship's water, when it was near being exhausted, like the rest of the fleet, Captain Hallo-well asked and obtained permission to remain at sea. Few incidents occurred to vary the sameness of a long cruise of six months. Now and then we exchanged a few broadsides with the French ships if, when they came out of port, they ventured beyond the very narrow limits to which we confined them.

In November, Captain Hallowell was sent to the coasts of Catalonia and Valencia, to see and report the condition of those places, still held by the Spaniards, and ascertain how far they were capable of offering resistance to Suchet, who, having subjugated Aragon and overrun the greater part of Valencia, was then before Tortosa, meaning, as soon as that place should fall, to pour down upon the coast, and sweep the whole line from Barcelona to Alicant.

The first place we visited was Taragona, which we found in a state of uncertainty and alarm, and but ill-prepared to resist so formidable an assailant as Marshal Suchet. At the urgent recommendation and entreaty of the English military resident, Colonel Doyle, the garrison had been reinforced, the advanced works were being repaired and strengthened, and the place itself, which was surrounded with a good wall, curtained and bastioned, but without a ditch or glacis, putting into as respectable a state of defence as circumstances would permit. We next touched at Peñiscola, which, from the nature of its position and vast strength if properly garrisoned and defended, seemed almost impregnable. We then ran along the coast to the westward, and in passing Alicant, at which we did not then touch, an explosion was distinctly seen from the ship, which, from the loudness of the report, and the great quantity of smoke and dust which filled the air, seemed to be of a very formidable character. We proceeded to Cartagena, which we found much better prepared to resist an enemy than Taragona; for, besides its being more regularly fortified, and a much stronger place, it had the good fortune, independent of a large Spanish garrison, to possess a British battalion (the 67th), with some English artillerymen and engineers, under the command of Brigadier-General Lambert, all of whom had, a short time before, fought at the battle of Barossa. In returning to the eastward, we looked into Alicant, which appeared to be secure from any sudden attack, the garrison being large, and General Joseph O'Donnel watching the line of the Xucar with a considerable force.

The explosion, which we noticed in passing a few days before, took place in the castle, a strong fortress that crowns a lofty and very remarkable rock, which backs the town to the north, but inclosed within the circle of its walls, and which dominates the surrounding plain, and every eminence within range of its guns. The accident was caused by the carelessness or stupidity of a gunner in filling shells; but although considerable mischief was done, several men having been killed and mutilated, and the barracks and other works a good deal damaged, still the injury was less extensive than might have been expected, the explosion having been confined to the shell-room, and leaving the principal magazine untouched. In pursuing our course to the eastward, the boats of the *Tigre* captured two feluccas, and destroyed a third, laden with grain for the garrison of Barcelona.

The object of his mission being fulfilled, Captain Hallowell steered for Mahon, where we arrived towards the middle of December, and where we found the commander-in-chief, with the body of the fleet moored for the winter months.

Not long after our arrival at Mahon, a report reached the Admiral that an attack, at first partially successful, but which resulted in most disastrous consequences, had been made upon a convoy of the enemy, which had put into Palamos on its way from Toulon to Barcelona. It consisted of a ketch of twelve or fourteen guns; two xebecks of three guns each; and eight merchant vessels, laden with grain and other provisions for Barcelona; and had sheltered within the mole of Palamos, in which was a detachment of French soldiers, estimated at a hundred or a hundred and fifty men, and further protected by a battery of three heavy guns, mounted *en barbet*, on the mole. Captain Rogers, of the *Kent*, who had under his orders the *Ajax*, 74, *Cambrian* frigate, with the *Minstrel* and *Sparrowhawk* sloops of war, planned the enterprise, whose object was to land a sufficient force to occupy the town; which done, a detachment of boats prepared for the purpose was to pull for the mole, and having spiked the guns and blown up the magazine, were then to destroy or bring out the vessels, according to circumstances.

The plan having been arranged, a force of three hundred and fifty seamen and two hundred and fifty marines left the ships in the forenoon, and pulled for the bay about two miles to the westward of the town, the whole being under the command of the captain of the *Cambrian*.

Some little firing took place between the men who first jumped on shore and the French piquet; but as soon as the whole had disembarked and moved towards the town, the piquet retired, and when the English force approached Palamos, the whole French detachment withdrew from the town without offering any opposition, and took post upon an eminence a short distance to the north-east, upon which stood a windmill.

The moment this movement was observed, the boats appointed for the service pushed for the Mole, and took possession of the battery and convoy without a struggle. They then commenced their allotted share in the business of the day by proceeding to spike the guns and destroy the magazine, and such vessels as were not to be brought away.

Meanwhile, the force under the captain of the *Cambrian* had marched through Palamos, and halted at the foot of the hill occupied by the French detachment. In that position each eyed the other for a considerable time without any movement or change on the part of either. But why the English detachment, which was so numerically superior to the enemy, did not attack them and drive them from the hill, I have never been able to conjecture, or heard explained. Possibly the commanding officer thought it sufficient to occupy the ground which he had taken up, thus interposing between the enemy and the boats at the mole, and securing them from interruption or annoyance in their work. If such were his intentions, and they had been well and steadily executed, perhaps it was the wisest plan to pursue; but that it was not so, the disastrous sequel of the expedition too lamentably attests.

After remaining in front of the enemy for a considerable time, and apprehending nothing less on his part than a movement in advance, the captain of the *Cambrian* proceeded himself to the Mole, to ascertain in person how operations were proceeding at that place. This was a most unfortunate step on his part.

Few men, if any, are to be preferred to sailors at a rush or an assault, when headlong impetuosity and daring courage are required; but take them out of their ships, and marshal them on shore, and they will be found to be restless and unsteady, and particularly impatient of inactivity.

With such knowledge of Jack's disposition and character, it behoves officers to be ever watchful of his eccentric movements, and at once to check and control the least deviation from order or discipline. The officer left in charge of the detachment by the captain of the *Cambrian* does not appear to have fulfilled this part of his duty; for the latter had been gone but a short time when the sailors began, first by ones and twos, and then in greater numbers, to leave their ranks, and stray towards the town.

This laxity and straggling was not unobserved by the French officer, who now only awaited the assured co-operation of the detachment at San Felice, to whom an express had been sent, to advance upon the British.

The latter, weakened by the defection of the men who had quitted their ranks, and expecting nothing less than to be assailed, were taken by surprise; and so sudden and furious was the onset, and being allowed no time to re-form their disordered ranks, they retired precipitately towards the town.

The French hotly pursued, and being soon joined by the party from San Felice, which equalized the contending forces, gave their opponents no time to rally; but after taking many prisoners, drove them with considerable slaughter to the boats.

They then occupied the houses, and every available point that looked to the Mole, where the boats were all assembled, embarking the fugitives; whence they poured upon them a destructive and unremitting fire until the last boat was beyond the reach of musketry.

The loss sustained in this ill-fated enterprise was very considerable, amounting to two officers, nineteen seamen, and twelve marines killed; fifteen officers, forty-two seamen, and thirty-two marines wounded; two officers, forty-one seamen, and forty-three marines prisoners; making a total of two hundred and nine *hors de combat* – nearly one-third of the force landed.

Amongst the prisoners was the captain of the *Cambrian*, who flew to put himself at the head of his men as soon as he heard that the French were advancing, and was taken in a vain attempt to arrest their flight and rally them.

Without entering into an inquiry as to the causes of so unexpected a failure, I have endeavoured to give as clear and impartial, though succinct, an account of the affair as I could learn from several of those who were personally engaged in it. When the result became known a gloom was cast over the whole fleet, and nothing was talked of for several days but the disastrous attempt at Palamos. So much, indeed, had the two line-of-battle ships suffered by it, that each ship in the fleet had to furnish them with a proportion of men to complete their crews, and restore them to a state fit for service.

The fleet had now passed a couple of winters in Mahon, and such officers as preferred '*la società de las señorinas*' to billiards and hotels had been always well and kindly received by the different families that formed the society of Mahon. They therefore bethought them that the best and most acceptable way of returning such civilities was by giving a series of balls. With this very laudable purpose in view, a number of subscribers assembled, and soon agreed that a ball should be given every fortnight at the Town-hall, so long as the fleet remained in harbour. And this resolution was fully accomplished, much to the delight and happiness of the fair of Mahon, – the very best and most indefatigable of waltzers and dancers I ever beheld. In addition to the subscription, we had many private balls also that winter, and, among others, a very gay masked one, given by the Commander-in-Chief of the Fleet. To this I went as the 'queridita' of my worthy friend, the doctor of the *Sultan*, who figured as a barbiero, though not he of Seville. My wardrobe was furnished for the occasion by our friends the Mottas, and I still remember the laughing and tittering the young ladies had as they helped to adjust my tucker, and pinned on my robaçilla. I had scarcely made the tour of the ball-room, leaning on the arm of my cavallero, when I was accosted by a certain Admiral, renowned for his devotion to the fair, who began immediately to compliment me on the gracefulness and elegance of my tournure, beseeching me to remove my mask, and let him see a face which equalled, if it did not surpass, he was sure, the beauty of my figure. Seeing me so well entertained, or perhaps fearing that we should be discovered, my companion abandoned me, and left me *tête-à-tête* with my new beau. For some time I sustained my character of young lady passably well, replying in a feigned voice, and in broken English, with some archness, to the little speeches of the gay and gallant Almirante: but when they began to assume a tenderer and more earnest character, I could stand it no longer, but laughing outright, and speaking in my natural voice, fled, leaving the bewildered Admiral, no; a little astonished and mortified at the mistake into which he had fallen.

The foregoing episode in the gallant Admiral's career reminds me of another, which may serve to diversify the history of his life. One morning four officers, myself amongst the number, called at our friends the Mottas, and after waiting a short time in the *salle de reception*, we were told that the young ladies were very busy in another room, but that they would admit us if we were disposed to see them at their occupation. We very gladly obeyed the summons, and when the door was opened, three ladies were discovered busily employed making 'sobresadas' – a piece of household work most necessary and important at Minorca. After laughing and chatting away for some time, it was proposed that we should assist the ladies in the operation which they had in hand, to which we, glad of the fun, very willingly acceded. Knives and choppers were immediately provided, and to work we fell, amid peals of merriment and laughter.

In the midst of our work and frolic the door opened, and in walked le père Motta followed by the before-named Admiral, Captain Hallowell, Captain Rowley, and another, whose name I forget. Never were astonishment and dismay greater than ours at being so caught by such a party of 'Bigwigs'. Happily there was a second door to the room, through which we bolted, followed by two of the young ladies, the moment our surprise permitted us to do so. But, from being seated at the opposite side of the table, poor Rita could not do the same.

When they saw our flight, and gave a few hearty laughs at the suddenness of our escapade, old Motta and the three Captains again withdrew by the door at which they had entered, leaving the Admiral and the young lady in quiet possession of the room. Now Rita, the youngest of M Motta's daughters, was an extremely pretty girl, shy and timid as a fawn, and our Admiral, as we have seen, was a gallant officer in more senses than one, and he thought that such an occasion as that which now presented itself was not to be neglected by a man who always professed such admiration for the '*beau sexe*'. Accordingly he drew near, with the intention of offering those little civilities and attentions which gentlemen of his disposition are in the habit of sometimes showing; but there was something in his *regard* that terrified Rita, and she shrank from his proffered hand, gliding backwards round the table as he advanced. Finding, however, that this repulse, together with repeated requests, expressed in good Mahonese, that he would keep his distance, did not check his approach, she at length seized a handful of the sausage-meat, and flinging it full in his face, flew to the door, opened it, and while he was clearing his eyes of the savoury mess, darted through, and so effected her retreat.

Thus passed the winter at Mahon. Rides and rackets, now and then diversified by a pic-nic, as spring advanced, in the mornings; and in the evenings, when no ball intervened, at the *Tertulla* where we were sure to find either music, dancing, or a game at '*gallinas ciegas*' to amuse us.

But a life like this, of mere idle amusement, was not to last long without interruption. A mind anxious and deeply thoughtful for his country's service, like Captain Hallowell's, could not but feel ill at ease at the long continuance of the fleet in harbour, particularly when he reflected on the strength, and state of readiness for sea, in which that of the enemy was kept at Toulon, and the many points in the Mediterranean, which, if left unguarded, seemed to invite attack, whilst there were others into which he only waited an opportunity to throw supplies. Moreover, Captain Hallowell belonged to a class of officers who believe that much sound doctrine is contained in the old aphorism which declares 'idleness to be the root of all evil' and more applicable to sailors than to any other description of mortals. His study, therefore, always had been to find out as much work for both officers and men as could be contrived, and by constant employment keep a certain elderly gentleman as far from their thoughts as possible.

As far as regarded the men this could be managed even in harbour; but to carve out work for the officers was a matter not so easily accomplished. 'Tis true those of the *Tigre* were kept pretty well at it during the day, few boats leaving the ship on duty for any purpose unless under the charge of a Lieutenant; and it was no uncommon thing to see a Lord or an Honourable seated on high in a launch-load of empty casks, going for a turn of water, – a piece of duty which modern improvement and refinement may deem beneath the dignity of even the mates of the present day.

This impatience of harbour would now and then betray itself involuntarily in some hasty exclamation of wonder at the supineness of the Commander-in-Chief, and the state of inactivity in which he kept the fleet. Sometimes it was manifested by declarations that neither officers or men would be worth a c–se if kept much longer without anything to do, and presently he discovered that the officers of the *Tigre* were the idlest young men in the fleet, who did nothing but philander on shore every night – a discovery that was speedily followed by an order, which directed that none should be on shore after gun-fire. This order was a sad privation to many of us, which, however, did not last very long, for in less than a fortnight after it was issued, the fleet at length put to sea.

Prior to the sailing of the fleet it had been announced that the *Tigre* was the first ship to return to England upon the arrival of a successor; an announcement which was hailed with pleasure by us all; for although none felt tired of the Mediterranean, which was always a favourite station, still the prospect of soon revisiting country and friends, from whom you have been any time separate, always cheers and gladdens the heart. In expectation of soon seeing our relief, Mrs Boxer, our second Lieutenant's wife, who had been written to, had arrived from Malta, and Captain Hallowell offered a passage to a Mr or Major S——, as he was generally called, who, with his daughter, a little girl of ten or eleven, was waiting at Mahon for an opportunity of proceeding to England, Mrs Boxer forming one of our mess in the wardroom, while the Major and his daughter were domiciled with the Captain.

The circumstances under which Major S—— found himself in the Mediterranean were somewhat peculiar. It seems he had made a bet with a friend that, before the expiration of a given time, he would kill a certain quantity of fish and game in the island of Sardinia. Having performed this feat and won his bet, he crossed over to Minorca, where he found his little daughter. At the time I write of, she gave promise of being a very lovely woman. She was tall for her years, and her form and movements were naturally both graceful and elegant. Although quite untutored, her mind seemed astonishingly quick and intelligent, and although she had been learning the language but a short time, she already spoke English remarkably well. Those early indications of wit and beauty were afterwards fully developed and realized; and before she attained her twentieth year, the young lady was married to a baronet of good fortune.

Our relief not arriving as soon as expected, we remained with the fleet off Toulon till the end of June or beginning of July, during which time nothing took place there, that I remember, which calls for observation. It was different on the coast of Valencia and Catalonia, where the co-operation and exertions of our ships under the command of Captain Codrington, of the *Blake*, retarded, but could not prevent the sweeping conquests of the French under Marshal Suchet.

At length our successor arrived, and the same evening we left the fleet, and steered for Mahon, where it was necessary to get a supply of water for the passage to England. We reached Mahon on the second morning after we left the fleet, and fearing that many a day might elapse before we had a similar opportunity, my friend and chum Bob Spencer and I agreed to give a parting dance to '*las hijas Mahonesas*' at whose houses we had received so much kindness and hospitality for so long a time. But the ship was to sail on the following morning, and how to manage it in so short a time was a matter for consideration.

Where there is a will, however, as the proverb says, there will always be found a means, so to work we went in downright earnest. One inspected the preparations for the ball-room, ordered the refreshments, and arranged for the music, while the other undertook to call at the several houses of our friends, and deliver the invitations orally, as there was not sufficient time to send written ones. And thus we contrived a very pleasant ball the evening of our arrival, returning to the ship at four o'clock in the morning, which in a few hours after was cleaving the ocean with her head directed towards Gibraltar.

Our passage home, though long, was cheered and enlivened by remarkably fine pleasant weather, and the addition to our society of Sir Samuel Hood, just appointed to the command in the East Indies, with several of his officers, besides the passengers already mentioned. On the 2nd of August, I think it was, our eyes were gladdened with a sight of Old England, and on the following morning the *Tigre* anchored at Spithead.

As soon as the ship got pratique, she was ordered into harbour for the purpose of being stripped and having her defects examined and repaired. Just at this time a general promotion took place, and Captain Hallowell became a Rear-Admiral. A short time before he left the old ship, he assembled the lieutenants in his cabin, when he told us that he was promised by the First Lord of the Admiralty, that he should hoist his flag in a short time, when he would willingly apply for such as were desirous to follow his fortunes in another ship. But if there were any who desired a change, he would use his best endeavours to have them appointed to that description of vessel which they should prefer; adding, that as a junior admiral his power of advancing officers would be necessarily confined, but such as it might prove, it should be exerted in favour of the deserving, according to their standing and seniority in the ship. Every one expressed his grateful acknowledgments for so kind an offer, and all but one declared their desire to adhere to the fortunes of the Admiral. The dissentient was Lieutenant Matterface, our third, who was tired of a ship of the line, and preferred a frigate; and soon after, at the Admiral's request, he was appointed to the *Rota*.

This choice proved an unlucky one, and cut short the career of poor M——, who was an active, enterprising, good officer, and as brave as a lion; for not many months after his appointment to the frigate, he was shot through the brain while standing up in the stern sheets of his boat, leading and cheering on his men to the assault of the *General Armstrong* American privateer, which was anchored at one of the Western Islands, and defended, as well from the vessel, as by a part of her crew, which had been landed, and were advantageously posted on shore.

Half the officers had been superseded, and a new Captain (Halliday) had joined the *Tigre* before she was stripped and taken into dock, leaving the first and second lieutenants and myself to carry on the war.

Although I had written to be superseded, several weeks elapsed without my successor making his appearance. The ship was fast getting ready for sea. I was heartily sick of Portsmouth, and began to sigh for home, where I had passed but three short weeks out of eleven years, which had gone over my head since the day I first left it. At last my relief made his appearance on board, and in a few hours afterwards I was on my way to Bristol.

I found my eldest sister at Clifton, who had been recommended the air of that place for her health; and after staying with her for a few weeks, I prevailed upon her to accompany me to Ireland. As her health was still very delicate, we travelled by easy stages through Wales, and embarked at Milford towards the end of October.

After a passage of twenty-four hours, no bad run when we consider that there was no steam to quicken it in those days, we landed at Cheek Point.

Time, which severs so many ties, and robs us of kindred and friends – which obscures our brightest visions, and disappoints our most cherished hopes, toppling down, with ruthless hand, the air-built castles of our early days; – time had not yet chilled the affections, or blunted the finer sensations of youth; and therefore it was with a feeling akin to rapture that I once more touched my native soil, after an absence of so many years.

A drive of six miles took us to Waterford, where we slept. The following morning, as my sister did not feel strong enough to travel to Lismore without rest, we took the road by Clonmel instead of that by Dungarvan, which is the more direct, as we despaired of comfortable accommodation at the latter town for the night. I did not regret this choice of route, for I had heard that, in all Ireland, nothing could exceed the dreariness of the road by Dungarvan. Unreclaimed bog, and wild uncultivated mountain divided, at this time, the inhospitable region between them, which for the most part belonged to the races Power and Baron, – a proprietorship that struck a punning Englishman, who once had the misfortune to travel that way, as so apposite to the unfruitfulness and desolation of the soil, that he gave it the name of the 'poor and barren' county Waterford. The road by Clonmel is as pleasing and interesting, as the other is the reverse, passing through a country which possesses all the features of the beautiful and picturesque, wood and water – mountain and valley – green slopes and well-cultivated uplands, meet the eye wherever it turns.

On leaving the 'Urbs intacta', the road crosses the long wooden bridge which connects the counties of Waterford and Kilkenny, and then ascends the left bank of the Suir, having that noble stream, with the rich and varied grounds of Curraghmore, Lord Waterford's splendid demesne, in view, until you come to Pilltown, a village which had started into existence within a short time, under the fostering care of Lord Besborough, whose property it is. The spot upon which this village stands, is as romantic and beautiful as the imagination of painter or poet could ever desire or conceive. Its situation indeed equals, if it does not exceed, anything of the kind I ever beheld in England; and, what perhaps is unique in Ireland, the cottages of which it is almost entirely composed are as neat and trim, and the little gardens in front of them as tidily kept, as they are in the sister country. Pilltown reposes in a rich and sheltered nook, enclosed on all sides by well-wooded and rather lofty hills, except to the south-east, where it is just sufficiently open to afford glimpses of the grounds of Lord Besborough. In front of the range of cottages, which comprise the greater part of the village, runs a clear and cheerful stream, which, being crossed at intervals by a few rustic bridges that serve as points of communication to the occupants of some cottages of greater pretension on the opposite bank, hastens to add its scanty tribute to the more majestic Suir, which flows at no great distance below. After leaving Pilltown, the road through Carrick-on-Suir loses nothing in interest or objects of attraction, until you come to Clonmel, where we slept.

We found Clonmel to be a large, but ugly town, possessing some share of traffic, and a superabundance of the atttributes of most Irish towns – viz., poverty in its humiliating form, rendered painfully apparent by the numerous beggars by whom we were everywhere beset, and by the sight of the wretched hovels which then composed a large part of this metropolis of Tipperary. We dined with an old and valued friend of my father. They had been chums at College, and had maintained ever after, a constant intercourse and correspondence. Both entered young into the church, soon after which they settled, the one at Lismore, the other at Clonmel. As their duties and avocations did not permit of constant personal intercourse, they hit upon a plan by which they could see each other at all events once a week. It was arranged that each should mount his horse every Saturday, and meet at Clogheen, a village half-way between their respective homes. Then, after an hour's chat, and having refreshed man and beast at the little inn, their horses' tails were turned to each other, and the friends again repaired to their parochial labours. Once established, this hebdomadal meeting was seldom omitted till the close of life; and a friendship begun in youth, never cooled or relaxed, but gaining strength with increase of years, survived, (rare occurence!) even infirmity and old age.

The road from Clonmel to Clogheen, still ascending the Suir, which it sometimes recedes from, is bounded on the left by the Comraghs, a chain of mountains which separate the counties of Waterford and Tipperary. To the left is Knockmeildown, which lifts its picturesque and stately form high above all its neighbours, while the rich and cultivated plain over which the road passes, is enclosed to the north by the line of the blue and lofty Galtees. Half-way we passed through the miserable village of Ardfinnan, when a sharp and sudden turn in the road displayed to view the extensive ruin of the castle of that name. Its situation, and the extent of the ruins, show that it was once a place of great strength and importance. It is now almost prostrate, and there is little left except some huge fragments of the walls, from which an opinion may be formed of its former consequence and grandeur. The castle of Ardfinnan stands, or rather stood upon a precipitous rock, which, like a huge elbow. pushes itself into the broad Suir, that chafes, eddies, foams, and then rushes by with great force.

This situation enabled the fortress to look both up and down the river, and present a face to whatever might approach from either quarter; and as it was not commanded by higher ground in the neighbourhood, it was not easily assailable from the land side, as the art of war was formerly understood. At Clogheen, where we changed horses, the road turns to the south, and then winding round a shoulder of Knockmeildown, mounts a long and steep ascent. At the summit is a pond or small lake, called 'Bay Loch', to which many a marvellous legend is attached. Among others it is said, that never line has been found long enough to fathom its depths, and that, the adventurous fisherman, who is presumptuous enough to cast his net into its enchanted waters, is sure to be scared from his task by sights and sounds of a terrific and unearthly nature – the lake becomes agitated in a strange and unusual manner – smoke issues from the mountains – the loud, hollow rumble of thunder and other wild and strange noises are heard, while, if the terror-stricken wight casts his eye below, the whole village of Clogheen appears wrapt in flames.

The descent towards Lismore is less rapid than on the other side of the mountain. The road soon joins a torrent, whose tortuous course it follows for a considerable distance, until at a sharp bend it crosses an arch where a second torrent unites itself to the first, and both together form the stream that bears the name of Ounasheadh (Anglicè, Fairy's Water). Until this point was gained, the mountain presented little to arrest the eye, save one wild outline, the nakedness of which was clothed with heather, but which the season had robbed of its purple bloom. Soon the road assumed a more attractive and interesting character. To the left, the mountain became loftier, but still bare of trees, except here and there some patches of dwarf oak shooting up from roots coeval with the mountains. To the right it rose steep and abrupt, and was covered to the summit with a cloak of thick copse through which trees of taller growth reared, from time to time, their statelier heads, while huge masses of grey rock would here and there protrude their nakedness.

The road, which enters the glen formed by these mountains, followed the torrent in all its twistings and turnings, which, swollen to no inconsiderable stream, swept hurriedly along. At one time its desperate course bore it to the brink of a precipice, over which it leaped and formed no mean cascade. Then, weary with exertion, it reposed for a moment, and filled to the brim with its inky waters a basin dug from the living rock. Anon, renewed in strength, again it started on its furious course, and chafed and maddened by the obstacles that vainly crossed its path, it stopped not till it found a resting-place in the bosom of the gentler and more placid Blackwater.

From the moment we entered the glen and commenced the descent of the mountain, our reckless driver of the yellow 'Po-chay' urged on his smoking horses with mimic fury, imitating the tortured river in all its writhings and twistings. A sudden turn in the road, as the carriage flew round a rock that projected from the mountain-side, at length revealed to my anxious gaze the church and castle of Lismore; and it would be difficult to analyze or describe my sensations at sight of those well-remembered objects. In an instant it recalled the scenes and occurrences of my childish days, and brought before my eye, in vivid colours, the forms and features of my friends, such as I saw them when last we parted. Then followed that throbbing aching sensation, which would annihilate all space and time: and although we flew along at down-hill speed, the horses seemed to my impatience, actually to creep, and that we should never arrive at my father's door. At length the bridge over the Blackwater is passed – the church and castle are left behind – the crazy carriage rattles through the long street of Lismore – it stops, and the next moment I am in the arms of my dear father and sisters.

17: The *Malta*

Many changes had taken place in persons as well as things at Lismore since I had seen it last. Marriages and births had occurred, and a few of the oldest inhabitants had been gathered to their fathers. The face of the country evinced considerable improvement. Agriculture, fostered by the demand for produce and the high prices of the war, was making rapid strides. The cottages and cabins of the farmers and peasantry had a more comfortable appearance, many being now provided with chimneys and glazed windows; and the homesteads and fences of the farms were better looked to, and kept in better order. Following the example of the manager of the Duke of Devonshire's estates, the gentry, in numerous instances, had begun to plant. A part of the castle, before ruinous and dilapidated, had been restored, and an entirely new quarter had replaced some of the older parts of the town, where the houses had been taken down, either as being inconvenient, or too near and too much in view of the ducal residence. The transported, who were very loth to quit their old haunts, not inappropriately denominated the new quarter Botany, or, as they pronounced it, 'Bottomy' Bay, a name by which it is known to the present day. I likewise found that a change had been wrought in the dress of the humbler classes of my countrymen and countrywomen. The men in general were better clad. Instead of the grey frize coat, a better description of cloth had been substituted, and cloth had also supplanted the sheep-skin breeches of their fathers. The younger women had adopted the English costume, and had substituted *frocks* of printed calico for the brown or green stuff *gowns* of old, open in front to display the gay yellow or scarlet *calamanco*, and having discarded the close-fitting cap, that just suffered the hair to be seen beneath, parted on the forehead, they had turned up the hair behind and curled and ringletted it in front, after the newest and most approved fashion. This change in female attire might have had a lighter and more airy character, but certainly it added nothing in picturesqueness of effect.

A few weeks flew quickly by in the society of my friends, and in renewing acquaintance with old faces and scenes of my boyish days. I tried my hand at the river's side, and found that eleven years' disuse had not robbed me of an angler's 'trick'. Though all unused to the perilous sport, I even ventured to bestride a hunter's back, and still live to record my escape with unbroken bones. But this holyday life was not to be of long continuance. I might have been at Lismore between three or four weeks, dreaming little of ships or service, when one morning, at breakfast, looking carelessly over the columns of a newspaper, my eye was arrested by a paragraph that the *Malta* was fitting at Plymouth with all imaginable dispatch, under the command of Captain Inglefield for the flag of Rear-Admiral Hallowell, who had already proceeded to the Mediterranean in the *Royal George*. Startled by this announcement, and recollecting that the authorities at the Admiralty must be ignorant of my *séjour*, inasmuch as I had neglected to inform them of it, I wrote immediately to Captain Inglefield, telling him how I was situated, and requesting him to let me know whether my name had been included in the list of officers appointed to the *Malta*. To this letter I received an answer by return of post, saying that my commission had been lying a month at the Commissioner's Office at Plymouth, and expressing surprise and disapprobation at my neglect in not having sooner joined my ship, which was now nearly ready for sea. On the receipt of this communication I took a hasty leave of my friends, and started immediately for Cove, in the hope that, should one of the cruisers be about to sail, I might get a passage direct to Plymouth. Disappointed in this expectation, I embarked in one of the Bristol traders, which fortunately was passing Cove the same afternoon, and which landed me at Clifton after a run of thirty-six hours.

I lost no time at Clifton, but started again the same afternoon at three o'clock by a 'six inside', the only public conveyance; but so slow was its progress that it did not reach Plymouth until five o'clock on the following afternoon.

The next morning, I waited on my new Captain, who received me with a good deal of stiffness, and expressed in words what he had written, much surprise at the coolness and indifference I had shown in taking so long a time before I joined my ship; but when I explained to him that I was really unacquainted with the fact that the *Malta* had been commissioned, and that I had been appointed one of her lieutenants, he seemed somewhat appeased, and we parted better friends.

It was a few days before Christmas, in the year 1811, that I joined the *Malta*, and having received the last draught of men to complete her crew, she went into Cawsand Bay on the following morning. And, certainly, the *Malta* was a noble ship – as fine, if not the finest vessel upon two decks at that time in his Majesty's service. Her armament was ninety-six guns, four of which were 68's, all the remainder, as well as the guns for the boats, carrying 32s and 24s.

As Admiral Hallowell had already proceeded to the Mediterranean, it was supposed that we should make no delay at Plymouth; but as the French squadrons of Rochefort and L'Orient were ready at any time to put to sea, it was judged more prudent that we should have a consort, and accordingly we waited two or three weeks for the *Edinburgh*, which ship was fitting at Portsmouth, and destined, like ourselves, for the Mediterranean. These few weeks of detention appeared tedious enough, for we were tired of harbour, and longed, with all sincerity, to return to our old station. The wished-for release at length arrived. The *Edinburgh* made her number, and before she had passed the Mewstone, the *Malta* was standing out to join her.

We crossed the bay, and rounded Cape St Vincent without a chase, or any occurrence worth recording. The *Edinburgh* had rather the advantage of us in sailing, and we observed that the *Malta* was uneasy, and laboured a good deal when the sea was rough. This circumstance, and the dullness of her sailing, we attributed to the great quantity of stores which she had on board for the fleet in the Mediterranean, in addition to her own supply, and six months' water and provisions.

The evening we entered the Straits was dark and lowering, and we passed the rock of Gibraltar the same night, with the wind on the quarter, blowing fresh at W.N.W. About two o'clock in the morning, after having had the first watch, I was startled from a comfortable sleep by the call of 'All hands shorten sail!' and at the same moment in came a midshipman of the watch to rouse the lieutenants. It took me but a few minutes to huddle on my clothes, and make my way to my station, which was the forecastle, and when I reached it, what a scene presented itself!

Courses clewed up, but unconfined by the brails, were flapping in the wind with the noise of thunder – the men were aloft, but the topgallant-sails still unfurled – and the topsail-yards, pressed by the force of the wind, and weight of the sails, new, and saturated with wet, against the lee-rigging, refused to come down. The wind, which had suddenly shifted several points to the northward, was increased to a gale, and the rain poured down in torrents. The sea had risen almost as quickly as the wind, and the ship, deep in the water, and out of trim, was rolling most fearfully.

Such is a brief description of the state of matters when I reached the deck. At length the topsails were clewed down, and the yards and sails secured, so as to permit the men to be ordered to lie out for the purpose of reefing and furling; but the rigging, which was new, and difficult suffi-ciently to stretch in cold weather, felt the effect of a motion so violent, and soon became so slack, as did also the parrels of the yards, as to endanger not only the safety of the masts, but also the lives of the men who were aloft. Happily, these last accomplished their difficult and perilous task without accident. The fury of the squall did not last very long, and by degrees the canvas was reduced, and things began to wear a snugger appearance. The sails being new, had escaped without a rent, but the fore-top-mast was found to be badly sprung, and the lower rigging of the fore-mast so slack that, unless immediate steps were taken to set it up, there was great danger at every lurch that it would go over the side.

Boxer, the second lieutenant, who supplied the place of the first, too unwell at the time to attend to duty, saw with a glance, and instantly sug-gested a method to effect this operation – an operation so difficult of exe-cution when rolling heavily in a sea, and one which no man in the ship had ever seen tried before. This seemed simple enough, when *explained* and put into execution, and consisted merely in clapping a luff-tackle upon each lee-shroud, and, when all was duly prepared in the chains, man the falls, and then, as the ship rolled to leeward, walk away, and take in the slack of the lanyards all together, until the rigging be deemed suffi-ciently taut, and the shrouds all bear an even strain. When this was done with the lee-rigging, and the lanyards secured, the ship was veered upon the other tack, and the same process pursued on the opposite side, and in this manner the foremast was saved, and the rigging almost as well set up as if the ship had been in harbour.

The foretop-mast had then to be shifted, and it was ten o'clock on the following day before the ship was quite to rights, and proceeding on her proper course.

I should have passed over this squall and its disagreeable consequences without notice, were it not for the opportunity it gives of, and the pleasure I now find in, relating this proof, out of many, of that quick apprehension, and ever-ready resource to meet difficulty and danger, how sudden soever they might be, or in whatever shape they might present themselves, with which my old friend and messmate, Edward Boxer, was at all times furnished.

We reached Minorca, without further accident about the end of February, or the beginning of March, 1812, after a much shorter absence than I calculated upon when leaving the island in July before. We found our consort, the *Edinburgh,* which had arrived before us, and the whole fleet, now under the command of Sir Edward Pellew, at Mahon.

On the morning after our arrival, Rear-Admiral Hallowell shifted his flag from the *Royal George* to the *Malta,* and being desirous to try the qualities of his new ship, he obtained permission to go to sea for a short trip for that purpose. We had scarcely time to visit our friends on shore, when we found ourselves again at sea, and steering in the direction for Toulon. Arrived off Cape Sicie, the first consideration was to see the number and condition of the enemy's fleet; and for this purpose the ship was steered under the immediate direction of the Admiral, whose knowledge of the harbours and arsenal of Toulon, as well as long and thorough acquaintance with that part of the coast, enabled him to place the ship just out of range of shot and shell, but in a position to command the inner and outer harbours, and distinguish the ships ready for sea from such as were refitting, or those upon the stocks.

The fleet was found to be in much the same state as when we left the Mediterranean eight months before, except that the two line-of-battle ships then building to replace the ones destroyed off Cette, in 1809, had been launched, and were now fitting in the inner harbour, and advancing fast towards completion. The weather proved boisterous and squally, and just such as was required to put the ship's good and bad properties to the proof, upon which, having satisfied his mind, the Admiral returned to Mahon. In this trial it was found that the ship had an unnecessary quantity of ballast – that she was too much by the head; and the Admiral was of opinion that by adding to the breadth of the rudder, she would steer more easily, and, on a wind in a head sea, carry a better helm.

The rigging had been fitted at the dockyard, and the service, having already become slack, required to be stripped and clapped on anew; and the dead-eyes having been turned in *cutter-fashion*, and the ends of the shrouds squared and pointed, to give them a neat appearance, had to be changed and turned in afresh. This practice, almost universal in the navy, of squaring the ends of the shrouds, was contrary to Admiral Hallowell's notions of security, and, consequently, good seamanship; for, in the course of a long service, during which he had seen numberless shrouds carried away, he had often occasion to remark that, from the custom of squaring the rigging, there was scarcely end enough left to form a knot if wanted, and, therefore, in those ships that he personally fitted out and commanded the ends of the shrouds were left just as they had been originally cut at the dockyard, simply capping them neatly, but without squaring or reducing them at all in length.

When we returned to Mahon, Boxer was still officiating as first lieutenant, and it was under his able management that these necessary changes and improvements were made; and when I mention that the ship was again ready for sea in four days, and recapitulate what was accomplished in the time, it must be acknowledged a performance of no ordinary nature. The ship was stripped, and, after taking off the service of the lower and topmast shrouds, re-rigged again. The hold was broken up, and entirely cleared, four hundred tons of water started, and every water-cask in the ship, to the ground-tier leagers, landed, rinsed out, and refilled; one hundred and eighty tons of shingle ballast – not thrown overboard, but put on shore by the ship's boats; the iron ballast shifted so as to change the ship's trim, and the hold entirely re-stowed. All this was done, and the ship ready for sea in four days, in March, when they are not the longest, and by a crew not three months together. When this piece of duty, which engaged the attention and active co-operation of every officer and man in the ship, was finished, we were indulged with some relaxation, and enjoyed ourselves with greater zest with our friends on shore.

Early in April the fleet sailed from Minorca, to resume the blockade of Toulon, and soon after its arrival on its station, Admiral Hallowell was appointed to command the advanced or inshore squadron. As well as I remember at this distance of time, this squadron consisted of the *Malta*, *Kent*, *Centaur*, and *Sultan*. The enemy's fleet, though rarely venturing a league from the land, whenever the wind was easterly, seldom lost the opportunity of getting under weigh, and coming out of harbour for the purpose of exercising the crews. Some of the boldest now and then stretched beyond the limit to which they usually restricted themselves; but whenever they showed themselves so hardy, they were instantly driven back by our advanced ships.

This sparring between individual ships of the hostile fleets reminds me of a tussle, or short action, of a somewhat similar, but far more brilliant character, that took place about that time – one that reflects the greatest credit on the memory of the distinguished officer, now unhappily no more, who commanded the British ship, and was a theme of general admiration to all who witnessed it. A French frigate and brig, coming from the eastward, had anchored in Hyères Bay, and were compelled, by the situation of the English fleet, to remain there until an opportunity should present itself of running for Toulon. To prevent this, if possible, Sir Peter Parker, in the *Menelaus*, had been selected to watch the Petite Passe, the only outlet by which the Frenchmen could effect their object. This duty he performed with his accustomed vigilance, and for several days they made no attempt to move. Early one morning, however, taking advantage of a fresh breeze from the north-ward, which had drifted the English fleet to some distance from the land, they at length got under weigh, and were seen from the *Menelaus*, which kept her station, steering in the direction of the Petite Passe, and soon after the Toulon fleet was observed under weigh, and working out of harbour. As soon as the enemy's frigate and brig had cleared the Passe, they hauled as close to the shore as possible, and then steered for the harbour.

Nothing daunted by the nearness of the French fleet, nor by the formidable array of batteries which bristled along the coast, Sir Peter stood boldly in, with the intention, I believe, of laying the enemy's frigate on board, if possible; but if not, to give her as good a hammering as time would permit, before she got under the protection of her friends. Though the wind was fresh, the water was smooth, and the two frigates steering, the one athwart the other's course, neared each other with great rapidity. When within little more than pistol-shot distance, the *Menelaus* bore up, and kept abreast, and as near her opponent as the proximity of the shore would admit. In this situation the two frigates engaged each other, and maintained an animated fire for a considerable time, the brig and batteries also taking part in the action, by which the *Menelaus* was much galled, until Sir Peter Parker observed that the French fleet had cleared Cape Sepet, and that their headmost ships were now so far advanced, while those of his own friends were full seven miles to leeward, that if he continued the action longer, it would expose the *Menelaus* to certain capture. He, therefore, reluctantly, I have no doubt, put his helm astarboard, and having brought the wind on his larboard beam, steered in the direction of the English fleet, then reaching in under a press of sail, the *Malta* being considerably to windward and ahead of the rest. The leading ships of the enemy pursued the *Menelaus* for some distance; but, although they could not fail to observe she was crippled, having furled her head-sails preparatory to striking her fore-top-mast, which was badly wounded, they did not dare to continue the chase, lest, by running further to leeward, they should expose themselves to be cut off before they recovered their windward position again. The moment the enemy's ships put their heads inshore, the *Menelaus* did the same, and hove-to, and then proceeded to shift her foretop-mast, with as much regularity and coolness as if no enemy had been present, and she lay quietly in harbour.

The *Menelaus* did not suffer as much as might have been expected from the closeness of the combat, and the force to which she was opposed – namely, a frigate of equal size with herself, a brig of sixteen or eighteen guns, and the powerful batteries which line the coast. Besides the loss of her foretop-mast, her rigging and sails were a good deal cut, and she received several shot in her hull; but I cannot call to mind that she had any casualties in killed or wounded. It certainly was a triumphant and spirit-stirring sight to witness the bold and masterly manner in which this single British frigate dashed at and encountered such odds, pressing her opponents to the shore, even to the muzzles of the guns of their batteries, and never relinquishing her quarries till she had driven them to the har-bour's mouth, and, I may say, into the very arms of their friends, who were hastening to their succour.

Some time in May – I think it was – a change took place in the con-struction of our mess in the *Malta*. Two or three lieutenants, not meant to belong permanently to the ship, left about that time, and were succeeded by others, who, with few exceptions, remained together as long as she continued on the station. And here, let me pause for a moment, whilst I call to mind the characters of some of those early friends, in whose society the happiest days of my life were passed – days chequered by duty that was little other than pleasure, and a relaxation from toil, which we con-verted into positive enjoyment.

Of the new-comers who joined the *Malta* at that time, there was one, whose frank and affable manners, gentlemanly bearing, good-humour, and almost constant flow of spirits, won for him the regard, and made him a favourite with all his messmates.

A congeniality perhaps of tastes and feeling, and a similarity of judg-ment and opinions upon different subjects, first drew Charles Christopher Parker* and me together; – hence, an intimacy that soon ripened into friendship, which knew no interruption while we remained

* Now Sir Charles C Parker, having succeeded to the baronetcy in consequence of the deaths of his elder brothers and nephews.

together, and still survives fresh and vigorous as ever, although for many years we have not been able to see much of each other.

I think I see C C Parker now, just as he was when he joined the 'Malta' – young, ardent, frank, sincere – slender in person, with a bloom and freshness on his yet unrazored cheek, that a girl might have envied; mirth and frolic laughed in his joyous sunny eyes; dulness (if a ward-room can be said ever to be dull) fled at his approach, and badinage and fun, with a repartee that leaves no sting, reigned in its place.

With all this airiness of a happy temperament, this *gaieté de cœur*, Charles was of a nature at once candid, generous, and sincere, capable, moreover, of strong and lasting attachments. His knowledge and love of his profession were hereditary;* and had opportunity been given, and his health permitted him to serve, his zeal and acquirements would doubtless have added to that fame, which a long line of illustrious naval ancestors has acquired for themselves and for their country.

Many and many is the *lark* (to use a cant phrase) Charles and I have had in harbour; and how often at sea has the weariness of a midnight watch been cheated by his droll and witty stories.

Those days are gone – swept, like their predecessors, into the abyss of time. And yet, who will say they are dead? for memory, the grand exorcist, evokes them at her will, arraying even now before the mind's eye, with the freshness and distinctness of reality, events and circum-stances around which the mantle of nearly thirty years oblivion has been rolled!

Before I knew him, and up to the present time, Parker had been subject to headaches of a most painful and distressing nature, rendering him, dur-ing the access, totally incapable of the least exertion. These headaches are the consequence of a serious fall, which he met with on board ship in the perfor-mance of his duty, and have produced an effect so injurious to his general health, as to render it a matter of less regret, that the numerous applications which he has made for active employment have been unsuccessful.

Of a character and disposition that differed *toto cœlo* from those of the friend I have just described, was S——n, another of our lieutenants, who joined the ship about the same time. Possessed of a certain kind of humour, you could not help at times being amused by his drollery, or for-bear a smile at many of his odd jests and sayings, though the latter were often of too broad a nature to leave a pleasing impression behind them.

He had been wrecked in a frigate early in the war on the coast of France, when he was taken, and remained several years a prisoner at

* Admiral Hallowell, upon re-hoisting his flag in 1815, applied for Parker to be his first lieu-tenant; but he had just before been made a commander.

Verdun, until, at length, he effected his escape into Holland, whence he was put on board one of our cruisers by a fisherman, whom he bribed for the purpose.

S——n's professional knowledge, it may be supposed, had not advanced by a five years' compulsory residence in an inland town in France. In fact, it would seem to have retrograded, although his nautical phraseology had lost none of its raciness since he left the midshipman's berth.

En revanche, however, he had picked up a little of the language, and gleaned a multitude of sayings peculiar to the *braves* of that nation; so much so, that some of those expressions used to petrify a French gentleman of somewhat fastidious manners, who was detained for a time on board the *Malta*, and who declared that a life passed amidst the *tambours* of the French army was hardly sufficient for the acquisition of so much knowledge of military cant as Monsieur S——n possessed. S——n, whose height and figure were good, could mimic, at pleasure, the strut and swelling air and ferocious look of a French *militaire*, and could imitate to perfection every beat and roll of the French drummers, and flourish his cane, and march with the measured step of that important functionary, the *tambour-major* of a French battalion.

A rare and invaluable addition to our society, was Archibald Murray,* who acted in the double capacity of Purser and Admiral's Secretary. He had long been known to Admiral Hallowell, with whom he sailed in the *Argo*, who fully appreciated his many estimable qualities. It is too much the custom in the navy to consider pursers as a money-loving and avaricious race, – a character which, as far as my own experience goes, they do not deserve, and if universally applied, is both unfair and unjust. But if such a disposition rightly attaches to any of his compeers, Murray's was quite the reverse. Liberal and generous to a fault, he set little value upon wealth, except in so far as it enabled him to increase his store of books, of which he had already a goodly collection. An avarice of knowledge, indeed, and a thirst for those fountains whence its riches flow, he certainly possessed: so sorely was he afflicted with the malady of bibliomania that he often indulged it to the detriment of his finances. When he joined the *Malta*, his library could not have contained less than four thousand well-chosen volumes; to which he made valuable additions whenever opportunity offered. Considering how limited are a sailor's opportunities, Murray's acquaintance with the literature of England, France, Italy, and Spain was varied and extensive; to which he added a love for the acquisition of languages, many of which he understood and spoke

* Elder brother of the late well-known and highly respectable publisher of Albemarle Street.

fluently. His critical acumen upon all subjects submitted to his judgment was seldom surpassed; and although no artist, he was well acquainted with the sciences of music and painting, and with the histories and works of their best masters. Indeed, his knowledge of and taste in pictures were both chaste and correct. With a mind so richly endowed, and with such stores – such an affluence I may say – of knowledge, it has often been matter of wonder to me that he did not give himself to the production of something which would have made his name better known to the world. The omission is only to be accounted for by attributing it to a modesty and diffidence which were inherent in him, and which are generally the companions of true genius and knowledge. Except the revision and last finish of Ciciloni's Italian Grammar, which the author, a friend of his, requested him to do, and clothing in chaste, elegant, and nervous language the vast research and profound sentiments contained in Sir John Malcolm's latest work 'On the Government of India', I know nothing that proceeded from his pen. Although little acquainted with its history, and almost ignorant of the statistics of that country, he consented to undertake the latter work at Sir John's earnest solicitation; who said that he could himself supply *raw material* in abundance, but that he could not devote the time and trouble necessary to arrange and polish it to his satisfaction. And how well and beautifully Murray executed his task, the world has an opportunity of judging.

Murray's disposition was naturally grave and thoughtful, and his manners were peculiarly gentle and attractive. The character of his mind was innocence itself, and to the unsuspecting simplicity of childhood was joined a correctness and strength of judgment which made his opinion be sought for whenever any serious or difficult point had to be solved. In him it may be truly said was united 'the wisdom of the serpent with the harmlessness of the dove'. Such was our Purser; and to have had such a messmate, and be able to count him among my friends, I regard as a high privilege, and one of the most fortunate circumstances of my life.

Our Master, Ben Hunter, was another variety of the *genus marinum*, – a noble specimen of the good old school of sailors. Ben was, indeed, a thorough seaman, and no contemptible navigator, at a time when that science was not as much attended to as it is at the present day. The possession of such essential qualities, with a rigid attention to all the duties of his station, gained him the good opinion and favour of the Admiral; and an evenness of temper, perfect good-humour, joined to unpretending, unassuming manners, soon won for him the esteem and regard of all his messmates. He was a silent, quiet man, naturally reserved in his habits, and went about his work with so little noise and bustle, that one was astonished to find so much accomplished in his department without any seeming trouble. In the ward-room even his voice was seldom heard, except he were particularly addressed, or some knotty nautical point that drew his attention, came under discussion. Upon such subjects his observations were always clear, apposite, and just. Or if anything unsailor-like, or which militated against his notions of ship-decorum or propriety, occurred in his presence, then, indeed, he became somewhat excited, venting his indignation in few but caustic remarks, that smacked strongly of his salt-water education. Ben, I dare say, was nearly a year in the *Malta* before he even expressed a wish to go ashore, all which time he conducted himself with the strictest propriety, nor were his messmates aware that one little failing partially obscured the brightness of a character otherwise so stainless. Fain would I pass this trivial weakness over in silence, but the truthfulness of these sketches compels me, alas! to reveal it. On board ship, and at sea, he was everything that could be desired in a sailor, an officer, and a man – sober, vigilant, attentive, and trustworthy; but on shore it was otherwise. There his honest unsophisticated nature was ill calculated to resist the many allurements and temptations, novel and attractive to a sailor immured in a ship for so long a time, by which he was beset; and the first time he landed from the *Malta*, which was at Alicant, the poor fellow remained so many days absent from the ship, that, ignorant of the cause, we became alarmed for his safety, fearing that, as assassination was no uncommon occurrence in Spain, some disaster had befallen him. Every corner of the town was searched, and the authorities applied to, but in vain – no tidings of Ben could be obtained. At length it was ascertained, when we began to despair of seeing him alive again, that he had been inveigled to a noted spot without the walls of the town, familiarly called 'El Vivar', or the 'Rabbit Warren', the resort of the vilest and most wretched characters of both sexes, who literally burrowed and lived under ground, from the nature of the soil. From this extraordinary locality old Ben was bolted by two ferrets in the guise of midshipmen, who with no little difficulty persuaded him to accompany them to the ship, where he appeared in a most pitiable plight, with not a *sou* in his pocket.

The following morning, when he was quite himself, and was pacing the half-deck in deep humiliation and contrition for all that had happened, one of his messmates, who felt a great interest in his welfare, spoke to him with much kindness and feeling about the disgrace attending, and the fatal consequences of a repetition of such conduct. Ben listened in silence, and for a time after he had ended his homily uttered not a word.

At length, upheaving a sigh, that more resembled a groan, there burst from him, with an energy that evinced the sincerity with which he spoke, this sole but characteristic response, 'I wish there wasn't a bit of b———y land in the world'.

By this time, the state of the First Lieutenant's health was such as to compel him to invalid, and Boxer was confirmed in that responsible office. Enough has already been said to show how well fitted he was for the situation, and in what estimation he was held by all in the ship, from the Admiral down to the youngest boy.

In summing up this account, it now only remains to observe that the rest of my messmates, though differing in degree, in temper, disposition, and acquirements, had each some peculiar property to recommend him, and thus we formed a united whole, that lived in harmony and perfect good fellowship all the time we were together in the *Malta*. Idle, indeed, we were, and fond of amusement when in harbour, and duty admitted of relaxation, – but yielding to none in zeal and true devotion, whenever the service called for our exertions. The cockpit and gun-room, too, could boast of as fine a set of Tyros as were ever collected together; and by their conduct and bearing gave promise of distinction, which time has not disappointed.

With such a ship, so commanded, and well manned and officered, as I have described, who could fail to be content? Not I, for one; and at this distance of time I look back with pride at having belonged to her, and with pleasure and thankfulness to the many happy days I passed in her.

18: Off Alicante

Nothing occurred in the spring of 1812 to diversify a blockading cruise, except an abortive attempt upon the town and harbour of Ciotat, – a small place situated between Toulon and Marseilles, in which there was a small frigate ready for sea, and some vessels building, one apparently a man-of-war. It failed, partly because the wind did not allow the ships and boats to get to their allotted stations in sufficient time, but chiefly because the management and direction of the enterprise had been taken out of the hands of Admiral Hallowell, the original projector of it. Had it remained with him, he would have chosen his own time, and not have given the enemy an intimation of his design, by a repetition of reconnaissances, and an unnecessary display of preparation. I notice the circumstance, to show that interference with the plans of an officer upon whose judgment and discretion full reliance may be placed, is likely to prove injurious, and also to remark that it was the only time in which an affair of the kind promised to be so tough a job, that I thought it necessary to write a few valedictory lines, bidding adieu to my best and truest, and most devoted friend through life, and containing some directions about the disposal of my very scanty worldly effects.

It was after the fall of Badajos, I think, that the Spanish government at length consented to confer the chief command of its armies upon Lord Wellington, and it was in the early part of the spring which followed that tardy and reluctant decision, that he arranged the plan of the campaign which led to the battle of Salamanca, and the occupation of Madrid. A part of this plan seems to have been to keep the armies of Soult in the south, and Suchet in the east, so occupied, that they should not be able to detach any men to reinforce Marmont, against whom it was the Commander-in-Chief's design to manœuvre, and fight him, when the wished-for opportunity should present itself. In furtherance of this plan, Lord William Bentinck, who commanded the English forces in Sicily, was invited to send what troops could be spared from that island to Catalonia or Valencia; and in conjunction with the Spanish armies in those provinces, give the troops of Marshal Suchet as much employment as possible.

Finding himself in a situation to comply with this request, Lord William assembled a force of twelve or thirteen thousand men, composed partly of English and Germans, and partly of Italian corps in English pay. This force, under the command of Lieutenant-General Maitland, made its appearance off Toulon about the middle of May; and Admiral Hallowell, who was appointed to the naval command on the coasts of Catalonia and Valencia, was directed to take charge of the convoy, and cooperate with the General in command of the troops. The same evening we parted company with the fleet; and in order to mystify the enemy as to its ultimate destination, the convoy steered in the direction of Sardinia. Having shown ourselves off that island, and given the people on shore an opportunity of observing the nature of, and counting the number of vessels of which the convoy was composed, sail was made the same night for Mahon, in which harbour we anchored on the third day after leaving the coast of Sardinia. Leaving the convoy there, Admiral Hallowell proceeded in the *Malta* to Majorca, where a Spanish division of between five and six thousand men, under the command of Major-General Whittingham, an English officer in the service of Spain, had been raised and disciplined. This force was meant to form part of the expedition, and it was to hasten its embarkation, that the Admiral went himself to Palma. Having pressed the necessity of dispatch, and embarked some Spanish officers of the Staff and Artillery, the *Malta* returned to Mahon, and all being at length arranged, we finally sailed early in July, for the coast of Catalonia.

We had fine weather, and made the land prosperously, with all the convoy around us, in a few days, somewhere in the neighbourhood of Palamos. No time was lost in communicating with the shore, when three Spanish officers came off to the ship; – Cabanis, the chief of the staff of the Catalan army, Manso, a celebrated leader of Miguelites, and the Baron D'Eroles, a General of distinguished reputation: and the information which those officers furnished, gave the chiefs of the expedition to understand that the moveable column of the French army was much stronger than they had been led to expect. By their computation, this column amounted fully to thirteen thousand men, while all the fortresses which they held in the province were amply garrisoned. To act against this force, long inured to war, and composed of some of the best soldiers in the armies of France, the British Commander could disembark but thirteen or fourteen thousand men, combining within themselves very incongruous elements, and forming a curious aggregate of English and Italians, Germans and Spaniards, Corsicans and Greeks.

Besides these disadvantages, the Spanish army at that time in Catalonia was weak, ill-appointed, and worse disciplined; and as it held not a single fortified place in the province, and as no dependence could be placed upon it for support, if the British army stirred from the coast, it would be thrown completely upon its own resources in a country, the military occupation of which was in possession of the enemy, and its safety compromised in case of reverse. Under those circumstances it was deemed not advisable to land in Catalonia, but to disembark the army at Alicante, where it would have a secure *point d'appui*, from whence it might operate so as to keep Marshal Suchet on the alert, and prevent him from detaching any men to reinforce the army of Portugal, or, if necessary, re-embark the troops with safety and at leisure. When this decision was come to, the convoy made sail to the westward, and anchored in Alicante Bay sometime in July. The army and all its *matériel* were immediately disembarked, the troops cantoned in the villages around, and the head-quarters fixed in Alicante.

To give an account of the movements of this army, except when the navy was in immediate co-operation with it, is foreign to my purpose, if I were enabled to do so, which I assuredly am not. It will be sufficient to observe, that soon after its disembarkation, one of the Italian regiments showed such evident symptoms of disaffection and treachery, that it was thought necessary to disarm it and send the men back to Sicily. At this time the French army of Valencia, under Suchet, was posted along the right bank of the Xucar, the advance under General Harispe occupying Almanza, while a strong picquet of cavalry, and a regiment of light infantry, were pushed forward to Yecla. This active and enterprising officer did not suffer our troops to occupy their cantonments long without giving them an alert or two; and upon one occasion he pushed a strong reconnaissance as far as the village of San Vincente, into which he did not penetrate, though he carried off an officer and some men of the Calabrese corps, which formed the outlying picket.

It was soon apparent that a command, which, more than any others perhaps, required consummate tact and ability, with great judgment and decision, was more arduous than the mind and nerves of General Maitland could support, and accordingly they soon gave way beneath a load so heavy. Indeed, it often happens that men who have physical courage to face any danger, are nevertheless deficient in that moral fortitude so requisite in a great leader of the art, either of government or of war, which more than any other quality shows a capacity for command, giving the possessor a proper confidence in his own abilities and resources, and, with unfettered judgment, leaving him at liberty to be guided, and to act according to his own decisions, without attaching an undue importance to what may be the opinion of the world in case his plans should fail of success. But how few are the men whose minds are so constituted, and what numbers have sunk under the responsibility of command! – men too, if placed in subordinate situations, who would carry out their chief's directions, even in the cannon's mouth.

General Maitland proceeded ill to England, before the army had been two months in Spain, and before long we heard that his mind was entirely gone. To him succeeded Lieutenant-General Campbell, the Adjutant-General to the forces in Sicily. During this time the opposing armies occupied their respective positions without approaching very near each other: and for some months I do not remember any operation that was undertaken by the British troops except an expedition that sailed coastways, under the command of General Donkin, the Quartermaster-General, against the town and castle of Denia, situated thirty miles to the eastward of Alicante, and a night march of the grenadier company of the 81st regiment meant, in conjunction with a Spanish battalion, to surprise the French detachment at Yecla, – both planned and undertaken at the suggestion of the Quartermaster-General, and both signally failed.

But though our operations were not of a stirring nature, Admiral Hallowell's ever-active mind did not slumber. The ships under his orders were stationed judiciously along the coasts of Valencia and Catalonia, as well for the purpose of keeping up a communication with the Spaniards, and gaining as much information as possible, as with a view to preventing the enemy from throwing in supplies by sea to the fortified places, which they held along the coast. The transports were classed and anchored in the order most convenient for re-embarking the army at a moment's notice. In making this arrangement, the Admiral found that a transport laden with ammunition for the Spanish division of General Roche, which was armed, paid, and clothed by the British Government, had been lying in the bay for nine months, her cargo still on board, except a small part of it, which had been landed from time to time. Finding how long this vessel had been kept idle under the plea that Alicante had no magazine wherein the ammunition could be secured, Admiral Hallowell was not a little indignant at such a flimsy excuse; and upon inquiry, he found that there was ample accommodation and perfect security for twice the quantity of ammunition in a vault or crypt beneath one of the churches. The cargo was then immediately discharged, and safely lodged, ready to be served out to the troops at any moment that it might be wanted, and the vessel herself thus made available for any service for which she might be required.

This is one instance, recounted among many others, of the culpable neglect, if not something worse, by which the servants of the Crown permitted the money and resources of the country, committed to their trust, to be wasted. At that time England was compelled to employ a multitude of transports, and in proportion to her necessity and the numbers required, was the amount of freight demanded and paid; notwithstanding which, we see one of those vessels kept at anchor unnecessarily and totally useless for nine months, at a great expense. If lightly considered, it may be viewed as an insignificant matter – as a drop added to the enormous expenditure of Great Britain during the late war. But what is the ocean itself but an aggregate of drops? And although perhaps the mind of man is not comprehensive enough to entertain even the possibility of the ocean being drained, we all can conceive that, if the drops which fall from heaven, and the rivers which pour their ceaseless waters into its bosom, were withheld or curtailed, its bulk would be sensibly diminished.

So with the expenses of the nation. Had every one in the public service felt a proper interest in their just repression, and in his own person avoided and checked all waste or unnecessary expense in others subjected to his control, the amount of money required for the sustentation of the war, would not have been nearly so great, – the debt which it has entailed upon the nation would not have been so large, and consequently the people's burdens at the present time would not be so heavy.

But to return. It early occurred to the Admiral that forage for the horses, and other draught animals of such an army, would soon be scarce, particularly as the extent of country into which foraging parties could be sent was much straitened by the proximity of the French army. Transports, therefore, under charge of an agent, were appointed to bring straw and barley from Majorca and the coast of Barbary, by which prudent foresight the animals suffered no want as long as the army continued at Alicante.

Anticipating the probability of the army being required to re-embark in haste, and finding upon examination that there was no other point of embarkation but the Mole, he lost no time in having a temporary wharf constructed to the westward of the town, and in the most convenient situation. This wharf was formed of piles, driven firmly into the ground, and run out into water sufficiently deep to admit heavily-laden boats to lay alongside. It was then planked over, and the whole made solid and strong enough to bear the weight of horses and heavy ordnance. Subsequently, when the army did embark, and celerity and dispatch were of great moment, this additional accommodation proved most opportunely convenient, by which great delay was avoided; for the whole of the horses and mules walked into the boats without the least confusion or accident, – whereas it would have been necessary to sling and lower them from the Mole, an operation that consumes much time, and is always attended with considerable risk.

The town of Alicante, though surrounded with a wall, has no fosse or glacis, and at the time I write of must have fallen as an easy prey to any force that presented itself before it, but for its castle or citadel. To remedy this weakness in some measure, a few additional guns were mounted on the neglected bastions as soon as the army disembarked, and the engineers were set to complete some unfinished works, which the Spaniards had commenced on two eminences to the north and west of the town. These works were mounted with heavy guns, drawn from the Artillery depôt, by parties of seamen landed from the *Malta* and *Fame*, and when finished presented formidable obstacles to the close investment of the place.

These matters being completed, little remained to occupy the time of us sailors, save the daily routine of duty of a ship at anchor. Much of our time was therefore passed on shore, and we soon became known to the principal people that remained in Alicante. Many wealthy individuals, among whom were several English merchants, alarmed at the neighbourhood of the French, had left the town, and were at that time waiting at Gibraltar, until more secure times should invite their return. Enough remained, however, to make the place sufficiently gay and pleasant, and we took an early opportunity of giving a ball at the town-hall to all the presentable people in the town, – a step which I strongly recommend to all soldiers, as well as sailors, arriving at a strange place, as one that will infallibly secure them a favourable introduction, and conciliate the good opinion of mammas and señorinas in most parts of the world.

Whilst off the coast of Catalonia, before it was decided to disembark the troops at Alicante, one of our brigs picked up a small boat, which had come off from Arens de Mar. On board this boat, besides two Catalan rowers, was a French gentleman, and the circumstances under which he was found induced the commander of the brig to conduct him to the Admiral. He was a well-looking gentlemanly man, of about forty-five, and, as well as I remember, the story which he told of himself was to the following purport. In consequence of an intrigue with a lady, who filled a high situation about the court, the Emperor had banished him, he said, forty leagues from Paris; and when it was afterwards discovered that he infringed this order, and made an attempt to see the lady, he only escaped being shut up in prison by a timely flight from Paris, and then, by means of friends on the frontier and in the army, in Catalonia, made his way to the east coast of Spain. His object, he declared, was to proceed to England, and there reside until the storm blew over, or until some fortuitous circumstance enabled him to revisit his native land, and obtain the Emperor's pardon for past peccadillos.

This gentleman's name was de Montron, and we have since reason to know that the account which he gave of himself was quite correct: but from long experience of their character, – such, perhaps, as elicited the Trojan's well-known exclamation, 'Timeo Danäos et dona ferentes', – the Admiral had a well-grounded distrust of the good faith of all Frenchmen; a distrust that was much strengthened by the exaggerated notions held at the time with respect to the almost impossibility of eluding the vigilance of the French police, and, further, by de Montron not only having escaped their surveillance, but also being supplied with a respectable wardrobe, and all *appliances* for a Frenchman's toilet, with a considerable sum in cash, and four thousand pounds in bills upon London.

All these circumstances considered, he thought it most prudent not to let him proceed direct to England, or, at all events, not before he had the Commander-in-Chief's authority for permitting it. De Montron was informed of this determination, and at the same time requested to consider himself as the Admiral's guest. At first the Frenchman was indignant at being detained a prisoner, and was still more furious, or affected to be so, at the truth of his statement being questioned. He had too much good sense to quarrel with his own comfort, and refuse the Admiral's proffered hospitality. This did not reconcile him, however, to his situation of a *détenu*. He exclaimed constantly and bitterly against the unreasonable hardship and cruelty of his case, loading 'ce vieux coquin d'Amiral', as he called him, with a torrent of abuse, as the cause of such unheard-of barbarity and injustice – concluding, however, after an explosion of bile, with 'Cependant, il faut avouer qu'il est assez bon enfant, – il est franc et généreux, et on fait très bonne chère, chez lui'. In time he was permitted to go on shore with any of the lieutenants who would be answerable for his safe return to the ship. Upon these occasions Bob Spencer or Sutton generally undertook the office of sponsors, particularly the latter, whose long residence in France made him cognizant of the habits and manners of the people, and, consequently, more companionable for M de Montron. His friends took him with them to the Tertulias, and introduced him to a certain Princesa del Pio, whose husband was absent, from some cause that I do not remember.

At these reunions in Spain it is not the fashion to give refreshments, – a bad custom de Montron remarked, and one that required amendment. One evening that a few of the officers were going to the Princesa's (as she was called), de Montron said that if the party would stay for a few minutes after the other guests were gone, he would try whether an experiment, which he had found upon one or two occasions successful in France might not prove equally so, in procuring a supper in Spain. They all laughed exceedingly, and thought the idea of getting a supper in a Spanish house good fun, and promised not to leave until he should give the signal for departure. The Tertulia met, and passed off as gaily and as happily as those very delightful assemblages generally do, – music, dancing, and forfeits, entertained the young, while their seniors of both sexes played at monti, a very seductive and inciting game at cards, at which much money changes hands in Spain. At the usual time, about eleven o'clock, the company began to thin, and this was the moment that de Montron selected for putting his scheme in operation. At first he complained of an unusual thirst, and begged the fair hostess's permission to ask for a glass of water. The water was brought, and then he remembered that his physician had cautioned him against drinking 'eau pure', and again he would take the further liberty of entreating that he might be permitted to mix the smallest drop of wine imaginable with the water, to prevent all mischief. When the wine made its appearance, and he had put the mixture to his lips, he removed it with a kind of shudder, exclaiming that he had the most rebellious stomach in the world, which always revolted against liquids, unless first tamed and quieted by a morsel to eat, and then overwhelming the lady with apologies for the immense trouble he was giving, and with compliments for her own amiable condescension and good nature, he begged to ask for a 'biscuit, ou bien un crouton.'

By this time the other guests had retired, and the party from the ship was all that was left with the lady. The Princess was *au fond*, hospitable, and obliging, and thinking that her supper would answer the Frenchman's purpose as well as a 'crouton', she begged, with many apologies for its extreme simplicity, that he and his friends would stay and partake of it. The invitation was at first very properly and *modestly* declined, – but upon being pressed very earnestly, the objections became weaker and weaker, until at length they yielded to her kind and urgent solicitations, and they all consented to remain. Then might be seen the triumph of de Montron's eye, as it glanced from face to face of his companions, asking applause for the complete success which crowned his well-laid scheme. During the repast, which was enjoyed by all with double zest, from the manner in which it was procured, his usual happy flow of spirits rose with the occasion. The Princess was charmed with his witty sallies and the agreeableness and vivacity of his conversation which shone with undiminished brilliancy to the last moment this delightful *petit souper* was prolonged.

Soon after this an order from the Commander-in-Chief directed that M de Montron might proceed to Sicily, if he pleased, but not to England; and, as he preferred *terra firma* to being cooped up in a ship, the first vessel sailing for that island conveyed him to Palermo. Whilst there, he became attached to the suite of the Duke of Orleans, and upon the Restoration, in 1814, accompanied that Prince to France. At Genoa, where they touched on their way to France, we renewed our acquaintance with de Montron, and Spencer, in writing to his brother, Lord Althorpe, then about to visit the continent, desired him to make inquiry for a certain M de Montron, and should he find him, *en société* to be sure to make his acquaintance.

Accordingly, when Lord Althorpe reached Paris, he made out his brother's friend, and found him to be not only an agreeable and pleasant fellow, but also of excellent family, and moving in the best circles. So much, indeed, was he pleased with his new acquaintance, that upon his expressing an intention of crossing over to England, he gave him a pressing invitation to Althorpe. The invitation was accepted, and the following autumn he proceeded to Northamptonshire, where in an English nobleman's country residence, even a Frenchman could hardly be *ennuyé*, so replete is it with all that can gratify the taste, or minister to the pleasure and amusement of a gentleman. In the mornings, there were the out-door amusements of hunting, shooting, or a drive or gallop through the country. Within are books, billiards, with numerous resources, and appliances besides; and at dinner, and in the evenings, will be found assembled a society at once accomplished, intellectual, and refined. In such a house, and surrounded with such a variety of *agrémens*, M de Montron could not fail to be amused, and he passed a month so delightfully, and made so many friends and agreeable acquaintances, that he ever after paid an annual visit to England, where he became a member of the Travellers' Club, at which he was almost as well known as his celebrated countryman, Prince Talleyrand.

There were four martello towers, which protected the Bay of Alicante, two to the eastward, and two to the westward of the town. As these towers were of no use to the Spaniards, who had then no enemy to apprehend from the sea, but, in the hands of the French, should they get possession of them, would prove a protection to any coasters of theirs which might attempt to move along shore, as well as an annoyance to British cruisers and their boats, Admiral Hallowell judged it wise to have them dismantled and destroyed. Having, therefore, obtained permission of the Spanish authorities for the purpose, the guns and stores were removed, and then a few barrels of gunpowder soon reduced them to a heap of ruins.

The autumn and winter passed over with nothing to diversify or disturb the quiet in which we lay; even the elements seemed that season in repose, for I do not remember that, during the time we were in the Bay of Alicante, which could not have been less than eight or nine months, we had occasion once to strike the topgallant-masts, or that the communication with the shore was at any time interrupted. All this time the troops remained quietly in their cantonments, and the *Malta* only lifted her anchors occasionally by way of exercise, and to water at Altea, a bay ten leagues to the eastward of Alicante.

This state of inaction produced in the officers of the *Malta* an increased love of idleness and amusement, and an unwonted degree of fidgettiness and irritableness in the Admiral, whose energetic and ever-stirring mind could ill brook the absolute quiescence in which both ships and army were reposing. Day after day, and night after night, were some of us on shore, until at length, for some cause or other which I do not remember – some neglect on our part, I have no doubt – the Admiral gave an order that the officers of the *Malta* should not be out of the ship after gunfire.

This order was a sad mortification, confining us to the ship at the time that we took most pleasure in being on shore, namely, the hours between eight o'clock and twelve at night; and some of the most refractory spirits, in which category I grieve to include myself, in order to show how much they thought the punishment exceeded the offence, magnanimously resolved to confine themselves altogether to the ship, and as they could not visit the shore at night, to avoid it by day also. And this species of martyrdom they submitted to for four or five weeks, with a constancy and self-devotion worthy of a better cause.

But this kind of sacrifice, half voluntary, half compulsory, was not to last for ever. In February, 1813, the Admiral shifted his flag to one of the small vessels in the roadstead, and sent the *Malta* to Cartagena, to assist in making a main-mast for the *Ganymede*, which ship had sprung her own. We all rejoiced at this move: it promised a reprieve from the confinement and restraint which we had endured for so many weeks; besides which, change and novelty have always a charm for the human mind. Trusting, therefore, that the embargo would be removed upon our arrival at Cartagena, and looking forward to a large indemnity for our long confinement to the ship, it was with light and gladsome hearts that we bade adieu for a time to Alicante.

We anchored at Cartagena a few days before the close of the Carnival, and the sails were scarcely furled, when an invitation was received from the officers of the 67th British Regiment to a masked ball for the same night. The officers of that regiment had a palace for their quarters – the Naval Academy – a noble building, destined in less stormy and perilous times for the reception and education of the cadets of the Spanish navy, but then, like most public buildings in Spain, allotted to some use far different from the original one, or suffered from total neglect to fall into ruin and decay. The hall of this building, which was appropriated for the ball-room, was a magnificent apartment, lofty, spacious, and finely proportioned, and when we arrived, was already thronged with company. Some wore masks, but the greater part did not. A few of the gentlemen appeared in character, but the numbers dressed in national uniform prevailed. There might be seen cavalry and infantry – sailors and engineers – Marines and Artillery – English and Spanish – all mingled together, without regard to nation or profession, and forming as curious and picturesque an assemblage as were ever crowded together before. Need I say that we of the *Malta* enjoyed ourselves that night. For my own part, I felt an elevation, a buoyancy of spirits, the effect perhaps of a lengthened abstinence from such amusements, as much as from the novelty of the animated scene itself.

Our stay at Cartagena was short, only four or five days, which sped like hours. During this time few of us thought of bed, the whole being passed in a whirl of gaieties and amusements, such as the closing days of carnival in Roman Catholic countries alone present, – at the theatre, at masquerades, at tertulias, – in short, wherever the sound of viol or guitar summoned the young, the giddy, and the gay.

Unquestionably, Spain is the country of bright eyes and graceful forms, and *las bellas Cartagenesas* are in that respect no way inferior to their charming sisters in other parts of the Peninsula. Where all are fair, it would seem difficult to choose; and yet a look, a simple expression, a tone of voice, a something felt, but which words cannot convey, – these, or any of them, will attract to some particular object, and the selection is made.

The first dance at the ball before described decided my fate, and for the few days we stayed at Cartagena, no knight could be more true to his lady-love than I was to the gentle Andrea Degueras. And yet Andrea could not be thought a faultless beauty. In person she was not tall, and for one so young was a little too much *en embonpoint*. Her features, however, were all most correctly cut; her hair was glossy and dark, and her fine large eyes, of the same hue, shed a mild and softened light, rather than the brilliant and lustrous ray, or dazzling flash, so characteristic of the daughters of the south. Her hands and feet were small and beautifully-shaped, and her complexion, without a tinge of red, except in exercise, was brune, but clear, healthy, and transparent.

Such was Andrea in person; but what won my especial homage was her gentle unpretending manners, united to a soft, melodious voice, which gave to her country's rich, magnificent language an expression and effect, that, much as I admired it before, I had no conception till then it possessed.

Her father was a captain in the Spanish navy, and, in returning from South America many years before, had the misfortune to be blown up in the ship which he commanded. Although rescued from death with a small part of the crew, he was so mutilated as to be disabled from serving any more at sea, and at the time I write of he filled the situation of Commandante de la Marina at Cartagena, an office somewhat analogous, I believe, to that of captain of the port with us.

During our brief stay at Cartagena, we fulfilled the promise we made to ourselves on leaving Alicante, – that of some indemnification for our long fast from *terra firma*.

At the season of Carnival no evening passes without a dance, and to the young in Spain dancing is a positive enjoyment. Unlike the labour and rapid whirl of the German waltz, badly imitated in England and France, in Spain the movement is smooth, graceful, and easy. Upheld at once, and borne along by the inspiration of soft, delightful music, the votary of Terpsichore seems to swim through the mazes and intricacies of the *contradanza*, or if it be the waltz, just aided by the light and elegant motions of the arms, to float round the room without toil or exertion.

Carnival was at an end, and we knew that the morning of Thursday was fixed for our departure. As we had met with much kindness and courtesy at Cartagena, we were therefore very desirous to offer the hospitalities of the *Malta* to our fair friends before we bade them perhaps a final adieu. There was only one day before we sailed on which an invitation could be given. This was Ash-Wednesday; and to persuade them to embark upon a party of pleasure on *Miercoles de Ceniza*, a day always observed with such strictness in countries professing the Roman Catholic faith, appeared so hopeless, that we quite despaired of being able to do so. We resolved, notwithstanding, to make the attempt, and, to our great astonishment, as well as pleasure, when we did so, found it a matter of far less difficult attainment than we feared it would prove.

At first, when the proposal was made to them, the ladies exclaimed, and declared it totally impossible to accede to our request. But their husbands and brothers came to our assistance, and partly by their persuasion, and partly by ridicule, aided no doubt by the secret inclinations of the young ladies themselves, we succeeded, and before we separated that night (Tuesday), it was arranged that boats should be on shore by noon on the following day to fetch the whole party to the ship.

To prepare a collation befitting the occasion was the real difficulty. This too was happily achieved, and before the appointed time on Wednesday a very respectable repast adorned our tables in the ward-room.

Soon after, the boats came alongside, when a goodly array of Spanish beauty assembled on the quarter-deck of the *Malta*.

Every part of the ship was then shown to them, and from the store-room to the captain's cabin, each object which they saw drew forth new and increased exclamations of pleasure and surprise; but when the elderly ladies, in their desire to examine everything within view, peeped into certain little boudoirs fitted on the quarters, their ecstasy and delight at the discovery knew no bounds. They actually shouted with admiration, calling to each other, 'Juana! Maria! – Vengan, vengan aqui, por amor de Dios! – Miren ustedes! – Que comodad! Que propriedad! – En mi vida no he visto cosa tan bonita, tan elegante. Seguramente los Ingleses son la gente la mas pulida, la mas ingeniosa del mundo.' 'Johanna! Maria! – Come here, come here, for the love of God! – Look what cleanliness! What convenience! – In my life I never saw anything so pretty, so elegant! – Certainly the English are the neatest and cleverest people in the world.'

When every part of the ship was inspected, we adjourned to the wardroom where the *déjeuner* was prepared, and although the day was considered as a rigid fast, we did not observe that our Spanish guests shunned *carne*, or practised much abstinence or self-denial.

To the repast succeeded dancing, which was kept up till eight o'clock, when we accompanied our friends on shore, and passed the remainder of the evening at the house of the Commandante de la Marina. By ten o'clock on the following morning the *Malta* was rounding Cape Palos, and the same evening, before eight was moored in the Bay of Alicante.

We found upon our return that things wore a brighter and more cheering aspect at Alicante. Three gun-boats, which, since the raising of the siege of Cadiz, consequent upon the victory of Salamanca, were no longer wanted there, had arrived. Rumours were in circulation that a move of the troops was in contemplation, and that as spring advanced more active operations would be undertaken.

This expectation had wonderfully helped to clear the Admiral's brow. It no longer had the grave, almost stern, expression which had settled upon it before we went to Cartagena. His countenance had resumed its open cheerfulness, and his keen, penetrating eye kindled from time to time as the hope of more active and busy times flashed across his mind. The embargo raised by our trip to Cartagena was not renewed – our delinquencies seemed all forgotten; the Admiral's manner was again cordial, frank, and kind, and our visits to the shore became as frequent and uninterrupted as ever.

19: The Siege of Tarragona

Sir John Murray had arrived from England, and assumed the command of the army, his predecessor, General Campbell, having returned to Sicily. Early in April the Anglo-Sicilian army was put in motion, and took up a position at Castalla, the advance, under Colonel Adam, consisting of the 2nd, 27th (a weak battalion), the Calabrese rifle corps, an Italian light infantry battalion, Captain Jack's troop of hussars, and two mountain light guns, occupying the village and defile of Biar. This movement in advance of the Allies was not unobserved by Suchet, who immediately concentrated his troops, and prepared to attack them in their newly-occupied position. For this purpose he advanced with his whole collected force, and early in the morning of the 12th of April made a furious assault upon the post of Biar, which was defended with great gallantry and resolution, until Colonel Adam, finding his flanks likely to be turned, was at length compelled to fall back before a force so overwhelming. This movement was effected in admirable order, the division retiring across the plain which separates Biar from Castalla, followed by the enemy's numerous cavalry, which threatened and pressed it close, but never ventured to charge home the serried ranks of the intrepid little column. The same afternoon it entered the lines of Castalla, and took its allotted position to the right of Wittingham's Spanish division. Considering the obstinacy with which the post was defended against assailants so numerous, the division did not suffer much, but it had to leave the two mountain guns behind, in consequence of the mules having been killed.

On the morning of the 13th, the army of Marshal Suchet was observed in front of the Allied lines, making dispositions which showed an evident intent to attack their position. A strong column, with the whole of the French guns, threatened the centre and right, which they cannonaded, but which was warmly and effectually answered by the British artillery. Meanwhile, two columns, one in support of the other, and preceded by a cloud of skirmishers, advanced against the left, a steep and rugged height, the key of the position, which was occupied by the Spanish division of General Whittingham. The nature and importance of this post, and the national troops to whom its defence was confided, were not unobserved by the enemy. Once in motion, their advance was steady, and although the ascent was exceedingly steep, and the ground difficult, on they pressed without a pause; nor did the heavy fire from the Spanish troops, which thinned their ranks, arrest their progress for a moment. The crest of the height was gained, and Whittingham's soldiers fell back before the gathering storm. The moment was critical. The post once in possession of the enemy, the left of the Allies was turned, and then a miracle could scarcely save the army from defeat; and such probably would have been the result of the day, had Spaniards alone been on the height. But fortunately the heroic little band, which had so much distinguished itself the day before, occupied part of the same ridge, immediately on their right. Here an abrupt dip in the ground concealed it from view of the ascending columns, and when the French gained the summit, instead of Spaniards alone, the blood-red uniform of England met their gaze. The sight of this new and unexpected opponent caused the enemy to pause; but no time was allowed them to recover from their surprise; a well-directed volley, within pistol-shot distance, added to their confusion, and before they had time to breathe, or close their ranks, loosened and disordered by the steepness and difficulty of the ascent, Colonel Reeves called on the 27th to charge, and placing himself at their head, rushed like a torrent upon the foe, who scarcely awaited the shock, but fled with the utmost precipitation, bearing with them, in their downward flight, the columns advancing to their support. Seeing the success of this charge, and how completely the enemy's columns were overthrown, Colonel Adam wisely restrained the impetuosity of his men, and re-occupied his former position.

Suchet, having failed in his attack upon the left, made no other serious attempt, but holding some strong columns in front of the right and cen-tre, which he continued to cannonade, till his discomfited battalions were brought into some order, he then drew off his army, retiring in the direc-tion of Biar. Sir John Murray then moved out in advance, but slowly and with caution; so that the French filed through Biar with no other obstruc-tion than what was occasioned by a distant cannonade. There were not wanting those who affirmed, that had the English General's pursuit been closer and more vigorous, the enemy's loss must have been very consider-able. He was provided with a powerful and admirably-appointed artillery, which, if sufficiently advanced, must have played with crushing effect upon the mass as it struggled through the defile, where at one time horses, guns, tumbrils, and men choaked the pass, impeding each other's movements. But of these matters, or by what motives the General's con-duct was guided, a sailor can be but a very imperfect judge; I only recount the opinions of several officers who bore a part in the operations of the day, and which were expressed at the time.

The loss of the Anglo-Sicilian army in the operations of the two days was inconsiderable; one officer, Captain Campbell, of the staff, was killed, and Colonel Adam, and three or four officers of the 27th were wounded. I am unable to say what number of men were *hors de combat*, but certainly not many. The loss sustained by the enemy must have been much greater, though the numbers were not precisely ascertained. They left several dead and wounded upon the field, and some prisoners were taken. From the latter it was gathered that the enemy's forces at Castalla amounted to between thirteen thousand and fourteen thousand men, including one thousand seven hundred cavalry. In point of numbers the Allied army was somewhat superior, with a strong position, partly entrenched, and a formidable and well-served artillery; but of cavalry it had little or none, two squadrons of the 20th Light Dragoons, two squadrons of the Brunswick Oels Hussars, and Captain Jack's troop of foreign hussars, comprising its strength in that arm.

The repulse of Marshal Suchet at Castalla was regarded by the English General as a victory, which he deemed of sufficient importance to be announced to Government immediately by a special dispatch entrusted to one of his Aides-de-camp. And perhaps this estimate of the day's advantage was not much overrated, if the constitution of the opposing forces be taken into consideration. The French army was composed of men of one nation, in perfect discipline, and inured to war; it was led by officers in whose skill and courage they had a just confidence, and the whole was commanded by a chief of consummate knowledge in the art of war, who had conducted them from victory to victory with scarcely a single check. On the other hand, the Allied army was compounded of men of five or six different nations – Calabrese, Sicilians, Spaniards, Germans, and English; the soldiers of the two latter forming scarcely a third of the whole force. And when it is considered that the French advanced to the attack with all the confidence which uninterrupted success is sure to inspire, while the Allied forces, with the exception of the British, fought under the disadvantage of conscious inferiority to their assailants – an inferiority impressed upon their minds from former disasters and defeat – it will be conceded that the result of the day was creditable to the combined army.

After the affair of Castalla, the opposing armies remained for some weeks in front of each other, occupying nearly the same positions which they did before the combat. Various were the conjectures during this interval as to the probable destination of the army in the approaching summer. That something was in agitation we felt pretty confident, and it was generally thought that Catalonia would be the scene of the ensuing campaign. This supposition gained strength from the circumstance of an officer having been sent to that province in order to communicate personally with Copons, the Captain-General, and make himself acquainted with the state of the Catalan army, and also ascertain, as far as that could be done, the numbers and positions of the French forces in Catalonia.

In May I was sent in a transport to Cartagena, with a letter to the Governor of that town, requesting him to furnish a supply of wood from the naval arsenal to the Engineer department of the army in Valencia, and when it was shipped, I was to return to Alicant with all the expedition I could use. A light but favourable breeze took us off the harbour in twenty-four hours, when, by the help of Tofino's Spanish Pilot, and his excellent plan and sailing directions for Cartagena, I took the ship in without any other assistance, and moored her alongside the jetty in the basin, or wet dock. This fine piece of water, of several acres' extent, situated in the heart of the dockyard, and capable of holding afloat from sixteen to twenty sail of the line fully equipped for sea, was then, like the rest of that noble arsenal, silent and deserted; no vessel, save our own English transport, rested on its still, unruffled surface. Here, as well as in all parts of the vast establishment, reigned the tranquillity of death, filling the thoughts with sadness, and presenting to the eye a picture of desolation and decay – true image of the departing glories of once powerful and haughty Spain.

In wandering around the dockyard, a solitary warder here and there, and the sentinels at the entrance gates, showed that the place was not quite abandoned. Not a soul was to be met to open the now useless and half-empty store-houses. The workshops and smithies were mute, and no longer rang with the sound of the sledge, the axe, and the adze; and in contemplating its then melancholy and forsaken condition, it was impossible not to contrast it painfully with the life, the stir, the busy activity, which it once exhibited, when it could boast of having laid down and built, launched, and fully equipped for sea, a 38-gun frigate in twenty-eight days.

When I waited on the Governor, with the letter with which I was charged, he received me with much courtesy, and he promised that inquiry should be made immediately in the proper quarter to ascertain how far he was enabled to comply with the English General's request. But I had soon reason to know how dilatory and procrastinating are all official proceedings in Spain. To my repeated inquiries, I was always told that the proper person had not made his report, and no answer could be obtained that day. It was the same the next, and then no Governor was to be seen.

For three days I was put off with the same, or some equally frivolous excuse, when, seeing no end to such prevarication, I at length demanded a simple answer, yes or no, as to whether I was to be supplied with the wood for which I had been sent, when I was told that none could be spared, as all that remained in store was required either for the service of the arsenal or for the repairs of the fortifications of Cartagena. Having got his final answer, which would have saved much time had it been given honestly at first, my preparations for departure were soon made, and in less than two hours we were clear of the harbour.

It would be difficult to account for the Governor's motive in thus refusing the request of the English General. Certain it is that the reason he chose to assign was not the real one. There were spars and gross timber enough and to spare for any purposes that they could have been wanted for at Cartagena. Perhaps it is not unreasonable to suppose that this churlishness sprang from that miserable petty jealousy, so constantly evinced by the Spanish authorities during the progress of the war, of everything English, and which so frequently impeded their operations, and sometimes defeated the best-laid schemes. We reached Alicant the day after we left Cartagena, and when I reported my proceedings, and gave copies of my correspondence with the Spanish Governor to the Admiral, he was pleased to express himself satisfied with my conduct.

When I returned to the Bay of Alicant everything bore the appearance of a speedy change. Transports were in motion; some shifting their berths to positions the most convenient for embarking cavalry, artillery, and stores, – whilst others were returning from or sailing to Altea, to complete their water. Just after the sailing of a batch of those transports for Altea, it was discovered that three seamen had deserted from the *Malta*; and as the Captain thought it not unlikely that they had escaped in one or other of those vessels, he directed me to proceed by land for the purpose of overhauling them. An order to the Postmaster being procured, I was furnished with a pair of mules, one for myself, the other for the guide, or 'conductor'. These were to take me to Los Baños, the first stage, when I was to be provided with a fresh guide and mules, and so on till I reached Altea.

It was noon before I set out, and I cantered quickly over a good road across the 'Huerta' of Alicant, a distance of six or seven miles. My companion was a young man, with a gay and cheerful, but somewhat arch expression of countenance. His stature was short, but well formed, lithe and active, and appeared to much advantage in his Spanish dress. This consisted of a jacket of Spanish brown cloth, and breeches of the same, which were met at the knee by tight-fitting leggings of smooth tanned leather, looped at the side by thongs of the same material. His purple velvet vest was ornamented with a multitude of silver buttons, of the kind called Talavera, and a gorro, or cap of scarlet worsted, that scarcely confined the luxuriance of his coal-black hair, the tassel of which hung over one shoulder, completed his attire.

The tract which we traversed was rich in all the products of a garden, and well deserved the name by which it was distinguished. Vines, and every variety of fruit and vegetables, were there in abundance. It seemed a fat alluvial soil, washed down by the rains of winter from the high land by which it is in great part surrounded. It is, or was, divided into numerous small properties, to each of which was appended a 'quinta', or farmhouse, with here and there the *casa de campo* of some wealthy Alicantino. The fields, vineyards, and gardens which compose these little properties were enclosed by low loose stone walls, bald and naked, and which detracted much from the appearance of the luxuriant fertility of the whole district. A pantano, or vast reservoir, is constructed in the hills to the north-west, in order to collect the waters of the small streams and drainings that fall from the uplands. A main aqueduct conveys these waters to the low grounds, and thence, by numerous conduits, to the different properties for the purpose of irrigation, for the use of which a small tax is paid by the owners of the estates. Where no river is at hand to supply the means of irrigation, reservoirs of this description are not uncommon in Spain; and, in a country subject to excessive drought, the consequence of a discontinuance of rain sometimes for months together, their utility is incalculable, furnishing refreshment and sustenance to vegetation, which without moisture must wither and die in the heats of summer.

It sometimes happens, however, though rarely, that these vast tanks or reservoirs burst their banks, when the immense body of water, released from confinement, pours down in one resistless overwhelming deluge on the plain below, sweeping all before it, and involving in promiscuous ruin whatever stands in its way – men, cattle, villages, cornfields, and vineyards – and leaving desolation, barrenness, and woe, where peace and happiness, fertility and abundance, smiled a few short hours before. An instance of the above kind took place near Orihuela, in Murcia, whilst we were at Alicant, and the distress and misery which it caused, plunging a whole district from comparative wealth and comfort, into hopeless poverty and ruin in a few hours, was quite appalling.

After crossing the Huerta, the road, which now becomes almost impassable for any vehicle upon wheels, enters upon a wild and naked country, interrupted and broken by large loose stones, and rocks imbedded in the ground, or knolls covered with moss or a scanty herbage. Here and there a dwarfed and stunted oak, or starveling algaroba, serves to add to, rather than relieve, the dreariness of the prospect. For seven or eight miles this road, though not steep, continually ascends, until it reaches Los Baños, a village consisting of a few miserable dwellings, scattered around the sides of a basin-like hollow formed in the side of the hill.

The village, as its name would imply, owes its origin to a mineral spring discovered there many years before. It is said to be efficacious in the cure of rheumatism and cutaneous disorders, and the poor inhabitants derive their subsistence in great measure from the strangers who resort thither for the benefit of the waters. I had no time, however, to examine them, or the accommodation and conveniency of the place where they were situated; for, being anxious to proceed on my way as far as I could that evening, I inquired for fresh mules immediately on my arrival. But to all my prequisitions I received the same answer, – not a mule was left in the village. All had been taken for the service of the army. I then asked to see the Alcalde, or chief authority of the place. He, too, was absent, or, at all events, could nowhere be found. I next told the guide that, as no mules were to be had at Los Baños, I should be obliged to take his on to Villa Joyosa, when he whispered me that he had just received a hint that two fine machos were secreted at such a house, pointing to one at a considerable distance, and that if I went myself, no doubt they would be produced. Upon hearing this, and charging the muleteer to be in the way in case of further disappointment, I proceeded to the house which he had pointed out. It took me ten minutes to get there, and then not a man was to be found about the premises, and the women declared they were all absent looking after their beasts, which had been impressed for the service of the army. And when I expressed a doubt of the truth of this statement, they showed me, without the least hesitation, two stables, one above, the other underground, in which animals had evidently been lodged, but which I found completely deserted.

Determined to make no further delay, but proceed to Villa Joyosa with the mules that brought me from Alicant, I now made all haste back to the place where I had left the guide, – but imagine my amazement, perplexity, and vexation, at finding the fellow gone. The moment he succeeded in starting me on my fool's errand, and I was fairly out of view, he was in the saddle, and, without waiting to give himself or his mule any refreshment, was four or five miles on his return to Alicant by the time I had completed the examination of the empty stables. I was now in a pretty dilemma, and began to think I had nothing for it but to wait patiently the Alcalde's return, or else start on foot for Villa Joyosa. Before I made up my mind, however, as to which course I should adopt, I resolved to try what effect storming and threatening would have on the people, who began to congregate and gaze at the stranger, and perhaps enjoy his perplexity and distress. So I threw myself into a towering passion, – fumed, and sputtered, and swore in bad Spanish, vowing that the Capitan-General, and all the authorities of the province, should know how a British officer, charged with an important mission, had been treated at Los Baños. Observing that this made some impression, I became still more voluble, swearing and threatening louder than before. There was now some whispering among the listeners; soon after which I was told that there was one sorry mule in the village, and that if I would have patience for a little, she should be brought out, when I could judge whether she was fit to carry me to the next stage or not. To this I very readily consented, and in a little time the animal made her appearance. She proved as miserable a creature as ever moved on four legs; but I was too happy even of such means to proceed on my journey, and leave the wretched village of Los Baños.

My guide, who was on foot, directed me across the moor. The way was rough, and perfectly trackless, but it cut off a considerable angle, and when we joined the high road I found it comparatively smooth. When we reached Villa Joyosa, it was eight o'clock. I went straight to the Alcalde, who received me with great courtesy and hospitality. He would not hear of my going to the posada, but insisted that I should be lodged and entertained at his own house; and for this civility I was not a little thankful, for I knew from experience what kind of fare was to be expected at a Spanish inn. Supper was soon served, to which we sat down a *partie carrée*, consisting of mine host, his wife, daughter, and myself.

My ride from Alicant, and fast since the morning, enabled me to do ample justice to a cheerful and social meal; soon after which, I was shown to a comfortable bed, where I slept like a top till five o'clock in the morning. At that hour I found mules and a guide at the door, and after taking a cup of chocolate, I proceeded over ten miles of a rough road to Altea. Without a moment's delay, I procured a boat on the beach, and pulled off to the transports, three of which were lying in the bay. I mustered the crews of each successively, and then searched every place below and aloft, where I thought a man could be concealed, but to no purpose – the deserters were nowhere to be found.

I was not a little chagrined at this unsuccessful result of my journey, especially when I noticed a grin of satisfaction on 'Jack's' countenance, and the knowing winks which they exchanged with each other at the man-of-war officer's disappointment.

It was still early when I returned to the shore; and getting to horse, or rather to macho again, I rode back to Villa Joyosa. There the worthy Alcalde gave me a good breakfast, and as I was determined to reach Alicant if possible before sunset, a fresh mule was ready for me by the time I had finished. As it was feared that I might again be disappointed in procuring a relay at Los Baños, this mule was to carry me all the way to Alicant; and as its owner was to accompany me on foot, and I was pressed for time, I thought that he would have found it difficult, if not impossible, to keep way with the mule for such a distance – more than twenty miles; but not at all. He kept up with the animal in a sort of slinging trot, without distress, and seemingly with perfect ease; and when a bit of good road enabled me to urge the beast to greater speed, he took hold of its tail as a tow-line, and so was lugged along.

We stopped a few minutes at Los Baños, and reached the barrier of Alicant just five minutes before the gun fired for sunset; and thus I lost my labour, and with it no inconsiderable portion of leather, the result of a kind of exercise to which sailors of the olden time were not much accustomed.

Conjecture was still busy as to the probable movements of the army in the ensuing summer, the most prevalent rumour being, that its destination was Catalonia, and that Sir John Murray only awaited the junction of the armies of the Duke del Parque, and General Elio, to break up from Castalla, and march to Alicant for the purpose of embarkation.

The last-named rumour was soon converted into certainty, for the second and third Spanish armies were in communication with that under the command of Sir John Murray, on the 28th of May, immediately after which, the first division entered Alicant; and between that time and the afternoon of the 31st, sixteen thousand men, with one thousand seven hundred horses and mules, and a competent field and siege train, were embarked, and sailed from Alicant. Prior to this the British garrison had been withdrawn from Cartagena. This consisted of the 2nd battalion of the 67th, and a wing of Dillon's regiment. The latter was incorporated with that of Rolle, and henceforward they bore together the designation of the battalion Rolle-Dillon. At the same time, six gun-boats, to be managed by English officers and sailors, were borrowed from the Spanish Government, and added to the force of the expedition. A moderate breeze bore the whole convoy off the Col de Balaguer by noon on the 2nd of June, when the brigade of Colonel Prevost, consisting of the troops that formed the garrison of Cartagena, with a proportion of artillery, hauled in and anchored under convoy of the *Brune* troop-ship, for the purpose of attacking St Felipe, a strong fort that commanded the high road (the only one practicable for artillery), from Valencia and Tortosa to Catalonia, Captain Adam, of the *Invincible* (than whom a better officer could not have been selected for such a service) having with him the *Thames* frigate, and the *Volcano* and *Stromboli* bombs, being directed to co-operate with Colonel Prevost. The rest of the convoy had all anchored by five o'clock of the same afternoon in the Bay of Tarragona.

It was intended to land the advance, and invest the place that evening; but upon examining the state of the beach, the Admiral gave it as his opinion, that as there was a little surf, and as no object would be lost by the delay, the disembarkation had better be deferred till the morning.

Early on the morning of the 3rd, the landing commenced. By noon the whole of the infantry, the field-train, some howitzers, and two hundred horses and mules, were put on shore; and by three o'clock in the afternoon, the place was invested without any molestation on the part of the enemy. Thus did everything combine to favour the success of the expedition. An army of sixteen thousand men, with the necessary *matériel* for siege and field, were wafted from the Bay of Alicant to that of Tarragona, a distance of more than two hundred miles, the men all disembarked, and the town invested, in the incredibly short time of three days! – a tide of prosperous circumstances unexampled, I believe, in the history of all former expeditions, and which must have produced the most fortunate results, if taken proper advantage of. But it was far otherwise. From the moment he had set his foot on shore, the General thought he had 'undertaken more than he was able to accomplish'. The natural consequence of this feeling in its chief was, that indecision and delay marked all the proceedings of this ill-fated army.

It was late in the evening before an order was given to land intrenching tools; and it was the 6th, three days after the disembarkation, before two batteries, the one of two 24-pounders, the other of four 8-inch howitzers, were opened on the Fuerte Real, an outwork five hundred yards in advance of the body of the place to the S. W., and which was the only one standing, the others having been destroyed some time before.

Our employment (I mean that of the Navy), was various. In the day, landing stores as they were required – an operation that was uninterrupted by the weather, or state of the beach, during the progress of the siege; and in the night, in keeping up a teazing flanking fire from the ship's boats on the Fuerte Real. The gun-boats were assisting the operations at Balaguer, or watching the coast roads to the eastward and westward of Tarragona. Whatever depended upon him, was thought of and provided for by our fine old Admiral.

He was in all places, superintending everything both ashore and afloat; and in order to be near at hand, in case his presence should be necessary, or the General should wish to communicate with him in the night, he had a kind of tent erected on the beach, under which he used to snatch a few hours' sleep, when he thought his presence was not required, or could be useful elsewhere. He had caused a temporary jetty or stage to be run out in a cove at the western extremity of the bay, for the more safe and expeditious re-embarkation of the horses and mules, similar to the one which had been constructed at Alicant for the same purpose. In fact, there was not anything which depended upon him, that his experience and sagacity did not provide for.

The force sent to reduce the fort at Balaguer found it a more difficult affair than was expected. Situated on a height that commanded every approach to it, and garrisoned by one hundred and twenty men, amply provided with stores and munitions of every kind, its speedy reduction could in no ways be effected. Besides which, the ground leading to it was so steep and rugged, that it was necessary to cut a road through the rock, before the breaching guns could be dragged up the height, and placed in battery. This, however, was accomplished with great labour, and a good many casualties; for there was neither brushwood, depth of soil, nor anything else, with which the working parties could cover themselves from the fire of the garrison. Both services vied with each other upon this arduous occasion; the exertions of Captain Carroll, of the *Volcano*, and of Lieutenant Corbyn of the *Invincible*, being conspicuously meritorious. When those difficulties were overcome, and the fire from the English batteries began to make an impression, and seeing no prospect of immediate succour, the fort surrendered on the morning of the 7th.

The possession of this fort was of great importance. It completely closed the coast road (the only one practicable for artillery), from Valencia and Tortosa to the eastward, compelling Suchet, when he advanced to the relief of Tarragona, to make a fatiguing détour through the mountains by ways little better than sheep-tracks, causing him a delay of at least forty-eight hours, and obliging him to leave his guns behind.

Up to the moment that Sir John Murray received the account of the fall of Fort St Felipe, the operations before Tarragona were tardy in the extreme; but when this intelligence reached him, it seemed to infuse a little more life into his measures, and the siege was pushed with somewhat more vigour. More guns and mortars were ordered to be landed; and on the 9th, two new batteries within four hundred and fifty yards of the walls, the one on the Oliva of six 24-pounders, and the other lower down to the right, of five 10-inch mortars, and five 8-inch howitzers, meant to enfilade the works on that side of the fortress proposed to be attacked, were commenced.

These batteries were ready to be armed on the night of the 10th, when four hundred of our 'Jolly Jacks', as a friend of mine in writing to England called them, were landed from the *Malta*, *Fame*, and *Bristol*, and were employed till daylight of the following morning in dragging guns and mortars to their allotted situations. The party from the *Malta*, under the command of the Captain, first assisted in placing two mortars in battery, and were then directed by the Admiral, who was ever present where work was going forward, to repair to the Oliva, and give their assistance in whatever way it might be required.

Four guns, which had been moved up from the depôt the night before, and left in readiness three hundred yards in the rear, were soon placed in the battery; but as the engineers were enlarging it for the reception of two more guns, our party had to wait until it was completed. The spot fixed upon for the mortar battery was so well chosen, that the nature of the ground and some brushwood which grew in its front, completely hid it from view, so that although within less than five hundred yards of the walls, the enemy was not aware of its being constructed, nor offered the least molestation to the workmen.

The battery on the Oliva was more open to view, and the night being perfectly still, the sounds, unavoidably made by the men at work, must have reached the town, for fire-balls, followed immediately by a discharge of grape, were thrown from time to time throughout the night, in the direction of the battery, though fortunately without doing any mischief. By dawn of day this battery was finished, and the last gun was rolling to its berth along the platform, when the sailors, a queer set of fellows, who seem swayed and ruled by feelings and impulses distinct from the rest of mankind, and are not much given to reflect or weigh consequences at any time, just by way, I suppose, of giving the Frenchmen on the ramparts a friendly hint that all was ready for them, and they might begin as soon as they pleased, raised one general hurrah that rang through the welkin, loud enough to startle the veriest sluggard within the walls of Tarragona from his slumbers.

The Frenchmen were not slow in convincing us that this well-meant intelligence had reached their ears, for in a few minutes a well-directed shot, followed by thud-thud-thud, from every gun that could be brought to bear, made the sand-bags fly, covering the battery and every man in it with clouds of dust; and the ammunition not being yet at hand, before the officer of artillery was ready to reply to this salutation, the enemy's fire had razed the parapet almost even with the platform. The fire from the walls was in a fair way of completely levelling the Oliva battery, and would most likely have prevented its reconstruction for the day, had not the mortar-battery now opened its fire, and with such admirable effect, that that of the enemy soon slackened, and in two or three hours had nearly ceased altogether.

This cessation enabled them to repair the damaged battery, and then the two together kept up a most crushing fire on the town for the rest of the day. When it was found that the presence of the sailors was no longer necessary, we were directed to withdraw – an order which we were not sorry to comply with; for the music of the shot, when we had nothing else to listen to, and nothing to divert our attention from it, began to sound anything but pleasant.

Early on the morning of that day (the 11th), reports reached head-quarters, that a column of the enemy amounting to seven or eight thousand men with artillery, and a small detachment of cavalry, was advancing from Barcelona, between which and the camp before Tarragona, five thousand men of Copons' army were interposed. In order to communicate personally with General Copons, and gain more exact information of the enemy's movements, Sir John Murray rode that morning to Vendrills, with the avowed intention of choosing a position, and fighting, if the report of their advance should turn out to be true. General Clinton, the next in command, was left in charge of the siege, with directions to make every preparation for storming the Fuerte Real that night, the breach in which had been practicable since the 8th. A fire was again opened upon it on the morning of the 11th, in order to clear and widen the breach more effectually, which was supported by the six Spanish gun boats, under the command of our first Lieutenant Boxer, which maintained a vigorous flanking fire upon the fort throughout the day, and also drew upon themselves the fire from the southern works of the town.

All now felt confident that the General was in earnest, and that the siege would, in future, be prosecuted with energy and vigour; and when we observed the terrible effects of the two advanced batteries, opened only since the morning, we calculated upon the speedy surrender of Tarragona with that confidence, which such advantages and the strength of the besieging force so justly inspired.

No sailors were landed from the ships, nor were any boats sent away upon service on the night of the 11th, and being aware that the Fuerte Real was ordered to be stormed, the officers collected on the quarter deck of the *Malta* soon after dark, watching with strained and eager eyes for the rocket which was to signal the advance of the storming party. About 10 o'clock, or a little after, a dropping desultory, fire was heard on the north side of the town, where the divisions of Clinton and Whittingham were stationed. This we knew to proceed from a false attack, meant to distract and divert the enemy's attention from the real point to be assailed, and we became, in consequence, if possible, more on the *qui vive*, expecting momentarily to see the concerted signal. All, however, remained quiet to the south of the town. No rocket went up; and soon the firing to the north ceased, when every thing around became once more perfectly still. The patience of some became now exhausted – they went below, but a few lingered still upon deck, hoping that the hour only was changed, and that the attack would yet take place.

About midnight, when we were still conjecturing what could delay the assault of Fuerte Real, the Admiral came on board. Without a word of observation he descended immediately to his cabin, and sent for the Captain and First Lieutenant. When the latter came on deck we all crowded around him to learn the news, when we heard with mingled feelings of astonishment and indignation, that the assault of the Fuerte Real was not only given up, but that the siege of Tarragona was to be raised, and the army forthwith embarked! Such then was to be the reward of our labours – the realization of all our visions of credit and renown! But no time was given us then to brood over our chagrin and disappointments. One was instantly dispatched to the agent of transports, and others to the different men-of-war, with orders to have all boats on the beach by daylight for the purpose of embarking horses, artillery, stores, &c.

The boats were all ashore at the appointed time, and the work of embarking guns and stores from the depôt commenced; but in its performance one could not help contrasting the downcast look, and dejected expression of officers and men, with the bold, and confident, and cheerful demeanour of the same people a few days before, when busy in landing the same *matériel*; and instead of the manly port, and erect and haughty carriage which distinguished them heretofore, the officers of the staff, in the execution of some necessary order, now moved about dispirited and crest-fallen, and in place of mutual congratulations for the success of last night's work, a shake of the head with 'It's a bad business', was the only salutation that passed between us.

At eight o'clock that morning (the 12th) the general commanding the army went on board the *Malta*. He staid but a short time, the purport of his visit being to tell the Admiral that 'he had staid too long, and that he had made up his mind to embark the men immediately, to leave the guns in the batteries, and his cavalry and artillery behind.'

The Admiral was terribly mortified, and at breakfast the officer of the morning watch, who partook of that meal with him, had an opportunity of observing how much hurt and distressed he seemed. For a long time he remained silent, apparently absorbed in deep thought. At length he exclaimed, 'I fear all is over, but I will make one effort more. I will try and get all the generals together, and go and represent to him their opinions of the measures which he is pursuing.' Then suddenly desiring his secretary to bring pens and paper, he dictated the following note:

Sir,

It being your determination to raise the siege of Tarragona, and embark your army at this place, at the risk of losing your artillery and cavalry, I hope you will not be offended at my suggesting a plan for their safe retreat and embarkation. It is, that they, with a column of infantry, shall be immediately put in motion for the Pass of Balaguer, and I will answer for their being got off.

This letter was immediately despatched, and the Admiral soon after went on shore. The General adopted, in part, the suggestion offered by the Admiral, and the field artillery, and the most part of the cavalry, marched for Balaguer.

The Admiral then, with some of the general officers, and the officers commanding the artillery and engineers, repaired to head-quarters, for the purpose of representing to the commander of the forces the propriety of marching to meet General Decaen, who was said to be advancing from Villa Franca, or at all events to suspend the embarkation of the troops until night, when all the guns could be brought down to the beach from the batteries, and embarked with safety.

To the first part of this representation he only answered by an ominous shake of the head, saying that 'it would not do', but he promised to wait till night in order to save his guns.

Having so far succeeded, the Admiral hastened to the beach, where, by his own indefatigable exertions, ably seconded by the zeal and promptitude of his own officers, and those of the other men-of-war and transport service, and in spite of frequent interruptions from the contradictory orders, and, as the second in command called them, 'that endless change of measures to be observed on that ill-fated day', he embarked all the heavy guns brought down to the beach, besides a considerable quantity of stores, by two o'clock in the afternoon.

While in the midst of this operation, what must have been his amazement and mortification at seeing a smoke ascend from all the batteries, which soon convinced him that the promise so lately made him of staying till night was not to be kept – that the General had again changed his mind, and that the guns in the batteries were to be abandoned. And if any doubt existed as to such being the case, it was soon dissipated by the arrival of the first division of the troops on the beach.

At three o'clock in the afternoon the embarkation of the men commenced, and by midnight the whole army was on board, except the advance under Colonel Adam, the field artillery, and part of the cavalry, which had marched to Salau and the Pass of Balaguer.

Sir J Murray, who went on board the *Malta* at eight o'clock on the night of the 12th, left early the next morning and proceeded in the *Volcano* with a division of transports to Balaguer, and the Admiral followed in the *Malta* soon after, having first seen that the horses and mules, whose embarkation had been stopped the previous day at the western cove, in order to have every boat that was possible to embark the men, were all safe on board.

Captain Bathurst, in the *Fame*, was left in the Bay of Tarragona with the rest of the transports, ready to weigh whenever the Admiral should send him orders for that purpose.

20: The Catalonian Campaign

When we anchored at Balaguer the division of troops which had accompanied Sir John Murray in the morning was in the act of disembarking. The General was on shore, but had left directions that the rest of the troops as they arrived from Tarragona, should be held in readiness to land. The infantry were all landed early on the 14th and the artillery and dragoons, which had been embarked on the following morning. A letter which the General received on the morning of the 13th, informed him that Suchet had quitted Tortosa with eight thousand or nine thousand men, and was in full march for Perello by the mountain pass. This information it was, which most probably induced him to disembark the army again, and by throwing himself with a superior force between the French Marshal and Tarragona check his advance, or engage him at a disadvantage, and thereby recover some portion of the credit which had been left under the walls of that fortress.

On the night of the 13th the enemy's fires were descried in the mountains in the direction of Bandillos; and our advanced patrols encountered those of the enemy in the neighbourhood of that village on the following morning, and drove them in. But I do not pretend to give an account of all the movements of this ill-fated army while on shore in the vicinity of Balaguer. It will be sufficient to observe that they were characterized by a greater degree of vacillation and irresolution than that which directed its conduct before Tarragona. Various and contradictory rumours of the strength and advance of the enemy reached head-quarters, and according to the tenor of those rumours, so were the movements of the army regulated. There seemed to be no fixed, steady plan of action, each change being governed by the last-received report, the truth of which was never clearly ascertained. One hour the troops advanced to meet the enemy, and the next they retired towards the beach. Now the General was all fight. He had selected his position and would give battle; and even a brigade of seamen, with two twelve-pounder carronades mounted on field carriages, were landed from the *Malta*, to act according to circumstances; and at midnight an order would come off to the ship to have all the boats of the men-of-war and transports on shore by daylight, ready to embark the troops; but by the time half a brigade was in the boats, a fresh order would be received to land, and the men countermarched from the beach, so that, in log-book phrase, we 'embarked and disembarked occasionally'.

Captain Carroll, of the *Volcano*, had been sent with the despatches announcing the failure of the attempt on Tarragona. The *Hyacinth* conveyed him to Alicant, whence he was to make his way to the head-quarters of Lord Wellington, and then proceed to England with the duplicate of Admiral Hallowell's letter to Sir Edward Pellew, detailing the proceedings of the conjunct expedition up to that time. Boxer was appointed to act as commander of the *Volcano* in the absence of Captain Carroll, and his removal made me senior lieutenant of the *Malta*.

From the moment the expedition reached the coast of Catalonia, everybody in the ship had been kept hard at work; but the six or eight days after my elevation to the post of first lieutenant proved the most harassing and fagging I ever knew at sea; not an instant were we unemployed. Orders and counter-orders followed each other so fast, that the utmost diligence and efforts could hardly keep pace with them. Stores and provisions were continually landing; and frequently scarcely clear of the boats, when they were ordered to be re-shipped again. Numerous working parties for various duties were to be selected and despatched, and the ship often left without sufficient hands on board to do the necessary duties; and at night none of us knew what it was to be in bed for an hour or two without being roused out for something or other.

On the 17th, the *America*, 74, arrived with Lord William Bentinck and a small reinforcement of troops from Sicily. Lord William went on shore as soon as the *America* had anchored. It was now ascertained that Suchet had quitted Perello, and was hastening back to Valencia, in which province the armies of the Duque del Parque and Elio were making alarming progress.

Upon learning the retrograde movement of the French marshal, Lord William decided upon destroying Fort St Felipe at Balaguer, and, re-embarking the army, to return immediately to Alicant; there it could be reorganized and brigaded fresh, and then act according to circumstances. This plan was put into execution, and the transports sailed by divisions under their respective convoys on the 19th and 20th.

The return passage of the fleet was of much longer duration, and not marked by the same good fortune which attended its descent upon the coast of Catalonia; – for in rounding the Alfaques, a dangerous shoal off the mouths of the Ebro, four transports and one of the Spanish gun-boats were totally wrecked. Fortunately the weather was moderate, and no lives were lost; but whatever else they had on board – guns, ordnance stores, and I think some horses – went to the bottom.

When all was clear off from Balaguer, we followed in the *Malta*. In passing Murviedro we saw the *Ganymede* in chase of a felucca, between that place and the Grao of Valencia. The water there runs off shoal a considerable distance from the land; and in his anxiety to close with the chase, the Captain of the *Ganymede* kept too near in, and ran his ship ashore: luckily the accident was seen from the *Malta*, for the sun was just sinking as it occurred. We anchored immediately, and sent all our boats, with stream anchor and cable, and hawsers to her assistance; and by dint of hard work, and receiving her guns, spare cables, stores, &c., into the *Malta*, succeeded in heaving her off by eight o'clock on the following morning. After this, we reached Alicant without further accident, and found the transports had all arrived, except the four which had been wrecked on the Alfaques.

And thus terminated the too famous siege of Tarragona, with the subsequent operations under the conduct of Sir John Murray; and that army, which left Alicant full of enthusiasm, and high in hope, returned to the same place in less than a month discomfited and crestfallen. But it was not dispirited, nor cast down; on the contrary, it burned with a desire for an opportunity of retrieving the credit which had been left under the walls of Tarragona. It felt that the disastrous result of the recent operations proceeded from no fault of its own; for composed though it was of such incongruous elements, including within its ranks men of such different nations, still, when put to the proof, it had shown itself equal to the occasion – witness the affair of Castalla, and the speedy reduction of the fort of Balaguer. The slow and cautious manner in which the operations of the siege were from the first conducted, and its sudden and precipitate abandonment just when more active measures were being adopted, and its speedy surrender might be expected, were matters wholly inexplicable to us, and I believe to everybody in the army unacquainted with the springs and motives by which the General's strange conduct was influenced. It was not till the 10th that he showed any disposition to press the siege with vigour. On that day more mortars and ordnance stores were landed. Two new batteries, advanced within four hundred and fifty yards of the place, were opened on the morning of the 11th, when he rode to Vendrills, and arranged with Copons, the Spanish General, a plan for fighting Decaen, who was expected to reach Villa Franca that night with six or eight thousand men. General Clinton was left in command of the siege during the absence of Sir John, with orders to make arrangements for storming the Fuerte Real that night. These arrangements were made, and everything now announced a determined perseverance. At nine o'clock in the evening, when the General returned to head-quarters, he told General Clinton that the arrangements, which the latter had made, were to be carried into effect at ten o'clock – and yet, in less than half an hour he had changed his mind! The storming of the Fuerte Real was countermanded: orders were given for abandoning the siege, and for holding the troops in readiness to embark in the morning.

It is bootless to repeat, as it is impossible to account for this decision, or the needless haste with which it was put into execution, still less, to use the words of a general employed on the expedition, 'for that endless change of measures which marked the proceedings of that ill-fated day'. Orders and counter-orders followed each other with such rapidity, that the greatest zeal and dispatch could not keep pace with them; the quarter-master-general giving directions in the name of the commander of the forces, which were denied by the latter as soon as he was made acquainted with them.

It appeared that soon after Sir John Murray returned to camp from his conference with Copons at Vendrills, he received letters from Villa Franca on the one hand, and Balaguer on the other, with information that Decaen had entered the former place with from six to eight thousand men, at four o'clock in the afternoon of that day (the 11th), and that Suchet had reached Tortosa on the afternoon of the 10th, with four thousand five hundred men. This movement of Decaen Sir John must have been prepared for, as it was only in the morning that he had arranged with Copons to oppose his advance to Tarragona, and fight him on the Gaya; but the approach of a chief so redoubtable as Suchet, seems to have alarmed him. And yet a moment's reflection must have satisfied him that the French Marshal would wait till he was joined by reinforcements before he ventured to descend into the plain of Tarragona, and when they came up, as we held the pass of Balaguer, he would be compelled to make a wide *détour* through the mountains by passes impracticable for artillery, which consequently must have been left behind. This circuit would have retarded his advance so much, that he could not have appeared before Tarragona sooner than the 14th; and in fact, it was not till the morning of that day that the patrols of the two armies encountered each other near the village of Bandillos, which is a long day's march from Reuss. By that time, had the General adhered to the promise which he made to the Admiral and Colonel Williamson of the Artillery, of remaining on shore the night of the 12th, everything would have been safe on board, twenty-four hours before, guns, stores, horses, and all. For this change of resolution there does not appear to have been any sufficient cause. No fresh intelligence could have influenced him; for at the moment, when we were precipitating the embarkation, and abandoning guns, stores, &c., Decaen, alarmed at the first intelligence of the appearance of Sir E Pellew's fleet in the Bay of Rosas, hastily fell back from Villa Franca, in order to be at hand to face a new assailant and protect his rear. Correct information seems to have been lamentably defective, nor were sufficient steps taken to procure better. Staff-officers of the British part of the force were not employed for the purpose, nor were patrols or detachments stationed upon those roads by which the enemy was expected to approach. The only one that had been sent out was posted at Valls, where Colonel Adam, with the advance, watched the road from Tortosa by Monblanc; as if Suchet, whose only chance of saving Tarragona was dispatch, would march by the longest route, or, as if a smaller detachment than the whole of the advance would not have been sufficient to watch that line. It has been a question whether the circumstances under which the Anglo-Sicilian army appeared before Tarragona, and the state in which that fortress was found, would not have justified an immediate attempt by escalade, without waiting the slower process of a siege and opening a breach. One outwork, the Fuerte Real, alone covered an angle of the fortress towards the sea to the S.W. Everywhere else the nature of the ground favoured the approach of an enemy. There was no glacis, and when the wall was reached, no ditch obstructed the immediate planting of the ladders. Then the garrison was known to be weak, consisting of at most one thousand six hundred Italians, whereas three thousand men would scarcely have been a sufficient number for so wide a circuit as the walls embraced. Besides time was of the utmost value to the English General; for it was to be supposed that, as soon as the object of the expedition was known, the enemy would make the most strenuous efforts to defeat it.

But if such a step were hazardous, or likely to cost more men than the prize, though gained, should be worth, still the slowness and want of decision manifested by the General cannot be justified. Thirteen thousand men, with what assistance could be derived from the co-operation of the fleet, having nothing to interrupt them, either from the weather or on the part of the enemy, lay for nine days before the town before a gun was opened on the body of the place! What a contrast does the conduct of the Duke of Wellington present! All his actions were marked by decision, energy, and rapidity of movement. He appeared before Ciudad Rodrigo on the 8th of January: it was assaulted and captured on the 19th of the same month. Badajos was invested on the 17th of March, and it fell on the 6th of the following April. And yet these were two of the strongest and most regularly fortified places in Spain – amply garrisoned and provided with all necessary munitions and stores, and commanded by officers of approved skill and resources in war in all its branches. The capture of these fortresses was also a question of time; for had not the rapidity of Lord Wellington's movements greatly outstripped the calculations of Marmont in both instances, the latter, in all probability, would have been able to have rescued them from the grasp of his bold and skilful adversary.

In consequence of the success of the Marquis of Wellington in the north of Spain, and the gloomy aspect of affairs in Germany, Suchet now thought his position in Valencia untenable. He determined, therefore, to abandon the province, and leaving garrisons only in Murviedro and Peñiscola, to concentrate his forces in Catalonia, where he should be prepared either to make a stand, or retire across the frontier, according to circumstances. In pursuance of this plan, and blowing up the works at San Felipe, he broke up from the Xucar, and withdrawing the garrison from Valencia, crossed the Ebro.

When the Anglo-Sicilian army was reorganized, and a fresh arrangement made of the brigades, Lord William advanced to the Xucar. The Admiral, who had provided himself with a couple of horses, accompanied the troops on the march, the *Malta* being ordered, after watering at Altea, to proceed to Valencia, whither the transports under their respective convoys were to follow. We anchored in the Grao of Valencia on the 14th of July, and the next day the advanced guard entered the city. The army halted in the vicinity for a few days to refresh, when all the officers of the *Malta* but myself visited the shore; but the duties of the first lieutenant tied me to the ship, and obliged me to forego the gratification of seeing the Queen of the Mediterranean.

The army again marched on the 17th, and we coasted to Vinaros, where we anchored with a division of transports. There we were employed till the 23rd in collecting boats, and other materials for a bridge to be thrown across the Ebro. On that day information was received that the enemy were about to blow up the works of Tarragona, upon which we sailed immediately with a division of four thousand four hundred men, under the command of General Clinton, to be in readiness to act according to circumstances, either by occupying the abandoned town, or harassing the enemy's retreat. Captain Bathurst, of the *Fame*, with the gun-boats and the rest of the transports, was left in the Bay of Alfaques, to further the preparations for the bridge; while Lieutenant Bowie, of gun-boat No. 23, an intelligent and experienced officer, who had seen much gun-boat services at the sieges of Flushing, Cadiz, Tarifa, and Tarragona, having with him two gun-boats and four light transports, ascended the river as high as Amposta, where the bridge was intended to be thrown across, and superintended its construction. It consisted of boats, with a few pontoons, lashed together, heading the stream, and the whole planked over. Not being quite long enough to reach from bank to bank, it was worked by hawsers from both sides, which were veered and hauled upon as necessary. Besides this mode of transit, there were three or four small rafts, each composed of a couple of boats planked over, and warped from side to side like the bridge. By this means, great part of the infantry, all the cavalry, artillery, and commissariat train, crossed in safety. The army continued its march to the eastward; but Bowie remained in the river to await the arrival of Sarsfield's division, which had not yet come up, General Villa Campa being left with four or five thousand men to watch the garrison of Tortosa, and protect the bridge.

On the night of the 4th of August, this General, deceived by a false report that a body of the enemy had left Tortosa, quitted the vicinity of the river in their pursuit, as he supposed, leaving the bridge and gun-boat entirely unprotected. Never dreaming of such an occurrence, and thinking himself perfectly secure under the guardianship of the Spaniard, who never apprized him of his movements, Bowie had taken no additional precautions, and placed no other look-out than the ordinary one on the deck of his little vessel; and the first intimation that he had in the morning, while washing decks, of this desertion of his friends, was by a volley from the ferry-house at Amposta, which brought down two of his men close by his side. When the firing commenced the gun-boat was within fifteen or twenty yards of the shore, to which she was steadied by a hawser. This Bowie immediately cut, and the vessel swung further out in the stream to her anchor. She was still, however, under fire, and before there was time to clear a gun, the enemy's musketry was so hot, and so well plied, that her decks were nearly cleared, three men being killed, and Bowie and several others wounded.

Finding it was now hopeless to attempt to save the craft, Bowie bethought him of saving himself and crew from a French prison, and his little vessel from becoming a trophy in the hands of the enemy. He therefore had his boat shifted to the side, where it was under shelter from the enemy's fire, and while he and the carpenter were scuttling the vessel, and laying a train to the magazine, part of the crew got into the boat, and the rest jumped overboard and swam to the north shore. When everybody was clear of the gun-boat, Bowie fired the train, and then flinging himself into the water, struck out after his men. A sharp fire was kept upon him as he swam, but though he was thrice touched, and his clothes were perforated in several places, he escaped without a serious hurt. When he reached the shore and looked round, he observed that a party of dragoons had got upon one of the rafts, and were in the act of hauling themselves across the river, upon which Bowie very coolly cut the hawser, and the Frenchmen, to their surprise and mortification, swung back to the spot from whence they started. His presence of mind upon this occasion saved the whole party from a prison; for had the enemy been enabled to cross at once, he and his men must have fallen unresistingly into their hands, as they were unarmed and perfectly defenceless.

A few minutes after he had touched the shore, Bowie had the satisfation of seeing his craft blow up, and then he and his crew moved off from the river as quickly as the condition of the wounded would permit them; and before the enemy had prepared another raft to follow them, they had found a cart and mules, into which the worst cases were put, and they were soon out of all danger. The enemy having effected their object by the destruction of the bridge and gun-boat, returned the same day to Tortosa. Bowie and his crew lost their all – books, papers, clothes, everything, and when they reached the *Malta*, they were in a very pitiable plight. The court-martial which followed, acquitted them all of blame, and the president, in returning his sword, paid Bowie a handsome, but well-merited compliment, on his coolness, gallantry, and judgment. The Admiral, too, was so much pleased with his conduct, that he appointed him to the *Malta*, which happened opportunely to want a lieutenant.*

When we arrived off Tarragona with General Clinton's division, we found the French flag still floating above the walls, without anything that indicated its being soon replaced by any other. We therefore prudently anchored out of range. The next night we suddenly weighed with the division of transports, and ran down to Balaguer, a report having been received that the garrison of Tortosa had escaped, and were in full march for Tarragona. The troops were landed at daylight in the morning (the 26th), and immediately occupied the pass. The report turned out to be false. The garrison had never left Tortosa, as Bowie found to his cost. The division was re-embarked, and we returned to Tarragona on the 30th, by which time the whole force, under Lord William Bentinck, to the amount of nearly thirty thousand men, including the army of the Duque Del Parque, had assembled before the town. The battering train was in the bay, and working parties were set to, to cut and prepare fascines; but

---

* Bowie is still a Lieutenant! Pity he did not serve in Syria or China. He might then have been a Captain, and mayhap a K.C.B. Since these sketches first appeared, Bowie was made a Commander; but I regret to say he did not long survive to enjoy his promotion. He died in a year after.

as Suchet's junction with Decaen had rendered his force nearly equal in point of numbers to the combined armies, Lord William considering the description of force which he had to wield, did not think it prudent to land his heavy guns. The town was therefore blockaded, and he watched the favourable moment to commence the siege with vigour.

Sarsfield's division of Spaniards was at Villa Franca, the nearest post to the enemy, who occupied the line of the Llobregat; while Colonel Adam with the advance, was stationed at Altafulla and Torredembarra, seven miles to the east of Tarragona. The coast road, which is the best and most direct from Barcelona, there approaches the beach so closely as to be, for a considerable distance, within grape-shot distance of the anchorage; and there the *Volcano* bomb and gun-boats were stationed to cover it. Suchet, seeing the jeopardy in which the garrison of Tarragona was placed, determined to withdraw it. For this purpose, he advanced with his whole force from the Llobregat, and driving the division of Sarsfield before him, the heads of his columns reached Torredembarra in the afternoon of the 6th. A fire from the bomb and gun-boats was immediately opened upon them, which checked their advance. Upon hearing the firing the Admiral instantly got under weigh, and in running down, we met the *Royal George*, which ship had been detached with eight hundred marines, by Sir Edward Pellew, with an offer of their services, if they could be usefully employed. The two ships anchored almost within pistol-shot of the shore, a very little to the westward of Altafulla, where the road comes close to the sea, and, with springs on their cables, were prepared to thunder on the enemy should they venture to pass that way. But checked, as they had been by the warm reception which they met with from the bomb and her companions, they did not dare to persevere in the face of the broadsides of a three-decker and an eighty-gun ship, and the near and menacing position, which they had taken up. The marines were immediately offered to Colonel Adam, but declined, his orders being not to defend Torredembarra and Altafulla, but to fall back upon the camp before Tarragona.

The ship's boats with their carronades, were away all night, and the men lay at quarters; but the enemy did not show themselves. It afterwards appeared that by a considerable *détour* to the right, they gained the road to Cressels, at which village they halted. Early the next morning, Lord William fell back from Tarragona to Balaguer, where he took up an exceedingly strong position with his whole force. We remained at anchor off Altafulla that day, and the following morning, in passing Tarragona, we observed the enemy's troops in great numbers on the heights above the town, which we saw them enter about ten o'clock. We then followed the army to Balaguer, and in a few days the enemy, having effectually destroyed the guns and carriages, and blown up the works of Tarragona, withdrew the garrison and resumed his position on the Llobregat. The army again advanced and entered Tarragona, where a great quantity of ordnance was found, chiefly brass, but rendered totally unfit for service.

The town presented a most forlorn and ruinous appearance. The walls had been breached in eight or nine different places, and the houses within them, which had greatly suffered from the fire of the French, when Suchet besieged it, still strewed the streets, which were in many places nearly impassable from rubbish, and scarcely a fourth of those left standing were inhabited. By degrees, however, the people began to flock in; the more respectable inhabitants – merchants and others – who had sought refuge at Majorca and Minorca, hearing that the enemy had abandoned the town and retired from the western part of the province, returned – shops were opened – a regular market established – the streets were cleared, and in less time than could be expected, the place exhibited signs of returning life and animation.

Lord William having occasion to confer with the Spanish General, who commanded to the south of the Ebro, proceeded in the *Malta* to Vinaros, and having arranged with that officer the business that called him thither, returned to Tarragona.

Having left a competent garrison in the town, with engineers and artificers to clear and repair the breaches in the walls, Lord William now marched to Villa Franca, where the head-quarters were established on the 4th of September, the advance under Colonel Adam occupying the village and pass of Ordal, a strong defile, eight or nine miles distant from the Llobregat.

The contending armies occupied the same positions till the evening of the 12th, when two Spanish battalions were ordered to Ordal, to strengthen the force under Colonel Adam. It was late in the day when they received the order to march, in consequence of which it was nearly eleven o'clock at night before they reached Ordal, and before they had taken up their allotted position, the post was attacked by an overwhelming force of the enemy.

Against such fearful odds the advance maintained its ground for an hour and a half with unflinching constancy, repulsing numerous charges of the French cavalry; and it was not until Colonel Adam, Colonel Reeves, and Major Mills of the 27th, and several other officers, had been badly wounded, that the enemy at last broke through, when the whole advance, with the exception of the Calabrese under Major Octavius Carey, was fairly dispersed.

As the principal attack was made upon the road, where the British were posted, the Spaniards were enabled to retire with very little loss to the mountains. The British, and the foreign corps joined with them, suffered considerably in killed and wounded; besides which, two six-pounders and two light mountain guns were lost, but not before they had done great execution in the ranks of the enemy.

Few prisoners were taken by the French; for although the brigade might be said to be completely broken and dispersed, the darkness of the night favoured the escape of the men, and before many days the greater part found their way back to head-quarters.

The enemy continued to advance, and early the next morning Suchet appeared with his whole army in front of the allied lines, making dispositions which threatened their left flank.

The ground which Lord William occupied presented no advantage of position; and as his army, although equal perhaps in point of numbers to that of the enemy, which was estimated at twenty-six or twenty-eight thousand men, was, for the most part, made up of foreigners, who were unused to act or move together in large bodies, he judged it more prudent to decline the offered battle, and to retire to a position more favourable for troops of the description such as his army was composed of. He therefore commenced his retreat, which was executed with but trifling loss, and without the least hurry or confusion.

The Spaniards moved off the ground first, and the division of General McKenzie, with the cavalry and a brigade of artillery, formed the rear-guard and covered the retreat. This was performed in masterly style, with the order and precision of a field day, one brigade halting to await the charge, often in square, of the enemy's numerous cavalry, amounting to two thousand sabres and more; and when they had repulsed them, passing to the rear of the next brigade, which halted and manœvred in the like manner as soon as the enemy again approached.

The artillery, too, played their part well, and the small body of cavalry, not a fourth as numerous as that of the enemy, executed several brilliant and effective charges. In one of them, Lord Frederick Bentinck, who commanded the allied cavalry, exchanged sabre cuts with the officer who led the enemy's horse, and a captain of the 20th Dragoons (I greatly regret I do not remember his name), whose impetuous courage bore him headlong, upon another occasion, singly into the thick of the enemy's ranks, after fighting his way clear again without a scratch, was shot by a trooper in the back as he trotted back to rejoin his comrades. He was a remarkably fine young man, of a tall and commanding figure, and not more than twenty-three or twenty-four years of age. He had joined his regiment only a few days before the retreat, from England, where he had been on leave of absence to recruit his health. He was a great favourite in his corps, and throughout that day his noble bearing and chivalrous gallantry were the theme of general admiration. His death was greatly lamented by all his comrades – a feeling that was, if possible, enhanced by the manner of the poor fellow's fall – shot when his back was turned by the hand of some ignoble trooper!*

The French Marshal, finding that he could make no impression on the retreating army, did not continue the pursuit beyond Vendrills, where he passed the night. The combined army then continued its retreat to the walls of Tarragona, except the rear-guard, which halted at Torredembarra and Altafulla.

The next morning the enemy's patrols showed themselves on the road near Torredembarra, but their further advance was immediately stopped by the fire of the *Malta* and gun-boats. In a day or two they withdrew altogether from the neighbourhood, soon after which Suchet fell back to his former position on the Llobregat. Sarsfield's Spanish division now formed the advance, being stationed at Villa Franca, with a picquet at Ordal, while the rest of the allied army was cantoned in and around Tarrangona.

In the two days' fighting, the Allies sustained a loss, in killed, wounded, and missing, of six hundred men; while that of the enemy, though not clearly ascertained, was supposed to be much more considerable. The Allies lost no prisoners on the retreat, while several were made from the enemy – a lieutenant-colonel among the number; and we heard subsequently that one hundred and two carts had entered Barcelona with the wounded.

An aide-de-camp of Suchet came to head-quarters to request an exchange of prisoners, and he spoke in high terms of the gallant and determined defence of Ordal, as well as of the skilful and soldier-like manner in which the retreat was conducted on the following day.

The works of Tarragona were soon placed in as defensible a state as before their recent destruction, and the affairs of Sicily requiring the personal supervision of Lord William about the same time, he sailed for that island, and left the command of the army in the hands of General Clinton.

The combined army lay quietly in cantonments all the autumn and most part of the winter, during which time we never left the Bay of Tarragona. Little occurred to vary our routine of duty on board, except that the Admiral contrived to diversify it somewhat by volunteering a

---

* I have since ascertained that the name of this officer was Hanson.

party of workmen from the ship to build a battery on a bluff to the eastward of the Mole, where no gun from the fortress bore upon that part of the Bay. Accordingly stone-cutters, masons, and hodmen were landed every morning, and worked away till sunset, under the superintendence of a lieutenant; and in process of time they turned out of hand a piece of masonry which would have done no discredit to any workmen.

Everything had now remained so quiet and undisturbed for many weeks, that several more families were induced to return to their homes in Tarragona, so that a little pleasant *société* was managed during the latter part of our sojourn there. We had sufficient leisure to make frequent excursions into the country, and often visited our friends of the artillery at Constanti, a village three miles on the road to Valls. Our rides sometimes led us to Reuss, a large town six or seven miles to the west of Tarragona, and once an *entrepôt* for the wine of that part of the province, many hundred tuns of which used to be shipped from the neighbouring Bay of Salou for Bordeaux and London, there to be remanufactured into most excellent port and claret. Occasionally we passed the night there, when we used to get billets upon the good citizens, the accommodation at the *posadas* in Spain being most villainous. On one of those nights we remained rather late at a *tertulia*, and in returning to our quarters we passed the house at which one of the party was billeted. We stopped for a moment to wish our companion good night, whilst the door was being opened; but to his repeated knockings no answer was returned, and although we lent a hand to make all the row we could, not a sound or movement from within gave evidence that the uproar had disturbed the drowsy inmates.

In despair of making himself heard, our friend was just turning to depart, fain to endure the miseries of a *posada*, when some one suggested the possibility of enteriug by the window, if the balcony could be gained. No sooner was this idea started, than, mounting upon our shoulders, and grasping the railings, he was landed in the balcony; then trying the window, to his great joy, it yielded to his touch, and wishing us good night, he passed through and we saw no more of him for the night. Next morning the whole party assembled to breakfast at the principal *café* in Reuss, when we learned the sequel of our friend's adventures.

It seems that he had no sooner passed through the window, than a gruff and angry voice shouted out, '*Quien es?*' and forth stepped the master of the house in his shirt, from an adjoining room, followed by his better half in habiliments almost as scanty. A torrent of abuse on either hand was immediately poured upon his devoted head, during which no epithet of opprobrium and scurrility was spared which the language of

Spain supplies, and in that respect its vocabulary is as rich and copious as that of any other country. To all his excuses and remonstrances a deaf ear was turned. The more quiet and apologetic his demeanour was, the more minacious and unappeasable they became, exhibiting in this the conduct of all true bullies, who commonly wax bolder and fiercer the more gentle and disposed for peace they observe you to be. When this scene had lasted some time, and from threats and abuse they seemed disposed to proceed to violence, the patrol happened opportunely to pass that way. Hearing loud and angry voices, the serjeant stopped, and demanded the cause of so much noise and turmoil. The master of the house instantly flew to the open casement, and told, in a voice almost incoherent from violent emotion, that *un Ingles* (sinking the officer) had broken into his house through the window, disturbing his family after they had all retired to bed, and what further mischief he might have committed he was as yet unable to say.

Fortunately our friend understood, and could speak the language tolerably well, which enabled him to put a very different interpretation upon this story, and the cause of his then situation, which otherwise must have appeared extraordinary and suspicious. As soon then as the angry and voluble saddler (such was the *métier* of the master of the house) had ceased, he told the serjeant that he was an English officer, billeted on the house. That on returning from a party of friends a short time before, he found the door locked; and when nobody would open it, or answer his repeated knockings, he then mounted to the balcony, and finding the window open, quietly entered where he was then standing: that all he required was to be shown to a bed-room according to his billet, which if not done immediately, the matter, as well as the master of the house's conduct, should be made known in the proper quarter in the morning. Upon hearing this version of the story, the serjeant sharply rebuked the saddler for his behaviour – cautioned him to be more respectful in future to King's officers, and then wishing both a good night, moved off with his party. The turn which matters had taken, and the serjeant's reproof, had a salutary and instantaneous effect in subduing the saddler's ire, and turning to his wife, he desired her to get a light and show the *cavallero* to his room. On descending in the morning, he found the saddler quietly at work in his shop, and disposed to be as civil and courteous as he had been rude and abusive over-night. Although I suppose I thought differently at the time, yet now upon reflection, I cannot help feeling that the man's conduct, however coarse and brutal, was in some measure excusable; for is it not hard and unjust that industrious people in business should have their quiet invaded, and be put to the expense and inconvenience of providing beds for officers, who, for pleasure and amusement, happen to pass a day in their towns?

In this way passed the months of autumn, except that twice or thrice I had been sent in a gun-boat to Sitges, for the purpose of communicating with a person there who sometimes furnished the Admiral with information. He had been a merchant at Barcelona, and left the town and his business when it was occupied by the French in 1808. He then retired to Sitges, a small place between Barcelona and Tarragona, where he lived retired and unsuspected, although he maintained a secret correspondence with the former town.

21: Napoleon in Exile

Upon one occasion that I was ordered to Sitges, upon this duty the gentleman happened to be from home. It being uncertain when he would return and having a few hours to spare, I thought it as well to employ them in visiting the division of General Sarsfield, at Villa Franca, as in idling them away at Sitges. Ordering the gun-boat to drop down to Villa Nova, where I purposed to join her the next morning, I got a mule, and rode by a bridle-path through the mountains to Villa Franca. As soon as I arrived, I called to pay my respects to the General, whom I had known before. He received me very politely, and pressed me to share a soldier's meal, adding that as it happened to be a 'field-day' at his quarters, I might chance to fare the better. At dinner I found assembled the commanding officers of regiments and heads of departments of his division, and also Captain Zehnpfinning, the British Military Agent in Catalonia, and an officer of the Quartermaster-General's department, stationed with the advanced corps for the purpose of forwarding to head-quarters the earliest intelligence of the movements of the enemy.

We had dined, and with our wine and dessert were discussing the wondrous events which then began to engross the attention of all, namely, the successes and advance of Lord Wellington into France, the campaign in Germany, so disastrous to the French, and their probable effect upon the issue of the war, and the ultimate fate of Napoleon, when a note to the General announced that the enemy was in motion in front of Ordal. He withdrew for a moment to give some necessary order, and then returned to the table, to all appearance as calm and undisturbed as before the communication. The bottle circulated as freely as before – too freely, I thought, considering the proximity of the enemy, and that cool heads and clear judgments are required more especially in those placed in advance, and charged with watching his motions. Another hour passed on, and from war and politics the Spaniards changed to lighter and gayer subjects, and the oftener the wine circled the table, the louder and more animated waxed the laughter and conversation.

Just when the merriment was at its height, another orderly gallopped to the door, who reported that the enemy had driven in the piquet at Ordal, and was advancing in force upon the road to Villa Franca. When this report became known, the noise immediately ceased, – the voices were hushed, all but the General's who gave a few directions, at once with clearness and precision. The officers then repaired to their respective posts, and the whole division was under arms, and on its march to meet the enemy, in an incredibly short time. The English officer of the Staff had retired some time before this alarm had dispersed our noisy party, and Zehnpfinning and I immediately proceeded to his quarters, to apprize him of what had taken place. We found he had gone to bed, having locked the door of his room; and, although we called and knocked, and made all the noise we could, for ten minutes or a quarter of an hour, we failed to make any impression on him.

Tired at last with our fruitless efforts, and having no more time to lose, we were obliged to leave him, convinced that should the enemy advance in sufficient force to compel Sarsfield to retire, he, as well as his papers and documents, would inevitably fall into their hands. We then got our steeds, and following the road which the division had taken, we soon overtook it. We had not proceeded more than a couple of miles when another report was received by the General, which informed him that the alarm was false. It had been occasioned by the accidental discharge of a sentry's musket, and although the enemy's piquets had been observed in motion in the early part of the night, he had not advanced. Upon the receipt of this intelligence the division was halted, and in an hour afterwards was faced about, and returned to their old quarters.

Arrived at Villa Franca, I threw myself on a bed for a few hours at Zehnpfinning's quarters, and early the next morning took the road to Villa Nova, where I arrived about six o'clock. Then, for fear false and exaggerated rumours of what had taken place the night before at Villa Franca might reach head-quarters, and cause unnecessary trouble and anxiety, I got on board the gun-boat as soon as possible, and made the best of my way to Tarragona, when I gave a true account of all that happened to the Admiral.

Here I will venture upon a brief notice of General Sarsfield, one of the few Spanish officers who bore a distinguished part in the struggle to rescue their country from French domination. General Sarsfield was born in the camp, being the son of an officer who held the rank of captain in the Regiment of Ultonia (Ulster), one of the battalions that formed the Irish brigade in the service of Spain. Young Sarsfield was educated at a military seminary, and got a commission in the same regiment with his father as soon as he was a fitting age. His father who never attained a higher rank than that of captain, died young, leaving his son, at the age of sixteen, to struggle with the world, and carve out a name and fortune for himself. I am not informed from what branch of the family General Sarsfield derived, – whether from the celebrated defender of Limerick or not. Certain it is, however, that it had been settled for some generations in Spain, where it was much respected. The General's mother, whom I knew at Alicant, after her husband's death, passed several years at Madrid, and filled some situation about the Court. Of this, as well as the salary attached to it, she was deprived when Napoleon usurped the vacated throne of Spain; and she hated him, and the whole French nation, with a hatred so much the more cordial and sincere, as through them she had been reduced from comfort, respectability and comparative wealth, to poverty and neglect.

At the time I write of, Sarsfield might have been twenty-eight or thirty years of age. In person he was tall and slight, with handsome features, fair complexion, large deep-blue eyes, and light-brown curly hair, in outward guise more like a Saxon than a Milesian, or a son of swarthy Spain. His address and manners were particularly courteous and affable, and although he had never been out of Spain, except once, when his regiment was quartered for a short time in Teneriffe, he spoke English fluently and perfectly, but with an accent as purely Irish as as if he had never strayed ten miles from Balinasloe, or the 'Devil's Bit', in the county Tipperary. Sarsfield was still a subaltern with his regiment in Catalonia when the French so treacherously made themselves masters of the strongholds in Spain, – and in the various skirmishes and struggles which the Spaniards subsequently held in the province with their powerful adversaries, the gallantry and daring of young Sarsfield were always eminently conspicuous.

Such conduct, at a time when it had but few imitators in Spain, soon attracted notice, procuring for him early and rapid promotion; and his bold and masterly relief of Figueras, when reduced to extremity, and on the point of surrendering, by which it was enabled to hold out five or six weeks longer won for him the rank of colonel. He was now generally employed on detached service, and always in command, during which he and his band were greatly distinguished. He was never worsted in any enterprise that he undertook, nor suffered himself to be surprised, or led into a snare, though the enemy made many attempts to do so, and would have gladly entrapped so bold and troublesome a leader.

In 1811, when Tarragona was besieged by Suchet, Sarsfield commanded in the Fuerte Real, in the defence of which he displayed his usual firmness and gallantry, maintaining his post with unshrinking resolution, and repulsing two assaults after the fort had been reduced almost to a heap of rubbish. Had Sarsfield been allowed to remain with the besieged, possibly the result of the siege might have been different; for it would not have been the first time that the presence, example, fortitude, and resources of one man have inclined the scale of victory, and decided a battle or a siege.

Unfortunately the Captain-General required, or fancied that he required, his presence at head-quarters, and sent him an order to join him; and although he twice excused himself for not quitting his post, a third and more peremptory injunction, which threatened suspension and further punishment if he hesitated longer to comply, at length forced a reluctant obedience. The night but one after Sarsfield left it, the fort was stormed; and by enabling the enemy to place their breaching-batteries, with little further molestation, within the required distance of the walls, led to the speedy reduction of Tarragona.

The fall of that fortress put the French in possession of every place of strength in the province, which now might be said to be completely subdued. The Captain-General, indeed, had yet the shadow of an army, and Erolles, Sarsfield, and Manso continued to harass the enemy's convoys whenever they ventured to move without a formidable escort, which was seldom the case. Still they were virtually masters of Catalonia, traversing the length and breadth of the land, whenever and wherever they pleased.

In this state of things, when reverses and misfortune everywhere pursued the Spaniards in Catalonia, and at the time when unanimity and concord were more requisite than ever to support their sinking cause, dissensions broke out among some of their leaders; and a jealousy of some standing that existed between Sarsfield and Erolles increased to such a height that it became necessary, if no means were found to allay it, that one or other should leave the province. Instead of standing aloof, or using his influence to reconcile and assuage these bitternesses and jealousies, an officer, whose situation placed much in his power, took a very decided part in favour of Erolles, the consequence of which was that Sarsfield was removed to Aragon. From that time little was heard of him upon the coast till he joined the Anglo-Sicilian army, after it crossed the Ebro; and when Suchet withdrew the garrison from Tarragona, and blew up the works, his division was the first that entered the town. Henceforward, as long as the English army remained in the province, his division was always placed in advance, in which he displayed his accustomed vigilance and activity. Subsequently, when intrusted with the blockade of Barcelona, he repulsed two vigorous sorties with very decided loss on the part of the enemy.

Marshal Soult, who, although fighting hard, but always beaten in the Pyrenees and South of France by his active and persevering foe, had been obliged to detach, from time to time, some of his best battalions to the assistance of Napoleon, then contending at the other extremity of the kingdom for empire and for life with the overwhelming masses of Austria, Russia, and Prussia, was in his turn compelled to draw reinforcements from the army of Suchet. The latter, thus weakened, saw, from the course which events had taken, that his advanced position in Catalonia was no longer prudent. Leaving, therefore, strong garrisons in Monjuic and Barcelona, and withdrawing the one in Girona, he fell back, occupying the line of the Fluvia, as he had done before those of the Xucar and Llobregat.

Previous to this movement on the part of Suchet, General Clinton had established his headquarters at Villa Franca, and when the former retired upon the Fluvia, he crossed the Llobregat, and by the 7th of March, 1814, established the blockade of Barcelona. The *Malta* moved with the provision and store transports to Castel de Fells, to be at hand to supply the troops, as it might be found necessary. The anchorage at Castel de Fells is quite open, and the beach exposed, so that when the wind blows at all fresh from the sea, the surf breaks upon it with considerable violence, in consequence of which, we often found the landing of stores and provisions attended with difficulty, sometimes with danger. Indeed, I remember that a transport had a man drowned one day by the upsetting of a boat when on that service.

While the army was before Barcelona, an officer of the garrison had held for some time a secret correspondence with General Sarsfield, who commanded the advanced lines. This person had been aide-de-camp to Suchet, but had made some pretence to remain behind in Barcelona, when the Marshal fell back towards the frontier. He was a Spaniard, of good family, and had been educated at a military seminary for the profession of arms. He had just finished his studies at the time of Murat's entry into Madrid, and, like others of his countrymen at the time, was dazzled and captivated by the splendour and prestige which attached to the 'Emperor' and his army, while he was disgusted with the quarrels, intrigues, and imbecilities of the Court and Royal Family of Spain. This feeling led him to join the invaders and oppressors of his country, and to become what the loyal termed in derision – an 'Afrancesado'.

In the campaign of 1809, when the war was renewed between France and Austria, he served in the Grand Army, and his intelligence and gallantry attracted the notice of Suchet, who, upon being appointed to a command in Spain, took him with him as one of his aides-de-camp. In this situation he continued to serve, with still increasing reputation, and so far gained the confidence of his superior, as to obtain the cipher which he used in carrying on his secret correspondence. Whether he now saw that the game was against the French, and, with the instinct of a rat, felt that it was time to quit a falling house, or (a far better motive) touched at last with remorse for having fought against his country, and helped to heap calamity and misfortune upon her, he was resolved, as some indemnity, and at great personal risk, to render her some signal service, I am unable to say. By whatever motive his conduct was influenced, however, he came to the resolution of abandoning the French service; and then, by means of a forged letter in cipher from Suchet to the Governors of Tortosa and Lerida, try to induce them to surrender those fortresses into the hands of the Spaniards.

His plans being arranged, one evening he made some excuse for riding out of Barcelona, and then, under cover of the shade, escaped to the British lines. Having held a short communication with the English General, he made the best of his way to Tortosa, and reported himself at the gate as an aide-de-camp of Marshal Suchet, charged with an important letter for the Governor. Being shown into the presence of General Robert, the Governor, he produced his despatch, which being in cipher, and expressed in Suchet's usual style and manner, and, moreover, intrusted to one of aides-de-camp, he was thrown entirely off his guard, nor for a moment entertained a suspicion of its genuineness. It simply directed him to evacuate Tortosa, having first capitulated for a safe passage for the garrison through the country, with arms and baggage, and then join him, with as little delay as possible, on the frontier. This order seemed rational and well-timed, at a moment when France required every soldier that could be spared for her own defence.

Having given due attention to the instructions which the despatch contained, General Robert, having been some weeks without hearing from France, or even from head-quarters, turned to the aide-de-camp, and anxiously inquired the news; and when, among other matters, he heard that a promotion had taken place in the French army, by which he was not only made a lieutenant-general, but also Grande Croix of the Legion of Honour, his rapture knew no bounds – he fairly skipped and capered about the room, cordially embracing the bearer of such gratifying intelligence.

The aide-de-camp next informed the Governor that he was charged with a similar letter for the Commandant of Lerida, and, after partaking of some refreshment, he hastened his departure, and took the road to that town, and well it was that he did so: had he delayed ten minutes, his life would have paid the forfeit of his temerity and treason; for the echo from his horse's hoofs, in passing the draw-bridge, had scarcely died away, when an emissary from Marshal Suchet, in the guise of a Spanish peasant, stood before the astonished Baron Robert. This person was the bearer of a true despatch, dated two days subsequent to the one which had been delivered to him not an hour before, and to which, of course, it made no allusion.

Although subjected to a most searching examination before he was allowed to pass the Spanish outposts, he contrived to elude their vigilance, and conceal the despatch. This he effected by rolling the slip of paper upon which it was written within the folds of a cigar, a few bundles of which he had for sale, and, by disposing of some to the Spaniards, and freely offering the rest for examination, he avoided all suspicion. This last order directed the Governor of Tortosa to hold that fortress at all hazards, and not to surrender so long as a day's provision lasted, or until contrary orders should be received. It would be difficult to say which were the feelings most prevalent in General Robert's breast when he read this despatch – rage and mortification at having been so duped and deceived, or satisfaction and delight at having escaped the trap into which he had so nearly fallen.

Meantime, the aide-de-camp pursued his way with the utmost diligence to Lerida. Arrived at that fortress, his stratagem had fuller success than at Tortosa. The Governor was completely deceived, and, as no counter-despatch revealed to him the treachery into which he was about to fall, and as he was but too happy to escape from the beleaguered town, he lost no time in concluding a capitulation with the Spanish officer before Lerida, who, aware of the *ruse*, threw no difficulties in the way of a speedy arrangement. That capitulation was in all respects similar to the one which the forged letter directed the Governor of Tortosa to enter into.

General Clinton had been made acquainted with the plan laid to entrap the garrisons of Tortosa and Lerida; but being no party to it himself, he did not think he was bound to observe its condition; nay, whatever might have been his personal feelings with respect to the deception practised upon the French Governors, his own duty was clear, and forbade him to allow so large a force to escape when he had them in his power, and add their strength to the garrison of Barcelona, or the army of Marshal Suchet.

A division of the army, strong enough to render resistance on the part of the French vain and hopeless, was accordingly marched to Martorel, at which place the garrison of Lerida, consisting of one thousand two hundred men, was intercepted, and compelled to lay down its arms, although not without strong and indignant remonstrance at what they called a flagrant breach of the terms upon which they consented to evacuate Lerida.

Towards the end of March, Bonaparte thought fit to release the King of Spain, Fernando Septimo, and on the 2nd of April, he passed through the cantonments of the army before Barcelona. Everywhere he passed, he was received with the greatest enthusiasm, and loud and general *vivas* testified the loyalty and affection of his faithful subjects. How requited, the history of Spain for the following nineteen years will record! In it will be handed down, to the latest time, that a nation's attachment and fidelity to its monarch, which no reverses could shake – no cumulation of misfortune subdue, was repaid by the foulest and most heartless ingratitude that ever prince was guilty of, and the most wanton and grinding tyranny that ever a loyal people endured!

Understanding that he had expressed a wish to visit a ship of the line, and willing to show all the attention and respect that were due to a person of his exalted rank, the Admiral moved to Mataro, through which town he was to pass, in order to be ready for his reception. The day of his arrival proved wet, and he did not embark; but the Admiral and several of the officers went on shore, to be presented and pay their respects to him.

From Mataro, Fernando travelled coast-ways to Valencia. Hitherto, he had disguised his real sentiments and intentions; but he only waited a fitting time to lay aside the mask, and show himself in his true colours – a ruthless tyrant, and the deadliest enemy to the least approach of freedom. By means of the Duke de San Carlos and others, who were more averse, if possible, than the King, to the order of things recently established in Spain, he had secured a considerable party favourable to his views before he reached Valencia, among the most powerful and important of whom was General Elio, then at the head of an army of forty thousand men

Backed by such support, he issued a proclamation a few days after he arrived in Valencia, in which he denied the authority of the Regency to alter or make laws which should bind him or his kingdoms; declared void the Constitution of 1812, established during his absence, and caused to be arrested the principal men of the city supposed to be favourable to it, although, not a month before in crossing the frontier, he had sworn in the most formal and solemn manner to observe it; proclaimed his own will and power absolute; that he was the sole judge of the laws and constitution best suited to the condition of his subjects, and that at a fitting time he would assemble the Cortes, and then propound such matters as came within their province to deliberate upon.

Soon after the promulgation of this manifesto he set forward for Madrid, which he entered escorted by a considerable body of dragoons. The members of the Regency, knowing themselves obnoxious, and fearful of the consequences of the King's displeasure, had quitted the city; but all those suspected of liberal opinions, and of being favourable to the Constitution of 1812, who did not follow their example, were arrested and thrown into prison; in short, the *ancient régime*, in all its plenitude, was restored, and an absolutism more despotic than that which reigned before the French invasion, replaced the abortive and short-lived efforts at freedom which the Spanish people had made.

It being ascertained that Marshal Suchet had now retired into France with the whole of his moveable forces, and the Spaniards being thought strong enough to watch and confine the French within the few fortresses which they still held in the country, the Anglo-Sicilian army was broke up about the middle of April, when part marched across the Peninsula to join Lord Wellington, and part – some destined for Sicily, some to reinforce Lord William Bentinck, who had proceeded against Genoa – marched to Tarragona to embark. In a few days the Italian and Sicilian regiments sailed for their own country; the *Pompée* with the troops destined for Genoa, on the 22nd April; and we followed on the 24th, having embarked a wing of the regiment of Rolle on board the *Malta*. As we entered the Gulf of Genoa, we passed at some distance from the *Undaunted* and could hardly credit our senses or believe that we read the signal a right when she made the following telegraphic communication: – 'I have got the Emperor Napoleon on board, going to the Island of Elba', – so great was our astonishment! To think that the man whose deeds and fame had filled the world for twenty years, whose levées kings attended, and whose behests they were wont to obey – the setter-up and puller-down of dynasties, at whose name Europe trembled, all but England, which singly and alone braved and resisted his gigantic power; whose accumulated force and energies were mainly directed to her subjugation, but which like the waves that rage and beat against her rock-bound shores, was broken and shivered in the vain attempt, – to imagine such a man 'cribbed and cabined' on board an English ship, was indeed matter of wonder as well as of exultation! And sure I am that there was not a man in the *Malta* whose heart did not swell with pride and thankfulness at the glorious termination of the fierce and desperate struggle in which his country had been so long engaged, his powerful and implacable enemy crushed and humbled, and now indebted to that generous country, against which his envy and hatred had burned with such inextinguishable fire, for safe conduct to his circumscribed dominions! All were anxious to see a man as remarkable, if not more so, than any with whom history makes us acquainted. But the Admiral gave us no opportunity to gratify our wishes, Either not choosing to show an idle curiosity, or thinking such deference from him unnecessary and uncalled for, – whatever was the motive, we did not close the *Undaunted*, but held on our course to Genoa, while she pursued hers for Elba.

Not many days afterwards we met the Commander of the *Merope*, who had dined on board the *Undaunted*, in company with Bonaparte. He said that his spirits seemed remarkably good, that he talked a great deal, and expatiated with much *sang froid* on the decrees he intended to have issued, and the measures he should have pursued, had affairs not taken the turn that they did. He likewise spoke of his intention of seeking an asylum in England, in case the fortifications of Elba had been destroyed: and turning to the Prussian officer, one of the Commissioners who accompanied him, he asked him what sort of reception he thought he should meet with from the English. 'What reception?' said the Prussian; 'oh! perfectly good; you never did them any harm'. At this reply the now small Emperor looked rather blank.

We reached Genoa one day too late; for in consequence of the plainly expressed determination of the inhabitants not to submit to the miseries of a siege, the garrison which was not large, considering the extent of the place, had surrendered the day before our arrival.

Viewed from the sea, Genoa and its bay form one of the noblest and most beautiful pictures I ever beheld, Constantinople and Naples not excepted. It is true, the latter boast many features of exquisite loveliness which are not to be found in the former; still, the rough, stern grandeur of the iron coast, deep within which the city shelters, and the lofty sweep of steep and rugged mountain at the back, at whose foot she seems to slumber, give a majesty and dignity (if I may so express myself) to the scenery around Genoa, which, for me, possess a far more attractive charm than the luxurious softness which is the leading characteristic of that of the bays and cities of Naples and Constantinople.

The walls of Genoa, which in their course climb hills and cross ravines, embrace an extent of twelve miles, within which are many beautiful villas and gardens, and, together with its noble buildings and unrivalled situation, claim for it the justly-deserved appellation of 'La

Superba'. Upon entering the town, and on nearer inspection, the visitor is a good deal disenchanted, for, like most cities, Genoa presents an union of the sumptuous and the mean, squalor and magnificence, poverty and riches. The lower part of the town and that bordering on the water is, for the most part, composed of an inferior description of houses, where the streets are steep, narrow, and tortuous, wretchedly paved, and excessively filthy. Here are congregated, with the miserably poor, the retail dealers and handicraftsmen of the various trades.

Far above the toil and turmoil of this busy part of the town are the noble streets Balbi, Nova, and Novissima. These 'streets of palaces and walks of state' bisect the town from east to west, which is built in form of an amphitheatre. Higher up still are the villas, with their beautiful gardens, at first thickly scattered, but more rare and at greater distances the higher you ascend. The churches are numerous, but gaudy, both within and without; two or three boast some tolerable pictures of the Genoese school, but few have any pretension to elegance or taste, either in ornament or architecture. The mansions of the old families – such as Doria, Durazzo, Serra, Brignoli, Pamfili, &c, – are splendid palaces, in which were now lodged the chiefs of the British Army and Navy, and other heads of departments.

Added to other sources of amusement, Genoa could boast a very good opera at this time, and the night before we sailed a ball, upon a magnificent scale, was given by the Municipality, to commemorate the expulsion of the French, and its fondly-imagined restoration to former sovereignty and independence. A day or two before it took place, the King of Sardinia and the Duke of Orleans (late King of the French) landed at Genoa, and their presence added not a little to the dignity and *éclat* of the scene. The *fête* was held in the Ducal Palace, the hall of which is a spacious and noble room, and was decorated and illuminated for the occasion in the most gorgeous and brilliant manner, and truly the *coup-d'œil* was most imposing. When seen from a raised platform at one end of the room, the mixture of beautiful damsels and gay cavaliers, the waving plumes and flashing diamonds of the one, and the variety and brilliancy of uniform and costume of the other, as they joined in the dance, or moved around the noble apartment, formed a spectacle the most dazzling and fascinating I ever saw.

Our stay was so short that we were not able to see much of the environs of Genoa; Murray and I, however, made a day to visit a few of the villas which lie scattered along the road that leads to Savona. In his search after literary treasures (a never-failing pursuit with Murray), he stumbled upon a publisher and bookseller, who happened to be one of the most eminent of his class in the city. This person was by birth a Frenchman, but had been established in business in Genoa for a number of years, and had been an eye-witness of each successive revolution which the republic had undergone since the year 1793. He was a well-informed, intelligent man, and Murray, thinking he would be an agreeable addition to our party, invited him to a seat in our curriculum. During our excursion, he related many anecdotes of events that occurred in Italy from 1793 to 1814, and gave us an interesting and graphic history of the siege and sufferings of the inhabitants and garrison of Genoa, when so obstinately defended in 1799 and 1800 by General Massena.

Two or three miles from Genoa, we stopped at the 'Albergo di Grotta', to order our dinner, which was to be ready by the time we returned from our excursion. This house had been built in a fanciful taste by some wealthy merchant of Genoa, and in the grounds attached to it he had formed an artificial grotto, encrusted with spar and shells, whence, when in the changes and revolutions of time it passed into other hands and became an inn, it derived its present name. I forget now whether it was at the Albergo di Grotta, or at one of the villas, that we saw the portrait of a noble dog, as large as life, beautifully painted in fresco on the wall of the dining-room, and for whose maintenance the owner at his death bequeathed a handsome annuity. This annuity, which was large enough to support a whole kennel, was to cease upon the dog's death, thereby ensuring good treatment to the poor animal as long as it lived.

In general we were not struck with anything remarkable in the country houses which we saw. The ceilings of most of the rooms were handsomely painted in figures or arabesques, and in the Villa Doria were some good pictures, particularly a portrait of the celebrated Andrea. The grounds, amidst which these villas stood, were neither extensive nor well kept; but their situations and the views which they commanded were fine, and the union of the Italian and English styles, in which they were disposed, had a good and pleasing effect. We passed a very agreeable morning, and returned to the Albergo di Grotta at six to dinner. The windows of our *salle à manger* opened to the ground and looked out upon a court, where the play and murmur of a *jet d'eau* soothed the ear, and cooled and refreshed the air. The viands we found excellent, the wines delicious, and a long fast and the day's exercise had well disposed us to do ample justice to both; added to which, 'the feast of reason', which flowed from the conversation and anecdotes of my literary friends, made it to me one of the most delightful and *memorable* repasts that I ever enjoyed. But in this life what happiness is there without its attendant misery? – what enjoyment without its countervailing *désagrément?* To calm and sunshine will succeed clouds and darkness, storms and tempest. The truth of these sage reflections we experienced when we came to balance accounts with mine host of the Grotta; for albeit well used to be fleeced in Spain, we were not yet fully prepared for the extortion of Italy. Even Murray, generally so calm and self-possessed, could not repress an expletive, which marked his astonishment at a bill so immeasurably extravagant as that submitted to his inspection. Upon being asked if some mistake had not been made in the charges, the Albergatore took the bill, and running his eye deliberately over the items, said that he could perceive none, but that it was possible that he had omitted to charge for some trifle; but as the 'Signori' were most likely in haste to return to Genoa, he would not detain them to have it rectified. He was then expostulated with upon the extravagance and unreasonableness of his charges, which exceeded those of Genoa three times over. But all remonstrances availed nothing; not a farthing would he abate, and leaving us to settle the matter in the best way we could, he quitted the room. What was to be done? To be cheated in a manner so barefaced, and then laughed at, was not to be endured. We therefore begged our friend to go and reason with him once more upon the exorbitancy of his demand, and explain to him that we were determined not to submit to so glaring an imposition. All this he did, but for a long time without effect. To whatever he urged the other sharply retorted, and asked what affair it was of his – he was not to pay the bill, and consequently had no business to interfere in the matter; that no arrangement as to price had been agreed upon – he therefore had the *forestieri* in his power, and that he would make them pay, and not abate a maravedi. At length, however, after much altercation, and being told that a magistrate must decide upon the reasonableness or unreasonableness of his charges, he consented to reduce his bill a third, which left it still three times more than just. This matter being settled, we returned to Genoa, very sincerely resolved, in ordering a dinner, never again to trust to the conscience of a Genoese, but always to fix the price beforehand, and in making the compact, never to forget that 'six Jews make a Genoese'.

22: Home and Promotion

After a sojourn of a week we left Genoa, and arrived at Mahon early in May, where the duties of the port devolved on Admiral Hallowell, his predecessor, Admiral Pickmore having already departed for England.

The war with France being at an end, a fleet was no longer required in the Mediterranean, the ships of the line were therefore ordered home to be paid off, while the frigates and sloops were for the most part sent to America, where peace was not yet re-established. Sir Edward Pellew, just created Baron Exmouth, soon took his departure, and left Admiral Hallowell in command of the station.

We remained some weeks at Mahon, where I was glad to have the opportunity of renewing old friendships and associations, after an absence of two years. We then sailed for Barcelona. The Admiral had offered a passage to that town to the Marquess de Matallana, formerly Ambassador at the Court of Naples; but who left Italy, and afterwards resided at Vienna when the French invaded Spain. He, with his wife and daughter, had now reached Minorca, on their return to their own country.

The Marquess was a reserved, quiet little old man, whose mind, as well as body, seemed enfeebled by age. Not so the wife and daughter; for, although neither could be called young, they both made up in energy of conversation, and vigour of intellect and action, for what was deficient in the gentleman. And, in truth, the Marquesa was a singular-looking personage. She was not particular in the style or material of her dress, which was usually soiled with snuff, of which she took an immoderate quantity. No mantilla or other gear, save a brown wig of Brutus fashion, adorned her head; and as she stood on deck, talking with energy to the Admiral upon the all-absorbing topic of Spanish politics, – one hand gesticulating and holding her snuff-box, the other thrust under her wig, which it pushed awry, her legs astride and firmly set, – she had nothing feminine in her appearance, and might well be taken for a little man travestied. In politics she was hyper-royalist, and, according to her creed, absolutism the most despotic should rule the land. The King's will alone should be the law, and she denounced, in unmeasured terms, the Regency and Cortes, which had dared to set bounds to it; and suiting the action to the word, by drawing her hand across her throat, she wound up every argument on the subject by exclaiming, 'Je leur couperais les gorges à tous, – à tous, – les scélérats!'

Barcelona from whence the French garrison had been allowed to retire a short time before by capitulation, is a large city, and prior to the war with France contained a population of eighty thousand. Many of the wealthiest and most respectable of the inhabitants, however, deserted it at the time of the invasion, so that the numbers were reduced below thirty thousand during its occupancy by the French.

Formerly Barcelona was a busy, commercial, and thriving place, and besides an active trade with South America, greater than any other town in Spain, it possessed several manufactories, particularly in silk. There is a lighthouse on the Mole, which runs out from the east part of the town three-quarters of a mile to the southward, and within which vessels of a certain tonnage have good shelter; but as a bar extends from its point to the foot of Monjuic, ships of greater draught of water than fourteen or fifteen feet cannot take advantage of it. At the time of our arrival, the town, though beginning to breathe, had still an empty and forlorn appearance. A song, very expressive of the deliverance from the incubus which had so long pressed upon the heart of the city, had already been composed by the Barceloneses, and was in everybody's mouth, the refrain of which, I remember, was, 'Pobre Barcelona ya pot respirar.'

Except the elevation of Monjuic, and towards the sea, Barcelona is surrounded by an extensive and fertile plain, inclosed within a belt of mountainous land, amid which Monsein to the north-east, and the rugged peaks of Monserrate to the north, form remarkable and conspicuous objects. Besides being rich in all the products of a happy climate and luxuriant soil, this plain was studded with the country-houses of the richer merchants of the city, particularly near the picturesque villages of Seria and Gracia, which stand nearly at the foot of the high land. We visited some of those *casas de campo*, and found the houses built, and the grounds laid out, much in the style of Italy. They were then in a sadly neglected condition; but with the return of peace it was to be expected that they would be refreshed, and restored to former neatness and elegance. Barcelona possessed some noble buildings, the most remarkable of which were its Cathedral, the Exchange, and the Governor's Palace. The Rambla, which intersects the city, is a very fine broad street, one end of which leads to the water, while the other conducts to the principal issue from the town to the north. There were no public amusements at Barcelona at this time, except the theatre. There we saw some comedies very well enacted, in the performance of which (albeit no great judge of such matters) I think both Spaniards and Italians excel.

A few days before we left Barcelona I stumbled upon an old acquaintance, La Commandante de Marina de Palamos, who, with one of her daughters, was waiting an opportunity to return to Mahon; and, as we were bound there (having first obtained the Captain's and Admiral's permission to do so), I offered her a passage in the *Malta*, and my own cabin for her accommodation. This she gladly accepted, and contrived to stow herself, her daughter, a maid-servant, with their bedding and a quantity of luggage, in my crib. After a smooth, calm passage of four or five days we arrived at Mahon, and on going on shore the lady thanked me over and over again for my courtesy and politeness. But it was not till I had resumed possession of my cabin, and slept some nights in my cot, that I discovered that, in going away, my friend had left me a present, for which I was ungrateful and ungallant enough not to be thankful. This present consisted of a whole colony of 'chinches', and before I could convince myself of the nature of the tormentors by whom my slumbers were so cruelly disturbed every night, they had fully established themselves in their new and pleasant location, multiplying, moreover so fast, that they very soon made their presence felt by my neighbours to the right and left who bestowed upon me many a benediction for bringing 'those l—y Spaniards into the ship'. But the mischief was done, and how to dislodge so active and tenacious an enemy was now the question. Every stronghold was already in their possession, – the crevices and joinings of the bulkheads and cot-frame – the folds of the cot itself, and even between the strands of the clews, were fully occupied. Nothing I found would do but to fling cot, frame, and clews overboard, and then by the application of a strong chemical preparation, which I got from the surgeon, to the crevices of the bulkheads, I succeeded in finally extirpating them.

Admiral Hallowell had been given to understand that the court-martial, before which Sir John Murray was to give an account of his proceedings whilst in command of the expedition which landed in Catalonia, in 1813, was to assemble shortly, either at Tarragona or Valencia, in consequence of which he remained some time at Minorca. At length two of the members, Generals Widdrington and Griffiths, arrived from Gibraltar, when we immediately sailed for Tarragona, expecting that the other members and witnesses would shortly assemble. But after the lapse of several days none made their appearance except Colonel d'Aguilar, from whom we first learnt that there were such difficulties in the way of the court assembling in Spain, that it was now intended to hold it in England, but that the time was not yet fixed. He himself had arrived at Tarragona for the purpose of collecting all the information that might be serviceable to Sir John Murray in his defence, which when the Admiral heard, he laughingly said, with all the frankness and candour which were the distinguishing features of his noble character: 'Well, come into the cabin, and you shall see everything that I have prepared, which can tell the other way.' In a day or two after a despatch arrived confirming the information which had been received from Colonel d'Aguilar, when the Generals departed for Gibraltar, and we returned once more to Minorca.

Having arranged for that part of the station, the Admiral sailed to the eastward, and after looking into Genoa, proceeded to Leghorn. The object in visiting Leghorn was to ascertain whether the English Minister had yet arrived at the Court of Tuscany, and if he had, whether he was the bearer of any instructions relative to the conduct to be observed towards Napoleon Bonaparte. We found that Lord Burghersh, who had been appointed to that office, had not arrived; but the Admiral saw Sir Neil Campbell, the English Commissioner, who had accompanied the fallen Emperor from France. This gentleman had been instructed to remain near him, – to watch his movements, and report his observations from time to time to the Foreign Secretary in England; but he could give the Admiral no light as to the manner in which the ex-Emperor was to be viewed and treated, – whether he was to be at liberty to come and go as he pleased, or whether he was to be watched, and rigidly confined to the island. In short, his appointment seemed of a nondescript character, and must be considered unusual and anomalous. Upon leaving Leghorn, however, the Admiral, in the absence of any instructions upon the subject, stationed the *Partridge* sloop in the vicinity, with orders frequently to visit Porto Feraïo, from which he was never to be long or far distant, and report any circumstances of a nature to excite suspicion as to the views and intentions of Bonaparte; and he took upon himself further to direct that, if Bonaparte should leave Elba, he was to use his utmost diligence, at whatever cost, to arrest him, whatever course he might be steering.

From Leghorn we proceeded to Palermo, where the Admiral intended to fix his head-quarters. There we remained several weeks, during which time a vessel arrived from England, bringing an account of the promotions in the navy consequent upon the peace. Though very extensive, they included but one officer of the *Malta*, Lieutenant Stirling.

The Commander of the *Wizard* having been promoted, Boxer was appointed to act in his place. This again made me the senior lieutenant, and also the first in the ship for promotion. Of this latter circumstance there was some probability at the time; for two captains on the station were unwell, and talked very seriously of invaliding. However, the invalids hung on, – their health improved, and, alas! my hopes which were pretty sanguine, were disappointed. Had either of them gone, the senior commander, Captain Edye, of the *Partridge*, would have got the vacancy, and I should have succeeded him in the *Partridge*. And sometimes in recalling those by-gone times to mind, I have imagined that a matter, so insignificant in itself as a change of captains of the vessel appointed to watch the movements of Bonaparte, might have altered the whole course of events that followed his escape from Elba. When that circumstance took place the *Partridge* happened to be in Leghorn Roads, and several hours elapsed before Captain Edye knew that Bonaparte had quitted the island. The moment, however, that he was made aware of it, both he and Sir Neil Campbell who embarked in the *Partridge*, agreed that France was his most probable destination, and decided to steer for the nearest point of that coast.

Subsequent events showed that this decision was judicious; for they were actually in the track of the Elbese convoy, when unluckily they fell in with a vessel which gave them such information as induced them to change their course for that of Italy. Now, in speculating upon these matters, I have thought it possible that had another officer been in command of the *Partridge* at the time, he might not have been at Leghorn, but nearer the island, and therefore likely sooner to be made aware of the movement which had taken place. The situation of the *Partridge* being thus different at the time of the departure of the convoy from Elba, it is also possible that the vessel whose false information led Captain Edye astray might not have been fallen in with; or, if she had, that her information might not have been acted upon.

The circumstances under which the pursuit would have been commenced and prosecuted being thus changed, it is not improbable that the convoy might have been intercepted before it reached Cannes, and if it were the duty of the Commander of the *Partridge*, of course, would have been to use his utmost endeavours to arrest Bonaparte. This, no doubt, he would have stoutly resisted; and as he had a brig of sixteen guns, besides five hundred devoted followers in the convoy around him, had the wind proved light, thereby offering his soldiers a facility of boarding, or using their musketry with effect, the issue of the struggle must have been doubtful. On the other hand, should the breeze have been commanding, thus enabling the English vessel to choose her position, so as to avoid too close contact with the enemy's lighter ones, or to run them down if opportunity offered, the probability is, that, dead or alive, their man would have been secured.

And if they had, how much would it have changed the current of events which afterwards took place! To say nothing of other matters, the money which was required and lavished for the assembling of forces in the Netherlands, would then have remained in the English coffers, and the blood which her sons poured out like water, on the plains of Waterloo, would have been spared, and many a heart and hearth, which that field made desolate, might still have been cheered and gladdened by the presence of a father, a husband, or a brother.

But to return from this somewhat long digression. The Admiral, who was still without any instructions relative to Bonaparte, received information, in October, that he was repairing and strengthening the fortifications of Elba, and had lately occupied an islet in the Piombino channel, upon which he was building a battery. This intelligence, together with the uncertainty in which he was placed, with regard to the conduct to be observed towards the ex-Emperor, determined him to proceed to

Leghorn, when he could see and form an opinion as to his goings on, and also communicate personally on the subject with the British Minister at Florence, who, he concluded, must have arrived at the Tuscan Court before then. Accordingly, we weighed, and steered, in company with the *Thunderer* and *Alcmene*, for Leghorn. Arrived at that anchorage, the Admiral proceeded, without a moment's loss of time, to Florence, to confer with the Minister upon the subject of Bonaparte, or, in his absence, with some member of the legation, if any such should have arrived; but, up to that moment, some time in October, not a soul had arrived from England who could give information on the subject, though it was known that a Minister had been appointed to the Court of Tuscany three or four months before. The Admiral, therefore, had his journey for nothing, returning to his ship as wise as he left her; then, seeing that the amusements of Bonaparte, in repairing old fortifications and throwing up new, could not be of moment, he returned to Palermo.

During our absence, Sir William A'Court had arrived, to fill the office of Minister at the Court of Sicily, vacated by Lord William Bentinck; but neither had he brought out any orders or instructions relative to Bonaparte. Thus matters remained for a fortnight or three weeks, and we had nothing to do but in crossing top-gallant yards, and loosing and furling sails, to contend for the mastery with the *Thunderer*, a ship which, from her smartness and perfect order, was a most fitting and worthy rival.

Early in the following month (November), we were all 'taken aback' by the arrival of Admiral Penrose, in the *Queen*, to supersede Admiral Hallowell; no previous intimation had been received that such a step was in contemplation. The usual courtesy upon such occasions had been dispensed with, and the Admiral found himself relieved from his command without notice and without preparation. The reason assigned for this summary mode of proceeding was, that, as the Admiral was a principal witness to be examined at the court-martial, before which Sir John Murray was to be tried, his presence was necessary in England.

The change of the venue, as lawyers phrase it, from Spain to England, was accommodating and very considerate towards Sir John; but how far it was fair and just to the Admiral, is another question. It deprived him not only of his command, and that in an uncourteous manner, to say the least of it, but also of the advantage of examining the witnesses in the country, where the transactions that gave rise to the inquiry took place, and of verifying on the spot any disputed matter as to the nature of the ground, distance and length of march from point to point, state and practicability of the roads, beach, &c. And to this may be added, that it was not till he arrived in England, and only ten days before the court assembled at Winchester, that he was informed that he was to prosecute upon one of the charges, up to which time he had been given to understand that he was only to be examined as a witness.

We left Palermo for England the day after the arrival of Admiral Penrose. The passage down the Mediterranean was tedious and boisterous, and when we reached Gibraltar, as the wind was blowing strong from the westward, and fever raging fiercely in the town and garrison, we anchored under Cabrita Point, to await a change, or until it should become more moderate. For several days, the wind proved most provokingly constant; at last it moderated sufficiently to invite us to get under weigh, and although it was still westerly, blowing right through the Gut, by keeping the Spanish shore abroad, where the indraught is less felt than mid-channel, or on the Barbary side, the old *Malta* behaved so well, working with the quickness and facility of a frigate, that we fetched so far to windward as to weather the Thisbe rock on the one tack, while we lay up for Cape Spartel on the other; another board or two would have taken us clean through, had not a dense fog, which hung all the morning on the side of the mountains bordering the Barbary shore, suddenly spread itself over the whole channel, concealing every mark and object from view.

Under those circumstances, the Admiral thought it not prudent to persevere, and we bore up for the Bay of Tetuan, which is more easily attainable, and where there is better shelter with a westerly wind, than the anchorage which we had left in the morning. This kind of weather so trying to the tempers of men in a hurry lasted some days longer, and it was not till the eleventh day after we had reached Gibraltar, that a change at last allowed us to pass the Gut. For the remainder of the passage, the wind was mostly favourable; but it was full six weeks from the time of leaving Palermo till we made the Lizard. A strong breeze at south-west swept the ship up Channel, and there was every prospect of her being snug at anchor that night in Cawsand Bay; but those anticipations were not fated to be realised quite so soon. The atmosphere was thick and murky, and the wind freshening fast.

Ben Hunter, the master, was not acquainted with the anchorage at Plymouth; daylight began to fail before we got as high as Penlee Point, and it was feared that old Penn, the pilot, might not see the ship. Under those circumstances, it was judged wiser not to run further in, but wait till morning before we ran for our port. Accordingly, to the manifest disappointment of many, we hauled our wind, and as it was blowing strong, with every indication of an increase of wind, the ship was put under reefed courses and close-reefed topsails for the night. Under that sail, with the wind at south-west, we were to windward of the Dodman by daylight in the morning.

And now, as I shall soon bid adieu to the old craft for ever, I may be permitted to remark, that few, if any, ships of her class and scantling ever surpassed the *Malta* in all the essential properties of a fine man-of-war; she berthed and quartered her men well, she was roomy and high between decks, she stowed four hundred tons of water in *cask*, with six months' coal and provision, and that with ease; besides all this, she was an admirable sea-boat, was very weatherly, worked and sailed well, carried her guns high out of the water – so high, indeed, that I have known her go eleven knots with the lower-deck guns run out, and the wind abeam; and if a further proof of her excellent qualities be wanting, I will only refer to the circumstance of her beating through the Gut of Gibraltar against wind and current, a thing never done before, I believe, by any ship, certainly not by a ship of the line; and again in a breeze that required such reduced sail as reefed courses, and close-reefed topsails, to claw to windward, in a night, the distance between the Ram Head and the Dodman.

At daylight we bore up, and before many hours were at anchor in Cawsand Bay. And with what heartfelt satisfaction we found ourselves once more in happy England, let those answer who have passed years in absence from its blessed shores! Yet, the night of our arrival, it gave us rather a rough salutation; for the wind had veered to the eastward of south before dark, and blew so hard as to oblige us to strike topmasts and let go another anchor, neither of which operations had the weather compelled us to do from the time of leaving England till we returned to it again. Before day, it had moderated, and by eight o'clock, everything was to rights and ship-shape like.

The morning was clear and frosty, and even the villages of Kingsand and Cawsand looked bright and cheery. The ship was soon surrounded by bum-boats, which, with the instinct of the raven, scent a ship from foreign afar off. These were laden with every comestible that could tempt the not over-fastidious appetite of a sailor, and the boatswain's pipe to breakfast was the signal for them to come alongside. Then might be seen Jack, resolved to reimburse himself for a long fast from such delicacies, making his way up the ship's side, with a loaf of 'soft tommy', of huge proportions, under one arm, whilst a leg of mutton dangled from the opposite hand.

We happened to have a young bear on board at the time, a native of the Pyrenees, and a gift from the Baron d'Erolles to the Admiral. This gentleman was attracted by the smell of the good things to the gangway, where he thrust his shaggy person among the crowd, and seeing one of those legs of mutton passing through the throng, he very unceremoniously relieved the man of his burden, and scampered away to the poop (his usual rendezvous) with his prize. A hue and cry was immediately raised after the thief, and he was pursued to his lair; but it was no easy matter to recover the stolen goods. To every blow, Bruin glared with his eyes, and answered with a formidable growl; still he kept fast hold of the mutton, and it was not until he had been well cudgelled with a broomstick, and had sadly defaced the once comely joint, that he was at last persuaded to relinquish it. These kind of rough pets, by the way, are not much to be desired on board ship; for, besides the difficulty, if not impossibility, of teaching them cleanly habits, they are at times extremely mischievous, and even dangerous. One instance I will mention, to show how little their general harmlessness and good tempers are to be relied upon.

From being petted and kindly treated by the sailors, Bruin was in the habit of paying a visit to the different messes, when they were at their meals. One day he lingered on the lower deck after the men had finished their dinners, and kept prowling about, and going from mess to mess, to see and pick up a few scraps more. In his perambulations, he thrust himself in the way of one of the cooks, whose business it is to put things to rights after all the others have dined. This man, to get rid of the interruption, gave the animal a sharp kick, when Bruin turned round, and not seeing from whence the blow came, seized the first thing he laid his eyes upon. This happened to be the hand of some poor fellow that hung below the stool upon which he had stretched himself to take a nap after dinner, and before it could be released from the brute's jaws, the man's hand was much lacerated, and one of his fingers had to be amputated.

It not unfrequently happened that, in attending to some duty on deck, the first intimation one had of Bruin being at hand, was finding your leg tightly clasped in the arms of the brute. This was by way of play; but it was a rough and unseasonable interruption, and sure to set Jack grinning, who chuckled to see the officer in limbo, and one that you could not easily shake off; for if you struck him, or even scolded him sharply, there was danger that he would resent the indignity, and in a manner that might not be at all agreeable. So the wisest way was to endure patiently, and let him enjoy his gambols unmolested, which seldom lasted long.

Two or three days after our arrival, the Admiral struck his flag, and then proceeded to London. Then, and not till then, was he informed that, instead of a witness at the court-martial upon Sir John Murray, now ordered to be held at Winchester, he was to prosecute and substantiate the third charge. This, he was told, had been framed from his official letter, in which he had inculpated the conduct of the Commander of the Forces for the manner in which he had raised the siege of Tarragona.

The breakwater at Plymouth was now so far advanced as to afford perfect shelter to the Sound, and therefore we shifted in a few days to that anchorage, as the securer. The Captain and some of the officers, who had received subpœnas to attend the court-martial as witnesses, left the ship about the same time, as did several others on leave of absence; and soon after we moved into Barnpool for the purpose of refitting, which brought us to the beginning of 1815. Those men whose service entitled them to it were now paid a portion of their wages, and got their tickets of leave, which left the ship with scarcely men enough to man the boats. Most of those poor fellows escaped the harpies of Dock and Plymouth, I believe, and reached their homes; but some ten or twelve having fallen into bad company on landing, were soon relieved of their cash, and in a day or two were glad to return to work, and to something to eat, on board the *Malta*.

Among the latter was a boatswain's mate, called Allen, and when I asked the reason of his being so soon tired of the shore, he made no answer for a moment, but scratched his head and looked sheepish. Then giving his trowsers a bit of a hitch, and rolling over a huge quid that boomed out his cheek like the toothache, he said: 'Ye see, Sir, this is as how it happened. The morning as we were paid, I landed at Mutton Cove, and right a-head a'most, not a cable's length off, I sees the Blue Anchor. So, Sir, as I hadn't tasted a drop of gin – no, not since we left England more nor three years agone – I says to myself, says I, I'll give you a hail, my hearties, and have half a pint, jist to get myself into trim. So in I steps, and gives 'em a cheer as made all sneer agin (warmed, either by his subject or his *morning*, Allen now grew eloquent), and calls for a half-pint of gin. When I'd nipped that off, I felt very comfortable-like; and so to keep all square and steady, I pours a quart of porter upon the top of it, and then got under weigh for a bit of a lark. At first I was as steady as a pump-bolt, and bowled along like an Ingyman down trades; but I wasn't long under sail, till I felt myself som'ut by the head, and yawed considerable. Jist as I had weathered Cove Street, and was getting clear of the narrows, I was hailed by one of them there pilot craft as is always cruising in Mutton Cove and North Corner, looking out for the home-ward-bound. "Hollo! shipmate," says she, "what's the matter? You steers rayther wild," says she. "Met with bad weather? – cargo shifted? – water-logged, or what? Come," says she, "I'll take charge of you," – and without another word, she sheers right alongside, and takes me in tow. Away we went, and steered right for the Lord Nelson, at the top of Henry Street, and there we had some'ut – but what it was I'm blowed, Sir, if I knows – no, nor I knows no more nor a babby where I was or what happened to me till I woke this morning in the Nelson, with my head on the table of the tap-room. All I knows is, as I lanted three days agone with seventeen pounds some shillings in my fob, and this morning I found in the same place jist eighteen-pence in silver, and five penn'orth of coppers. Bill, says I to myself, your company has not a been of the genteelest – that's as plain as a pike-staff – and my advice is, to cut and run from such a nest of pirates, as bad as the Malays in the Straits of Sunday. And then I shook my feathers, and when I put my head in a bucket of water, I got a mouthful of bread and cheese, and a drop of gin to keep all smooth – and here I am, Sir, and if them there sharks catches me ashore agin, till the ship's paid off, and they turns me adrift, they may call me so'ger, or say my name isn't Bill Allen.'

There was little work for shipwrights or artificers; but the ship was unrigged, the hold cleared, and a variety of duty, in returning old and drawing new stores from the dockyard, which, with few men and short days and very wet weather, was found laborious enough.

After the court-martial on Sir John Murray, Captain Inglefield did not rejoin the ship, and Captain Fahie was appointed his successor. Soon after this, orders came down to get the *Malta* ready for sea with as little delay as possible, which was soon done, and the ship in the Sound, with powder and everything on board for a six months' cruise, many days before her services were required.

Some of the lieutenants had now left the ship, and of those appointed to succeed them, two were senior to me. After having worked my way to the top of the ladder, and then to find myself, without any notice or reason assigned, suddenly lowered from senior lieutenant to the position of third, and that, too, after having had the entire fag of refitting, and getting the ship ready for sea, was truly galling, and I felt it keenly at the time.

And now, when I can take a calmer and more dispassionate view of the subject, I think such perfect disregard of officers' feelings, to say nothing of their deserts, as was shown in my case, is unwise, impolitic, and unjust, tending to discourage and disgust officers with the service, instead of, what should be the earnest endeavour of the Board of Admiralty, inspiring all with content and satisfaction, and a confident dependence upon its justice and consideration.

Under the circumstances I did not think that it was incumbent upon me to serve in a junior capacity; but before I decided to apply to be superseded, I wrote to Admiral Hallowell for his opinion and advice.

From his answer I gathered that an application to be relieved could not prejudice me at the Admiralty, and that he considered I was fairly entitled to some relaxation after so many years' service without a week's leave of absence.

Fortified by this opinion, I wrote, through Captain Fahie, to be super-seded, and in a week my successor arrived. The next day I bade adieu to the old ship, not without regret, though the feeling was much lightened by the consideration that most of my old messmates had already preceded me.

Before my departure for Ireland, I was rejoiced to have an opportu-nity of seeing and shaking hands with Charles Parker. He had just returned from leave of absence, and was on the point of rejoining the *Malta*, after an ineffectual attempt to obtain that promotion which his own, to say nothing of his ancestral, claims so justly entitled him to; and which promotion, though it took place soon after (about the time of the *Malta*'s departure from Plymouth), did not save him the trouble and expense of a trip to Gibraltar and back again. I passed a couple of days with my friend, and then embarked for Cork in the *Phœbe*.

I took the coach from Cork to Fermoy, and a drive of a couple of hours along the banks of the beautiful Blackwater, every bend of which revealed some feature of loveliness that brought by-gone times fresh to my recollection, landed me in Lismore. There once more, after thirteen years' wandering, I found myself in the home of my father, surrounded and made much of by kind and indulgent friends.

And who is there that would not feel as I did? The first burst of joy at meeting, succeeded by a more sobered, but full contentment and satisfac-tion, when I had leisure to look around and see all those happy smiling faces grouped about me, and to think what a blessed haven I was shel-tered in after my pilgrimage.

The first few weeks flew rapidly away, nor did a thought or care intrude themselves to disturb the perfect harmony of my happiness. But at last the reflection would force itself upon me, that I was still a lieu-tenant – that England was now at peace with all the world, a peace not likely to be soon disturbed – and that promotions had just taken place to such an extent, that, to use the words of Lord St Vincent, 'the door to any more was shut for many years to come'. When once such thoughts found an entrance into my mind, I could not shake them off, and I began to con-sider what course or plan of life I had better adopt.

After turning over various schemes, I found that my own profession, the sea, was the only line of life for which I was now fitted, and I directed my attention to South America. There the struggle was still going on between Spain and her colonies, and the services of British officers, both of army and navy, were eagerly sought for and rewarded with advance-ment by the latter.

But in the midst of these cogitations, and before I had come to any decision, all Europe was startled by the sudden appearance of Bonaparte in France, and his unopposed and triumphant entry into Paris.

This at once put every notion of entering into the service of a foreign power to flight. There was again seemingly work enough for us all cut out at home; and as I concluded that Admiral Hallowell would immediately hoist his flag, I wrote to him to request that I might again have the honour and pleasure of sailing with him; and as I was about to accompany my eldest sister to Bristol, whose husband had just returned from America, I begged that he would address his answer to the Post-office there.

My sister's health was too delicate to admit of much fatigue, so we travelled by easy stages through Wales. The morning after our arrival at Bristol, I was all impatience to call at the Post-office for my letters, and the moment I had finished my breakfast I started off. Upon inquiry at the office, I found two letters waiting my arrival, one of which bore the Admiralty seal and address. This I tore open with some anxiety, supposing it might contain an appointment to the ship in which Admiral Hallowell was to hoist his flag: but when my eye glanced at the auspicious words, 'My Lords Commissioners of the Admiralty have been pleased to nominate and appoint you Commander'. I read no more, but to the amazement no doubt of the astonished bystanders, uttered an exclamation of joy, and in three skips cleared the corridor of the Post-office, the happiest fellow at the moment in all Bristol.

When I became a little sober, I opened the other letter, which proved to be from Admiral Hallowell. In this he explained how it was that he managed my promotion. Upon his return to London from Winchester, he found that Boxer whom he had left acting in the *Wizard*, in the Mediterranean, had been superseded, and not confirmed in the rank of Commander. He immediately called upon Lord Melville, the First Lord of the Admiralty, and remonstrated with him upon the injustice and hardship of Boxer's case, as well as the little attention which his own services had met with from the Board.

At first Lord Melville said the Admiral must be mistaken – that Mr Boxer was promoted, for he thought he remembered giving directions about it himself. But when the Admiral assured him that he had seen Mr Boxer an hour before, and that he was still a lieutenant, his Lordship expressed great surprise, declaring that there must have been misconception or neglect somewhere, for that he fully meant that Mr Boxer should have been promoted. 'And now', continued he, 'Admiral Hallowell, if there is any midshipman whom you wish promoted, you have but to name him, and it shall be done.' 'Pardon me, my Lord,' the Admiral replied, 'if I first remind you that Mr Boxer's promotion has taken place, I humbly conceive, in consequence of his own services and mine, whilst in the Mediterranean. I now claim, as the invariable compliment paid to an Admiral upon striking his flag, the promotion of another lieutenant on that account: and in asking for the advancement of two, I require nothing more than what has been granted already to two or three flag officers who served upon the same station as myself.' This, too, was conceded, and thus, by a steady and respectful upholding of his own just rights, and a watchful regard to the interests and fair claims of his officers, does the writer of these pages entirely owe his promotion to the rank of Commander.

Also available in the 'Sailors' Tales' series

THE NARRATIVE OF WILLIAM SPAVENS
A CHATHAM PENSIONER, BY HIMSELF
A Unique Lower Deck View of the 18th Century Navy
This remarkable first-hand account of life at sea by an ordinary seaman
of Anson's time is one of the most fascinating, and rarest,
autobiographies to emerge from the Age of Sail
216 × 138 mm, 192pp, paperback
ISBN 1 86176 083 3 £9.95

NELSONIAN REMINISCENCES
A Dramatic Eye-Witness Account of the War at Sea 1795–1810
Lieutenant G S Parsons RN
Lieutenant Parsons served throughout the Napoleonic Wars, but the
highlight of his career was his time under Nelson's command in
the Mediterranean, during the great naval hero's controversial
time at Naples, with Emma Hamilton.
216 × 138 mm, 200pp, paperback
ISBN 1 86176 084 1 £9.95

A SAILOR OF KING GEORGE
The Journals of Captain Frederick Hoffman RN 1793–1814
In a long career at sea, Captain Hoffman saw action in all theatres of the
Napoleonic wars, including Trafalgar. Full of fascinating stories, and
written with wry humour and candid charm, this book gives a true
sense of what it was like to serve in Nelson's navy.
216 × 138 mm, 224pp, paperback
ISBN 1 86176 107 4 £9.95

For a full illustrated catalogue of all Chatham Publishing books, please contact:
The Marketing Department, Chatham Publishing,
61 Frith Street, London W1V 5TA
Tel: 0171–434–4242. Fax: 0171–434–4415